Viceroy Güemes's Mexico

Diálogos Series
KRIS LANE, SERIES EDITOR

Understanding Latin America demands dialogue, deep exploration, and frank discussion of key topics. Founded by Lyman L. Johnson in 1992 and edited since 2013 by Kris Lane, the Diálogos Series focuses on innovative scholarship in Latin American history and related fields. The series, the most successful of its type, includes specialist works accessible to a wide readership and a variety of thematic titles, all ideally suited for classroom adoption by university and college teachers.

Also available in the Diálogos Series:

The Struggle for Natural Resources: Findings from Bolivian History edited by Carmen Soliz and Rossana Barragán

At the Heart of the Borderlands: Africans and Afro-Descendants on the Edges of Colonial Spanish America edited by Cameron D. Jones and Jay T. Harrison

The Age of Dissent: Revolution and the Power of Communication in Chile, 1780–1833 by Martín Bowen

From Sea-Bathing to Beach-Going: A Social History of the Beach in Rio de Janeiro, Brazil by B. J. Barickman

Gamboa's World: Justice, Silver Mining, and Imperial Reform in New Spain by Christopher Albi

The Conquest of the Desert: Argentina's Indigenous Peoples and the Battle for History edited by Carolyne R. Larson

A Troubled Marriage: Indigenous Elites of the Colonial Americas by Sean F. McEnroe

From the Galleons to the Highlands: Slave Trade Routes in the Spanish Americas edited by Alex Borucki, David Eltis, and David Wheat

Staging Frontiers: The Making of Modern Popular Culture in Argentina and Uruguay by William Garrett Acree Jr.

A Woman, a Man, a Nation: Mariquita Sánchez, Juan Manuel de Rosas, and the Beginnings of Argentina by Jeffrey M. Shumway

For additional titles in the Diálogos Series, please visit unmpress.com.

Viceroy Güemes's
MEXICO

Rituals, Religion, and Revenue

CHRISTOPH ROSENMÜLLER

UNIVERSITY OF NEW MEXICO PRESS | ALBUQUERQUE

© 2024 by the University of New Mexico Press
All rights reserved. Published 2024
Printed in the United States of America

ISBN 978-0-8263-6588-0 (cloth)
ISBN 978-0-8263-6589-7 (paper)
ISBN 978-0-8263-6590-3 (ePub)
ISBN 978-0-8263-6641-2 (webPDF)

Library of Congress Cataloging-in-Publication data is on file with the Library of Congress

Founded in 1889, the University of New Mexico sits on the traditional homelands of the Pueblo of Sandia. The original peoples of New Mexico—Pueblo, Navajo, and Apache—since time immemorial have deep connections to the land and have made significant contributions to the broader community statewide. We honor the land itself and those who remain stewards of this land throughout the generations and also acknowledge our committed relationship to Indigenous peoples. We gratefully recognize our history.

Cover illustration: Juan Manuel de Ávila y Velasco, *Juan Francisco de Güemes y Horcasitas*, Count of Revillagigedo, painted after August 12, 1749, oil on canvas. (Source: The collection of the Salón de Cabildos del Antiguo Palacio del Ayuntamiento, Ministry of Culture of Mexico City, photo by Jorge Moreno Cárdenas [Jojagal], CC0, Wikimedia Commons public domain, https://commons.wikimedia.org/wiki/File:40_Francisco_Guemes_Horcasitas_(Palacio_Ayuntamiento_M%C3%A9xico).jpg.)
Designed by Felicia Cedillos
Composed in Minion Pro

Contents

List of Illustrations vii
List of Tables viii
Acknowledgments ix
A Note on Terms xi

    Introduction 1

    CHAPTER 1. The Education of a Bourbon Viceroy 9

    CHAPTER 2. A Passage to Mexico 23

    CHAPTER 3. From Viceregal Rituals to Informality
        The Court in Mexico City 45

    CHAPTER 4. "The Indians and Castes ... Long for Change"
        Wresting the Rural Priories from the Religious Orders 67

    CHAPTER 5. Friends, Foes, and "Specters Spreading at Court"
        How Güemes Seized the Mexico City Alcabala *Tax in 1753–1754* 89

    CHAPTER 6. One Kingdom to Rule the Other?
        New Spain versus New Galicia 109

    CHAPTER 7. Güemes's Endgame
        Helping the King and Helping Oneself 125

    Conclusion. Bourbon Brawn and Brain 141

Measures and Weights 151
Dramatis Personae 153
Glossary 169
Notes 173
Bibliography 235

Illustrations

Figures
Figure 1. Unknown artist, southeastern Mexico City in 1752 35
Figure 2. Juan Patricio Morlete Ruiz, *View of the Main Square of Mexico City*, 1770 58
Figure 3. Unknown artist, façade, lower floor, and horse stable of Güemes's palace on Mostenses Square, Madrid 135

Maps
Map 1. Colonial Mexico in the mid-eighteenth century 6
Map 2. Güemes's entry to colonial Mexico 28
Map 3. Important sites during the fight over Native *doctrinas*, 1749–1755 75
Map 4. Approximate viceregal itinerary from Mexico City to Veracruz 130

Tables

Table 1. Güemes's Entry to Colonial Mexico   29
Table 2. Güemes's Friends during the *Alcabala* Tax Conflict   101
Table 3. Mexico City *Alcabala* Yields, 1750–1760   103
Table 4. Approximate Viceregal Itinerary from Mexico City to Veracruz   130

Acknowledgments

My gratitude goes to series editor Kris Lane, Christopher Albi, and acquisitions editor Michael Millman for their valuable suggestions on publishing this manuscript in the Diálogos Series of the University of New Mexico Press.

Thilo Billmeier, Mark A. Burkholder, William Connell, Miguel Costa, Susan Deeds, Marc Eagle, David Rex Galindo, Hari Nair, Renate Pieper, Frances Ramos, Susan Schroeder, and William B. Taylor insightfully commented on chapters of this book. The seminar on the Long Eighteenth Century at the Universidad Nacional Autónoma de México, El Colegio de México, and Instituto Mora, composed of Iván Escamilla, María Teresa Álvarez Icaza, Patricia Díaz, Olivia Moreno, Guadalupe Pinzón, and Estela Roselló Soberón perspicaciously reviewed chapter 3, while the seminar Corporations, Commerce, and Service to the King, Seventeenth to Nineteenth Centuries, at the Instituto Mora, composed of Guillermina del Valle Pavón, Antonio Ibarra, Viviana Grieco, Iliana Quintanar, Ernest Sánchez Santiró, and Sergio Tonatiuh Serrano Hernández commented perceptively on chapter 5. Álvaro Armada Barcaiztegui, Iván Alcántar, Linda Arnold, James Córdoba, Udo Grub, Sherry Johnson, Pilar Latasa Vassallo, Horst Pietschmann, Álvaro Recio Mir, Javier Sanchiz, Dorothy Tanck de Estrada, and the late Guillermo Náñez Falcón advised helpfully over the years. Allan J. Kuethe graciously gave me copies of the French ambassadorial correspondence from 1754, which he culled from the Archive of Foreign Affairs in Paris. Any errors that remain in this book are mine.

The University of Florida Library, Special Collections, supported my research in the microfilmed Archivo de los Condes de Revillagigedo (Archive of the Counts of Revillagigedo) with a travel grant in 2006, while Middle Tennessee State University awarded me two summer research grants.

An early and shorter version of chapter 4 appeared as "'The Indians . . . Long for Change': The Secularization of Regular Parishes in Mid Eighteenth-Century New Spain, 1749–1755," in *Early Bourbon Spanish America: Politics and Society in a Forgotten Era*, ed. Francisco A. Eissa-Barroso and Ainara Vázquez Varela (Leiden: Brill, 2013), 143–64; and a revised and expanded Spanish translation of this chapter was published as "La 'langosta que arruina': Clero regular y secularización durante el gobierno del primer conde de Revillagigedo," *Historias*, no. 103 (May–August 2019): 29–50. A more exhaustive version of chapter 6 appeared originally as "Two Kingdoms in a Multi-Tiered Empire: New Spain and New Galicia in the Mid-Eighteenth Century," *Max Planck Institute for European Legal History Research Paper Series*, no. 10 (2018): 1–29.

Most importantly, my gratitude and love go to my wife, Marcela Saldaña Solís, for her unwavering support that allowed me to finish this study.

A Note on Terms

The term "Nueva España" (New Spain) had at least three distinct meanings in the eighteenth century. The first referred to the viceroyalty of New Spain or colonial Mexico. The viceroyalty bordered in the south on the kingdom of Guatemala including Chiapas and expanded northward into what is now the United States, comprising provinces such as Texas and New Mexico. The viceroyalty contained the northwestern kingdom of New Galicia with its capital Guadalajara.[1] While the president and judges of the *audiencia* (high court) of Guadalajara enjoyed great autonomy, the viceroy could overrule them in military and financial matters. Yucatán in the east also managed most of its own affairs, although appeals to lawsuits went to the audiencia of Mexico.

Second, the *reino* (kingdom) of New Spain resembled current central Mexico and formed part of the vast viceroyalty. The viceroy and the audiencia largely controlled the kingdom. Third, another concept of New Spain referred to the entire Spanish North America, including the Caribbean, in addition to the Philippines. This concept was mostly at play at the Council of the Indies in Madrid, where a prosecutor and an *escribano* (notary secretary) reviewed the correspondence from these regions. Another prosecutor and escribano worked on Peru, which signified South America in that sense. Nevertheless, these work assignments in Madrid did not give the viceroy any jurisdiction outside of the viceroyalty. Guatemala, Cuba, and the Philippines reported to their own audiencias and governors, for instance, and only took orders directly from Madrid. As an exception, the Crown may have mandated the viceroy to gather information or to get involved in some fashion. These were rare instances, however.

Primary sources of the mid-eighteenth century rarely if ever used the term "colony" to label the viceroyalty of New Spain. Therefore, many academics especially in Mexico shun the term or its adjective "colonial" for mischaracterizing the viceroyalty's significance in the Spanish Empire. Yet scholars in the United States commonly write "colonial Mexico," and I also use this term interchangeably with "New Spain," while the residents also appear as "colonial Mexicans" or "colonial residents." Those originating from the Spanish peninsula are labeled "peninsular Spaniards," and the inhabitants of the empire are called Spaniards for lack of a better word.

Furthermore, *alcaldes mayores* and *corregidores* were district judges who adjudicated conflicts, collected taxes, and governed in their districts, while the *alcaldes* and *alcaldes ordinarios* of the Native and Spanish-speaking municipal councils served as magistrates of the first instance. The audiencia consisted of *oidores* (civil judges), *alcaldes de crimen* (criminal judges), a *fiscal del crimen* (criminal prosecutor), and a *fiscal de lo civil* (civil prosecutor).

Moreover, most humans of the old society belonged to some corporation, which usually appeared in the sources as *cuerpo* (body) or *tribunal* (tribunal). Examples include the *cabildos civiles* (municipal councils), trade guilds, and religious orders. These were not businesses as today but self-governing social units with jurisdiction over their members. Members lived within the social hierarchies of their corporations and rarely acted as free individuals making their own decisions. Finally, viceroys communicated with many people of New Spain. I loosely label close viceregal collaborators as friends or allies, unless they were clearly dependents who profited from patronage, when I call them clients.

Introduction

Critics have long denounced viceroys (chief administrators of colonial kingdoms) as the root of autocracy in Latin America. In 1970, the poet Octavio Paz, for instance, lambasted Mexican presidents for continuing the "centralist and authoritarian" tradition of the Spanish viceroys. Paz argued that "there is a bridge from the *tlatoani* [Aztec ruler] and the viceroy to the president."[1] In part, the violent government crackdown on student protesters before the 1968 Mexico City Olympics enraged him. Likewise, this great power of one "strong and elevated person, institution, or myth" was for the Peruvian novelist Mario Vargas Llosa the "main reason for the delay of our continent and our economic underdevelopment."[2] Even today, activists and politicians attack the chief of state for grabbing power like the viceroys.[3]

While viceroys may have acted in authoritarian fashion, pinning modern misfortunes on the apex of colonial government oversimplifies the matter. Eighteenth-century viceroys saw themselves as defenders of justice and protectors of Natives. Viceroys wielded great but not unlimited authority and grappled with significant counterweights. The law restrained them, the *audiencia* (high court) in Mexico City vitiated their orders, and the king and his advisers monitored them, albeit from far away. Occasionally, regional elites and pueblos (Native polities) ignored or opposed orders coming down from Mexico City. In this book, viceroys emerge as cultural and political actors embedded in a complex society. Residents supported, constrained, and conditioned their work.

The viceroys asked colonial Mexico to shoulder more of the empire's burden, as the economy expanded in the mid-eighteenth century. The viceroyalty's population burgeoned, agricultural production grew, and the great mines boomed. Colonial Mexico entered a period of prosperity and sent a stream of silver pesos to upgrade the royal armada, strengthen fortresses in the Caribbean, and fill the royal coffers. Madrid harnessed colonial Mexico's wealth even further as it sought to contain its imperial competitors and stave off military decline. France and Britain outpaced Spain, for instance, while Habsburg Austria, Portugal, and the Netherlands remained potent contenders. The king of Spain, Philip V of Bourbon (1700–1746, with an interruption in 1724) and his ministers ordered a series of reforms to unleash growth, streamline the administration, and end unmerited entitlements. As part of the program, the king appointed Juan Francisco Güemes y Horcasitas (Juan Francisco Güemes for short) as viceroy of colonial Mexico. He, his family, collaborators, and enemies are the focus of this book.[4]

Little indicated originally that Güemes would one day steer the viceroyalty. He was born on May 16, 1681, in Reinosa, Cantabria (northern Spain) as a scion of the lower nobility. After receiving an education at the local Franciscan priory, he joined the infantry as a cadet in 1700. Güemes rose through the ranks by fighting many battles for Philip V. Later, on February 21, 1733, the king appointed him governor of Havana (Cuba). Before embarking, Güemes married Antonia Padilla Pacheco in the Church of San Sebastián in Antequera (Andalusia, southern Spain) on December 26, 1733. He was fifty-two, while she was the twenty-five-year-old daughter of an elite family in that city. In the following years, Padilla Pacheco and Güemes resided in Havana and had eight children. On June 21, 1745, following Güemes's sixty-fourth birthday, the king tapped him for the viceregency of colonial Mexico. After arriving in Mexico City, the viceroy and his supporters overcame significant resistance and brought about incisive change between 1746 and 1755. Scholars have largely overlooked the importance of these reforms.[5]

For instance, Güemes (pronounced GWEmes) believed that the religious orders, such as the Franciscans and Dominicans, skirted supervision and owned too much land. They also took advantage of the Natives in their mostly rural *doctrinas* (parishes). Güemes and the first minister in Madrid, the Marquis of la Ensenada (served 1743–1754), dealt the orders a serious blow. They ousted the friars from 109 doctrinas and replaced them with diocesan priests, who served under the watchful eyes of a bishop. The religious orders opposed their losses vigorously, but the Natives acquiesced or welcomed the successors in most cases and contributed to the friars' defeat.

In addition, Ensenada set his eyes on the profitable *alcabala* (sales tax) of Mexico City. At that time, the powerful *consulado* (merchant guild) acted as a tax farmer and collected the alcabala from most traders who brought merchandise to the city gates. The consulado tried to extend the profitable arrangement, and Güemes cautioned against sweeping change, as he feared turmoil at the gates. Yet Ensenada demanded significantly higher payments, and negotiations with the consulado stalled. Ensenada then ordered the viceroy to seize the alcabala administration, and Güemes complied. Despite significant pushback, royal officials began to levy the tax, and they oversaw a spectacular rise in revenue.

Furthermore, Güemes sent inspectors to review the treasury of Guadalajara, the capital of the northwestern kingdom of New Galicia. The inspectors caught several officials red-handed stealing money from the king's coffers. Güemes also wrested the mining camp Bolaños (about 450 miles northwest of Mexico City) from the audiencia. He appointed loyal treasury officials and a district judge to control silver production and taxation. The ongoing power struggle with his opponents in New Galicia vexed the viceroy considerably. He called for shutting down the audiencia of Guadalajara altogether. Madrid signaled agreement. Yet Ensenada fell from office in 1754 because of a palace intrigue. Thus, the audiencia of Guadalajara continued largely unscathed and recovered Bolaños, although treasury officials and the district judge in the mining camp gained autonomy from local powers and supervised silver production more faithfully.

Güemes carried out these trenchant reforms with the help of family, friends, and clients, as patron-client relationships undergirded colonial society. For example, Ensenada essentially promoted Güemes to the viceroyalty and relied greatly on viceregal expertise when crafting policies. In one instance, Ensenada proposed appointing royal officials to buy the coveted dyestuff cochineal in colonial Mexico and send it to Spain. Ensenada was convinced that the scheme would garner additional revenue for the Crown. Güemes resisted the plan as too risky, however, because of the unpredictable swings in production and prices. Ensenada followed suit and dropped the idea. At the same time, Güemes used his influence in Madrid to pull strings for his own friends. The treasurer of Mexico City's ecclesiastical chapter, for example, counseled the viceroy during tough conflicts, such as the fight with the consulado over the alcabala. In exchange, Güemes proposed promotions for the treasurer, and Ensenada complied. One official in Madrid noted that his "boss" was even willing to entertain further wishes of Güemes in this regard.[6] Finally, Güemes never lost sight of his own interests. While handing out awards, he also expected gifts and other perks in return. This was business as usual in the colonial period, and Güemes remained true to Ensenada.[7]

Güemes arrived in New Spain at a time when the lavish entry rituals of viceroys showed the first signs of decline. He still rode into five cities with great fanfare. These processions forged deep ties between the lord and his vassals. Baroque pomp and circumstance stood out from the daily routine and buttressed the viceroy's prestige, which helped him carry out controversial reforms. Nonetheless, viceregal austerity slowly advanced and undercut lavish gestures. Güemes himself hailed from humble origins and had served elsewhere in the Americas before coming to New Spain. He brought only his immediate family and a handful of companions. Most predecessors, by contrast, had boasted impressive pedigrees and presided over extensive entourages traveling with them. In addition, kings increasingly exalted their symbolic role over the viceroys. During the eighteenth century, kings rode in coaches with eight horses, while viceroys sat in six-in-hands. This trend toward greater viceregal modesty continued after Güemes. Later viceroys entered New Spain even less prodigiously.[8]

Much of viceregal life unfolded in the palace of Mexico City, where informality often reigned. Friends and other colonial residents visited Güemes and Padilla Pacheco. The couple hosted soirees with conversations and music, and they occasionally danced until late in the night. The viceroy also gambled in his quarters with his clients. In addition, Güemes enjoyed walking on Alameda Square. Once, he kept inquisitors waiting in the antechamber while he was strolling in the city, and he had to apologize to the ministers. Moreover, the viceroy, his wife, their six daughters, and two sons spent ample time on the haciendas of local heavyweight Jacinto Martínez de Aguirre. Friends and ministers joined them on these occasions, because conduct in the countryside was more relaxed than in the palace.

New insights into shifting viceregal ostentation and political conflicts rely on rarely consulted primary sources. Whereas most private papers of viceroys have vanished over the centuries, Güemes returned to Spain with a trove of letters that have survived in a family archive. They range from copies of lost official communications to confidential letters. These papers often laid out Güemes's views candidly and depicted daily life minutely.[9] I also draw on state, church, and private collections, mostly in Mexico City, Seville, and Madrid, while including a regional perspective from Guadalajara. These combined sources help to foreground a bottom-up perspective: they cast light on viceregal connections with colonial residents and detail the magnitude of the fight over the doctrinas. The documents also allow for a glimpse of palace life. For instance, the notaries of the Holy Office minutely recorded their audiences (formal meetings) with viceroys in the main hall. What is more, inspectors interrogated treasurers and witnesses in Guadalajara and Bolaños and reported irregularities. Finally, Güemes's contemporary José Manuel de Castro Santa-Anna wrote a distinctive diary on gossip, mundane activities, and state actions. He sometimes sniped at the authoritarian practices of Güemes and Pacheco Padilla. The diary, combined with two chronicles on the viceregal entry, notarial records, and colonial résumés, round off the image of a viceroy deeply enmeshed in society.[10]

Güemes, Padilla Pacheco, and their children departed Mexico City when his term ended in mid-October 1755. They sailed to Spain, where he became an important adviser to King Charles III in 1759. A few years later, the king sent another sweeping judicial investigation to scour the viceroyalty for abuses (1765–1771). Many historians see the ensuing Bourbon Reforms as a game changer that woke up the empire from a deep slumber. Nevertheless, this view is no longer tenable. This book shows that Güemes and his supporters initiated incisive changes before 1765 and cast the foundation for later measures. I therefore join other scholars in abandoning the traditional consensus of a watershed between 1759 and 1765. In fact, Güemes continued a long tradition of enhancing royal power.[11]

While this book draws a vivid portrait of one assertive viceroy, I also glance at the origins of his term and the changes brought about by his immediate successor, the Marquis of las Amarillas (1755–1760). For example, examining viceregal embarkation papers of the early eighteenth century shows that their entourages declined in number with the notable exception of Amarillas. This approach also throws into relief Güemes's small retinue in contrast to the other coteries of followers. In addition, this book shows that the alcabala tax revenue had increased substantially after 1576 and leaped ahead again substantially in 1753–1754. Finally, I provide evidence that the Crown offered the regular orders breathing space after Ensenada's fall from power in 1754 and Güemes's return to Spain the following year. Analyzing the context of Güemes's viceregency therefore yields significantly more insights than focusing exclusively on his term.

Studying the top echelon of the colonial administration debunks modern myths about the high-handed and corrupt satraps of colonial times. While viceroys such as Güemes did not shy away from authoritarianism, they also relied on the help of colonial residents. Güemes championed reforms, and probity and prosperity expanded. Critics and supporters of the Mexican presidency today would therefore do well to recall the eighteenth-century predecessors of the institution. Discarding flawed preconceptions about them helps us to better assess Mexico's challenges today.

Map 1. Colonial Mexico in the mid-eighteenth century. (Designed by Ana Gabriela Arreola Meneses.)

CHAPTER 1

The Education of a Bourbon Viceroy

Introduction

Juan Francisco Güemes has a bootstraps story to tell. He joined the army in 1700, just when the last Habsburg king of Spain died. During the ensuing War of the Spanish Succession (1702–1715), Güemes fought for the Bourbon cause. He saw combat in Naples, Italy, and was promoted to major upon returning to Spain. He and his Segovia regiment successfully charged English forces holed up in Brihuega (north of Madrid) on December 10, 1710. Just two days later, the soldiers stood their ground against Austrian troops at Villaviciosa, suffering heavy casualties. The two battles largely decided the war for Philip V, the first Bourbon king of Spain. Güemes subsequently continued to campaign. Commanding officers and influential ministers noted Güemes's no-nonsense attitude. Among them was the Marquis of la Ensenada, first minister of the empire (1743–1754). Ensenada became Güemes's patron and appointed him as viceroy of New Spain (1746–1755), as colonial Mexico was then known. Güemes looked out for the king, and the king repaid the favor. Güemes returned to Spain rich and attained more top positions in government. This chapter examines Ensenada's ascent and fall from power, the patronage that Güemes received on his way up, and the significant political and economic changes in the Spanish Empire in the first half of the eighteenth century.[1]

The Rise of Güemes and His Patron

In some ways, King Philip continued the policies of his Habsburg predecessors to intensify royal rule. He dissolved several great councils in Madrid to weaken the influence of the aristocracy, while the remaining councils evolved into appellate courts of justice. Meanwhile, the first minister and the secretaries of state expanded their influence. One of their goals was to improve the administration and raise tax revenue overseas. For that end, they set up a tobacco monopoly in Cuba and established the viceroyalty of New Granada (consisting of modern Venezuela, Colombia, and Ecuador). The opposition did not stand by idly, however, and temporarily dismantled several initiatives after 1719. Nevertheless, José Patiño became first minister in 1726 and put the earlier program back on track. He reinstated the Cuban tobacco monopoly and restored the viceroyalty in New Granada. Patiño also confirmed relocating the consulado (merchant guild) from Seville to Cádiz. That move eased up the stranglehold of the Seville elite on the sclerotic Spanish trade with the Americas.[2]

In addition, Patiño promoted capable people. In 1720, he visited the navy arsenal in southern Spain, where a young scribe called Zenón de Somodevilla (1702–1781) impressed him. Patiño ordered him to review the naval administration, and he carried out the mandate with aplomb. Somodevilla later coordinated the attack on Habsburg Naples in Italy to install Philip's son Charles as king in 1734–1735. In exchange for the Spanish victory, Charles awarded Somodevilla the title of Marquis of la Ensenada. The newly minted aristocrat originally hailed from modest origins in northern Spain, just as other officials in Patiño's network. The region had remained largely loyal to the Bourbons during the War of the Spanish Succession, and the king rewarded his faithful followers.[3]

Juan Francisco Güemes was one of them, and he continued his ascent. In 1732, Güemes joined Patiño in the conquest of the city of Oran in North Africa. Patiño saw Güemes's potential and appointed him as governor of Havana, Cuba. There, Güemes carved out a name for himself by suppressing contraband trade. In 1734, for instance, he sent soldiers to search a British vessel anchoring in Havana. The soldiers seized slaves, tobacco, and the ship itself, and forced contraband traders to dock elsewhere. The French consul witnessed Güemes's actions and noted that "the English have not run into anything like this here in the past eighteen years."[4]

Two years later, on November 3, Patiño passed away in Madrid, yet his network of people endured. After an interlude of nearly seven years, Ensenada succeeded him as first minister in 1743. He continued Patiño's policies and forged a broad coalition at court. That included, among others, the king's Jesuit confessor, who served as virtual secretary of religious affairs. The confessor protected his order at a time when public opinion was turning against it. For instance, fake coins circulated in Naples and Rome with the profile of an imaginary king Antonio I, whom the Jesuits had crowned in Paraguay. The proclamation of that king would have been treasonous, had it been true.[5]

Güemes's family noted the rise of Ensenada. Güemes's nephew knew about "Your Lordship's friendship" with Ensenada's immediate predecessor, a *montañés*, that is, a native of the northern mountainous region of Spain. Güemes had been born there and considered himself a montañés, too. The nephew observed that "the king instead appointed a *riojano* [from La Rioja] called don Zenón de Somodevilla with the title of Marquis of la Ensenada . . . and we are not aware that he considers the *montañeses* the same way as the deceased." Yet although they came from different regions in northern Spain, Güemes had become Ensenada's protégé by this time and profited from his patron's meteoric rise.[6]

King Philip's death on July 9, 1746, threw a monkey wrench into Ensenada's machinery, as the new King Ferdinand VI retooled the government. Ferdinand sidelined Philip's widow Elizabeth Farnese, while the new queen, Barbara of Bragança (1711–1758), initially opposed Ensenada for being "indecorous to the Majesty and too despotic."[7] Barbara wielded much influence over her husband; so much even that the French ambassador quipped that "it was rather Barbara who succeeded Elizabeth than Ferdinand following Philip."[8]

In this uncertainty, the aristocrat José de Carvajal y Lancáster (José Carvajal for short, 1698–1754) seemed poised to replace Ensenada as the first minister. Carvajal directed foreign policy as secretary of state, traditionally the most important of the secretaries. He also heard the affairs of the Councils of War and Treasury and became governor of the Council of the Indies (Spanish America) in January 1748.[9] In addition, Carvajal had spun a wide network of allies, although he was not particularly sociable. He led a rather solitary and austere life and locked himself up in his study for long hours. Meanwhile, the smooth-talking Ensenada, although of more humble extraction, schmoozed up the royal couple. He soothed the anxious king by administering bad news in homeopathic doses or left him in the dark entirely. Ferdinand was satisfied with the arrangement, and Ensenada continued in his role as first minister, holding the three key portfolios of secretary of finance, war, and the navy with the Indies.[10]

Ensenada, the Economists, and the Empire

Roughly at that time, economic philosophers in France—later called physiocrats—advocated a freer market with fairer taxes to create more prosperity. The physiocrats sought to understand the laws of economics and apply them, above all, to agriculture. They challenged the widespread belief that the soil only yielded a fixed quantity since output always plateaued at some level. Instead, physiocrats argued that agriculture could well expand beyond traditional expectations when owners better managed their lands and took advantage of opportunities. The state should therefore liberate tenant farmers from excessive charges and shift the burden to owners of large estates, merchants, and manufacturers. These social groups were either too idle or merely transformed the tenant farmers' products into merchandise, the physiocrats said. These economists also largely discarded the notion of state as entrepreneur. The king should rather stand back and "laissez faire et laissez passer" (allow to act, allow to happen), so that farmers could raise production and garner profits.[11] The physiocrats laid the foundation for classical liberalism as later synthesized by Adam Smith. Nonetheless, they shied away from fully freeing trade and manufacturing, as they ultimately desired to shore up agriculture and the absolutist regime.[12]

Their convictions left a mark on the Spanish Empire. An unknown author belonging to the team of Ensenada's predecessor, for instance, wrote the influential manuscript *New System*. That author singled out Natives as the oppressed group in the Americas. Natives chiefly tilled the land, while their own nobility, the clergy, and the *alcaldes mayores* (district judges) took advantage of them. Natives also chafed under the tribute while enjoying special protections, akin to minors, paupers, and old people. For the author of *New System*, the special status and oppression were a sign of the past, however. Instead, Indians "should become an industrious nation" and "useful vassals and Spaniards."[13] They should be equal to others, wear European dress, and learn the Spanish language. Consequently, they would work harder, purchase Spanish goods, and aid in Spain's recovery while helping to end the "immoral and cruel" trade with African slaves. Natives should also be consecrated as parish priests more frequently. Creating such opportunities could well be popular among many, although the author also clearly frowned upon the diversity of Native languages.[14]

In addition, the author proposed closer supervision of the Americas. More bishops should keep wayward clergy in check. A judicial investigation should scrutinize Spanish America from north to south to root out abuse, with intendants (well-paid administrators) keeping tabs on large provinces. Some of the ideas, such as breaking up internal trade barriers and barring foreign competition, were part of contemporary economic thinking. Other thoughts, however, pointed towards physiocracy, which favored the productive agricultural workers over landholders and merchants. The manuscript had a significant impact on Ensenada's government, although printing was delayed until 1789. Ensenada probably held off from publication because of rivalry with his predecessor, whom Ensenada had incriminated in an inquisition trial.[15]

In 1748, the naval officers Antonio de Ulloa and Juan Jorge expressed similar ideas to those expressed in *New System*. Ensenada commissioned them to write up their insights after they had returned from a French scientific expedition in Peru. Ulloa and Jorge criticized the landowners who stole Native land, selfish aristocrats who controlled political office, and abusive clergy. Natives suffered from lack of access to education and the "excessive vanity, presumption, and pride which pervade the Creoles" (Spaniards born in the Americas).[16]

Toward the end of Ensenada's government, Bernardo Ward, a protégé of the king, advocated absolute royal power as the remedy for Spain's problems. Ward, like many Enlightenment ministers, believed that the king and his advisers were best suited for resolving political challenges. He did not fully confide in the views of the people, who often acted in uneducated or self-interested ways. Instead, the king and his advisers should read and hear petitions and carefully deliberate the entire information available. Then they could wisely clear obstacles to the common good and remove the outmoded privileges of the few. In this sense, Ward argued that Spain was "a nation of high spirit, enlightened, full of love for its Sovereign, and very obedient to his orders: A constitution of government that gives the king absolute power to do all the good that he wishes."[17] Such ideas about unbridled royal power to improve the lot of the people were common during the Enlightenment, although they seem ominous to us today.

The midcentury reformers did not look too kindly at marginal groups. Both Ensenada and the Council of the Indies continued a policy of arresting and expelling the Roma, for instance. The council maligned the people in 1746 as "lacking religion, failing, thievish."[18] Ensenada demanded that the Roma should work in useful occupations; those who refused would be declared outlaws, and "it will be licit to use weapons and take their lives" if they were encountered armed. In fact, the Crown should separate men from women and "put them in fortresses . . . so the wicked race will disappear," the first minister argued.[19] Orders were sent throughout the empire to deport any Roma to Spain. They reached even smaller cities in colonial Mexico, where few Roma lived. Yet Ensenada and a special committee also acknowledged the difficulties of distinguishing poor people from the Roma, many of whom were well integrated into society. The term "gypsy" became a vague catch-all for nonconformists.[20]

Moreover, Ensenada's government again reviewed an incisive tax reform, long a topic for economists and ministers. One plan had emerged in 1655 to replace the cacophony of levies in Spain with one single tax on wealth and wages. The idea regained traction when Philip V ordered a census for the provinces of Aragon (eastern Spain) at the beginning of the eighteenth century. The census provided the basis for a 5 percent charge on landholdings and personal income from work, manufacturing, and commerce in 1716. In exchange, the Crown phased out most other levies in Aragon. Meanwhile, things moved at a slower pace in Castile, where resistance to the single tax ran strong.[21]

Regardless, Ensenada desired to overcome the roadblocks and collect revenues more fairly and efficiently. He particularly aimed at undoing the sales taxes, among them the alcabala. That levy raised prices on merchandise, which was counterproductive to economic recovery. If the alcabala endured, "this realm will never thrive, carry on active trade, or be populous," Ensenada feared.[22] Instead, he felt that the large landholders and rich clergy should step up and contribute their fair share. Many of them rejected hard work as ill suited to their status, and they contributed less to the state and economy than reasonably possible. For that purpose, Ensenada probably ordered a reprint of the book *Representation to the King*, which had praised the single tax in 1732. Ensenada also attempted to introduce the single tax in Castile in 1747. A royal decree from October 14, 1749, mandated a census of population and wealth in the province of Guadalajara, Spain (north of Madrid). Yet the opposition fought back, and it took almost seven years to complete the census. The measure lurched on until the Crown abandoned it in 1779.[23]

As Ensenada failed to make headway with the single tax, he unified alcabala collections in Castile. He terminated most tax farming and instead appointed royal officials to gather cash throughout the kingdom. The first minister also reintroduced the provincial intendants in 1749 to oversee the royal officials. In addition, Ensenada and Carvajal cut back royal debt payments, laid down nascent career patterns, and provided retirement pensions to set incentives for loyal ministers. Finally, Ensenada streamlined the apex of the treasury in Madrid, largely converting the Council of the Treasury into an appeals court of justice. The reform was successful. Crown revenue tripled, and the treasury in Spain remained virtually unchanged for the next fifty years.[24]

As opposed to Carvajal's thinking, Ensenada combined a hands-off approach to the economy with a dash of physiocracy. Ensenada was not a bullionist who prized precious metal output over all other sectors. Instead, he believed that trade was "the principal good of the monarchy."[25] Merchants should go about their business with little interference besides paying taxes. The first minister only favored Crown monopolies when necessary to supply the military or to market profitable luxury goods. For this reason, Ensenada ordered royal officials to buy and sell tobacco in Peru, although the agricultural producers remained independent. He also toyed with the idea of appointing royal officials to collect the precious dyestuff cochineal in colonial Mexico and ship it to Spain. Güemes opposed the scheme as too risky, however, and Ensenada abandoned the idea. Meanwhile, Carvajal differed by advocating for a stronger role of the state in the economy. For instance, he provided money to establish royal textile factories, among other things. Yet the factories failed because of low productivity and poor sales and eventually went out of business. Ensenada typically shunned such direct intervention.[26]

Ensenada and Carvajal also disagreed on foreign policy. Ensenada followed in Patiño's footsteps when proposing to beef up the Spanish armada to a fearsome size of sixty ships of the line and sixty-five frigates. With this plan, Ensenada aimed at making Spain stronger than Habsburg Austria or Portugal and powerful enough to serve as "the arbiter of peace and war between France and England, and even Europe."[27] Despite deep misgivings, he favored continuing the alliance with France to contain Great Britain's ambitions, especially in the Americas. Meanwhile, Carvajal proposed a diplomatic realignment; he distanced himself from France and instead resolved the quarrel over Italian territories with Habsburg Austria, France's nemesis. Carvajal also forged a peace accord with Portugal by redrawing the boundary between the two empires in South America. Finally, he espoused a working relationship with Great Britain to protect Spanish America. Consequently, Carvajal resisted Ensenada's clandestine orders to harass British settlers in the Americas and opposed ballooning the armada at the expense of the army.[28]

The king himself mostly desired peace to advance reforms in the empire. He observed the Treaty of Aix-la-Chapelle (or Treaty of Aachen) in 1748, which ended hostilities that had begun in 1739. The treaty achieved the Spanish goal of ending the British annual ship. That annual ship had whisked away hapless slaves from Africa and sold them to Spanish Americans, along with copious amounts of contraband merchandise. By ending the annual ship, Spain also abandoned its own sluggish convoy that schlepped European merchandise across the ocean. Instead, the Crown allowed individual registered ships to supply the Americas. The registered ships revived trade and filled royal coffers with taxes.[29]

A New Cut of Viceroys for the Americas

Ensenada tightened the screws in the Americas by improving the administration and tackling entitlements. For instance, the religious orders, such as the Augustinians, lost an unprecedented number of doctrinas (parishes among the indigenous population; see chapter 4). Ensenada also expanded the power of the viceroys in Peru and New Spain, after the office had bled authority during the first decades of the century. In addition, the first minister increased remittances from the Americas to Madrid as well as to fortresses on the northern frontier and in the Caribbean. Furthermore, Ensenada responded to frequent complaints about the alcaldes mayores in the Americas by phasing out the sale of their appointments.[30] In 1755, a satirical "imp of Mexico" censured despotic alcaldes mayores for evading the judicial review of their time in office:

They tyrannize the vassal,	Tiranizan al vasallo,
cheat the worker,	defraudan al jornalero,
oppress the poor widow,	oprimen la pobre viuda,

and leave the orphan naked.	dejan al pulpilo en cueros.
During their judicial review,	Llégales la residencia
the defendants strike a deal	pero como el juez y el reo
with their judge,	se ajustan, queda frustrado
thwarting such powerful remedy.[31]	tan poderoso remedio.

Career officers in part resolved that challenge by replacing alcaldes mayores and other district judges in strategic positions. In the late seventeenth century, the Crown began naming more senior officers, including brigadiers, to important ports such as Havana in Cuba. After the War of the Spanish Succession, the Crown stopped selling these appointments and increased salaries. In 1731, for example, the separate positions of the district judge of Veracruz and the warden of the fortress merged and provided a better income. Güemes himself applauded the two career officers who superseded the previous alcaldes mayores in Puebla and Sinaloa in 1754. Many of these military commanders had gained ample experience on the battlefield and in governance, just like Güemes. The process foreshadowed the changing selection criteria for viceroys. Eighteenth-century royal advisers increasingly opposed naming stiff-necked aristocrats for the viceregencies, because several of them had turned out to be disobedient, grasping, and underperforming over time. The advisers rather tapped hard-nosed officers of modest origins to carry out stringent reforms.[32]

Meanwhile, colonial Mexico lacked good leadership. Viceroy Count of Fuenclara (1742–1746) obtained the job to an extent because his wife, María Teresa Patiño, belonged to the influential Patiño clan and served as the queen's lady-in-waiting.[33] Yet Ensenada had suspicions about Fuenclara, and he ordered an inquisitor in Mexico City to report secretly about the viceregal conduct. The inquisitor replied that Fuenclara gambled and preyed upon residents too much. For instance, Fuenclara expelled the butchers from downtown ostensibly to improve public health. He ordered the demolition of "the pigpens, where the pigs were kept and killed, and free the neighboring houses and territory from the plague of lice . . . which penetrates the walls and passes to the other houses and buildings, besides the bad smell." Fuenclara also clamped down on the large copper cauldrons used to boil pork bones for soap. As a result, one soap boiler's house became nearly worthless, as its value dropped from 9,000 to 2,000 pesos. The butchers were up in arms against the order and collected 6,000 pesos to distribute at the viceregal court. The inquisitor dryly observed "that the viceroy received all or the largest part of that quantity" and revoked the order. The butchers then presented another 1,500 pesos to Fuenclara in gratitude for the felicitous resolution of the conflict.[34]

As a result of this and other missteps, Ensenada recalled Fuenclara and chose Güemes for the position on June 21, 1745. The Crown also confirmed raising the salary of viceroys from 27,573 to 40,000 pesos per year in 1746. Ministers who received better salaries served more faithfully, the thinking went. In addition, the higher pay compensated for the declining opportunities of illicit self-enrichment for viceroys, at least to a degree. An exuberant Ensenada soon cheered that "one cannot improve" the viceroys of colonial Mexico, Peru, and New Granada, "while some of their predecessors have been quite useless."[35] Güemes's social rise did not stop here. In 1748, the king admitted Güemes to the military order of Santiago as a sign of distinction. On August 12, 1749, the king also titled him as the first Count of Revillagigedo, elevating him into the aristocracy.[36]

While in office, Güemes prodded the municipal council of Mexico City to improve public safety, among other measures. He exhorted the council's public order committee to maintain the cobblestone streets in the urban center. Its members demurred because they had to "chase after stone masons" to fix the streets. After some cajoling, the committee members agreed, however.[37] Güemes also initiated a bare-bones fire brigade. On April 6, 1747, he ordered the municipal council to buy a water pump, sixty shovels, twenty-five axes, fifty buckets, and other tools. The steward had to set these tools aside in his home for any emergency and review them once a year. The councilors resisted again, citing lack of funds, but ultimately complied when pressured by Güemes.[38]

Ensenada's Fall from Power

Meanwhile at the court in Madrid, tensions simmered between Ensenada and Carvajal. As early as 1748, Carvajal lamented the lack of royal favor, as Ensenada began sticking his nose into Carvajal's business of foreign affairs. When Carvajal passed away on April 8, 1754, the conflict exacerbated. Most of his clients joined the opposition. They convinced the queen and the king to appoint Ricardo Wall, the former ambassador in London, as the new secretary of state on May 15, 1754.[39]

Wall detested Ensenada, whom he called the "great mogul," and sought to oust him. Wall and an important aristocrat reported to the king on July 14 that Ensenada had undermined the Treaty of Madrid (1750) with Portugal. The treaty handed seven Jesuit missions among the Guaraní people on the eastern bank of the Uruguay River to the Portuguese in Brazil. In exchange, Spain gained the important trading port Colonia del Sacramento (now in Uruguay) with the aim to contain contraband commerce. Ensenada, however, surreptitiously encouraged the Guaraní and the Jesuits to defend their valuable homelands. The subterfuge infuriated the king. Wall also produced Ensenada's clandestine directives for warships in Cuba to attack British settlements in Honduras and Nicaragua. The British ambassador had received the papers from a spy and slyly passed them on to Wall. The secretary of state claimed that Ensenada's course invariably led to war with Britain.[40]

That frightened the king and the queen. They felt betrayed and finally dropped Ensenada. At one o'clock on the morning of July 22, royal guards surrounded Ensenada's residence in Madrid and arrested him. They put him on a coach to Granada, which was chosen mainly because it rhymed with Ensenada and could be read as the *Gran Nada*—the great nothing. The soldiers rummaged through Ensenada's papers and turned up more incriminating news. The Austrian ambassador, in league with Wall, reported that in Ensenada's home, "indulgence and voluptuousness reigned; he swam, so to speak, in a sea of riches." One golden centerpiece had just arrived with compliments from Paris, and its "middle part is so magnificently and artfully crafted that the king in France himself clenched his shoulders when he saw it."[41] Yet King Ferdinand and Queen Barbara had qualms about the whole affair and stopped short of prosecuting Ensenada, despite Wall's pleas. Ensenada lived comfortably in exile, and he saw his fortunes rise again after the passing of the royal couple.[42]

The regime change in Madrid reversed some reforms. Wall succeeded Ensenada as first minister, and Julián Arriaga, president of the House of Trade (1752–1754), switched sides effortlessly and became secretary of the navy and the Indies (1754–1776). According to the optimistic French ambassador, Arriaga was an "intimate friend of Ensenada and very honest."[43] He lived up to his reputation as a moderately conservative administrator with ties to the consulados of Cádiz and Mexico City. One of Arriaga's first measures was to resuscitate the sluggish fleet that shuttled between Spain and colonial Mexico and confine the registered ships to the rest of Spanish America. The first convoy arrived in Veracruz in 1757. Both consulados lauded the change, because they recovered much control over the Atlantic commerce, mostly to the detriment of other residents. Güemes, meanwhile, received notice of Ensenada's fall in mid-January 1755 at the latest. Disenchanted, he requested relief from office. Arriaga acceded to his wishes and named a successor. Güemes had served nine years and four months as viceroy of colonial Mexico.[44]

Conclusion

Important reforms in colonial Mexico began earlier than many historians have acknowledged. Traditionally, scholars have focused on the period after 1759, known as the period of the Bourbon Reforms. This view is no longer valid, however. Historians now maintain that reforms in various shades took place throughout the early part of the century. Ensenada contributed to this process by authoring a series of sweeping transformations during his term as first minister.

Ensenada originally joined José Patiño's pack in 1720 and succeeded in the naval administration. He put together the campaign against Oran in North Africa in 1732, where he met Güemes. Ensenada also organized the attack on Habsburg Austrian possessions in Italy and seized Naples for the future King Charles III. Subsequently, Ensenada became first minister in 1743 and inherited Patiño's legacy. Ensenada streamlined the treasury and replaced tax farmers with royal officials, as he needed cash to finance the growing navy. Proto-physiocratic thinking inspired him, and he sought to unburden Natives in colonial Mexico from oppression. He felt that they should prosper and integrate more fully into Spanish-speaking society. The state would then be able to tax them more fairly. Bernardo Ward, who loosely belonged to Ensenada's circle, added that Natives and other individuals should become useful to the nation and entrust their well-being to a wise king with absolute power. Such love for authoritarian ideas foreshadowed the decline of the old order, which was dominated by entitlements of the aristocracy and oligarchic groups to a varying extent. Most people also belonged to corporations (self-governing social units with jurisdiction) that both protected and constrained them. Many of the vestiges of the old society were a thorn in the side of Ensenada and his people. They instead favored opening markets and allowing more self-determination and opportunities for individuals, as long as these measures did not challenge the Crown. At the same time, the reformers prized homogeneity and cared little for marginal groups or indigenous languages. Their utilitarian ideas turned especially against the Roma minority in Spain. Many Roma were rounded up for forced labor in the shipyards or persecuted in other ways.

Part of Ensenada's program consisted of sending hard-charging military commanders to the Americas. Among them was Juan Francisco Güemes. He was an offspring of humble nobility, akin to Ensenada, and embarked on a successful soldierly career. After helping to conquer Oran, Güemes obtained the position of governor of Cuba in 1733, a glowing sign of Patiño's trust in him. Thirteen years later, Güemes took the reins of the viceroyalty of colonial Mexico. Its population and economy thrived, and Ensenada believed that the viceroyalty could contribute more to imperial defense. Güemes largely succeeded in raising revenue for the Crown and reining in the religious orders, such as the Dominicans and the Franciscans. Yet when Ensenada's colleague and rival Carvajal passed away in 1754, Ensenada could not keep himself in power for long, either. The king dismissed him, and his successor struck a different political course. Güemes returned to Spain in 1756. Although his patron was sidelined, Güemes nevertheless obtained prestigious appointments at the apex of royal administration.

CHAPTER 2

A Passage to Mexico

Introduction

In May 1746, Juan Francisco Güemes, his wife, Antonia Padilla Pacheco, and their eight children sailed from Cuba to colonial Mexico. They disembarked in Veracruz and rode toward the colonial capital on a path of meaning originally forged by the Spanish conquistadors. Güemes and his family entered the pueblos (ethnic polities) and cities that had played a key role during the onslaught. A wave of excitement washed over these places. The people thronged the streets to cheer the viceroy designate, while the colonial capital glorified him in allegories as Atlas, the titan of Greek mythology. The ritual intertwined religious and secular elements, including Native contributions, and the public approval undergirded the accession.

Yet baroque pomp increasingly yielded to modesty over time. Unlike his predecessors arriving from Spain, Güemes came as a seasoned administrator from another posting in the Americas. Only his immediate family and a handful of companions rode with him instead of the sprawling entourages of the past. Güemes was not a titled aristocrat either at that time. Instead, he had risen through the military ranks because of his aptitude and relations with important ministers. In addition, the Spanish kings increasingly curbed the lavish rituals overseas while accentuating their own superiority over the viceroys. For instance, the kings began riding in coaches with eight horses, while viceroys traveled in six-in-hands. That transition to greater royal spectacle in Spain and New Spain accelerated after Güemes's term, as most viceroys altogether abandoned the sumptuous entries outside of Mexico City. The aim of this chapter is to chisel out this process by studying how Güemes arrived in the viceroyalty. With sources that are scarce and scattered, the chapter draws on Güemes's correspondence and two rare diaries reporting on his successor's entry rite in 1755—the year of Güemes's departure.[1]

Departing Spain

Little is known about how viceroys traversed the Atlantic Ocean. The voyage from Cádiz, Spain, to Veracruz in colonial Mexico at that time lasted typically between six weeks and three months.[2] A rare chronicle recorded the crossing of an early seventeenth-century Peruvian viceroy designate, although his trip was surely more lavish than Güemes's. The Peruvian dignitary embarked on the flotilla flagship, where he occupied the stern chamber. Rosebuds in vinegar perfumed the room and kept bad odors at bay. The ship also loaded plenty of fare—thirty jars of clean water, three hundred chickens, thirty hams, and a dozen mutton legs in addition to other roasted, smoked, and marinated meats. The provisions provided the viceroy with choice cuisine, while his dependents munched on cod, tuna, and other fish. About a dozen retainers and seven slaves joined the viceroy aboard the flagship. They dressed him, cleaned his quarters, cooked, and looked after other daily needs.[3] A retainer also recommended bringing "a Black woman from Lisbon who knows how to preserve food and cook . . . and other slaves to help her as washerwomen."[4] Moreover, seamless and glued sheets contained bedbugs. The viceroy also changed his silk shirts daily because of the heat and to check lice infesting the ship. When rising to the main deck, sombreros and a canopy shielded him and his family from the sun.[5]

Like the Peruvian dignitary, most Mexican viceroys left Spain with stately entourages, although these declined in the eighteenth century. For instance, thirty-six nobles, a similar number of non-nobles, and forty-eight Black slaves boarded ships with Viceroy Marquis of Cerralvo (1624–1635). Most nobles served in positions such as personal secretary or master of the horse, for instance, and they hoped for lush appointments overseas. The other travelers usually toiled in the household. Vicereine Marquise of Cerralvo also took along several ladies-in-waiting to serve her.[6] Yet splendor lessened in the early eighteenth century. The Duke and the Duchess of Alburquerque were both grandees; that is, they belonged to the upper crust of the aristocracy. Nevertheless, they arrived in 1702 with a smaller retinue than the Cerralvos. Up to one hundred people accompanied the Alburquerque family, including four Black slaves. Shortly afterward in 1716, an incoming viceroy brought sixty-six clients—considerably fewer than his predecessors.[7]

Even more modest groups emerged in 1722, when the Marquis of Casafuerte braved the ocean with twenty travelers. Casafuerte represented a new cut of viceroys. Unlike most of his high-born precursors, he was born in Lima, Peru, into a family of lower nobility with a long track record of military service. Casafuerte also excelled in the army and by 1700 had ascended to the position of lieutenant general, the second-highest rank in the army. The Crown named him viceroy primarily for his achievements and political ties rather than his birth. Madrid had high expectations, and Casafuerte did not disappoint them. For instance, when he brought fewer clients than his precursors, he assuaged tensions with colonial residents over providing desirable positions.[8]

Viceroy Güemes rose from a more humble background than Casafuerte, and he took another step toward smaller coteries. Güemes served as governor of Cuba before sailing from Havana to Veracruz in 1746, whereas most viceroys had departed from Spain. His wife and eight young children, two clients from Spain, and perhaps a handful of others escorted Güemes—a reduction even compared to Casafuerte's smaller cortege. Afterward, some of Güemes's successors also arrived from postings in the Americas. They, too, brought only a few companions—a striking departure from the days of the Cerralvo family.[9]

Some viceroys bucked the trend, however. Güemes's immediate successor, the Marquis of las Amarillas (1755–1760), reported an entourage of sixty-eight clients and their family in 1755. The most important reason for that sizable group was the second Marquise of las Amarillas. The vicereine came from a more distinguished family than her husband, who had obtained the title of nobility by marrying her. She needed her own staff, including ten women, bringing more than any other vicereine of the eighteenth century. The clients came from places outside of Castile, such as Genova and Milan in Italy. The marquise and the marquis had previously served important missions for the king in Italy, where they met the assistants.[10]

Notably, the chronicler José Manuel de Castro Santa-Anna questioned Amarillas's official roll call. Castro Santa-Anna penned that "besides the most excellent lady, his wife, their young son, an extended family of eighty-one people" arrived in Mexico City. Additional viceregal retainers apparently flocked to New Spain without registering in Spain before departure. This was probably true for many other viceroys, too. Castro Santa-Anna sniped at these newcomers, because many of them would occupy posts that should have gone to his compatriots, in his view.[11]

The subsequent coteries also varied somewhat in size, although they did not usually exceed thirty-five retainers. In 1760, an interim viceroy traveled to colonial Mexico from Cuba, where he had served as governor. His wife, daughter, and five clients joined him on the voyage, making this one of the smallest groups of the century. On the other hand, the late-century vicereine María Antonia de Godoy again relied on her own ladies-in-waiting. She was the sister of the king's favorite minister, and she and her husband arrived in colonial Mexico with thirty-four assistants in 1794, more than their immediate predecessors. Nevertheless, the days of the great entourages had passed by then.[12]

Entering New Spain

Symbolic significance couched Güemes's arrival in New Spain. His ride to Mexico City commemorated both the Spanish Conquest and the medieval homages to the kings. The homages in turn built on two archetypical scenes—the triumphal marches of the Roman legions and Jesus's entry to Jerusalem on Palm Sunday. Jesus rode a donkey to the temple, as the people acclaimed him as their king. Meanwhile, the Roman army camped on the Field of Mars outside the Eternal City before entering through a triumphal gate. The army marched past the jubilant residents and stopped to salute the Circus Maximus and other symbolic places. The procession concluded at the Capitol, where the leader worshiped Jupiter.[13]

The two archetypes combined with the desire to create personal bonds between vassals and lords of Spain. As a result, when the kings or queens of medieval Castile acceded to the throne, they usually traveled to the cities to take the vows of loyalty, setting up camp in the vicinity. The city's representatives came out to offer homage in exchange for a confirmation of city privileges. After negotiating the terms, the king entered through a gate, hailed by the people in a similar fashion to Jesus in Jerusalem. The king and retainers also recast the Roman procession in Christian garb when they honored the patron saint and worshipped in the principal church. By doing so, the king affirmed the city privileges, while the public expressed consent to the accession. Over time, negotiations among kings and cities diminished and increasingly yielded to an enactment of absolute royal power in the early modern period.[14]

Güemes's entry to colonial Mexico in 1746 mostly followed the established viceregal protocol that built on the Castilian royal accession. He and his family left Havana on May 24, 1746, and sailed into Veracruz on June 6. As their ship pulled up to the pier, the fortress artillery fired welcoming salvos, which the flotilla guns answered. Bells rang in the city. Municipal councilors, fortress officers, and clergymen in formal dress boarded the ship, climbed below deck, and welcomed the viceregal family. Shortly afterward, they emerged and disembarked on the dock. The councilors presented the incoming viceroy with the keys to the city, symbolizing lordship. The viceroy accepted and returned the keys. Güemes and the ministers then passed soldiers in the line as they walked through the festively adorned city. They arrived at the entrance to the Church of Our Lady of the Assumption on the main square. The clergy received the viceroy and offered him a *palio* (portable canopy), which was rejected, however, for being a royal prerogative. Then they jointly entered and heard mass, while the choir sang the "Te Deum Laudamus," which was a service reserved for joyous occasions and royalty.[15]

Meanwhile, the wives of the governor and municipal councilors consociated with the vicereine in her coach. She sat alone on her side facing her two companions as a sign of distinction. They rode to the home of a rich nobleman on the main square, where she, Güemes, and their children stayed about four nights to recover from the voyage. During that time, the incoming viceroy inspected the fortress in Veracruz and hammered out the travel plans with the sitting viceroy. That viceroy ordered pueblos and cities to improve the roads and prepare fiestas and lodging for the viceregal family.[16]

Incoming viceroys sent most of their retinue and baggage ahead, because the rest stops could not accommodate them. Several clients, among them the master of the horse and the pastry maker, remained with the dignitary. As the time had come, the viceregal family left Veracruz along with a company of mounted dragoons of the palace guard. The family struck out in coaches toward the north, riding along the beach for about five miles. Then they switched to litters, carried by mules that negotiated the rivers and the increasingly rugged terrain. The outgoing viceroy in Mexico City and the bishop of Puebla had sent the litters to make the trip more comfortable. When Güemes's family and clients passed a pueblo, Native governors and nobles sallied forth to receive them with flowers, music, and a few words. They bent their knees in a sign of allegiance and walked with the travelers to the next jurisdiction. As the night fell, the alcaldes mayores (district judges) welcomed the travelers into their wooden homes. After a few days, the group departed from the coast and climbed up into the cooler highlands. The ascent was steep, and the mules carrying the litters strained under the load. The group reached the city of Xalapa following some strenuous days and rested. The viceroy dined with select people, while others joined them and merely watched.[17]

Subsequently, the procession left Xalapa. Güemes, his family, and some noble retainers switched back to coaches just outside the city as the quality of the road improved. Others rode on horseback. Along the way, the viceroy received delegates from surrounding cities, and Natives welcomed him with dances at the hacienda known as San Antonio Virreyes (Viceroys). Afterward, the procession entered the territory of Tlaxcala, a major polity that had early on supported the Spanish conquistadors against the Aztecs. The viceroy halted in Atlihuetzian to commemorate the forging of that alliance. A cross had appeared that day to bless the enterprise, according to legend. The travelers left that site and reached the largely Native city of Tlaxcala on June 21. The entry recognized its lasting importance.[18]

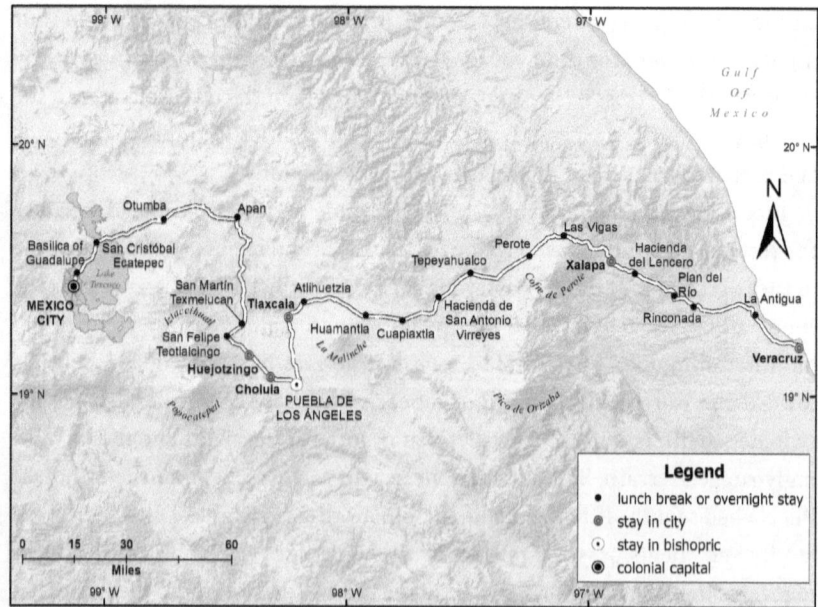

Map 2. Güemes's entry to colonial Mexico. (Designed by Ana Gabriela Arreola Meneses.)

TABLE 1. Güemes's Entry to Colonial Mexico

TRAVEL STOP	EVENTS
Veracruz	The viceregal family arrived on June 6, 1746, and rested several days. Some viceroys stayed in Veracruz fifteen days or longer to inspect the fortifications and the military.
La Antigua	Public lunch, overnight stay.
Rinconada	Public lunch.
Plan del Río	Reception by the alcalde mayor of Xalapa, overnight stay.
Hacienda del Lencero	Public lunch.
Xalapa	The travelers stayed several days, joined by the master of the horse of the outgoing viceroy, a government secretary, and constables of the acordada (summary court).
Las Vigas	Public lunch; travelers exchanged litters for coaches.
Perote	The viceroy received Puebla's municipal council representatives; overnight stay.
Tepeyahualco	The viceroy received representatives from Córdoba, Orizaba, and neighboring pueblos; public lunch.
Hacienda San Antonio Virreyes	Native dances, overnight stay.
Cuapiaxtla	Public lunch.
Huamantla	Overnight stay.
Atlihuetzian	Brief commemoration of alliance with Tlaxcala.
Tlaxcala	Public entry on June 21, at 11:00 a.m.; the travelers spent three nights.
Puebla de los Ángeles	Public entry on June 24; the travelers departed on July 3.
Cholula	Public entry, overnight stay.
Huejotzingo	Public entry, overnight stay.
San Felipe Teotlalcingo	Public lunch, overnight stay.
San Martín Texmelucan	Public lunch.
Apan	Overnight stay.
Otumba	Exchange of baton with outgoing viceroy on July 7; public lunch and dinner, overnight stay.
San Cristóbal Ecatepec	Reception hosted by the consulado (merchant guild) joined by the archbishop, ecclesiastical chapter, and representatives of the municipal council; several women welcomed the vicereine; overnight stay.
Basilica of Guadalupe	Reception hosted by Mexico City's municipal council on July 9.
Mexico City	Viceregal arrival and swearing in during the early evening of July 9; public entry on July 10.

Sources: Based on García Panes y Abellán, *Diario particular*, 73–111; Ahumada y Vera, *Diario de viaje*, 38; and Güemes to Ensenada, Mexico City, July 10, 1746, AGI, México 1506, no. 7. According to Inquisition to Fuenclara, Mexico City, October 10, 1742, AGN, Inquisición 889, fol. 31, Viceroy Fuenclara spent four nights in Veracruz. García Panes y Abellán noted Alahuazan instead of Atlihuetzian, Coapiastla for Cuapiaxtla, and Huexocingo for Huejotzingo. Today, Otumba is also called Otompan, while Las Vigas is officially Las Vigas de Ramírez.

The public entry to Tlaxcala featured a fusion of Spanish and Native imagery. Silk and brocade draped the windows and balconies along the main street. Militias lined the way as the procession formed half a league outside the city limits. Four dragoons marched ahead with their swords drawn. Then Native officials followed, wearing white cotton capes embroidered with their coat of arms. They were "splendidly dressed according to their old use," as the chronicler noted. The officials walked in the order of the pueblo governments, each displaying their insignia on poles. More Natives came afterward playing drums, horns, and flutes. Then came Güemes's page bearing the standard, showing the royal coat of arms on one side and the viceregal colors on the other. Finally, the viceroy rode on a great horse gifted by the municipal council. That horse was rubbed in "sky blue that drew much admiration from the people . . . a proof of the skill of the Americans," as the chronicler observed. The municipal officials of the city of Tlaxcala walked alongside, with the Native and Spanish governors both holding the horse's reins. More dragoons brought up the rear.[19]

The magnificent acclamation in Tlaxcala and elsewhere transformed an important nobleman into the king's representative overseas. Entire families traveled from far away, and a multitude packed the streets. Others watched from their balconies, as this was an opportunity to see and be seen. Most never attended a grander fiesta in their lives. When they beheld the viceroy, the people shouted, "May God protect you," or "how handsome and how gallant."[20] By doing so, they endorsed the viceregal accession. Expressing consent was important because the people could well refrain from applauding or even stay away from the ritual altogether. While the king had legally appointed the incoming viceroy, the festive spectacle sealed the bond between viceroy and vassals.[21]

The parade ambled through the principal street and reached the center. The viceroy stopped before a large wooden slab painted to appear like a triumphal arch, depicting allegories of the viceroy's life. Güemes listened to a speaker praising his exploits, and then the gates of the arch swung open. He and his companions passed through the gate and rode up to San Francisco Church just off the city's main square. The viceroy dismounted, entered the sanctuary, and sat under a canopy, attending mass with a "Te Deum Laudamus" that implored divine support for his governance. Afterward, fireworks cracked on the square and bullfights entertained the crowds, with admission fees paying for expenses. The viceregal family stayed in the city for three days during the celebrations. They used the time to ride in a coach to the sanctuary of Ocotlan on a hill overlooking the city. Güemes also received well-wishers, among them the provincial heads of the religious orders residing in Mexico City. They had traveled to Tlaxcala because it had been the first bishopric of New Spain and still boasted an important Franciscan priory. Moreover, Güemes exchanged letters with other corporations (self-governing social units with jurisdiction, such as a municipal council) in the colonial capital.[22]

Afterward, the entourage marched out to Puebla, which welcomed Güemes on an even grander scale with its own customs. The city had eclipsed Tlaxcala over the years as the episcopal see and largest city of the region. Over time, Puebla developed its own traditions in receiving viceroys. Unlike in other cities, the bishop and the ecclesiastical chapter rode out to salute the viceroy on the city's edge and then returned on a different route. Afterward, Güemes bathed in the multitude on the way to the main square, where he passed through another triumphal arch, richly painted. After he dismounted and entered the cathedral, a few choirboys welcomed the viceroy. They took off his spurs, challenging the master of the horse to recover them, which was yet another custom of Puebla. Similar to Tlaxcala, the vicereine arrived in a coach at the city palace, home of the municipal council and the alcalde mayor. She ascended to the balcony, where other women of distinction joined her to view the festivity. Concluding the ritual, Güemes retired to the city palace. The family stayed eight nights in Puebla, longer than anywhere else on the voyage, and met many residents. The family attended plays and participated in dances and lavish banquets offering exquisite meats, sweets, and barrels of white wine. They also visited the priories of friars and nuns and received representatives of the corporations, among them two delegates from Mexico City's municipal council.[23]

The viceroy left Puebla on Sunday, July 3, and publicly entered the cities of Cholula and Huejotzingo. Large crowds again welcomed the viceroy and his entourage. A similar ritual unfolded, with Cholula gifting the viceroy a harnessed horse for the entry, too. The cities also featured bullfights, music, and fireworks. Yet these two cities had fallen on hard times after the Conquest, and they paled in comparison to the splendor of Puebla and Tlaxcala. The viceregal family stayed only one night each and moved on.[24]

On July 7, 1746, Güemes reached Otumba in the northeastern Valley of Mexico, where outgoing and incoming viceroys usually met. Sometimes this was not feasible. Several early eighteenth-century viceroys died in office, for instance. Other viceroys promoted to govern Peru had also traveled westward toward the Pacific Ocean. Yet since 1580, the departing and arriving viceroys mostly coincided in Otumba, which symbolized victory over the Aztecs. The conquistadors and their Native allies had reached that place after suffering terrible losses during their escape from Mexico City in the Night of Sorrows. They held off the pursuing Aztecs in battle on July 14, 1520, and captured their adversaries' standard. That victory allowed the conquistadors and their Native allies to regroup and renew the assault. More than two hundred years later, Güemes conversed with the departing Count of Fuenclara in that pueblo. The two dignitaries entered a hall in the municipal council building, and each sat down on a canopied throne. Other dignitaries gathered, among them the Inquisition constable from Mexico City. The viceroys exchanged the baton of authority, indicating the new helmsmanship.[25]

The viceregal family and most guests lodged in the Franciscan priory and the council building of Otumba, although both were in disrepair by that time. When they left, they traveled about twenty-two miles to San Cristóbal Ecatepec (Mexico State). The archbishop, the ecclesiastical chapter, and the municipal council welcomed the viceroy at that site. The consulado threw a rich reception for the guests. After the meal, the viceregal retainers spread out in the alcalde mayor's residence and in the priory of San Francisco.[26]

The choice of the destinations along the entry route was meaningful but changed according to necessity. In the past, for example, viceroy and retinue traveled from San Cristóbal Ecatepec to the mansion in Chapultepec just outside of Mexico City in preparation for the grand entry. In 1642, however, the municipal council favored welcoming the viceroy near the basilica of Guadalupe. Yet its lodgings proved insufficient, and the council forsook the plan. In 1739, the Crown prohibited viceroys from spending the night in either Chapultepec or Guadalupe to save money. Instead, they had to leave San Cristóbal Ecatepec, lunch with dignitaries near the basilica, and arrive at the palace in Mexico City in the afternoon. Later viceroys even skipped Otumba entirely as they exchanged the baton in Guadalupe or elsewhere and then parted ways.[27]

The audiencia as a body welcomed Güemes, as he arrived in the palace on

Saturday, July 9, 1746. The viceroy stepped out of his coach at the bottom of the main flight at 6:00 p.m. The audiencia ministers raised their hats to salute him. Then they covered their heads again. They were entitled to that privilege, because they jointly represented the king as a corporation. Most others uncovered their heads in the viceroy's presence. The ministers walked upstairs to the meeting hall and sat down. At that point, the court chancellor entered with the viceregal appointment title. He, too, represented royalty for an instant by carrying the document with the king's signature, and he briefly wore a hat as well. All ministers rose in the presence of the royal document, and the chancellor handed the appointment title to the viceroy. At that moment, the chancellor relinquished his special role, took off his hat to show deference, and left. The viceroy rendered his oath, and the senior civil judge gave a speech. Then the other corporations came to the palace to greet Güemes.[28]

Many residents near the main square adorned their houses during the entry celebrations, similar to Tlaxcala. Other than embellishing their homes with fabric, they also kept a covered candle at their doors or windows for three nights. This was also the case on other occasions, such as the accession of a king or the marriage of a princess. Three days had symbolical importance for most Christians, as Jesus rose from the dead after that period.[29]

On the day of his grand entry on July 10, Güemes rode on horseback without the palio, symbolically subordinating himself to the king. The palio had originally covered the host and church prelates during processions but evolved into a symbol of royal power in the fifteenth century. In 1573, the Crown reserved the palio for the king, yet the custom survived, and Mexican viceroys still rode under the canopy in the mid-seventeenth century. The *Law of the Indies* again prohibited the practice in 1680. While the Crown formally allowed the second Duke of Alburquerque to enter Mexico City under the palio in 1702, he allegedly lacked the opportunity to do so. Other viceroys equally rejected its use. By the early eighteenth century, the use of the palio distinguished kings from viceroys.[30]

Other elaborate elements elevating viceroys disappeared over time, too. The municipal council, for example, demanded in the late sixteenth century that the governors of the Native barrios turn the main square of Mexico City into an impromptu forest. They had to release deer and rabbits to stage a memorable hunt within the city for the incoming viceroys. Eighty knights on horseback also featured mock jousts until the late seventeenth century, when the custom waned. By the mid-eighteenth century, viceroys no longer swore oaths at triumphal arches to uphold the privileges of Tlaxcala and other cities, either. These practices were too lavish, no longer fashionable, and opposed to the rising royal power.[31]

Güemes and his noble companions left the palace in Mexico City in the afternoon of the official entry. They rode in coaches to Santa Catarina Church (today Lagunilla), about nine blocks away from the main square. The municipal council had set up a canopied stage in front of the church. The viceroy ascended the stage with a few companions and sat down. Delegates of the council and other corporations rose to the stage to exchange courtesies, and then descended. University professors donning gowns and caps seated themselves on their mules, while audiencia ministers straddled black horses. Titled nobles, municipal councilors, and viceregal retainers joined them, carrying the standard. Meanwhile, the religious orders as corporations barely played a role in this procession. Finally, the viceroy mounted his white stallion. Mexico City's *corregidor* (district judge similar to an alcalde mayor)—as the king's representative in the city—on the right and the senior *regidor* (municipal councilman) on the left held the reins.[32]

The train started moving through the city. As the artillery fired rounds, bells rang and fireworks exploded. The procession ventured through the festively decorated streets and arrived at Santo Domingo Square, where the municipal council had set up a triumphal arch draped with flowers. That arch measured about eighty-three feet in height by forty-eight feet in width, if a later account is to be trusted. The viceroy and his entourage halted and passed under the arch. Then they rode west for several blocks, veered twice to the left, and returned toward the palace on stately San Francisco Street (now Madero). The parade stopped at the great Franciscan priory, the Jesuit Profesa Church, and significant secular corporations. Upon entering the main square, the viceroy paused briefly to greet the vicereine, who played a prominent role in the act. Doña Antonia, her daughters, and other women of distinction were sipping refreshments on the balcony of conquistador Hernán Cortés's former palace. They rose and exchanged salutations with the viceroy, who then resumed his stride toward the arch of the ecclesiastical chapter facing the cathedral.[33]

Figure 1. Unknown artist, Southeastern Mexico City in 1752, on an eastward-facing map. The viceregal parade marched toward the palace on San Francisco Street, here shown on the very left of the image, following number 6 to 1. The procession also stopped at the Franciscan priory (marked with number 6) and the Jesuit Profesa Church (number 4). (Source: Mapas, Planos e Ilustraciones [280] / MAPILU / 210100/4423 Ciudad de México [4150] / originally in AGN, Civil 1496, fol. 242; courtesy of the Archivo General de la Nación.)

Viceregal Virtue and Glory

The arches of the ecclesiastical chapter and the municipal council lionized viceroys by comparing them to classical heroes, gods, and virtues. The arches, for example, depicted viceroys as Mercury, the divinity of mental acuity and trade, and Neptune, the god who ruled the sea and soothed the storms. Neptune also reined in the winds as the mythical founder of Rome crossed the Mediterranean, like the viceroys journeying to colonial Mexico. Meanwhile, the kings frequently appeared as Apollo or Jupiter—roughly representing reason and justice, respectively, in the eighteenth century.[34] In addition, the archbishops entered in similar albeit smaller rituals than the viceroys. A late seventeenth-century arch compared the prelate to the Greek god Proteus, a learned judge, shape-changing shepherd of seals, and son and subordinate of Neptune. One humanist even compared Proteus to Jesus, although eminent critics tore into this view. The metaphor displeased the austere archbishop, in part because of the implied subordination to the viceroy. Many other beholders understood the allegories to varying degrees, as some ambiguity in the messaging was desirable.[35]

The arch commissioned by the ecclesiastical chapter in 1746 praised above all Güemes's strength and justice. The viceroy beheld fourteen images on the arch, showing him as Atlas, the titan of Greek mythology who bore heaven on his shoulders and kept it apart from earth. A professor of the theological seminary at that point declaimed a poem on the arch's meaning. He hailed Güemes's martial heroism for despising clouds of steel on the Italian battlefields and inflicting on the British "human terror with giant valor."[36] According to the professor, Atlas also mingled with his lover Hesperia, their children, and his brother. Regardless, justice reigned, since Atlas was "not conquered by blood" and banned his brother to Italy for committing an offense. Justice was a cardinal virtue and God-given undergirding of society. Viceroys upheld justice, just as judges had to live in "fear of God" to resolve conflicts fairly.[37]

Finally, the poem proposed a union of strength and gentleness, an axiom of early modern thinking. The professor suggested that the outgoing Viceroy Fuenclara had shouldered Mexico and then ceded the "Mexican heaven" to Güemes—akin to Hercules, who briefly stood in for Atlas. Early modern allegories often showed Hercules representing manly virtues. The hero also stood in for the king and even emulated Jesus Christ and divine principles.[38] By introducing these characters, the professor referred to the popular play *Love Tames Beasts*. In the play, Hercules first frees Hesperia but spurns love for being a chimera. He then goes to battle in exchange for a promise to marry Yole, the daughter of the king of Libya, home of Atlas Mountain. Yet Hercules mainly seeks to humiliate Yole for rejecting him as a brute. In the end, she attains Hercules's love and triumphantly breaks his power by entrapping him.[39] The professor hastened to deny that Fuenclara was a beast, instead saying that he behaved like a "courtly Hercules."[40] The play mainly alludes to the principle that gentleness, love, and beauty should temper the ferociousness of a great warrior. By speaking these lines, the professor also confidently requested that Güemes not exaggerate his military rigor in comparison with the more accommodating Fuenclara. The arch equally implored harmony between Güemes and New Spain, which the professor proudly praises as resembling Atlas's celestial sphere:[41]

> This kingdom, Lord, is home to all . . .
> this spacious treasure and ark embrace all
> this great part of the universe,
> where beauty is shown by the diverse.[42]

> Este Reyno, Señor, patria de todos,
> este tesoro y arca que espaciosa por si todo lo abarca
> esta parte mayor del universe
> donde prueba hermosura lo diverso

After passing through the arch, Güemes worshipped with other dignitaries in the cathedral, where the archbishop blessed him. The viceroy then returned to the palace in a coach, hindered by the multitude of people gathering on the main square. The artillery continued to fire salvos, and the cathedral bells struck periodically until two o'clock in the morning. For the next two weeks, the viceroy and his wife attended banquets, comedies, and musical performances. The municipal council also held bullfights next to the palace, charging admission to pay for expenses. The viceregal family watched the games from the palace or joined others in a VIP box that was served with refreshments.[43]

Evidently, the viceregal entry was modeled on the royal accession in

Madrid, which also interspersed secular and religious imagery. A key element of that ritual consisted of the waving and planting of the royal standard in front of the vassals. That secular piece was inherited from Rome's armies. The king also rode out to seek the consent of the people. He left the palace in Madrid in the early evening, traveled to the Puerta del Sol (Sun Gate), and passed through triumphal arches adorned with allegories. Multitudes lined the streets, shouting "Viva!" as the king passed. In addition, the delegates of the Cortes (the much-reduced parliament of estates) met to swear oaths with the king, which was followed by kissing the hand of the new ruler. Furthermore, the ritual integrated practices of the faith. The archbishop received the king outside a large parish church and offered blessed water. The prelate said mass with a "Te Deum Laudamus," "imploring the help and powerful protection of the sacred image of Saint Mary." After the meeting of the Cortes, the archbishop concluded the ritual with another mass.[44]

While Spanish kings claimed that they served by the grace of God to defend the faith, other monarchies featured even more sacred symbols. In the Holy Roman Empire, for example, the archbishop of Cologne anointed and crowned the emperor during mass. French kings even wielded the supernatural powers of thaumaturges, who healed petitioners by laying their hands on them. Yet Spanish kings did not profess such transcendence.[45] In fact, several religious elements such as crowning and anointing kings fell out of use in the late medieval period, and rulers refused to bow symbolically to the clergy during accession. As a token, the kings also dropped the address "Sacred Catholic Royal Majesty" in the sixteenth century for the simple "Señor" (Lord).[46]

Because of that strong secular component of kingship, colonial authors merely glorified ideal conduct without deifying king or viceroy.[47] The erudite Carlos Sigüenza y Góngora stressed in 1680, for instance, that princes should "serve as mirror to observe the virtues adorning" them. Mirrors were effigies that reminded the beholder of both virtues and vices, without being identical to the original. Sigüenza y Góngora even added that princes were "less so God's vicars . . . but His living image, or an earthly God." Sigüenza y Góngora did not equate the king to the Christian God, however, since "earthly God" refers to classical non-Christian figures, which abound in his texts.[48] In fact, Sigüenza y Góngora directly drew on a late sixteenth-century jurist, who stated more cautiously that the prince is "in a sense like an earthly god." That jurist continued that "the prince ought to surpass others in virtue as much as he precedes them in dignity."[49] A prince must, therefore, behave in a way that reflects his social station and embody a standard that others can aspire to. That call for good leadership, although by no means always achieved, inspired Sigüenza y Góngora.

Viceroys shared many other tokens of power with the kings. Contemporaries labeled the viceroy the "alter ego" or the "living image of the king," who acted as a royal simulacrum, for instance.[50] Most viceroys also belonged to the aristocracy, and their aura buttressed governance until the early eighteenth century. They usually grew up in courtly society and quickly became accustomed to "representing the person of the king," as a chronicler put it in 1666.[51] In addition, when visitors came to the palace, they kissed the viceroys' hands, which was a gesture performed for the king in Spain. Viceroys also enjoyed the protection of Black soldiers, a mounted force, and a guard of twenty halberdiers with their captains. Viceroy Linares even expanded the guard to three hundred soldiers—more like the royal guards in Madrid—but the Crown quashed the project for parsimony.[52]

Toward Viceregal Austerity

Nonetheless, eighteenth-century Mexicans recognized the difference between the king and his representation only too well. While the jurist Juan Solórzano likened viceroys to kings, for instance, he noted that other jurists compared them to lesser Roman provincial governors. Solórzano also observed that viceroys could not ennoble people or appoint and remove audiencia judges. They had no formal say in audiencia rulings, while the court regularly reviewed and rejected viceregal mandates. Solórzano's view remained influential, as his legal commentary was republished in 1739. Meanwhile, the king did what viceroys could not: alter the law and recall audiencia judges and viceroys at his pleasure.[53]

In addition, the imagery of likening viceroys to kings dissolved over time, as viceroys became heads of bureaucracies, and both practice and law clarified boundaries. A conflict from 1719 illustrates this point. In that year, the Council of the Indies ordered the viceroy to surrender jurisdiction over a criminal case to the audiencia, with the prosecutor advocating for a reprimand of the viceroy. The dignitary replied bitterly that "viceroys have less jurisdiction than a municipal magistrate" in New Spain.[54] In addition, eighteenth-century viceroys did not typically receive the ambassadors of other sovereigns and conducted very limited foreign policy, if at all. Residents also knew that the viceroys were not of royal Bourbon blood. Viceroys had to request approval from Madrid for major changes and were subject to judicial investigations. Moreover, the king's patronage power to appoint alcaldes mayores in the kingdom of New Spain grew markedly in the late seventeenth century at the expense of the viceroys. In 1702, a disgruntled observer accused viceroys of a power grab to make themselves kings. He exaggerated, however, as his aim was to further diminish viceroys.[55]

This process continued. Mid-eighteenth-century entry arches equated one viceroy to a Roman general serving the emperor and another to Hercules, who appeared here as the son of Jupiter, who often represented royalty. The two arches demonstrated the subordinate role of viceroys to the king.[56] Portraits of viceroys in Mexico City also depicted mere high dignitaries. Güemes appears (see this book's cover) as a slightly plump yet vigorous man in middle age (although younger than he was in reality). He wears a fashionable *casaca* (an embroidered, long, and tightly fitted jacket), vest, and white shirt with a powdered wig. The viceroy holds the baton of command and a document indicating just governance. In the background, the royal armada sails past a fortress whose guns discharge a volley. That demonstrates Güemes's resolve to defend the unity of the empire, be it in Spain, the Caribbean, or colonial Mexico. The painter also hints at Güemes's patron Ensenada, who was known for rebuilding the armada against considerable opposition. The top left of the painting displays the viceroy's coat of arms and several weapons symbolizing Güemes's military career. The elements point to an officer hardened in the king's service without inferring royalty.

More evidence points in this direction. Officer Diego García Panes, who chronicled the viceregal entry of 1755, spoke of "the general who truly holds the post of viceroy of New Spain" and "the distinguished office of a viceroy of Mexico, who represents the person of the Sovereign in that kingdom." García Panes considered the viceroy a senior officer without equating him to the king.[57] Furthermore, Spanish viceregencies in Europe had almost entirely vanished by this time. Seventeenth-century aristocratic viceroys still hobnobbed in elite milieus in Italy. They appointed multitudes of people to coveted offices. A viceroy of Naples allegedly named at least two hundred people to plush positions and pensions in the 1630s, surely extracting favors in return. Yet the Crown increasingly frowned upon these viceregal excesses and curbed their powers. As a result, a Sicilian aristocrat commissioned a work in 1644 excoriating viceroys for lacking majesty and poorly copying the king. Ultimately, Spain lost its Italian possessions in the early eighteenth century and suppressed most viceregencies in the Spanish peninsula.[58]

As the institution declined in Europe, the Crown also reined in the considerable expenses of viceregal entries in New Spain. In 1612, the audiencia capped costs at 14,000 pesos, and seven years later, the Crown set the bar at 8,000 pesos, ordering councilors to shoulder more costs themselves. Despite the measures, the viceregal accession rite of 1640 surpassed precursors in grandeur.[59] Just over one hundred years later, the municipal council officially contributed 8,000 pesos for wining and dining the viceroy, improving the roads, and staging the ritual.[60] Yet the council drew on additional clandestine funds in defiance of the law. The chronicler Castro Santa-Anna reported that the council paid 16,000 pesos for the spectacle in 1755, excluding the individual expenses of the councilors in organizing the event and riding out in full attire. Moreover, the consulado spent 2,000 to 4,000 pesos for the viceregal reception in San Cristóbal Ecatepec, although the Crown curtailed that expense as well.[61]

The burden of pageantry also fell on the Natives. The municipal council of Tlaxcala, for example, paid a total of 2,000 pesos for the grand entry. Its councilors charged all subjects of the jurisdiction the equivalent of three reales (three-eighths of a peso) for the triumphal "arch, fireworks, and horses" in the late seventeenth century. The Crown at that point prohibited drawing on Natives and their community funds for the ritual.[62] Nonetheless, Güemes and the civil judges noted in 1746–1747 that the governor of Tlaxcala continued to demand money. The small pueblo Moras (probably near San Francisco Ixtacuixtla), for instance, contributed "a dozen hens, a dozen roosters, and four dozen eggs," worth about one peso, to the governor, while Santa María Acuitlapilco paid five pesos. The surrounding pueblos chipped in 355 pesos.[63] At that point, the authorities once again enjoined governors and alcaldes mayores of Puebla and Tlaxcala from exacting cash or services from residents. The complaints continued, however, until the viceregal entries in the two cities faded away.[64]

In fact, the Enlightenment slowly undermined the ritual. In general, baroque opulence decayed as sensibilities shifted. Rambunctious processions in the streets, bloody flagellations of the faithful, and risqué dances on religious holidays declined. A sober mood spread across New Spain, and the great gestures lost attraction. Many residents accepted modest entries as a commitment to reason and the public good rather than a confirmation of an obsolete lord-vassal relationship. As a result, ritual acclamation mattered less than before. Güemes's entry, while still exuberant, took some steps in that direction, as we have seen—his humble background differed from that of his predecessors, and he arrived with a small entourage. Other displays of lavishness, such as deer hunting on the main square, had already been squeezed out earlier.[65]

Entries continued to downsize in the second half of the century. The interim viceroy broke with tradition when traveling in 1760. He forewent comfortable lodgings in Veracruz and slept in the rugged San Juan de Ulúa fortress instead. That viceroy also rode straight to Mexico City, skipping the festivals in Tlaxcala and elsewhere. While his successor opted again for ostentation, the ensuing viceroy dispensed with most protocol in 1766. He also dreaded Otumba's discomforts and handed off the baton in San Cristóbal Ecatepec in 1771. Most successors afterward forewent the parades outside of Mexico City.[66]

The use of horses also accentuated the king. The viceroys originally emulated royal conduct when riding into a city on horseback. By the seventeenth century, however, kings forsook the practice and remained in coaches. In New Spain, the viceroy arriving in 1783 could barely saddle up for his old age, and subsequent viceroys sat in the carriage, too. Originally, six white horses drew the coaches of both kings and viceroys. The president of the Council of the Indies confined viceroys to four-in-hands in the early seventeenth century, but the order was widely ignored. By the early eighteenth century, however, kings traveled in eight-in-hands, separating them visually from the viceroys.[67]

In addition, royal accession rites trumped viceregal entries as part of a larger change. Kings sought to rule a more unified empire by focusing loyalty on themselves. They downplayed the political autonomy of overseas realms and their viceroys. Royal accessions in turn became more elaborate, as the advent of King Charles IV in 1788 exemplified. The municipal chapter of

Mexico City commissioned wooden painted façades to cover its building as part of the celebrations. The corporations of Mexico City also organized dances on the occasion, and some lasted until four in the morning. Stores remained closed for three days. As part of this process, the ostentatious viceregal rites declined in stature.[68]

Conclusion

Güemes and his family rode a path of meaning from Veracruz to Mexico City, hewn by the conquistadors. Native officials briefly joined the procession, bending their knees and offering flowers, while visitors from other cities came from afar to welcome them. The viceregal entourage stopped at Atlihuetzian to commemorate the alliance with Tlaxcala against the Aztecs. That city, although much reduced in size, pompously received the viceroy. Güemes, and other viceroys of the period, then festively entered the cities of Puebla, Cholula, Huejotzingo, and Mexico City, reminiscing medieval homages to the Castilian kings. The entries transformed a career officer into the king's representative, and the people and corporations witnessed and approved the accession. Baroque bombast legitimized Güemes's governance, glorifying him in largely secular allegories. The extravaganza also affirmed the unity of the Spanish Empire, as people of diverse ethnic backgrounds congregated.

Yet austerity advanced at a time when Güemes prepared to carry out reforms and ruffle feathers. He rejected the palio when riding into town, just as his predecessors had done. The Crown also repeatedly reined in expenses and continued to inquire about excessive Native payments for the 1746 spectacle in Tlaxcala and Puebla. Madrid had also earlier cut an overnight stay in the Valley of Mexico to save on expenses. Moreover, when not riding on horseback, viceroys traveled in six-in-hands in New Spain. Meanwhile, the king switched to coaches with eight horses in the eighteenth century, symbolically stressing their difference.

Likewise, viceregal entourages dwindled notably during the eighteenth century, but not in as linear a fashion as assumed. While Viceroy Alburquerque brought a sizable entourage in 1702, Casafuerte introduced modest retinues comprising around twenty retainers in 1722. Even fewer clients accompanied

Güemes in 1746—his wife, eight children, two clients from Spain, and perhaps a handful of others. And yet, the cortege of the Marquis of las Amarillas shattered the trend toward modesty when arriving with sixty-eight followers in 1755. The Marquise of las Amarillas contributed significantly to this reverse. She was entitled to bring several ladies-in-waiting, as she descended from a more illustrious family than her husband. Additional clients flocked to New Spain to bask in viceregal patronage, sidestepping controls in Cádiz. Although smaller entourages returned after Amarillas, a late eighteenth-century viceroy, his politcally well-connected wife, and thirty-four companions marched to a different drummer once more. Retinues sailing the Atlantic declined unless vicereines of high social standing were aboard.

The interim viceroy of 1760 even rode straight to Mexico City, eschewing any fiestas along the road. Six years later, a full-fledged viceroy followed that model of modesty, although the entries in Mexico City continued until the end of the century. Meanwhile, royal accession rites increasingly eclipsed viceregal rites, as Madrid directed attention to the king of a more unified state at the expense of the regional autonomies. The traditional ritual forging bonds between a lord and his vassals slowly fell out of use.

CHAPTER 3

From Viceregal Rituals to Informality

The Court in Mexico City

Introduction

In 1755, Vicereine Marquise of las Amarillas arrived in Mexico City and settled into the palace. Shortly after, she received the ministers of the Inquisition, who welcomed her to the city. They exchanged courtesies, and she remarked that she was "very grateful and satisfied with the inquisitor's expressions." Amarillas then continued the conversation by briefly pondering the travails of coming to New Spain, since "it was a much hardship to sail, and she preferred traveling on land, even if it meant more effort."[1] That was unexpected. Usually, visitors merely traded formulaic pleasantries during the audiences (formal meetings) and then departed. For that reason, there are few records of what participants said during meetings in the viceregal palace. The mere existence and duration of an audience mattered more, because the attention of both vicereine and viceroy was a scarce good that many residents vied for. However, Amarillas's "flattering affability" broke the mold and graced the Holy Office with special attention. Her favor also starkly contrasted with the chilly conduct of her predecessor, Antonia Padilla Pacheco, toward the inquisitors on a similar occasion in 1746.[2]

Generally, much life at early modern courts was tightly choreographed. The royal family, the aristocracy, and many clients raised in the palaces had internalized complex guidelines and knew how to behave in public. Meanwhile, the etiquette was often opaque for the uninitiated and awed them purposefully. That was also true for the viceregal court in Mexico City.[3] Yet ingrained guidelines did not curtail spontaneity or informality. Life in the apartments of the royal palace in Madrid was more relaxed and even ludic. King Ferdinand VI of Spain and Queen Barbara of Bragança (in power 1746–1758/59) often played music or met with friends in casual settings at late hours. Kings and aristocrats also went hunting in the countryside, where a more permissive atmosphere reigned in various ways. Informal conduct marked smaller European principalities, too. Many at the court of the archbishop elector of Cologne in the Holy Roman Empire, for instance, ignored their own printed ceremonial etiquette. Such smaller courts resembled the Mexican one in size, more so than the well-studied royal courts of Madrid or Paris.[4]

There are reasons to believe, then, that much conduct at the viceregal court was not tightly regimented, as the Marquise of las Amarillas showed. Viceroy Güemes at least occasionally sidestepped protocol when receiving visitors. He was tardy twice when the inquisitors came calling on him. In addition, most viceroys rose from their seats without moving away when seeing off visitors. That indicated their superior status. However, one dignitary slightly altered this protocol to gratify his guests by taking four steps toward them at that point. What is more, the viceroy and the vicereine gambled, danced, or dined with guests and family, indicating a frolicsome life in the viceregal apartments, at least occasionally.

This chapter distinguishes between informality, ritualized conduct, and rituals. Unlike informality, ritualized conduct refers to standardized gestures that are meaningful and frequent such as greeting others, observing table manners, or asking for forgiveness. These gestures signal respect, social standing, and belonging. While important, ritualized conduct does not rise to the level of rituals, which stand out from everyday life. Their festive performances contain sets of elements such as imagery, ornate dresses, and formulaic speech, which repeat in similar ways. Performing rituals entertains, legitimizes, and transforms reality. Güemes's viceregal accession, for example, broadcast colonial power and amused the crowd. More importantly, the public witnessed and confirmed a high-ranking officer's accession to the viceregency as a representative of the king, which had important legal ramifications.[5]

In this regard, historians now widely accept that rituals expressed the intentions of both the central government and the colonial residents. The Spanish Crown, for instance, controlled important rituals overseas to convey the idea of a strong dynastic rule. Meanwhile, residents celebrated their corporations (self-governing social units with jurisdiction, such as municipal councils) and underlined their standing in society. They also uttered grievances and bickered over arrangements even while performing the ritual.[6] Despite their significance, frequent rituals, especially the sacred ones, tired the individual members of the corporations. Several municipal councilors repeatedly clashed with Viceroy Güemes for shunning processions. This chapter explores such conduct ranging from rituals to informality at the viceregal court.

An Informal and Unruly Court

The law collection *Siete partidas* (Seven Parts) defines the court as "the place where the king, his vassals, and his officials are, who counsel him daily and receive others from the kingdom to honor him or to attain justice."[7] By and large, the Spanish court complied with this idea. The king and the queen in Madrid met daily at noon with ministers to consult over important state affairs. They crafted politics and dispensed favors. The royal couple also participated in many public acts and set a standard for art, fashion, cuisine, language—good taste in general.[8]

At the same time, much quotidian life in the royal apartments was informal. Queen Barbara conversed with her ladies-in-waiting during the mornings, for instance. After lunch, she deftly composed and played music, while Ferdinand chimed in occasionally with more effort than talent. During his better days, he conversed affably with the courtiers and their wives. Ferdinand also frequently hunted until nightfall. After dinner, the queen and king played cards, listened to opera, or danced. Later at night, they met with the first minister Ensenada and the celebrated castrato singer Farinelli. They took off their wigs, drank French wine, sang, and joked at the expense of the court jester. Afterward, the royal couple usually prayed and retired to their separate bedrooms.[9]

Yet few colonial Mexicans ever made it to Madrid, and many instead visited the protean viceregal court. This was the home of the viceregal family and several clients. Visitors usually ascended the grand staircase to the second floor of the palace. They met with the viceroy or the vicereine in their own halls. Only close confidants passed through the antechambers to access the separate bedrooms of the viceregal couple. In addition, audiencia ministers and royal officials regularly came to work in their offices, which nestled around the palace patios. Litigants, attorneys, and testators also pleaded their case and moved paperwork through the bureaucracy. Natives and their procurators (legal agents) entered the building and ascended a back staircase to a room behind the viceregal apartments, where a special Indian court heard their matters. Prisoners dwelled forcibly on the lower level of the palace, as did some jailers, although they did not participate in courtly events. A large park for bullfights and horse riding delimited the premise from the city.[10]

Güemes and his family usually received people of distinction at court. He invited ministers of important corporations and their wives to festivities or audiences. Many nobles, officers, clergy, and others with a university degree flocked to the palace, too.[11] Supplicants also solicited meetings. The details are unknown, but admission depended at least on clean, quality clothes. A viceregal page at the gate barred entry for unsuited commoners. They could deposit a letter in a box at the entrance of the halberdier guard and pick up a viceregal response from the sergeant within two days. The responses did not necessarily resolve the issues and sometimes merely directed petitioners to an office for further inquiry.[12]

Desperate to get Güemes's attention were offenders seeking pardons. They frequently lived in church asylum or hid elsewhere to escape secular justice. For instance, Güemes visited the Santo Domingo priory on December 8, 1752, on the day of the Immaculate Conception. At that time, a coppersmith inhabited the church, because he had wounded an officer in a quarrel. As Güemes entered the patio, the coppersmith rushed past the viceregal retinue. He threw himself at the viceroy's feet and begged for mercy on account of the holiday. Güemes, however, called him a "brazen scofflaw" and repelled his request. The stricken delinquent remained in asylum.[13]

Formal rules often yielded to informality at court. In 1603, for example, the president of the Council of the Indies in Madrid gave the departing viceroy a manual of good behavior. The manual encouraged the dignitary to represent the king with gravitas and command deference from residents. The viceroy was to keep social distance from visitors and maintain hierarchies when dining with others. While the Marquis of Gelves (1621–1624) confidently carried out these rules, his successor flouted them often and met with civil judges in rolled-up sleeves, to some chagrin.[14] In addition, the meeting space of their regular reunions, called the *real acuerdo*, became more informal. The dedicated room collapsed in the palace fire of 1692. Instead of switching to the viceregal hall, however, the real acuerdo assembled in the antechamber of the viceroy's bedroom until the 1720s. The antechamber was barely adequate, because it lacked a table for proper proceedings, and poorly designed doors invited passersby to listen in.[15]

In addition, condoling the viceroys for the death of a king should have been an orderly event governed by rank. Long before Güemes's arrival, on June 4, 1666, the corporations lined up in the palace at eight thirty in the morning for the funeral rites of Philip IV. The audiencia judges gathered in their hall as commissioners ushered treasury officials and municipal councilors into the other offices. When it was their turn, the ministers walked two by two down the corridor and around the audiencia courtyard. Important corporations, such as the merchant guild, went first, ascending in rank until the audiencia. Then the Inquisition and lesser corporations followed. Retainers admitted them to the viceregal hall. The members of a corporation saluted the viceroy, and the higher-ranked representatives kissed the viceroy's hand, as was customary. They sat down, while members of lower station remained standing. The senior member rose again and extended the corporations' condolences. Afterward, the ministers moved to the vicereine's hall, where they again expressed their sympathy. Concluding the act, they descended to the ground floor of the palace and drove off in their coaches or walked away. The ministers' wives also arrived in coaches at four thirty in the afternoon and commiserated with the vicereine.[16]

Yet even these obsequies demanding decorum descended into noisy discussions over preeminence. People thronged the hallways. Arguments broke out over the proper rank and sequence in the line of procession, as was often the case in the old regime. The clergyman writing the chronicle noted that the commissioners had to "impose decency and prevent strife or confusion that would disturb the stillness and silence, which such a majestic act called for." In fact, it was necessary to use "the hard hand of the soldiers of the guard to avoid spoiling the dignity" of the funeral. The clergyman underlined with satisfaction that the ecclesiastical chapter walked in perfect order and silence through the palace, while others undermined etiquette.[17]

In the early eighteenth century, Viceroy Duke of Linares (1710–1716) tried to curb such unruliness by appointing a palace usher, akin to the extinct viceregal court in Naples, Italy. The usher's job was to observe social hierarchies among participants and enforce ceremonial rules that few remembered. The Crown, however, opposed the additional salary for the usher and quashed the position in Mexico City. The usher, who also served as audiencia porter, may still have continued his work and received a stipend from other funds.[18]

Decades later, the Inquisition prepared to meet with the viceroy in his hall. On Christmas Eve of 1743, the inquisitors sent a messenger to inquire about an appropriate time. A viceregal page replied that four o'clock would be fine. In the afternoon, the inquisitors left their residence on Santo Domingo Square, crossed the main square, and entered the palace. They walked up the great flight, lined up according to rank in the corridor, and stepped into the hall. The viceroy came out of the bedchamber at that point. "After the initial customary bows, his Excellency, the inquisitors, and the other officials sat down according to rank," the Inquisition notary observed.[19] The viceroy rested on a cushioned velvet chair in the middle of the hall. The fine red cloth was associated with royalty, highlighting the viceroy's rank. This arrangement to an extent mirrored the royal court, where the king usually sat on an elevated and cushioned throne that raised him above others. Canopies covered both king and viceroy and lent additional authority. In addition, the senior inquisitors did not merely sit on benches but on backrest chairs "covered with damask."[20] They exchanged well-wishes for the holiday with the viceroy, who then got up to bid farewell. The inquisitors "fittingly bowed to his Excellency who replied similarly, and the gentlemen did so again at the door of the main hall."[21]

Now consider the lackadaisical conduct of Güemes toward the inquisitors two and a half years later. Güemes and Vicereine Antonia Padilla Pacheco had just arrived in Mexico City, and the Holy Office expressed its desire to welcome them. On Sunday, July 10, 1746, in the morning, a messenger came to the palace and requested an appointment for the ministers. Güemes sent a note setting the meeting at three thirty in the afternoon, because the Tribunal of the Crusade Indulgence (a board of clergymen who sold indulgences to fight non-Catholics) would visit at four o'clock. At the timely moment, the inquisitors walked up the flight. As they lined up in the corridor, however, a viceregal page stepped out to inform them that Güemes was delayed, because he had just eaten. He invited the ministers to move into the antechamber and wait.

Güemes then sent a note asking "to excuse him and give him the chance to put on his wig."[22] The inquisition notary recorded that

> the inquisitor and the other ministers entered the main hall at that point, where his Excellency was standing without parting from his cushion and seat . . . and his Excellency began to apologize, reasoning that it seemed to him that the Holy Office would not arrive before four o'clock. The inquisitor satisfied this point by stating that this was the hour appointed for the Tribunal of the Crusade Indulgence, while three thirty was set for the Holy Office, which his Excellency recalled and fully acknowledged.

The viceregal couple then followed up with another snub toward the inquisitors, when the Holy Office

> suggested to welcome the most excellent lady vicereine. His Excellency replied that they had eaten late, and the ladies did not usually prepare themselves so quickly to receive people, although he would pass on a message if the Inquisition preferred. The inquisitor answered that the tribunal merely desired to meet its timely obligation without discomforting his Excellency.[23]

The vicereine's refusal to meet the inquisitors differed starkly from the Marquise of las Amarillas's conduct, and yet Güemes continued his informality the next day. On that Monday, July 11, the municipal council commissioned a comedy in the Coliseum Theater on account of the viceregal arrival. Güemes's page crossed Santo Domingo Square after one o'clock. He entered the Inquisition palace and communicated the invitation to join the viceroy at the performance, as the notary noted with some pride. Perhaps Güemes tried to compensate for his earlier tardiness. In any case, the inquisitors lined up in the palace corridor after the evening prayer around six o'clock. At that point, a page stepped out to inform them that Güemes had not returned yet but invited them to enter the hall and sit down.[24] Shortly afterward, Güemes joined the ministers,

> apologizing for not being there, because he went out to see Alameda Square and San Francisco Street. Then they conversed for some time,

refreshments were served, and soon after finishing the conversation and having been advised that it was time for the comedy, the Inquisition left in its usual order according to their rank. The inquisitor accompanied his Excellency to his right."[25]

When they arrived at the Coliseum, Güemes and Padilla Pacheco went in and sat down in the middle. The Inquisition ministers walked to their assigned seats on the left side of the theater, while the lesser officials sat on benches in the rear. After the comedy had finished, the ministers waited for the viceroy and the vicereine and noted that no litter stood ready to take them back to the palace. The ministers fell back in line and walked the couple home. They accompanied them up the flight and said good-bye in front of the antechamber. The evening concluded agreeably despite previous tensions.[26]

Despite the slight, the relation of the inquisitors with the viceroy recovered. The subsequent audiences occurred uneventfully. Perhaps Güemes's missteps occurred because he had become more forgetful as he grew older. Apparently, no other retainer kept track of his schedule, either. When he was late enjoying his walk on the Alameda, however, the viceroy willingly snubbed the Inquisition. He knew that the power of the Holy Office had declined substantially in that century. The Enlightenment increasingly frowned upon persecuting heretics, and kings restricted inquisitorial jurisdiction. Under these circumstances, the viceroy could cold-shoulder peevish inquisitors, who minutely recorded their allegedly flawless conduct with the viceroys.[27]

Details of the palace audiences also changed, sometimes to indicate favor toward visitors. In most cases, the viceroys stood and remained near their seat when welcoming and seeing off people. Yet after Viceroy Fuenclara's arrival in 1742, the inquisitors noted with satisfaction that the "viceroy began to take four steps away from the cushion" toward them to invite them to the comedy as they were leaving.[28] In addition, visitors frequently entered the hall first, whereupon the viceroy left his bedroom to join them. In one instance, however, Güemes stepped out of his wife's bedroom. Neither did the Inquisition ministers always visit the palace in the same fashion. In 1746, for instance, an *alguacil mayor* (chief constable) accompanied them to welcome Güemes to the colonial capital. In 1747, the secretary acted as constable, while in 1753, the secretary noted with some consternation that the constable had missed the Christmas audience entirely.²⁹

Family and Daily Life

Viceroys regularly gambled in nocturnal reunions. The law prohibited the practice, especially for judges and prosecutors, but to no avail. An inquisitor reported that Viceroy Fuenclara hosted card games, "although they do not last beyond ten o'clock. They continued a few times past this hour in the room of the *mayordomo* [steward]." Fuenclara escaped a rebuke but was recalled soon after.³⁰ Güemes may well have heard of the report. He reminded the public that gambling was prohibited, unlike proper entertainment in elite homes. He also caught a member of his retinue "in the royal palace dealing with contraband cards and dismissed him from service," mainly making a statement against contraband goods.³¹

While residents showed a little more public restraint, Güemes relished playing cards as much as Fuenclara. The Council of the Indies in 1750 lambasted that "gambling and wagering continued in the viceroy's room in the palace, causing notable scandal."³² After this attack on Güemes, the council suggested altogether prohibiting the sale of playing cards in New Spain. The discussion resulted in one ostensible change. The consul of the merchant guild offered refreshments and harmless entertainment for his 1753 New Year's reception, while in previous years, "many lost considerable amounts of money when gambling."³³

In addition, the royal table in Madrid became more family oriented in the eighteenth century, which must have influenced Mexico City. The Habsburg kings often ate in silence and on their own as others looked on and witnessed the exalted stature. Yet manners softened up over time. The first Bourbon king, Philip V, and his first wife Maria Luisa married in 1701 and began sharing meals. They also joined their households and even bedrooms, an unheard-of practice at that point. Their successors continued the practice. Afterward, King Charles III (1759–1788) often sat at the table with his wife Maria Amalia and their children. In addition, while an ambassador occasionally dined with him, most important ministers merely conversed as they watched the king munching.³⁴

The abundance at the royal table did not always mean excess. King Ferdinand and Queen Barbara savored too much meat and not enough vegetables or salad, as contemporaries fretted. Yet Charles III refrained from gobbling down great quantities and rather chose carefully from the great offer. His servants prepared three soups, more than ten meat dishes, and four desserts. He usually picked soup, roast beef, egg, and salad for dinner, washing down his fare with a cup of sweet wine from the Canary Islands. Charles III also tried fricassee and nibbled on a doughnut. The king consumed almost the same food every day, for he considered routine healthy.[35]

How far this trend impacted the viceregal court is hard to grasp, although eating habits were surely more modest than in Madrid. Since audiences with visitors usually started between three thirty and four o'clock in the afternoon, the viceregal family probably lunched sometimes around two in the afternoon. In addition, an early seventeenth-century retainer recommended that viceroys in Peru forego dinner for health reasons, especially when traveling. If that was not possible, they should only consume cooked salad and fresh eggs or fish instead of meats that likely rotted. Water should be boiled and topped off with a dash of wine to cover any putrid taste. A jar wrapped in a bag of salt cooled the water. If a stomach bug or vomiting ailed the viceroys, their retainers should prepare a broth of "fowl with bacon, chickpeas, garlic, and many spices, and take frequent sips." That was the best remedy.[36]

The vicereine typically played a prominent role in the rituals, and she mattered even more in the palace. As we have seen, the viceregal parade stopped to hail Padilla Pacheco on the main square. Her predecessor, the Duchess of Alburquerque, had followed the procession in coach during the 1702 entry.[37] Invitees also dressed in gala to congratulate her on her birthdays. They walked into the vicereine's hall, where they saw her sitting on a cushion—just like the viceroy. Most men took off their hats and women showed signs of deference to salute, and then they offered gifts. Padilla Pacheco "expressed her gratitude with the customary politeness."[38] Afterward, she and the court played cards, conversed, quaffed refreshments, and danced until two in the morning in at least one instance. The vicereine and her daughters also attended banquets at convents and visited male priories in Mexico City.[39]

Some colonials, however, chafed under Padilla Pacheco's character, although this may have been for political reasons. During the consecration of a bishop on May 1, 1754, for instance, she sat in her gallery near the cathedral altar "with all the *señoritas* her daughters, and the ladies and dames" of society.[40] The gallery had black lattices that allowed her to view mass without being fully seen. Padilla Pacheco found this secrecy untimely, however, and ordered the removal of the screen. The ecclesiastical chapter cried foul, as it felt insufficiently consulted about the change. The vicereine also demanded signs of respect that the clergymen only afforded her husband. Some residents agreed with the clergy's complaints. When she left for Spain, for example, the chronicler carped that few women bid her farewell, as "more would have come if her character had been more sociable and affectionate"—a striking difference from the Inquisition's view about her successor.[41] Yet Güemes clashed with church and other corporations over reforms, and Padilla Pacheco probably stood by him. That may have riled the chapter and chronicler more than her alleged capriciousness.

She and her husband also groomed their offspring for the court in Madrid, as was usual in noble families of aspiration. They had two sons and six daughters—María Francisca, Juana María, Antonia, Francisca Javiera, Teresa, and Josefa Cayetana, the latter passing away in 1749. The children received an education in faith, languages, dancing, good conversation, table manners, personal appearance, and courtship. Juan Vicente and Antonio took Latin classes with a priest, and they learned how to ride and master arms. In 1748, Juan Vicente joined the military order of Santiago. Two years later, Güemes appointed him captain of the cavalry in the palace guard at the age of twelve, while his younger brother Antonio attained the title of lieutenant colonel of the infantry.[42]

Güemes's birthday on June 24 was celebrated with pomp, too. The viceroy, the vicereine, and the invitees promenaded on nearby Alameda Square. They entered the palace afterward. Many visitors attended and saw a painting of the king and the queen in the viceregal hall. Visitors must also have heard the "peculiar parrots that speak and sing." They had been sent to Madrid and probably inhabited the palace in Mexico City, too.[43] In the evening, invitees witnessed "an exquisite celebration with the most skilled musicians, which the viceroy and vicereine opened with a dance, followed by various lords and gentlemen." The musicians played until midnight. A palace theater had earlier served such purposes, but the fire of 1692 destroyed it, and festivities were moved elsewhere. The next day, all dignitaries attended mass, which included the "Te Deum Laudamus." The guard marched on the main square and fired three salves of gunshot and artillery.[44]

In addition, Güemes clamped down on informal dress at work but yielded to local custom. The viceroy himself frequently wore the *casaca* (an embroidered long and close-fitting jacket; see Güemes's portrait on the cover of this volume) with vest, tie, and pants, because the traditional Spanish *golilla* (black jacket with waistcoat and stiffened white neckband) had fallen out of use at the beginning of the century. Some ministers also wore the casaca on important holidays or birthdays, but many officials usually appeared for work in short suits with a white handkerchief at the collar. Güemes found the outfit too lax in 1745, but the audiencia and other tribunals convinced him otherwise. The viceroy grumbled about having to tolerate the "vice of liberty" in attire.[45] Later on in 1749, the Tribunal of Accounts took umbrage about the dress code, too. At that point, the viceroy ordered the cutting of the salaries of the tribunal's attorneys. Almost as disrespectful, however, was that a notary clad in the short suit delivered the decree to the tribunal.[46]

Outside of Mexico City, viceroys spent time at haciendas belonging to their friends, where life was more casual. As the *Law of the Indies* prohibited visiting with locals, Güemes ostensibly traveled to the outskirts of the capital, "seeking cures for his failing health." From there, however, Güemes dispatched orders, unabashedly revealing his location.[47] His preferred destination was the lavish hacienda near the main square of San Agustín de las Cuevas (Tlalpan, south of Mexico City). His wealthy friend Jacinto Martínez de Aguirre owned the hacienda, and he "exquisitely embellished and restored it, as the climate is more favorable to his Excellency's health." Güemes's family joined him at the hacienda, and he went deer and turkey hunting with his sons. Clergymen, ministers, and businesspeople also came to socialize.[48] Güemes's ostensibly pious predecessor, the Duke of Linares, allegedly preferred San Ángel (southwest of Mexico City) to savor drinking, illegal cockfighting, and other debaucheries. Güemes's successor later frequented Tacuba (just northwest of the city), because his secretary owned a house there. Viceregal families also crisscrossed the canals of Mexico City on merry boat rides, sometimes sponsored by local ministers.[49]

Contested Processions

Colonial Mexicans stopped and greeted the viceroy and other ministers in the streets to express respect and curry favor. Juan Patricio Morlete Ruiz's painting of Mexico City's main square captured this moment fifteen years after Güemes's return to Spain. In the idealized painting, orderly tranquility reigns on the square, cloaking its everyday bustling nature. The viceroy rides out of the palace in a coach drawn by six white horses, followed by audiencia judges in carriages each pulled by four black horses. Meanwhile, the archbishop readies his four-in-hand in front of his palace. They roll to mass in the cathedral, barely two hundred yards away from their respective main gates. Morlete Ruiz here dispels complaints about viceroys who tarried for mass. The image also shows soldiers standing in line while viceregal clients clear a corridor for the coaches. Passersby stop, uncover their hats, and bow; women may curtsy. Horsemen also keep at bay the general population beyond the corridor. Those people show little sign of heeding the viceroy and go about their business.[50] While Morlete Ruiz largely depicts appropriate conduct, some ministers in fact demanded too much when encountering people. Güemes singled out one audiencia minister of Guadalajara. When the residents saw him, they quickly resorted to "shutting the doors when he walked on the streets to avoid conflicts over whether or not to take off the hat, get up on their feet, and other peculiarities of this kind."[51]

The audiencia often accompanied the viceroy in public, with differing roles for civil and criminal judges. When the viceroy and the audiencia ministers rode together in coaches, the ministers got out after their arrival and walked with the viceroy to the main staircase of the palace. The viceroy ordered the civil judges to remain at the bottom of the stairs, an instruction that they politely ignored. The viceroy then repeated the command, and only the criminal judges followed him upstairs, because they represented the king's justice in matters of life and death. The criminal judges had lower status than the civil judges and had to exert themselves climbing stairs. At the same time, they gained by escorting the viceroy. When on horseback, however, the civil judges surrounded the viceroy, which underlined their status as the senior members of the foremost court of justice. Upon arriving on the main square, they remained in the saddle. The criminal judges meanwhile dismounted and accompanied the viceroy up the stairs.[52]

Figure 2. Juan Patricio Morlete Ruiz (1713–1772), *Vista de la Plaza Mayor de México* (View of the Main Square of Mexico City), 1770, oil on canvas. Morlete Ruiz depicts Viceroy Marquis of Croix's ride to the cathedral. (Courtesy of the Photographical Archive Manuel Toussaint, Instituto de Investigaciones Estéticas, Universidad Nacional Autónoma de México.)

While seventeenth-century viceroys demanded that audiencia ministers accompany them anywhere outside the palace, this was no longer true for Güemes's period.[53] When the Inquisition ministers walked Güemes and his wife to the theater in 1746, they did so without audiencia ministers. Güemes, his family, and a cathedral prebend also walked to San Francisco and three other important priories in Mexico City on December 8, 1753. A "footman carried a beautiful lamé parasol" to offer shade from the sun. The audiencia was nowhere to be seen. The chronicler also noted that the party returned to the palace in a carriage after visiting the friars, showing the various modes of viceregal transport.[54]

Proper conduct displayed the standing of clergymen and ministers. For instance, the archbishop sat on a throne covered by a canopy during mass. While walking, a page followed the prelate and raised his gown. The page had to lower the gown when reaching the viceregal hall, however, to avoid any gesture of superiority. Güemes and audiencia judges also attended mass in the cathedral, and the prebendaries showed respect by receiving them at the entrance and showing them inside. The viceroy ascended to a platform and rested on a canopied throne. Some of his noble clients, among them the chaplain and captain of the guard, sat on benches right behind him. The audiencia judges also placed their chairs on the platform if they appeared as one body, because they, too, represented the king. Nevertheless, judges attending mass individually stayed on the floor. Their servants placed a carpet below their seats and furnished a cushion for kneeling. The wives of the judges and the public sat on benches in church.[55]

Most residents also cared deeply for the marching order. The standing of corporations in rituals mattered, and participants emphasized their own rank within them. Issues of sequence could get out of hand and take empires to the brink of war. The emblematic entry of the ambassadors in London in 1661 turned into a bloody melee, for example, as Spanish and French retinues pulled swords over precedence.[56]

The municipal councilors of Mexico City smarted from lesser slights. After the death of a former corregidor (district judge), for instance, the councilors visited the family to express sympathies. When the councilors departed, palace guards marched out, too. The council's procurator raised his voice to stop the soldiers, demanding precedence, but the junior officer of the guard ignored the calls and advanced. The incensed council later sent two delegates to Güemes, who said that "he would settle the matter and give satisfaction." Then the captain of the guard, Güemes's son Juan Vicente, personally called upon the councilors to deplore the junior officer's "precipitous actions." He added that "if he had been there, the council could have gone wherever it liked." Juan Vicente assured them that he would express this sentiment in a council session. At that point, the councilors felt that the offense had been sufficiently atoned for.[57]

In part, the corporations worried about demotions to their status. As an example, the leadership of the consulado (merchant guild) in Mexico City expected to be greeted as "Your Lordship" and sit on chairs with a backrest and canopy during public events. They had obtained that privilege as part of their contract to collect the Mexico City alcabala (sales tax). Yet when that tax administration reverted to the state in 1754, Güemes rescinded the privilege, too. The consulado complained bitterly "that this viceroy, who is so indisposed toward the tribunal, tries to deprive its preeminence." This was not just empty whining; the leaders suggested that their agents grease palms liberally in Madrid to preserve public standing.[58]

Participating in these rituals was a frequent and important duty. The municipal council in Puebla attended about fifty public acts per year, which amounted to almost one event per week. Their Mexican colleagues probably matched the number. Their presence and that of a sizable audience mattered, because they witnessed and tacitly approved of the performance of a ritual and pleaded for divine intervention when necessary. Failure to appear could imperil the ritual's goal and undermine the reputation of the participating corporations. For this reason, the Crown repeated orders that municipal councilors and other ministers had to show up for all "holidays and mandatory functions."[59]

Nevertheless, the frequent public acts were time consuming, costly, and probably tiresome, especially for the elderly and the ill. Petitioning to be excused, sending representatives in one's stead, joining late, or outright skipping was common. Meanwhile, viceroys and other authorities stemmed the tide and punished truants for disrespecting the faith, the Crown, and themselves. In 1747, for example, the governor of New Galicia denied pleas from out-of-town delegates to waive their presence at the proclamation of King Ferdinand VI in Guadalajara.[60] Güemes also ordered notable penalty fees during the 1750 procession on Saint Ferdinand's Day—the king's namesake. The viceroy chided the "absence of some officials, especially of the Tribunal of Accounts, the lower financial officials, and the larger part of the municipal councilors." They hid as the procession slowly assembled in front of the palace. When the ceremonial train had snaked around the main square and reached the cathedral, they furtively slipped into the ranks, to the viceroy's dismay.[61]

The municipal councilors also refused to attend additional religious processions, despite the fines threatened by their council and the viceroy. Güemes had earlier detained six councilors for missing the Saint Francis's Day procession in 1748. He also threatened punishments of 500 pesos for anyone failing to ride out for the day of Our Lady of Remedies.[62] In 1754, the municipal council and the viceroy clashed again over this issue. Güemes detained several councilors on Carnival Monday for missing mass in the Jesuit Profesa Church and imposed a fine of 25 pesos each. The chronicler commented that this "caused great surprise among the public that the gentlemen were arrested for such a minor thing."[63]

The councilors subsequently risked another confrontation with the viceroy. Güemes mandated attendance at mass on Wednesdays, Fridays, and Sundays during the following forty days of Lent. The councilors replied that they would take turns accompanying the viceroy, because some of them were ill. The viceroy demurred. He again detained some councilors on September 2 and held them until the following day, because they had missed mass on the day of Our Lady of Remedies. On September 6, the councilors were "requesting to release them from attending so many functions, as there are plenty, and many others are not for the city patrons or another urgent duty." One councilor even suggested appealing Güemes's unjust verdicts to the king.[64]

Over time, the urgency of the matter declined. Tardiness and truancy irked Güemes just as much as they did his aristocratic predecessors, as exemplified by complaints against overbearing viceroys.[65] Yet the councilors' outcry against Güemes's demands portended change. Later viceroys no longer saw the need to attend many acts themselves. On the king's birthday on November 12, 1792, for instance, a chronicler noted disapprovingly that the viceroy did not receive the corporations "for the hand kiss and did not go out to promenade or to the comedy or anything else." The Enlightenment slowly pulled the rug from under frequent or ostentatious rituals.[66]

Stricter Work Rules

During that period, royal ministers and officials began working more effectively. The audiencia of Mexico reflected the change in the early century. While Viceroy Linares thought in 1711 that the criminal judges lacked experience and focus, the dogged judicial investigation of 1716–1727 dismissed more than two-thirds of audiencia ministers for malfeasance. This sharpened ethics on the bench.[67] In part because of the punishing outcome, Güemes found the ministers rather industrious in 1752. In fact, he asked to release them from afternoon assignments in intestate matters, as "they are tired from working continually in the audiencia since eight in the morning, and they cannot rule anymore on the complex resolutions" of that sort.[68]

The audiencia ministers usually labored harder in the mornings than in the afternoons. After attending mass, they convened in their palace hall at 8:00 a.m. in the winters. During the summers, they began working at 7:00 a.m. so they could leave earlier and avoid the early afternoon heat. A clock rang every hour to indicate time. Judges read lawsuits, heard litigants, and ruled for between three and four hours. The ministers usually ended the morning duties between ten or eleven, except on Tuesdays and Fridays, when public audiencia hearings ended at noon. In addition, the civil judges met with the viceroys on Monday and Thursday afternoons for the real acuerdo.[69] There were other tasks. Criminal judges regularly visited the jail to check on prisoners, although some delegated the duties. Most judges also took turns for three months to serve on the provincial court of the first instance. Another judge sat as *semanero* (magistrate on weekly rotation) to handle jobs that did not require sentencing. He swore in royal ministers or recorded testimonies and petitions of Native communities, for instance.[70]

In contrast, the Tribunal of Accounts, which reviewed the record of treasuries and tax collectors, cherished its work-life balance. The accountants worked for three hours in the morning between eight and eleven o'clock, and for two hours in the afternoons on Mondays, Wednesdays, and Fridays.[71] In the late seventeenth century, the tribunal petitioned to leave office at 11:00 a.m., alleging that the audiencia did not usually attend to its duties in the afternoons either. This was not entirely true, but the tribunal campaigned for years to improve its status in comparison to the audiencia. The Council of the Indies rejected the plea at that time. The accountants continued to beseech the viceroy for relief. They claimed that they had little time to go home before the afternoon rains that so ruined their health. Viceroy Duke of la Conquista (1740–1741) relented, provided the accountants add the six afternoon hours to their morning schedule. At that point, the accountants left the palace around noon every day. The short workday exacerbated the backlog of unresolved cases, however. Consequently, Güemes decreed a return to afternoon work in 1753, much to the tribunal's grief.[72]

Besides insisting on longer hours, the Crown also pruned the number of holidays. According to canon law, Catholics worked from Monday to Saturday and heard mass on Sunday. At the same time, Spaniards observed an ample thirty-three church holidays, which included the patron saint days of the local church and the cathedral. The law set a differing bar for Natives. When poverty forced them to make a living, they only had to observe seventeen holidays including mass.[73] Yet the audiencia of Mexico was more generous with its own holidays by the mid-eighteenth century. The court celebrated Saint Ferdinand's Day for being the king's namesake. Its judges and other corporations also attended mass on the king's and the queen's birthday, and the viceroy afterward received the ministers and other well-wishers. In addition, many colonial Mexicans also celebrated royal successions and the anniversary of the Conquest on August 13.[74]

The audiencia of Guadalajara in the northwestern kingdom of New Galicia championed even more extensive breaks to honor its many patron saints. Anecdotal evidence from that period suggests that the king ordered more workdays for the court, since the excessive recesses aggravated slow sentencing. The court's civil prosecutor, however, invited the king to rethink. He pointed out that holidays included the days of the important local patron saints, the birthdays of the royal family, and any time Guadalajara received news of their good health. In addition, the court took off from Christmas to Three King's Day (December 25 to January 6) as well as Easter and the subsequent week. Neither did the court work on the day of Our Lady of the O, whose image adorned the neighboring pueblo Zapopan, because the virgin helped against the "harsh heat" and the "lightning storms."[75]

The argument for powerful patron saints was not scurrilous. The patron saints in Guadalajara differed from those of other locales, and they merited proper worship to be effective, even when they were not officially sanctioned. For instance, the judges observed the days of Our Lady of the Rosary (February 10) and Saint George (April 23), "because in this city scorpions and other venomous animals are plentiful." They also participated in the procession to the Carmelite nunnery in June and celebrated Saint Martin (November 11), because of his abilities against "ants and locust that abound in such way that they destroy the seeds." Saint Clement (November 23), meanwhile, was "patriotic against the continuous lightning and fire sparks." The audiencia finally took off on the birthdays of all living presidents. How the conflict of the audiencia with the Crown over holidays ended is unknown, but their number probably shrank in the following decades—despite the need to humor powerful saints.[76]

Conclusion

Much of life in the palace was informal and sometimes even unruly. For instance, Güemes was late twice when the Inquisition ministers came calling. He enjoyed his walk in the park too much in one instance and confused his meeting time in a second. Güemes and Pacheco Padilla also played cards, conversed with friends and clients, and at least occasionally danced into the wee hours of the morning. In addition, the viceregal family relaxed at a hacienda outside the city. Güemes conducted business and received visitors despite the legal prohibitions against socializing with residents. He and his sons also hunted deer and turkey during these sojourns. A pious predecessor was even rumored to have indulged in drinking and cockfighting. This conduct mirrors on a smaller scale the frequent informality of the royal court of Madrid. King Ferdinand VI and Queen Barbara jested with ministers and confidants until late in the night. The king and many aristocrats enjoyed the countryside, too, where they were more at ease.

Apart from that, much conduct with the viceroy was ritualized. When he went into the streets, people stopped and greeted him by bowing or drawing their hats, for example. Most visitors in the palace also exchanged formulaic courtesies. It mattered less what people said during these audiences, since most residents competed for the scarce viceregal attention. Even then, Viceroy Fuenclara and Vicereine Amarillas broke the mold by flattering visitors with unexpected attention. Fuenclara took some steps toward them as they were leaving, while Amarillas struck up a conversation about traveling. The audiences also differed in detail. The viceroy frequently came out of his bedroom after visitors had entered the hall, but in some instances, he left his wife's bedroom or waited in the hall. The Inquisition ministers in turn came occasionally with insignia such as their staff of authority, while dispensing with the gestures during other meetings.[77]

Rituals stood out from the daily routine in space and time. They featured adorned dress and speech, commemorative constructions, and pageantry such as games, horses, and coaches. Many of these elements remained identical over the years, although Crown and residents both shaped messages. Quarrels broke out frequently over crafting symbolism of the important rituals. Corporations and individuals vied over preeminence, and the conflicts even marred the ceremonies in the palace.

Yet mid-eighteenth-century residents also tired of frequent processions, especially the religious ones. Residents skipped them or arrived late, sometimes clandestinely slipping into their position after the multitude of people had already tottered forward. That conduct threatened the effectiveness of rituals, which depended on the ample participation of actors and audience. Participants legitimized rule, pleaded for divine intervention, and approved transformations such as the accession of a viceroy. Therefore, Güemes, although himself rather cavalier toward visitors, did not tolerate truancy or lackluster participation. He punished absent municipal councilors and other ministers with house arrest or fines—in part, because absenteeism undermined his own public standing.

Furthermore, Güemes homed in on the work ethic of officials. For instance, audiencia judges mostly ruled on cases in the mornings. They also met with the viceroy to deliberate policy, while others heard first-instance cases and recorded Native petitions in the afternoon. While early-century ministers had flirted with mediocrity, Güemes objected in 1752 to afternoon assignments in the intestate court for hardworking judges. At the same time, the Tribunal of Accounts managed to go home at noon while unreviewed treasury reports towered in their offices, concealing fraud and errors. Güemes ordered the tribunal to return to afternoon work for three days a week. The accountants resisted, as the unhealthy afternoon downpours would vex them on their way home, but the viceroy did not budge. What is more, most Catholics worked on Saturdays, and they observed about thirty-three Church holidays, above and beyond today's practices. Yet the audiencia of Guadalajara took off even more days to honor the city's patron saints. The Crown attempted to bring the court's holidays in line with the Council of the Indies' practice, but Guadalajara insisted on tending to its powerful saints. The struggle over workloads and appropriate religious duties most likely did not end there.

Finally, Güemes's and Pacheco Padilla's personalities contributed to the atmosphere at the court. He had trained in the military for decades and was as exacting with others as he was doughty on the battlefield. She came from an elite family in Antequera and was of higher social status by birth than her husband. She also suffered criticism for being abrasive and unsociable, as opposed to her aristocratic successor, the Marquise of las Amarillas. In the end, however, the sources do not reveal as much as we would like about the personalities of the viceroys and vicereines and how they shaped the court.

CHAPTER 4

"The Indians and Castes . . . Long for Change"

Wresting the Rural Priories from the Religious Orders

Introduction

Franciscans, Dominicans, and Augustinians—these religious orders of the Catholic Church arrived in Mexico shortly after the Conquest (1519–1521). They set up *doctrinas* (parishes) among the Natives to teach the faith and administer the sacraments. The friars chose their own superiors and vowed to live in poverty and obedience, as their rule (Latin: *regula*) commanded. Known as the regular orders, they usually defended their rights with verve and kept a wide berth from the Crown. For that reason, the Crown often preferred secular priests for the ministry after the conversion of the Natives. The secular clergymen lived among the faithful under the supervision of a bishop, who was selected by the Crown. The bishops also selected, examined, and invested most priests, and the viceroys confirmed the proposed candidates.[1]

By the mid-eighteenth century, most reformers around the first minister Ensenada and Viceroy Güemes believed that too many regulars were defrauding the Natives. Ensenada and Güemes tackled the orders. They seized many vacant doctrinas and turned them over to the secular clergy, a process called secularization. The feisty friars fought the forfeiture of their spiritual and economic foundation and called in significant support. Nonetheless, the Natives in most cases backed or at least acquiesced to the change. That helped Güemes to switch more doctrinas to secular hands between 1749 and 1755 than in any other period. This chapter analyzes the political alliances of the viceroy, bishops, Natives, and friars during the sweeping secularization drive.

The Hubbub in Capulhuac

Augustinians and dozens of Natives noisily protested the transfer of the doctrina San Bartolomé Capulhuac (thirty-five miles southwest of Mexico City) to the secular clergy in 1750. The regular priest of the doctrina had passed away, and an Augustinian vicar administered the sacraments without royal confirmation. Güemes got wind of the situation and ordered the ousting of the friars on November 10. Three days later, an interim secular priest, an ecclesiastical judge, and another clergyman appeared in the pueblo (Native polity). They notified the Native governor of their arrival and demanded that the Augustinians vacate the premises. The friars resented losing their rich doctrina, especially since the other regular orders continued unscathed at that time. The friars opened the church to the seculars but refused to surrender the conventual buildings. Tension rose in San Bartolomé Capulhuac.[2]

Meanwhile, the alcalde mayor (district judge) of the jurisdiction dallied in the house of one doña Alfonsa, as a friar slyly remarked. The friar implied that the alcalde mayor should have hastened to the priory instead of remaining with a woman in the pueblo of Santiago Tianguistenco (one mile south of San Bartolomé Capulhuac). The alcalde mayor instead sent word that he would arrive the next day with a notary and a constable to record the delivery of the doctrina.[3] The alcalde mayor was most likely a client of Güemes, who had appointed him to the position in 1748. They both came from the same region in Spain, and the viceroy knew that he could rely on the alcalde mayor. That probably contributed to choosing the pueblo for the showdown with the friars.[4]

In any case, the ecclesiastical judge refused to wait for another day, and he summoned the deputy alcalde mayor. That official, probably a local notable, wasted little time. He sent "a resident of Santiago Tianguistenco to call for help in the pueblo, and he did so with such diligence that a large number of people came right away, equipped with arms, and in a way that the Natives of San Bartolomé Capulhuac justly feared their destruction," as a friar put it.[5] As a response, dozens of Natives from San Bartolomé Capulhuac hurried to the square, and "a great gathering of Indians occurred at the priory, men and women alike, raising their voices that they did not want the priest but the friars, adding threats and the women tears, claiming that the fathers should not leave."[6] What was worse, a Native interpreter saw the friar Nicolás Graneros enter the priory brandishing a knife and screaming in "the rage of a madman, and behind him were a great number of *indias* [Native women]." Yet the seculars contributed to the commotion. Two indigenous witnesses claimed that a secular priest unsheathed a sword and slapped an Indian in the face for not taking off his hat in the priest's presence.[7]

During the standoff, José Meninde, the Augustinian vicar, set off and rode more than thirty miles to downtown Mexico City to consult with the order's provincial. Meninde was running a fever when he reached the great house by midnight. The next day, the alcalde mayor arrived in San Bartolomé Capulhuac and threatened to deport the friars to the grueling fortress in Veracruz if the hubbub did not end. Calm returned slowly to the pueblo, and the seculars whiled away the time playing cards, an illicit activity, according to the Augustinians. Meanwhile, after receiving guidance from the provincial, Meninde left Mexico City on November 16 and rode back to San Bartolomé Capulhuac. He arrived at nine in the night. The next day, he handed out the letter of the provincial, ordering the surrender of the entire priory. The friars complied on November 18 and withdrew from the pueblo.[8]

That day, Güemes received notice of the ruckus and concluded that the Augustinians were guilty of "formal resistance for seducing the Indians to oppose such a just and appropriate order." Güemes ordered Nicolás Graneros to the fortress in Veracruz for violently opposing the seculars. He would ship out to Madrid to stand trial. The viceroy also demanded that the Augustinians punish the two leading friars. On November 21, the provincial detained Meninde and the prior in Mexico City. The provincial appointed a special judge, who began investigating the uproar on November 26, 1750. The special judge was expected to rule whether the regulars had deliberately incited the Indians to resist the secular priests and the deputy alcalde mayor.[9]

During the investigation, the prior defended himself and his fellow suspect by stating that they had had no intention of causing evil. At worst, they may have erred in their judgment, which was a lesser offense. In part, this error arose because the prior had not received the provincial's order to vacate the priory when the seculars appeared in San Bartolomé Capulhuac. Therefore, the prior "delayed yielding, although not with the aim of disobeying the viceregal decree, but rather with the intention of gaining time to reconcile" it with the expected provincial's order.[10] The prior's attorney added that when Meninde returned from Mexico City to San Bartolomé Capulhuac, the friars complied and handed over the priory. They only retained the keys to the *sagrario*, the room where the host was kept, but an acolyte opened its doors for the seculars. In this fashion, the friars executed the "material or physical surrender of the sagrario," although perhaps not the full "judicial surrender."[11] The prior concluded that "if his decision had been sinister, it would only have been a mistake of understanding rather than intent," because "postponing is not canceling."[12]

The defense strategy was to downplay the friars' motivations and actions and to foreground those of their opponents. In this view, Graneros never deliberately threatened a royal minister or clergyman. He rather suffered a "serious accident that seized his senses, causing him to utter indecorous words and acting precipitously, without being able to be corrected." This madness precluded willful acts, and that lessened any guilt. In fact, the prior shifted the blame for Graneros's momentary lapse of judgment and the whole turmoil to the deputy alcalde mayor, the secular clergy, and the Indians of Santiago Tianguistenco. They had marched "with such tools, audacity, and weapons" that the Indians of San Bartolomé Capulhuac "believed beyond doubt they are preparing some mischief against them and their brothers, raising their fears, in addition to the impatient anger of" the interim secular priest.[13]

As much as he sympathized with his coreligionists, the Augustine provincial largely rejected the defense, because the viceroy was breathing down his neck. The provincial assigned the former prior and Meninde the "punishment for the most serious guilt," which meant that they had intentionally committed a serious wrong. These were stern words, although the punishments were more humiliating than stringent. The provincial sent the former prior to another Augustinian house in the highlands to serve in menial chores for three months, while Meninde had to do the same for four months.[14] The viceroy softened up in January 1751 when he saw the leaders punished. He noted that the prior and Meninde "had been detained during the trial, and it seems that they have atoned for their guilt." He also approved releasing Graneros from the damp dungeon in Veracruz. The physicians confined him to the cooler highlands, too. In the end, Güemes had attained his goal, and the Augustinians did not seek to escalate the conflict.[15]

Neither did the viceroy forget to reward the faithful alcalde mayor for his actions. Güemes appointed him to another jurisdiction in 1751. Three years later, the viceroy promoted him to the position of interim treasurer of the audiencia (high court). That was a desirable and well-paid position that could well turn into a permanent post.[16]

A New Wave of Secularizations

Secularization had a long trajectory, dating back to the medieval period and advancing in colonial Mexico. The bishop of Puebla ousted several regulars during the mid-seventeenth century, for example, while the bishop of Oaxaca sequestered twenty-two doctrinas in the early 1720s. Secular priests nevertheless continued to press for a greater share of the wealthy doctrinas administered by the orders.[17] Other supported these claims. The influential pamphlet *New System* excoriated the friars for leeching on the Natives, and the regulars did not come off well in a satirical pamphlet of that time, either. The "imp of Mexico" lampooned their conduct:

The kingdom has hallowed laws,	Leyes tiene el reino santas,
and books are full of these,	libros hay de ellas completos,
but how about compliance?	¿más cómo anda la observancia?
just ask in the priories![18]	¡pregúntese en los conventos!

Opinions on secularization clashed during several meetings in Madrid during 1748–1749. In one meeting in November 1748, the archbishops designate of Mexico and Lima (Peru) proposed that the viceroys dissolve priories in Peru that had been damaged by the earthquake of 1746, or at least delay rebuilding them. The prelates also desired broader jurisdiction over the orders, which the friars would fiercely oppose.[19] Another meeting on March 28, 1749, raised the question of what to do with the understaffed doctrinas dotting New Spain. A papal bull from 1611 required that at least eight friars be in residence to prevent closure. The king's confessor demanded a tougher course by raising the bar to twelve friars in residence. The viceroys elect of Peru and New Spain also endorsed far-reaching goals. Yet José Carvajal, governor of the Council of the Indies, resisted. He stuck with eight friars in residence as a minimum and recommended that the alcaldes mayores make a head count. That would have delayed the issue once more. Carvajal also suggested confining further secularizations to the archbishoprics of Mexico and Lima, excluding the other dioceses. Consequently, that meeting only proposed that the bishops "begin separating some parishes when they fell vacant."[20]

On October 4, 1749, the king issued a royal cédula (communication) to seize doctrinas in the archdioceses of Mexico, Lima in Peru, and Santa Fe de Bogotá in New Granada (now Colombia). This cédula upheld to an extent Carvajal's suggestion to exclude most bishoprics. This also divided the orders. As we have seen, the Augustinians stood to lose many doctrinas around Mexico City, while the other orders initially held ground. In addition, the cédula dampened acrimony by mandating the taking of vacant doctrinas of lesser value first. Furthermore, Madrid obtained another papal bull in 1751 that once more legitimized secularization, blunting any protest of the regulars.[21]

By early 1753, Ensenada had shored up his position sufficiently to ratchet up pressure on the orders. He ignored Carvajal's objections and the recommendations of the 1749 meetings. Instead, Ensenada convinced the king to issue a far-reaching royal cédula to secularize doctrinas in all dioceses of Spanish America. A year later, Viceroy Güemes obtained the new cédula and passed it on to the bishops. The struggle over secularization hit a critical juncture.[22]

Ensenada and Güemes largely agreed on the course against the orders. The first minister believed that too many friars feigned cloistered life, forgot about poverty, and fleeced the Natives.[23] Güemes also shared Ensenada's view that the church owned too much land and money, hampering state and economy. According to the viceroy, especially the regulars sought to

> reduce everything to temples and foundations, and they dominate . . . the foremost residents, richest merchants, and even the audiencias of these kingdoms, as they gather the best haciendas and flourishing funds and persuade others to establish chaplaincies, foundations, and pious works.[24]

Therefore, Ensenada and Güemes expected profound resistance to secularization. They were right. The friars and their allies left no stone unturned to avert their fate, availing themselves of courtiers in Madrid. Güemes reported that

> these orders go there with significant amounts of money to see if they can

stem or suspend the blow, because they found the doors shut here. If they do, there will be no shortage of protectors who consume their cash without achieving anything.[25]

Despite the regular opposition, secularization progressed well beyond the boundaries of the kingdom of New Spain. The Franciscans lost pastoral assignments in Yucatán, for instance. The Jesuit general in Rome also suggested yielding twenty-two older missions in the northern viceroyalty to the secular clergy. This way, the Jesuits could concentrate on proselytizing Natives in California. The Jesuits turned over the older missions between 1753 and 1755 despite considerable internal resistance against the move.[26] Meanwhile, the orders succeeded partially in Guatemala. Its governor suspended secularization, much to the dislike of the archbishop of that diocese. To avert such actions, Ensenada excluded district judges and the audiencia from hearing any appeal to the process. In addition, the first minister relieved the Council of the Indies, and that also meant to a degree Carvajal, from jurisdiction in this respect. The only complaint against secularizations went straight to the king, and that meant in effect to Ensenada.[27]

Initially, the hammer stroke fell hardest on the Augustinians, who had a strong presence in the archdiocese of Mexico. They lost six doctrinas in 1750, and these included, arguably against the royal cédula's mandate, the rich parish of San Bartolomé Capulhuac and two desirable ones in the capital. The order surrendered nineteen more doctrinas in the two following years.[28] In 1753, secularization applied to all dioceses in the Americas and began eroding the Dominican and Franciscan presence, too. The regulars lost ten doctrinas in New Spain that year. The heaviest onslaught came in 1755, when fifty-two doctrinas changed hands. From the beginning of secularization in October 1749 to 1755, Güemes ordered the sequestration of a total of 109 doctrinas in New Spain. The Augustinians ceded almost as many doctrinas as the two other orders combined. Never had the orders lost so much in such a short time.[29]

Güemes backed the bishops in several instances, which was a departure from the period before 1749 when the bishops had frequently faced heavy headwinds. Now, Güemes and Archbishop Manuel José Rubio y Salinas had "the best communication and harmony, which I cultivate by all possible means," as the viceroy put it. In fact, he even shielded the archbishop from direct attacks by the orders.[30] The archbishop also noted the "general applause and inexplicable joy of the Indians" about ousting the regulars. The prelate of Puebla largely agreed. Secularization advanced quickly when Güemes and the bishops collaborated.[31]

Meanwhile, some bishops dragged their feet. By 1756, the prelate of Oaxaca had seized only eight doctrinas before recommending taking six additional ones. In part, the diocese lacked candidates with sufficient command of the Native languages to supplant the regulars, and the bishop's predecessor had already sequestered almost two dozen doctrinas by the early 1720s. The fall of Ensenada and the change of government in Madrid played a role in the bishop's caution as well. In addition, the bishop of Michoacán hesitated, while praising the "good reputation" of the Franciscans who lived "according to the rules of their patriarch while fulfilling their duties." He needed some coaxing to take nine parishes in his diocese.[32] In the meantime, the bishop of Guadalajara, outside of the kingdom of New Spain, had secularized mere five Franciscan doctrinas by 1755. Episcopal opposition in some dioceses hampered the process considerably.[33]

A Conflict of Natives and Friars

Güemes typically seized a doctrina by denying the request of a provincial to confirm a candidate for a vacancy. The viceroy then asked the bishop to name an interim secular priest instead. That interim priest and other clergymen, the alcalde mayor, and, in at least some cases, armed constables appeared in the pueblo to occupy the doctrina shortly after. In most cases, the transfer was peaceful. In one instance,

> a great quantity of people was afoot along with the Indian officials of the republic of the doctrina, and having received the priest at the door with great benevolence, humility, and courtesy, they all entered the church where they prayed in front of the main altar . . . and the assistant vicar read from the pulpit the titles of the priest as vicar and ecclesiastical judge . . . and they took possession of the parish for the priest . . . who closed the sagrario, ascended and descended the pulpit, sat in a confessional, went to recognize the

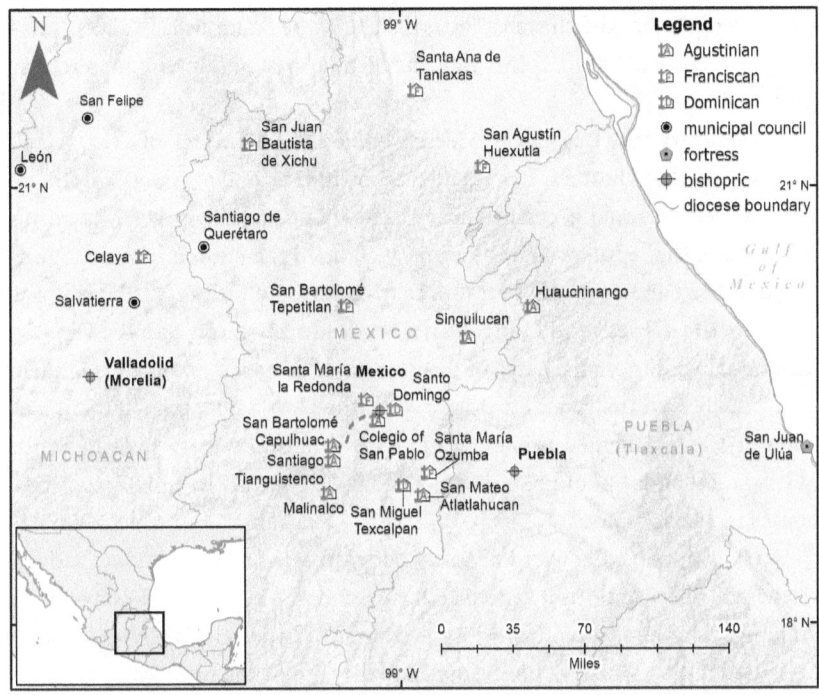

Map 3. Important sites during the fight over Native *doctrinas*, 1749–1755. (Designed by Ana Gabriela Arreola Meneses.)

baptismal font, which he opened and closed . . . peacefully and without any opposition . . . while the aforesaid [regulars] fraternally demonstrated that they were religious and ministers of the Lord, and they ate together at a table, and proceeded to make an inventory of all church goods.[34]

In several cases, however, Natives and the orders clashed over the priories, their estates, and valuables when the regulars left. For instance, the parishioners of Santa María la Redonda in Mexico City demanded in 1753 that the Observant Franciscans return the church treasury after departing from the doctrina. The church had owned a votive "silver, large, old lamp, used in the sacristy of this priory with four candle holders, and five chasubles." The friars sent that part of the treasure to Celaya in the diocese of Michoacán, where the bishop was friendly toward their community. The Franciscans also acknowledged that the church's "missal went to the Santa Ana Tanlaxas mission" near San Luis Potosí. This way, the friars warded off attempts to return the vessels.[35]

Sending away the treasury was legally dubious. The Council of Trent (1545–1563) stated that the mendicants could not individually possess anything beyond their personal necessities, because of their vow of poverty. According to this rule, the regulars should not have claimed the church treasure at all. While other canon law allowed orders to have some property, that did not apply to the Observant Franciscans, who administered Santa María la Redonda. In addition, the papal bull of 1611 stated that friars should bring their own valuables to their nearest priory when they lost a doctrina. The Madrid junta of 1749 reaffirmed this bull, and accordingly, any vessels from Santa María la Redonda should have been deposited in one of the nine Franciscan houses in Mexico City.[36]

Furthermore, the *Law of the Indies* added that when the regulars moved elsewhere, they could not take anything from the church and conventual buildings that were "conjoined with the church."[37] Especially when objects had been used in the ministry, they belonged to the church and had to stay. Güemes therefore underlined that "the beautiful silver lamp had been donated by the Duchess of Alburquerque to the image of Our Lady that is venerated in this church" of Santa María la Redonda. In his view, the former vicereine had intended the lamp for the ministry and not the order. Even the Observant Franciscans admitted that the objects had been used in mass. In the light of most laws, then, the vessels should have remained. For that reason, Güemes fumed that "a commissary general mandated on his own authority to send to their college of Celaya the golden chalice that shortly before served in the church along with the adorned vestments which had been the best of the sacristy."[38]

Güemes reported to the king in terms that made the friars look rapacious, and they were probably not keen on this kind of publicity. Güemes claimed that it was difficult to understand the Franciscan arguments on the church vessels, "except recurring to the principle that in the morals of the friars there are opinions for everything."[39] The point was particularly arduous, because the parishioners were mostly Indians and entitled to special protections. Despoiling these "miserables," as they were called, made the friars look nefarious and vitiated their claims of serving the Indians better than the secular clergy. Güemes insisted on controlling the friars in the future when they withdrew from a priory, "without allowing them to remove anything but the valuables of their own use."[40] The order dampened quarrels, although Natives demanded the return of the pearls in one priory and sought to regain control of a chapel in another.[41]

Did the parishioners of Santa María la Redonda consider themselves Indians? Clearly they belonged to one of the six doctrinas in Mexico City that tended to Natives. Its chapter and the donations of forebears and the duchess enshrined its corporate identity. The Franciscans also downplayed any ethnic mixture of the flock in order not to jeopardize their ministry. The friars sometimes even chided the Indians as *ladinos*, by which they referred to astute Spanish speakers. This way, the order hoped to remain indispensable.[42]

Nonetheless, while most people living on the fringes of the Spanish city center identified as Indians at the end of the seventeenth century, population mixture was considerable. About one-third of the Native population had moved to their parish from another, and many Indians dressed as Spaniards, while the castes (people of mixed ancestry) also donned Indian garb. Later, in 1772, the Crown combined the separate Spanish and Indian parishes. In the ensuing census of 1773, only 30.5 percent of the population of the combined parish of Santa María la Redonda self-identified as Indians. Of course, the constituency had changed since 1753, and tactical motives about status and taxation played a role in these auto-labels, too. Natives typically had to pay tribute, while others did not, for instance. The census, however, showed that ethnic blending had advanced notably in the community.[43]

In August 1753, several Indian officials complained about the secularization of the Augustine doctrina San Mateo Atlatlahucan (forty miles southeast of Mexico City). According to the Native governor, the secular priest "does not know the Mexican tongue which is so necessary to administer the Holy Sacraments in our pueblo, since we are Natives and there are no people of reason [Spaniards] here." In the governor's view, the secular priest had to bring an Indian student as an interpreter to hear confessions in Nahuatl, while bilingual Franciscans and Augustinians from adjacent priories assisted as well.[44]

The secular priest was also lazy and thieving, according to some locals. One magistrate of the nearby pueblo of San Miguel Texcalpan added that the priest insufficiently administered the sacraments, and "María Rosario..., the former governor Sebastián Antonio, and María de la Trinidad" died before confessing, while one child "passed away without receiving baptism."[45] In addition, the secular priest stole from the church treasury, and "he made us pay a half real every Sunday, collecting between twelve, eighteen, or even nineteen pesos... and during six and half months, they handed the priest about 600 pesos or a bit less... and he spent it all in Mexico City, while his predecessor, the interim priest, took the largest part of the silver from our church."[46]

Yet the regulars were behind this complaint, too, which fell on deaf ears. The guardian of the nearby Franciscan priory of Santa María Ozumba orchestrated the testimonies to criticize the misconduct and insufficient language skills of the diocesan priest. More importantly, however, the archbishop and the viceroy ignored the accusations. They had decided that enough people in San Mateo Atlatlahucan understood Spanish, and they appointed a monolingual secular priest for the pueblo. Archbishop and viceroy saw the opportunity to replace Nahuatl with Spanish and disregarded the protest.[47]

Furthermore, political support for the friars dropped off in most cases after they left. For instance, when the special Augustinian judge investigated the commotion in San Bartolomé Capulhuac, he interviewed ten residents from that pueblo and Santiago Tianguistenco. None of the municipal officials, save for a notary, participated in the inquiry, however. Neither did the council of San Bartolomé Capulhuac or elsewhere demand the return of the friars in the 1749–1755 period.[48]

The regulars had conducted a series of inquiries in doctrinas almost twenty years earlier to showcase their usefulness. At that time, several locals praised the friars' spiritual labor. In San Bartolomé Tepetitlan (sixty miles north of Mexico City), eight indigenous *principales* (nobles)—five of them had served as governors at some point—and ten Spaniards applauded the Franciscans.[49] Despite that vote of confidence, the Natives welcomed the diocesan clergy when the pueblo changed hands on January 11, 1754. Then,

> various men of all qualities and the Native governors of several pueblos in the doctrina came out to receive the secular priest, praising him with their *xuchiles* [flower offerings] that are customary in these acts, and waiting

for the priest on the hill about half a league before arriving at the *cabecera* [head town] was . . . the larger part of the pueblo . . . showing its happiness . . . while the bells were ringing.⁵⁰

Similarly, the Franciscans held an inquest in Huejutla (about 170 miles northeast of Mexico City) in 1734. One former Indian governor, a Spanish hacienda owner, and a mestizo (of mixed ethnic ancestry) vouched for the friars. Nevertheless, the diocesans equally summoned a great number of Indians in 1751, "and the sierra rallied to the sound of their drums and horns, and they appeared in Huejutla with raised banner"⁵¹ to evict the friars. As long as the regulars were the ecclesiastical authority in town, many expressed loyalty until the diocesan priest appeared.⁵²

Old acrimony also built new alliances. Over time, the friars had demanded excessive fees and labor obligations from pueblos and seized land for their priories. The religious also policed religious conduct and clamped down on drinking. These measures triggered lengthy conflicts that predisposed some pueblos against the orders. Güemes could therefore count on Native acquiescence or support in most cases. Many alcaldes mayores, their deputies, and secular priests also worked to break the regular resistance. That was one reason for the general calm that reigned during secularization. Almost all pueblos received the seculars quietly.⁵³

In addition, it was easier for a parish to sustain one secular priest, perhaps aided by a vicar, rather than several friars. Güemes claimed that in the priories without endowment, several regulars in residence required services from the locals as though they were the parish priest. The indigenous men in Puebla served in turns "in the refectory, as bell-ringers, gardeners, sextons, and in other tasks, for free" while the women did much of the cooking for the regulars.⁵⁴ Thus, the "Indians . . . and the other castes . . . are very badly served by the friars and long for change," the viceroy opined.⁵⁵ Gaining some relief was one reason why most Natives readily accepted secular priests.

Nonetheless, during the next decades, new secular curacies were carved out of the former doctrinas so that the locals supported additional clergymen. This process had begun in the sixteenth century, when secular priests and Natives constructed churches to improve spiritual care and supervision. Yet as opposed to many friars, these clergymen often lived side by side with their parishioners and entitled their communities to greater autonomy from the head town. Moreover, the legitimacy of the king and the church remained intact. The combined factors made for a smooth expansion of curacies.[56]

Conversely, many friars deeply resented the loss of the doctrinas that the orders had founded two centuries earlier. An anonymous friar stated that "the white men (generally called Creoles) of the Indies (if they are poor) have no other way to ascend than the regulars, but with the new mandate to seize the doctrinas, they cannot become regulars or seculars." Instead, the secularized parishes mostly went to the bishop's clients from Spain. Under these conditions, "the Creoles have hope but no curacy, at least a good and livable one. Those who know a Native tongue and are at least somewhat studious will at most become sacristan or vicar."[57] The anonymous friar continued that the kings of Castile had chosen the orders as best suited for conversion, since they "were not the moth that feasts or the locust that laid waste." Meanwhile, the seculars were rapacious when driving out the regulars from their doctrinas, as "they took away the cushions and kitchen tools from the Franciscans." What was worse, the secular priests expelled the friars of the doctrina of "Coyoacan and seized the food that they had prepared for that day."[58]

The stance evoked much sympathy. The chronicler Castro Santa-Anna wrote that "seeing the religious removed from their priories, which they have had since the beginnings, gave rise to much compassion."[59] The municipal council of Mexico City also demanded an end to secularization. In addition, a stream of protests poured out from municipal councils when the viceroy secularized the Franciscan doctrina of San Juan Bautista de Xichu (near Guanajuato).[60] The social groups represented in the municipal councils exerted significant influence on regional politics and trade. Meanwhile, the Natives of the doctrina remained mute. The secular priest succeeding the Franciscans found them later recalcitrant, but such complaints were also heard in regular parishes.[61]

Moreover, secularization spelled the end of the doctrina of the Chapel of the Rosary in the great Santo Domingo priory in Mexico City. The doctrina ministered mostly to the Zapotecs and Mixtecs, two major ethnic groups from the bishopric of Oaxaca who lived in the colonial capital, and those from the pueblo Metztitlan, one hundred miles north. These groups had founded the chapel in 1620 and received their own chapter in the 1670s. Controversy arose because the "Creole nation of this city," that is, another *cofradía* (sodality), resisted the chapel's foundation in the priory.[62] Conflict continued because the other parishes of the capital served either Indians or Spaniards and castes. They competed with the chapel and its priest for ecclesiastical fees paid by parishioners. In addition, Güemes attempted to make a headcount of all residents for tax purposes at that time. It must have irked him that the chapel did not have a list of tribute-paying Natives, allowing some to shirk their obligations. Güemes observed, too, that "the Indians of those castes or nations ... no longer exist or gather in this city."[63]

Shortly after the regular priest of the doctrina passed away, the archbishop's vicar general, a constable, and notaries marched to the Dominican priory on May 22, 1753. They demanded that the interim priest destroy the baptismal font, and "gather the holy unction and books of the parish and deliver them to the priests of the sagrario of the Cathedral."[64] The sagrario was the newly built parish church next to the cathedral that ministered to Spaniards and castes in the surrounding neighborhoods. The Dominican complied. Nonetheless, while the doctrina ended, both chapter and chapel survived. Soon after, the chapter tore down the wall separating the chapel from that of the third order of Santo Domingo, composed of Spaniards.[65]

A Brake on Cloistered Life

The strident secularizations boded ill for new urban houses for the regulars. The Crown had opposed new mendicant foundations on several occasions since the seventeenth century and ordered the demolition of houses that lacked royal permits. While the orders nevertheless continued to grow during the eighteenth century, Ensenada and Güemes worked against the trend. The viceroy received a royal cédula shortly after taking office, mandating him to review any foundation that lacked approval. As a result, he and Ensenada derailed several projects and delayed others.[66]

Ensenada and Güemes supported some houses with charitable purposes or those that directly fed into the mission on the northern frontier. That explains why the order of San Felipe Neri established a house for abandoned women in Mexico City and a teaching college in San Miguel el Grande (now Allende). In addition, the girls' orphanage of San Miguel de Belén, founded in 1684 in Mexico City, came under scrutiny for lack of a royal permit. Regardless, the institution survived because of its charitable purpose. Güemes also endorsed a college for indigenous women and a hospice for the grievously ill in Mexico City.[67]

Yet the Franciscans suffered setbacks because of their internal divisions and Ensenada's opposition. For example, the Discalced Franciscans failed to found a hospice in Valladolid (now Morelia) because of resistance from another Franciscan colegio in the region. The colegio feared more competition for religious donations and fees.[68] In addition, the Discalced Franciscans made little headway in converting the hospice of Nuestra Señora del Destierro (Our Lady of the Exile) just outside of Puebla into another colegio. The Crown had issued a permit, but the site lacked access to water, and the commissary proposed moving the colegio (an entry-level university) into the city. Ensenada, however, scuttled the project.[69] Güemes sharply noted that the

> Jesuits in Puebla have three populous colleges, the Dominicans three priories, the Augustinians one, the Mercedarians one, the Franciscans two, one each for the Observants and the Discalced, one for the Carmelites, then three belonging to the Hospitallers of San Juan de Dios, the Bethlehemites, and those of Saint Hippolytus, in addition to six priories, and the parishes have four seminars to educate the youth as well as a great number of churches and shrines, and all of these in a poor city that has no mining or considerable commerce.[70]

The female Capuchins, a reformed branch of the Franciscans, ran out of good luck, too. They attempted to establish a convent in Lagos (Jalisco) in 1752, for which a local priest promised to pay with his own money. In his words, the house was meant for "young women of quality who could not take the vows in another province because of their lack of means, and they would be forced to marry below their station causing opposition and scandal among the parents who abandoned them." Both the bishop and the Council of the Indies accepted the project. Yet Güemes advised against the matter, and the Crown still demanded corroborating information on August 13, 1755.[71]

Even the reformed orders that observed strict vows encountered stumbling blocks, although Ensenada and Güemes generally approved of them. Güemes and his wife supported the Discalced Carmelites, for example, who emphasized penitence and extensive prayers in their cells. Vicereine Antonia Padilla Pacheco bequeathed more than 2,000 pesos to their priory in Madrid, for instance, and Güemes was eventually laid to rest there.[72] In colonial Mexico, the Carmelites sought permission to build five houses, including a second one in Puebla. Both the former bishop of Puebla and Güemes's predecessor had backed the idea. The king approved various petitions in the fall of 1746, but a royal decree from September of that year changed course and delayed the foundations. By that time, Ensenada was firmly in power.[73]

Although Güemes and Ensenada initially still supported friars traveling from Spain to missionize on the frontiers, their enthusiasm cooled in 1751 at the latest. In that year, Ensenada ended financial support for the Augustinians, Dominicans, and Observant Franciscans, and even those going to the northern frontier received less. Güemes also suggested cutting in half the number of friars coming from Spain.[74] In 1752, Güemes commented acerbically that the friars never teach the "languages of the Indians to the young people joining them here or to the subjects that they bring from Spain at the expense of the royal treasury, and they do not send them to accompany the missionaries to learn the holy ministry... and they never leave to look for the infidels, because they find the frontier rather remote."[75]

Three councilors of the Indies met on December 21, 1752, to parry attacks on the friars. They argued that the leadership rotation in the orders among peninsular Spaniards and colonial residents had to continue. In their view, the peninsular Spaniards restrained the colonial residents, "so they do not stray from their profession's path, driven by the inconsistency and laziness of their minds."[76] The following year, however, Ensenada insisted that any friar leaving for colonial Mexico needed royal approval, while peninsular Spaniards who had served more than ten years abroad had to return to Spain. A newspaper in Madrid even reported on July 20, 1754, that the king prohibited anyone from joining the orders for a period of ten years. Yet, Ensenada fell from power the next day, and King Ferdinand VI walked back his order three years later.[77]

A Challenge to the Secular Church

While Ensenada and Güemes generally curbed regular foundations, they were on better terms with the secular church. For example, Güemes looked kindly on the basilica of Our Lady of Guadalupe. That basilica neared completion on the storied Tepeyac Hill, where the Virgin Guadalupe had allegedly appeared to the Native Juan Diego. In part, Güemes supported the new church, because the king appointed thirteen prebendaries and its abbot, while the cathedral chapter elected only three.[78]

The new basilica originated when a clergyman donated half a million pesos in the early eighteenth century. Despite the cash infusion, the project limped along, and its chapter convened for the first time in 1750.[79] In 1753, Güemes allowed the staging of a bullfight in San Diego Square (now part of the Alameda) to raise additional funds. The adjacent priory, however, objected to a gathering of a rowdy crowd. The regulars dug out a royal cédula prohibiting such a spectacle in front of their house. Yet Güemes ignored them, and the games began on February 19. One bullfighter was killed in the arena, while two soldiers died when somebody bellowed "earthquake" and provoked a panic. The chronicler wondered afterward why the viceroy had allowed so "many deadly sins" that mostly benefited criminals.[80]

Nonetheless, the secular church faced growing state power, too. The king's confessor, for instance, insisted that the pope chose too many church prelates in Spain, assailing the concordat with Rome as the "murder of the nation."[81] Ensenada and Carvajal demanded the right to select the prelates, and they followed up on the attack with diplomacy and plenty of palm greasing. Rome agreed in 1753 on a new concordat. The king now presented most senior clergymen in the peninsula. Critics decried the outcome, however.[82]

A satire arrived in Veracruz ridiculing the pope, Ensenada, and King Ferdinand for the new concordat. According to the pamphlet, they met with the cardinals on April 1, 1753, in Rome. The king said, "All power is given to me in heaven and on earth," while the attending Spaniards nodded: "We now have a pope." The pope then stated: "I acknowledge my fault, and my sin is ever before me, I have sinned only against you." The satire ends when the Protestant king of England appears, claiming, "I absolve you of your sins." The satire implied that the pope illicitly yielded his rights to the king. It drew on Bible sections, such as Matthew and the Psalms, yet blasphemed by assigning these passages to living leaders, including the Protestant adversary.[83]

Güemes also traced church obligations to the state more carefully. One-ninth of the tithe was for the king, for example. Güemes sensed in June 1747 that much of this money had gone elsewhere, but he made little headway in recovering the dues.[84] In addition, Ensenada insisted that the church hand over current and past salaries of vacant prebendaries. He threatened to confiscate private property or the entire tithe if the ecclesiastical chapters failed to cooperate. The first minister even sent twenty blank royal orders to deport any clergyman opposing the measure. The chapter of Mexico City nonetheless stalled, and Güemes largely gave up. His friend Ignacio Cevallos, the chapter's treasurer, suggested in October 1750 to ascertain at least the value of the current vacancies.[85] This satisfied Güemes, who observed that

> to tighten this business further could result in a never-ending affair without yielding much, because confiscating the funds would mean entering into an obscure labyrinth that we would never leave, besides causing a scandal. We would have to uncover the estate of each individual . . . while some wealth has turned into alms or pious foundations, from which nothing can ever be retrieved . . . and instead of pursuing this, I have cautiously computed what the living can contribute . . . allowing us to recover 60,000 pesos . . . and I believe I have achieved more than the Cid Campeador [the medieval crusader] in this matter without any fuss or even a minor uproar.[86]

After Ensenada's Fall

The demise of the secretary of state, José Carvajal, on April 8, 1754, ushered in a volatile phase at the court in Madrid. The regular orders lamented the loss of a protector and worried about Ensenada's aims. At that point, Franciscan procurators (representatives) traveled across the Atlantic to Cádiz and finally reached the royal court in Aranjuez. The chief clerk of the secretary of the Indies, one of Ensenada's clients, received the procurators for an audience in early June 1754. They expressed their fears about the "extinction of the province" in Mexico, and the chief clerk suggested that they write up a memorandum to the king with their concerns. This calmed the procurators, and they left the meeting "much consoled and believing with good reason that despite the death of Lord Carvajal, blessed be his heart, the theater is not that horrible, and our fortune looks on us more favorably."[87] They were right. Carvajal's followers were abandoning Ensenada and aligned with his detractors. As a result, the king dismissed the first minister on July 20, 1754.[88]

The new secretary of the Indies, Julián Arriaga, softened the course against the regular orders. He replaced Güemes with a viceroy who was more friendly to the friars. Arriaga also stipulated that when secular clergy took over a doctrina, the friars could hold on to church and conventual buildings if at least eight friars resided on the premises and they possessed a royal permit for the foundation. The solution was onerous for the Natives and the secular clergy, because they would have to construct a new church. In any case, the regulars could retain two wealthy doctrinas in each diocese to take in their displaced brothers. In addition, the viceroy and the bishop should confer about the wisdom of additional secularizations, seek linguistically qualified candidates in the synods, and allow interim regular clergy to serve the doctrinas in the meantime. Arriaga also allowed the Council of the Indies to hear complaints against the process, which would slow it down.[89] Moreover, some regulars, such as the Carmelites, could finish their new foundations. As a result, the order completed the priory in Tehuacan de las Granadas (Puebla), for example. This new policy eased the pressure on the orders.[90]

This period of acquiescence with the regulars ended in 1763, when yet another government took the helm in Madrid. Three years later, a new archbishop and a new viceroy, both ardent supporters of secularization, arrived in Mexico City. With their help, secularization surged ahead. In that period, the bishop of Puebla alone seized thirty-four doctrinas from the regulars, for instance. By the end of the century, secularization in rural New Spain was almost complete.[91]

Conclusion

This chapter has examined the interactions among the Spanish court, central and local authorities in New Spain, and the popular response. The analysis shows that the period before José de Gálvez's judicial investigation (1765–1771) was all but stagnant. In fact, Ensenada, Güemes, and their allies dealt a blistering blow to the regulars by secularizing 109 doctrinas in New Spain in the period 1749–1755, significantly more than historians have assumed.[92] The Augustinians relinquished fifty-three parishes, almost as many as the Dominicans (twenty-nine) and the Franciscans (twenty-seven) combined. In addition, secularization proceeded beyond the viceroy's direct influence on the northern frontier and in Yucatán. The regulars ceded more pastoral assignments in this short period than at any time before.

Ensenada and Güemes (and others) held that secular priests should administer the sacraments to the faithful, while the orders should focus on conversion, especially on the northern frontier, or on rigorous spiritual exercise in their priories. The friars therefore had to cede most rural doctrinas in the kingdom of New Spain to the secular clergy. Only urban priories whose aim was not primarily the ministry and those houses directly serving the mission or charity, such as supporting abandoned women, would remain. The urban priories also needed to show a royal permit for their foundation. Under these circumstances, the Franciscans held on to their great house in Querétaro, while the Augustinians lost the imposing priory in Yuriripundaro in Michoacán.[93] Moreover, Ensenada and Güemes ended or delayed new regular priories in the cities, even if they had received royal approval. The Discalced Carmelites, a reformed and austere order, for instance, tried to establish five new houses in that period. Some of them had already received royal permissions, but the first minister and the viceroy stalled the process.

The Augustinian friars mobilized the Natives of San Bartolomé Capulhuac to oppose secularization of their priory. Yet the alcalde mayor, one of Güemes's appointees, his deputy, and the Natives of neighboring Santiago Tianguistenco, ousted them. Some Indians of San Mateo Atlatlahucan also rejected a monolingual secular priest, and the Franciscans happily instrumentalized the complaint for their own purpose. The complaint fell on deaf ears, however, because archbishop and viceroy agreed that Natives in that pueblo spoke enough Spanish for pastoral care. These were the few instances of opposition in that period; in most other cases, the Indians welcomed the change, because they were chafing under the work and land demands of the regulars. In addition, secularization proceeded because many rank-and-file secular clergy clamored for more curacies, and the bishops usually agreed. The viceregal alliance, however tacit it was, broke the resistance of the religious orders and the Creole elites.

This chapter also shows that the Bourbon kings did not pursue a consistent policy toward the regular orders in the eighteenth century. Policy depended rather on the government in Madrid and the collaboration of the viceroy with bishops and residents in New Spain. For that reason, the discord that was revealed in the 1749 meeting in Madrid contributed to Ensenada's fall in 1754 and ended the phase of rapid secularization. A new secretary of the Indies charted a more cautious course, ordering Natives and secular clergy to construct new churches if the regulars held royal permits for their rural priories. Güemes's successor also shielded the orders on other occasions. As a result, the Carmelites completed their project in Tehuacan de las Granadas, while the Capuchins ultimately constructed a house in Lagos.

The following stages need further research, although the pace of secularization recovered again. The appointment of the Marquis of Esquilache as first minister in 1763, and the arrival of a new viceroy and archbishop in 1766, gave another jolt to the process in colonial Mexico. The friars continued to bleed priories until the end of secularization in the highlands in the late 1790s.

CHAPTER 5

Friends, Foes, and "Specters Spreading at Court"

How Güemes Seized the Mexico City Alcabala Tax in 1753–1754

Introduction

In 1753, Viceroy Juan Francisco Güemes contended with the powerful consulado (merchant guild) over the highly profitable alcabala (sales tax) of Mexico City. At that time, merchants paid the tax at the city gates according to the volume of the goods they were hauling into the colonial capital. The vagaries of trade and grasping tax collectors often hampered a steady revenue stream, however. For that reason, the Crown preferred renting the administration of the alcabala to the consulado, which paid a fixed annual sum in exchange.[1] By 1753, the consulado had gathered the alcabalas for decades, and money ran freely into its pockets. That irked the first minister, the Marquis of la Ensenada. He concluded that the consulado should pay considerably more or relinquish the tax farm. The Crown would then divert the revenue stream into its own coffers.[2]

Not surprisingly, the consulado protected its turf. Its leaders offered additional money to renew the contract. They also used their informal influence in Mexico City and Madrid to sway opinion, helped along by generous bribes.[3] Yet Ensenada negotiated from a position of power and rejected the consulado's offers. He ordered Viceroy Güemes to seize the administration for the Crown. The viceroy drummed up support from a consulado minority faction and other merchants and clergymen. They skillfully carried out the order despite trenchant resistance.

Güemes also oversaw the public auction of the alcabala administration in

Veracruz, the most important port on the Mexican Gulf. Two groups of merchants rivaled each other in bidding for the administration in 1740. When the contract ended nine years later, another businessman threw in his hat and improved upon his competitors' offers. He finally gained the tax administration in 1753. Yet he had overestimated tax proceeds and ran into trouble. Royal officials stepped in to collect the alcabala until another tax farmer took over. This episode was hardly a case of consensus building with local elites. Instead, Güemes used a competitive and even acrimonious process to press for more Crown revenue.[4]

This chapter shows that the viceroy kicked off a significant tax reform in the 1750s, continuing a process of revenue hikes and administrative changes that had originally begun with the introduction of the alcabala to Mexico in 1576. While the 1760s are often seen as the game changer for fiscal expansion, Ensenada, Güemes, and their allies got the most important job done earlier by seizing the Mexico City alcabala and improving the Veracruz auctions. In fact, by doing so, they laid the foundations for the later reforms.[5]

Seizing the Mexico City Alcabala

With the alcabala well established in Spain, the Crown began levying the tax in colonial Mexico in 1576. Later, during the Thirty Years' War (1618–1648), the empire needed more funds to feed the colossal appetite of the military. Consequently, in 1628, the viceroy nudged Mexico City and Puebla to double their alcabala rate from 2 to 4 percent. In 1636, the king again asked for more cash to build fifteen warships. These battleships were needed to flush out pirates in the Caribbean, escort the silver fleet to Spain, and defend the Spanish peninsula. At that time, the viceroy successfully coaxed the municipal council of Mexico City to charge 6 percent on the alcabala. When the municipal administration went bankrupt in 1677, however, the king appointed a superintendent, who raised the revenue to a steady 259,226 pesos after expenses. In 1693, the consulado began administering the tax in exchange for a payment of 260,000 pesos per year.[6]

The Crown successfully pitted the consulado against the municipal council or a royal superintendent to raise alcabala proceeds significantly over time. As a result, the alcabala gained in comparison to other sources of royal income.

While mining taxes and the Native tribute generated most revenue in the late sixteenth century, by the end of the next century, the alcabala and other taxes drove more than 40 percent of royal income. Overall tax receipts expanded consequently, strengthening the monarchy.[7]

Later in 1707, a merchant promised to pay 325,000 pesos annually to collect the alcabala in the entire kingdom of New Spain. The Crown tentatively approved the offer to force the consulado's hand. Its representative in Madrid floated the idea of paying 280,000 pesos and a one-time donation of 50,000 pesos to the Crown for the Mexico City alcabala. At that time, Spain was embroiled in its War of Succession (1702–1715). King Philip V needed cash to defend his throne, but he also worried about unrest in the Americas. He ultimately accepted the consulado's offer, because it guaranteed reliable payments and peace at the tax gates.[8] The Crown renewed the tax farm contract in 1724 after the consulado donated 50,000 pesos. In addition, the consulado greased the wheels by loaning the Crown one million pesos without interest in 1726. In the late 1730s, the consulado bribed many courtiers in Madrid, and the Crown renewed the contract in 1739 without raising payments. After another even larger loan at favorable terms in 1742, Ensenada called on the viceroy to provide an additional two million pesos during the War of the Austrian Succession (1740–1748).[9]

Viceroys typically enjoyed some leeway in implementing such orders. They rewarded collaborators and cajoled the unwilling. Viceroy Fuenclara used that script in 1744 to serve up some fine arm twisting. He called a meeting with important treasury officials and the consulado leadership. When all members had arrived, the viceroy asked the consulado ministers to step out. The remaining officials deliberated Ensenada's orders and agreed on raising the alcabala rate from 6 to 8 percent. Then the consulado ministers rejoined the meeting and protested vehemently on being informed of the agreement. The municipal council joined them, but to no avail. Fuenclara had followed protocol by hearing all the involved parties. He raised the annual consulado payment from 280,000 pesos to 373,333 pesos for a period of five years. Yet as things are with taxes, the king could not do without the additional income even after hostilities had ceased. Ensenada even obtained another sizable loan in 1746.[10]

By midcentury, the consulado levied the alcabala fairly effectively. Armed guards charged the alcabala according to the volume of goods and livestock. Merchants and mule drivers reported their goods at one of the twenty gates of

Mexico City, which were located on the main roads on the fringes of the urban center. One checkpoint, for example, sat on the highway toward the basilica of Guadalupe, while another controlled access to the market in San Francisco Tepito. Canoes also zigzagged through the city on myriad canals and paid taxes on their merchandise at designated bridges. Eleven guards on horseback traveled the outskirts of Mexico City to enforce payments and catch tax evaders. In addition, consulado representatives used an honor system to collect the alcabala in surrounding districts, right from Tula (Hidalgo) in the north to Chalco (Morelos) in the south.[11]

At the same time, the consulado favored friends and special corporations, and tax evasion remained rampant. Many circumvented the collection by using smaller, unchecked venues. The artful "mule drivers, carriers, and cartwrights" particularly riled the consulado.[12] Clergymen also brought tax-exempt crops from their haciendas into town to feed their coreligionists. They imported more than they consumed and sold the untaxed products in the city. In addition, wholesale merchants doing business with clergy, private tax farmers collecting tithe, and suppliers to the missions and forts often negotiated a reduction by claiming that serving the church was not business. Even laymen who joined the lower orders dodged the taxman. Güemes quipped that anything with the "odor or color of the Church was free of alcabala."[13] Yet in his and Ensenada's view, the priests were meant to save souls instead of making money on trade.[14]

Nonetheless, Güemes and Ensenada disagreed about extending the contract with the consulado for fifteen years. The first minister pointed out that tax farm proceeds in other cities had risen by 220 percent in the past decades, while revenue from Mexico City stagnated. Yet Güemes believed that the people would see significant change as "an imminent pest or an army of Moors attacking them" and expected resistance.[15] Güemes believed that the consulado could pay an additional 20,000 or 30,000 pesos annually to the Crown. The consulado would not be able to raise the payments at the same rate as elsewhere, however. In any case, if Ensenada insisted on seizing the alcabala, Güemes suggested returning the tax rate to 6 percent.[16]

Meanwhile, the consulado emphasized its leniency. Its leadership claimed that Spanish merchants selling bulk or luxury goods paid the alcabala. Meanwhile, Indians and castes (offspring of racially mixed families) who retailed minor amounts of maize, grain, and seeds were exempt. The consulado also forewent taxing most sales within the city, especially on retailers who bought smaller quantities of merchandise from wholesalers. The exchange of real estate, slaves, and auctions in ecclesiastical courts was taxable, too, and so was property sold outside the city if the owner resided in the capital. Nevertheless, the consulado mostly ignored the transactions unless it received notarized accounts. This "waiver was so appreciated because of its age, that it was assumed to be Mexico City's particular privilege," Güemes noted.[17]

The consulado also bemoaned its financial woes while secretly stashing away a tidy slush fund. The consulado pointed out that it had raised 5,772,732 pesos from 1739 to 1750. It had paid the Crown 3,360,000 pesos from this amount. The consulado also donated funds to the king and coped with the bankruptcies of several merchants who had failed to pay their dues. "This year," agreed Güemes, "two of them have died, one owing 36,000 pesos and the other more than 50,000 in alcabala" to the consulado.[18] Deducting all expenses, the consulado garnered a net profit of 281,856 pesos during that period. The consulado claimed that it used most of the remainder for charity and the public good. Güemes agreed that the consulado supported the "hospitals and religious communities, the widows, unmarried women, and other poor folks."[19] Despite these pretensions, the collection was highly profitable, and much money seeped away into hidden funds. In 1776, a dissident member of the consulado incriminated the leadership for hoarding over one million pesos from the alcabala administration. The consulado by no means effectively supported charities or restored public buildings as it said.[20]

Because the alcabala was so lucrative, the consulado asked for a renewal of the contract lasting from 1754 until 1768. Its agents gave away at least 100,000 pesos to grease palms and influence opinion in Madrid. The leadership also offered to raise annual payments to 354,000 pesos per year on the 6 percent tax. If the king kept the alcabala at 8 percent, the consulado would deposit 472,000 pesos, provided it also collected the tax at the fair in Xalapa, where the Spanish fleet merchants sold their merchandise.[21] In addition, the consulado sought the monopoly on selling pulque, the popular fermented agave brew. At that time, hundreds of pulque taverns peddled their potions in Mexico City, yet Güemes took measures to remedy public drunkenness. As a result, the annual fee for the pulque monopoly declined. Nonetheless, the consulado offered the original price when tied to the alcabala administration.[22]

At roughly that same time, a competing project emerged. The merchant Juan Bautista Belaunzarán submitted three memoranda to the Crown during 1751–1752, proposing to add 255,000 pesos per year to the consulado's offer. He may well have acted as Ensenada's straw man to turn on the heat on the consulado. Güemes was wary about this course of action, however, since Belaunzarán had ruined his reputation in the business community. Most did not trust him to keep commitments, and Belaunzarán would fail to get bondsmen to put up the required deposit. In the viceroy's view, Belaunzarán's "proposals are . . . the daring of a man who is drowning and thinking of any means to reach the shore."[23]

On June 23, 1752, after considering all pleas and ploys, Ensenada ordered the wresting away of the alcabala from the consulado.[24] In September 1753, Güemes informed the public, and the consulado relinquished the collection on January 1, 1754. The viceroy appointed a superintendent to administer the alcabala, while armed guards continued to review merchandise at the gates. In total, eighty-seven officials gathered the proceeds and entered them into a chest that could only be opened with three separate keys held by different royal officials.[25]

Most officials from the consulado administration remained on their jobs, although Güemes seized the opportunity to appoint twenty new officials. No viceroy before him had named as many officials to treasury positions in such a short time. These appointees tended to return the favor and loyally serve the viceroy. Some of the appointees were viceregal clients, such as his personal treasurer who had accompanied him from Cuba. The Council of the Indies objected in his case to appointing "family of young age and no experience with papers," although Güemes also needed to rely on some trustworthy people in the tax administration.[26] Appointees also came from other sections of the royal treasury, such as the superintendent. He had traveled to colonial Mexico before Güemes's term and must have impressed the viceroy in some fashion.[27]

The collection tightened and improved. For instance, the superintendent ordered that the clergy be checked with "tact and vigor."[28] The guards had to calculate the quantity of goods that the clergy declared at the gates against the number of coreligionists dwelling in the city. The friars paid taxes on anything beyond their consumption capacity. In addition, the viceroy mandated necessary repairs of inspection gates and storage buildings.[29]

The new collection did not stir any major trouble, although discontent was palpable. Many wholesalers had already shipped large quantities of goods into Mexico City in the last days of the old administration to avoid the new levy. Meanwhile, the Jesuit provincial pleaded with the king's confessor in Madrid to derail the measure. A friar in Mexico City even dared lambasting the new rules in a sermon. When Güemes heard of that, he asked the archbishop to come to the palace, and the prelate "promised to punish and correct" the friar. The archbishop "instantly revoked the licenses for preaching and hearing confession and threatened others with the same if they incurred in the same nonsense." When the regulars backed down, Güemes asked the archbishop to reinstate the clergy's licenses. Meanwhile, the secular church largely kept quiet.[30]

The consulado resisted the new administration stridently, which Güemes attacked as "a direct challenge and recrimination of the king's rights."[31] The consulado sent a stream of petitions to Güemes, its representative at the court, and the king. The merchants deplored the loss of their checkpoints and bridges, which they had built at their expense to collect the alcabala. They alone were worth 120,000 pesos. The consulado also contested orders that it had to continue supporting the rural mounted police force with 5,000 pesos per year. Güemes shrugged this off and mandated the consulado to draw on other income.[32]

Besides, the municipal council of Mexico City opposed the new administration. In late 1753, the council reminded the king that it had agreed to giving two sizable loans and to increasing the alcabala rate in 1636 under conditions. These included doubling the amount of goods and money that the galleons carried between Acapulco and the Philippines. The conditions also included legalizing trade between colonial Mexico and Peru, importing more Black slaves, and providing additional leadership positions for Mexican-born friars. According to the municipal council, the viceroy had accepted these terms, but the king disregarded them, vitiating the council's consent. What was worse, the king had seized the tax collection on leather hides and sweetened ice—brought from the volcanos to Mexico City—without offering any compensation.[33]

As these complaints were fruitless, the consulado added that levying the tax in the city was unjust. In its view, the Spanish fleet merchants imported merchandise wholesale to Mexico City and then retailed the goods, paying the alcabala only once.[34] Meanwhile, the modest hawkers inside Mexico City would have to pay additional alcabala when buying from the wholesalers. According to the consulado, "the richest in this line of merchants are the peanut sellers, whose property is usually limited to the small amount of 300 pesos or less." The consulado added that the "cloth and rag sellers and used goods peddlers are so poor that we believe that most cannot sustain themselves," while "the chocolate vendors have twenty-five pesos of capital or less, perhaps loaning from a merchant one *arroba* [twenty-five pounds] of cacao, one and a half pound of cinnamon with the corresponding amount of sugar, and they earn their meals with this misery." Many of the hawkers would go out of business and switch to crime, the consulado feared.[35]

What is more, special rules undermined an efficient collection in the city. Bakers, for example, paid the alcabala when bringing their ingredients into the city but not on their sales. Similar exemptions applied to selling "fresh and salted meats with coal, firewood, lime, stones, and many other lines of goods that together are worth millions" of pesos. Thus, the resale tax would barely yield 100,000 pesos and not be worth the significant effort of tracking sales. Finally, the consulado feared that the new tax regime would ruin the colonial capital. In its view, the city of Puebla had suffered a downturn when the Crown took over the alcabala there decades earlier.[36]

Güemes rejected the demands in December 1753 as "exorbitant, odious, and unheard-of."[37] Ensenada agreed, since the residents of Madrid shouldered a higher tax burden by paying 8 percent on goods sold within the city in addition to other surcharges. Nonetheless, the merchants in Mexico City continued to press their demands in 1755 by stressing their role in "supplying the palace" of the viceroy.[38] By May 1755, the consulado had handed several reports to the viceroy about the "most serious damages" caused by the new levy. Two representatives also embarked for Spain to plead their case, although some merchants advised restraint, because Güemes's voice counted for more in Madrid than the consulado's.[39] All the same, the senior consul invited the municipal council to join protests in 1755. Most municipal councilors agreed and voted to send a representative to Madrid. Yet three councilors opposed the motion. One of them was a relative of an audiencia judge who had befriended Güemes. As a result, the municipal council was divided, which helped Güemes to deny a travel permit for the representative without appearing unduly authoritarian.[40]

At that time, Güemes devised a census to better collect the tax in the city. Back in May 1753, the viceroy had ordered two municipal magistrates to produce the head count. This caused unrest, as many feared that the viceroy intended to "ship them out to Mobile [Alabama] to fight the French" or "order the vagrants to prisons."[41] In the following year, the superintendent of the alcabala drafted a list of shopkeepers to track sales and to quantify the commercially active population. While in favor of the work, Güemes cautioned against these street vendors. They would eventually have to pay taxes, "but that will be the last thing to try, because these people have nothing to lose, and they are ready for any kind of disorder."[42]

The Spanish fleet merchants supported the new administration because they had often quarreled with the Mexican consulado over assessing the alcabala. For instance, they had originally paid a flat fee of 12,000 pesos per merchant fleet that pulled into Veracruz. Since 1740, however, individual registered ships began replacing the fleet, sailing on their own schedule from various ports in Spain. As more registered ships disembarked their goods, commissioners began recording the quantity of boxed merchandise in Veracruz. The merchants afterward presented records and merchandise at the gates in Mexico City. According to critics, grumpy consulado guards rummaged through the merchandise to check for discrepancies. Allegedly, they assessed luxury goods differently from bulk merchandise and destroyed or stole goods. In 1747, the fleet merchants complained indignantly that the guards discriminated against them and preferred the Mexican wholesalers.[43] The consulado retorted that the fleet merchants "forged records to deliver goods and defrauded the royal alcabala" administration.[44]

Moreover, the fleet merchants objected to paying a higher tax than 12.5 pesos per *fardo* (about 150 pounds) of merchandise, while the consulado insisted on charging at least 21 pesos. Güemes finally nudged the parties to agree on 16 pesos per fardo.[45] The viceroy also threatened all merchants with a penalty of 500 pesos or two years of forced military service if they tinkered with alcabala records issued in Veracruz. Repeat offenders lost their entire "mule team, carts, or cars" or served eight years in a fortress.[46] Notwithstanding these measures, the fleet merchants held their grudge, and they welcomed the royal alcabala administration in 1754.[47]

Friends, Foes, and "Imagined Misgivings"

Several people helped Viceroy Güemes to seize the alcabala administration. They were members of a minority faction of the consulado, other merchants, administrators, and clergymen. Most of them did not belong to established families of Mexico City; instead, they had migrated from other parts of the empire. They helped the viceroy to obtain important information and build support for measures, while clearly banking on receiving viceregal patronage in return.

Ignacio Cevallos served as Güemes's most important adviser. Cevallos was born in Guatemala, where he attended a Jesuit colegio. Later, Cevallos became a prebendary at the Cathedral of Mexico City and counseled the viceroy in financial matters.[48] For his part, Güemes recommended Cevallos to the Crown in 1749, and in the following year, the latter became cathedral treasurer. Cevallos also drew on backing from Madrid, such as from the chief clerk of the secretary of the Indies. In 1751, both the chief clerk and Güemes championed another promotion for Cevallos, but they squared off with the king's confessor. The chief clerk reported to Güemes that

> our Cevallos's merits are well known, and he well serves the treasury, although there has been ample resistance . . . and when I came from my boss [Ensenada] and seeing the father confessor, I mentioned him [Cevallos] on his behalf and also favored him on my behalf, and added Your Lordship's [Güemes's] meaningful recommendation, and we then had a varied and long disagreement and argument, and the following day, he [the confessor] told me in fairly unpleasant terms that Your Lordship already has Cevallos as treasurer. In the current state, I believe it is very difficult that we progress another step, even if an opportunity arose again.[49]

Güemes listened to Cevallos, much to the consulado's chagrin.[50] The consulado chided Güemes for ignoring its own advice and that from experienced treasury officials. Güemes did not follow the consulado's arguments, because "he was not aware of them, he had forgotten them, and he did not receive notice of them from the person he consulted." That person was Cevallos, who in the consulado's opinion was a subject of "no knowledge in government and even less in the affairs of the alcabala, because he was born in the province of Guatemala three hundred leagues away and has been in Mexico City only in passing without managing any important affairs."[51] The consulado exaggerated Cevallos's lack of knowledge, but it shared with others its disdain for clergy intruding in state affairs. The satirical "imp of Mexico," which circulated in New Spain in 1755, may well have been aimed at Cevallos. The clergymen:

better not meddle in politics,	no los metais en negocios,
because they will fail ...	porque esto será perderlos ...
As a safe rule,	Tened por regla segura
the most respectable among them	que en la gente, que refiero,
is the person	el mas respectable es
who least enters the palace.	El que entra en Palacio menos.
I do not say	No digo, que alguna vez
never listen to their honest advice,	no oigais sus avisos rectos,
but let it be in matters	pero sea en los asuntos
of their own profession and law.	De su oficio y de su fuero.[52]

For the consulado, Güemes's supporters faced serious conflicts of interest. Cevallos, for instance, was friends with the merchant Juan Bautista Belaunzarán and the regent of the Tribunal of Accounts, who were brothers-in-law. According to the consulado, "they are involved and have a stake in the offer that they made in Madrid in Belaunzarán's name" for the alcabala administration.[53] Güemes also originally distrusted the regent, who had bought his appointment in 1740. In 1748, Güemes observed caustically that the regent and his colleagues fell short of "punctual and swift conduct," adding: "I am presented with the challenging and inappropriate appointments of these ministers on the Tribunal, who were named by His Majesty, because they have served Him with large sums" of money.[54] By 1752, however, Güemes changed course completely and recommended the regent as one of two non-lawyers to a prestigious seat on the Council of the Indies.[55]

In addition, the viceroy could not legally socialize with residents, so his oldest son Juan Vicente forged family ties with the Count of San Bartolomé de Xala, among others. San Bartolomé de Xala was among the richest merchants in the kingdom. He built a fortune by producing pulque and importing Venezuelan cacao, especially after the Venezuelan monopoly collapsed in 1749. His daughter married Güemes's personal secretary, and Juan Vicente godfathered their child.[56] The chronicler reported that in the afternoon of December 21, 1752, the baby girl was christened Antonia Josefa, and

> Ignacio Cevallos, currently judge of testaments and treasurer of this Holy Church, baptized her, and the Lord colonel don Juan Vicente Güemes Horcasitas y Padilla, captain of the royal mounted guard and firstborn son of

said most excellent Lord viceroy, held her in his arms as godfather.... [T]he turnout was great, money was distributed to the poor with splendor, and the refreshments were ostentatious, because the principal subjects of this city attended.[57]

Güemes's friendship with San Bartolomé de Xala continued. The viceroy's sons attended the baptism of María Josefa Ignacia, the count's granddaughter. In July 1754, Güemes also conferred the captaincy of the consulado's grenadier battalion on San Bartolomé de Xala's son. The chronicler commented acerbically that "various lieutenants and cadets of the battalion, who already served as such when that gentleman was born, deeply felt this."[58] In turn, San Bartolomé de Xala repaid the honors. When the viceroy arrested several council members for truancy during sacred processions, the council protested and voted to demand "satisfaction" from him. Notably absent from that vote was Bartolomé de Xala, who served on the council at that time. The viceroy had not arrested him, either. Such internal divisions in the council helped Güemes to dispel opposition without appearing despotic.[59]

Güemes's coalition consisted of recent immigrants to New Spain, mostly from northern Spain and some American-born ones. San Bartolomé de Xala, for example, grew up not far from Güemes's birthplace. Ignacio Cevallos hailed from Guatemala. Yet Güemes's group was by no means anti-consulado or marginal. San Bartolomé de Xala served as consul during 1739–1740, and another influential merchant of the group held that position in 1743, before Güemes's viceregency. They probably belonged to a minority faction within the consulado that favored accommodation over confrontation with the viceroy.

Most members of the alliance continued to communicate with Güemes after his return to Spain for mutual benefit. Güemes frequently wrote to his "dear friend" Cevallos and asked him in 1762 to "express his fondest affection to my Count of San Bartolomé [de Xala] ... and the regent."[60] The bonds were even passed down to the next generation. During 1763–1764, Güemes corresponded with Belaunzarán's son and expressed friendship, for instance. The son of another merchant wrote in 1763 that the Crown had seized the pulque monopoly. He stated that the family had lost most of their fortune after his father's death and sought Güemes's help at court.[61]

When the Marquis of la Ensenada fell from office on July 21, 1754, the consulado sensed an opening in alcabala matters. Its representative in Madrid

TABLE 2. Güemes's Friends during the Alcabala Tax Conflict

NAME	ORIGIN	IN NEW SPAIN SINCE	RELATION TO THE CONSULADO
Juan Crisóstomo Barroeta y Barrenechea, regent of the Tribunal of Accounts	La Rioja	about 1728	
Juan Bautista Belaunzarán, merchant	Basque (Guipúzcoa)	1723	
Ignacio Felipe Cevallos Villagutierre, treasurer of the ecclesiastical chapter	Guatemala; parents were from Salamanca (León)	mid-1720s	
Manuel Cosuela, merchant	Basque (Vizcaya)	1723	member in 1761
Jacinto Martínez Aguirre, merchant	Basque		member 1735–1741, consul in 1743
Manuel Rodríguez Sáenz Pedrozo, Count of San Bartolomé de Xala, merchant	La Rioja	no later than 1718	member 1727, 1735–1741, consulado's deputy in 1736, consul 1739–1740, prior in 1759

Sources: Sanchiz and Conde Díaz Rubín, "Familia Monterde y Antillón," 101–2, 115–18; Tutino, "Creole Mexico," 62–81; Velasco Mendizábal, "Familia, poder y negocios," 762–68; and Hausberger, "Matrikel Consulado." See also endnotes 48, 53–56, and 60–62 in this chapter.

wrote a letter to Güemes, beginning on a personal tone about his personal tragedy. He apologized for not writing himself, as "his wife had just passed away because of spotted fever that overcame her two days after giving birth to a boy who lives, and for that reason, and for having a strong headache, a scribe is writing this letter." The representative could then barely hide his schadenfreude, claiming that "those opposed to the marquis seized on the unrest among businesspeople and those living in that city, when introducing the royal administration of the alcabala, and its possible bad consequences, especially when rigorously charging the 8 percent and the tax within the city."[62] Güemes, however, largely refuted the claim. He replied by equally apologizing for not writing himself, since some "fluid is bothering my eyes, and my many occupations have prevented me from penning this letter with my own hand." Güemes then defended the royal alcabala administration against "specters spreading at court and imagined misgivings." He believed that "the rumor circulating in public that this matter separated the Marquis of la Ensenada from his office is apocryphal and invented."[63]

Nevertheless, Ensenada's and Güemes's successors responded to the consulado's pressure and sought more accommodation. On September 4, 1754, Secretary Arriaga ordered that the alcabala be lowered.[64] Viceroy Amarillas complied on March 22, 1755, by reducing the tax on goods produced in colonial Mexico and cacao imported from Venezuela and Cuba. He also exempted the Mexican consulado and "all mechanical trades such as cobblers, blacksmiths, chocolate makers, and others" from the tax in the city, except for "factories and productions and manufacturers of silk cloth, cotton, and wool," much to the applause of the consulado and the municipal council.[65] In September 1756, the consulado also suggested exempting "iron, copper and other metals, wax, and tallow," because craftspeople working with these materials suffered when paying the alcabala twice.[66] The Spanish fleet merchants probably did not oppose this move since they imported many of these goods. Arriaga agreed and lowered the alcabala to 6 percent across the board, where it remained for the next decades.[67] More importantly, Arriaga yielded to the wishes of the consulados of Mexico City and Cádiz in southern Spain and prohibited registered ships from sailing on their own. Instead, in 1756, he restored the outmoded fleet departing every two or three years for New Spain. This benefited the consulados, who largely controlled fleet commerce. Most other colonial Mexicans lost out, and even other Spanish ports that competed with Cádiz saw their fortunes wane for some time.[68]

A Rise in Revenue

Güemes's reform triggered soaring revenue. In the early 1750s, the consulado deposited 373,333 pesos into the treasury every year. After relinquishing the alcabala in 1754, proceeds almost doubled to 739,056 pesos. Tax receipts in the following year hovered near that mark. In June 1756, the Crown lowered the alcabala rate from 8 to 6 percent and ended collecting tax within the city. The outbreak of the Seven Years' War in that year also undercut trade and tax revenue, since European luxury imports provided most of the alcabala. The proceeds

TABLE 3. Mexico City *Alcabala* Yields, 1750–1760

YEAR	ALCABALA PROCEEDS OF MEXICO CITY IN PESOS AFTER EXPENSES	IMPORTANT EVENTS
1750	373,333	
1751	373,333	
1752	373,333	
1753	373,333	
1754	739,056	End of the tax farm
1755	738,792	
1756	448,765	Alcabala lowered to 6% and the ending of most collection within Mexico City; outbreak of the Seven Years' War (1756–1763)
1757	533,292	
1758	860,652	
1759	486,261	
1760	420,601	

The data in column 2 shows alcabala proceeds from 1750 to 1760, which was the last year before the separation of the alcabala and *alcabala de viento* (tax on smaller quantities, esp. textiles) in 1761. The consulado paid 280,000 pesos annually from 1709 to 1745. In 1754, gross proceeds were 778,487 pesos and net proceeds 712,408 pesos after administrative and facility expenses of 66,079 pesos, according to Fonseca and Urrutia, *Historia general*, 2:57–60, and foldable overview, 2:119–20, based on Güemes, *Reglamento de alcabalas*, fol. 44v, also fols. 23–47v. This amount, however, excludes some income, especially 35,560 pesos from the resale alcabala in Mexico City. In 1755, administrative costs were 52,550 pesos per year, and the data does not include the unknown amount of resale alcabala in 1755. Colonial data is not always complete, and similar imprecisions probably also affect subsequent alcabala proceeds. Castro Santa-Anna, *Diario de sucesos notables*, 5:114, reports 600,000 pesos income for 1754, probably after expenses. For the period before 1754, the chart also draws on consulado to king, Mexico City, January 4, 1753, AGI, México 2501; and consulado to king, March 1, 1754, AGI, México 2093. TePaske and Klein, *Ingresos y egresos*, 16, and sections S2131 and S2026, confirm the trends, since the combined alcabala and *armada de Barlovento* receipts from all regions reporting to the Mexico City *caja real* (treasury), including cities such as Puebla and Oaxaca, grew from 896,079 pesos in 1753 to 1,468,656 pesos in 1754, dropping slightly to 1,245,475 pesos in 1755 and 1,020,683 pesos in 1756. In 1760, they stood at 922,885 pesos.

spiraled down by 39 percent in that year. Yet income rebounded in the following two years, probably caused by a more consistent collection in response to the earlier drop. Proceeds then dropped again and hovered below 500,000 pesos until 1760. Table 3 shows the Crown receipts during the period 1750–1760.[69]

The alcabala net gains also increased slightly, because Güemes cut the salaries of the officials. While the consulado had paid 64,505 pesos in wages annually, Güemes reduced this amount to 52,550 pesos.[70] Nonetheless, the top positions still received ample income. The superintendent of the alcabala, for example, earned 5,000 pesos per year, which was 1,000 pesos more than a civil judge of the audiencia, the most prestigious position in New Spain next to the viceroy. Lowering wages for important treasury positions conflicted with Güemes's idea of setting incentives for good conduct, but he probably felt that the consulado had overpaid its officials.[71]

Alcabala Auctions in Veracruz

The Council of the Indies urged the viceroy to review the alcabalas outside of Mexico City, too. Most collections worked on an honor system, as merchants declared their sales to a tax farmer. Since the revenue was rather low, the council instructed Güemes to interview trustworthy people about the likely value of the local collections and farm out the alcabala at that level.[72] Güemes was not impressed by that thought, however. He favored more competitive bidding in auctions instead. In 1747, he proudly announced that proceeds from provincial alcabala had risen by 30,000 pesos as a result. Then he set his gaze on Veracruz, the most important port of the viceroyalty.[73]

Trade coalesced in this harbor, and merchants outbid one another to collect the alcabala. The tax farmers levied 6 percent tax on the goods that were taken into the city, while merchandise leaving the port paid the alcabala elsewhere. In the seventeenth century, the Veracruz alcabala yielded between 17,000 and 21,000 pesos per year, rising to 23,000 pesos at the beginning of the eighteenth century. By 1728, the tax farmer paid 33,750 pesos in those years when the Spanish fleet arrived and 32,500 pesos in all others. In the same year, however, the royal officials in Veracruz complained that the tax farmer shortchanged them and recommended seizing the collection.[74] The Crown nonetheless auctioned off the administration again. In 1740, Juan Bautista Belaunzarán, probably acting as a straw man for for the crown, made an appearance. Yet a group of other merchants claiming residence in Veracruz offered 45,600 pesos per year and outbid him. In 1749, the Crown again posted the tax for auction. On July 10, 1749, the merchants started the bid with 40,600 pesos annually, while attaching thirty conditions to the contract. Another group of businessmen offered 65,730 pesos per year. When it was Belaunzarán's turn, he outdid the second proposal by adding an annual donation of 500 pesos. At that point, the auction ended. Güemes, his legal adviser, and the civil prosecutor approved Belaunzarán's offer.[75]

The merchants then claimed the moral high ground to drum up support in a divided city. They presented a petition in their favor signed by fifty-four residents of Veracruz. Afterward, on October 30, more than one hundred residents gathered. They applauded the merchants' attempt to match Belaunzarán's offer and pay the first year up front. The meeting lent credence to the merchants' assertion that they represented the community of Veracruz and looked out for its public good. In addition, the municipal council of Veracruz met on November 20, 1749, to back the offer. The governor, a municipal councilor, and the constable favored giving power of attorney to a representative in support of the merchants. Nevertheless, three councilors and three other officials opposed the motion. As the discussion turned ugly, the governor struck down the opposing votes. He disqualified one of them for being Belaunzarán's relative, while the two others could not agree among themselves. The governor ordered the issuance of the power of attorney. The losing party challenged the case and took it to the audiencia in Mexico City. The civil prosecutor concurred on Christmas Eve 1749 that the governor had acted lawfully, since the dissenting votes "were not in agreement, but conflicting." After reading the verdict, Güemes handed the tax farm to the merchants.[76]

Belaunzarán then appealed the case to Madrid. The civil prosecutor of the Council of the Indies suggested overruling the Mexican authorities on February 30, 1751. The prosecutor maintained that the merchants only ostensibly represented the community of Veracruz, because its members pursued their own financial interests just as much as Belaunzarán. The council finally approved the recommendation on November 3, 1752. Almost three years after Güemes's verdict in favor of the merchants, Belaunzarán obtained the tax farm of Veracruz in early 1753.[77]

Belaunzarán subsequently paid 88,140 pesos annually to the treasury, because the alcabala rate in Veracruz had also risen by 2 percent to 8. He now paid almost twice as much as the previous installment. Consequently, Belaunzarán had to tighten the collection. Many merchants balked at the terms and looked for loopholes. Some declared that they merely disembarked merchandise and paid taxes elsewhere. Others purportedly provisioned the garrison in the fortress and the fleet, which was tax free. The matter went to Madrid again. Belaunzarán requested prohibiting any carriage of goods to the fortress or the fleet without his written approval. Arriaga agreed and issued a royal order, although Güemes and the port officials in Veracruz remained skeptical. Güemes even toyed with the idea of reducing the alcabala in Veracruz to 3 percent to set an incentive for paying the tax in the port instead of in some other place.[78]

Failure loomed before Belaunzarán, as he could not pay his annual installments. In 1754, Güemes "considered him in arrears in business, and this is true even in the public eye." The merchant locked himself up at home, and his son-in-law took over.[79] In lieu of the annual payment to the treasury, which was due in June 1756, the son-in-law simply issued invoices to those merchants who had sold goods in Veracruz without paying the full amount. The merchants appealed the measure, and Belaunzarán and his son-in-law acknowledged failure. On September 11, 1756, royal officials recovered the administration, two years before the contract would have ended. Subsequently, they collected about 70,000 pesos annually. Despite Belaunzarán's failure, the Crown benefited substantially from the rising alcabala proceeds.[80]

The episode did not damage Belaunzarán, in part because the Council of the Indies had supported his bid in full knowledge of the risks. In fact, the merchant strengthened his friendship with Güemes over time. In 1764, Belaunzarán requested him to use his influence at court to recover 5,000 pesos that Belaunzarán had lent the Crown in 1747. Güemes promised to help, citing the "particular affection that I have always had for Your Lordship."[81]

Conclusion

The Crown successfully raised the alcabala rate and revenue in Mexico City beginning in the sixteenth century. The tax rate rose from 2 percent in 1576 to 4 percent in 1628, 6 percent after 1636, and 8 percent in 1744. The revenue grew from originally 77,000 pesos to 373,333 pesos after 1744. This was possible because the Crown alternated the tax administration between the municipal council, the consulado, and a superintendent. The changes allowed royal officials to fathom the tax yield, while the king credibly threatened an end to the tax farm if the consulado or municipal council refused to raise their bids. The results show that the financial administration of the empire did not stagnate in that period.[82]

Building on that experience, Güemes again seized the alcabala for the Crown with a notable outcome during 1753–1754.[83] He remained true to himself as a loyal and energetic, yet cautious reformer. The viceroy initially supported the consulado's quest to continue its administration. He feared unrest at the gates if the state seized control with a heavy hand. Yet Ensenada insisted on a higher revenue, and he probably encouraged the merchant Belaunzarán to act as straw man and force the consulado's hand. Negotiations with the consulado stalled, and Ensenada and Güemes abandoned building a consensus, in the sense that most participants agreed. Instead, the viceroy followed Ensenada's promptings and ended the consulado administration in 1753. Royal officials stepped in, and the alcabala receipts skyrocketed to 739,056 pesos in 1754 and 738,792 in 1755 after expenses—these were unimaginable numbers under the previous administration. Subsequently, receipts hovered below 500,000 pesos per year after 1758, mostly because the government lowered the tax rate to 6 percent.

Güemes collaborated with a network of recent immigrants to Mexico City. His allies provided information and assisted in confronting the consulado, the municipal council, and the regular church. Most other colonial Mexicans acquiesced. It helped that few disputed the king's right to charge the alcabala, since royal superintendents had administered the tax before. Seizing the alcabala without major upheaval was a breakthrough for Güemes and the Crown. The alcabala administration collected significantly more, and Güemes carved out a name for himself as an able reformer.

"Regime change" mattered too. Ensenada took a hard line on Mexico City's tax rate because it was still below that of Madrid. In 1753, the first minister only lowered the taxes on Spanish wine and brandy in Mexico City by way of concession. Yet Güemes even suspended that order because the municipal council needed cash for the drainage system.[84] Subsequently, Ensenada's successor, Arriaga, and his new viceroy in Mexico changed course. They lowered the alcabala rate to 6 percent and forewent collecting the tax on sales within the city. Arriaga also restored the cumbersome merchant fleet sailing to Veracruz, while restricting the travel of individual merchant ships. By doing so, Arriaga gave a nod to the consulados of Mexico City and Cádiz, which together largely controlled the trade. Regardless, the profitable alcabala administration of Mexico City never reverted to the consulado, showing the limits of colonial consensus building. In addition, the change of course also responded to

Arriaga's moderately conservative political aims and reflected the typical back-and-forth of early modern state reforms. Once a first minister and his clique had reached a political goal, their successors adjusted some points of contention to diffuse conflicts.[85]

Besides, Güemes presided over more competitive alcabala auctions in Veracruz. Several merchants claimed to represent the common good when squaring off with another group of businesspeople in 1740. The merchants won the contract by promising to pay 45,600 pesos per year to the Crown. Nine years later, however, the other group of businesspeople outbid the merchants. At that time, Belaunzarán, well known from the Mexico City imbroglio, joined the fray and offered slightly more than his competitors. Güemes handed him the contract until the audiencia heard the case and recommended awarding the merchants. Belaunzarán then took his case to the Council of the Indies and ultimately obtained the tax farm in early 1753. He paid 88,140 pesos per year, a considerable jump in proceeds, in part because the local alcabala rate had risen to 8 percent. He tightened the collection to make ends meet, while merchants moving merchandise into Veracruz actively used subterfuge to evade the alcabala levy. His tax farm failed. The royal officials stepped in briefly before auctioning off the administration once more. Subsequent contractors paid around 70,000 pesos annually. In the end, the viceroy and the royal officials oversaw a significant revenue rise in the port city, with the help of Ensenada's straw man Belaunzarán.

Güemes's success in Mexico City and Veracruz set the course. The results convinced him, and he proposed applying that model to Antequera de Oaxaca and elsewhere in the kingdom. In these places, tax farmers usually relied on the sworn reports of businesspeople, who declared their local sales. Instead, Güemes championed royal officials to take over there and charge the alcabala at the city gates.[86] Güemes's experience laid the groundwork for the later reforms between 1764 and 1766, when royal officials replaced private tax farmers in forty districts of the viceroyalty, although merchants continued to administer the remaining two dozen alcabala districts. King Charles III finally deprivatized all tax farms in 1776. Proceeds rose, by more than 200 percent in some northern mining cities. It can be said, however, that Güemes had pioneered this process by seizing the alcabala of Mexico City for the Crown and making the Veracruz alcabala more competitive.[87]

CHAPTER 6

One Kingdom to Rule the Other?
New Spain versus New Galicia

Introduction

Incessant tussles marked the kingdom of New Galicia (northwestern Mexico) in the mid-eighteenth century. In 1752, for example, a councilman of the capital, Guadalajara, sued the former president of the audiencia, Fermín Echeverz González. The councilmember alleged that Echeverz González had propositioned his wife, Juana Zedano, and "satisfied his depraved appetite." That hurt the councilman's "renowned reputation in all America." Echeverz González, however, rejected the accusation and demanded that "the fellow receive the special punishment that he deserves."[1] Echeverz González continued to raise eyebrows when he attended a bullfight in early 1753. He pulled up the carriage next to his successor, José Basarte (1750–1758), and asked him "why he only had two mules in his team," even though presidents were entitled to four. Basarte replied, "so as not to embarrass anyone." Echeverz González rebuffed him, however, by saying that "the seams hurt only those who don't use underwear." Echeverz González came from an illustrious family and quoted poetry to insult Basarte for his lowly origins, lack of refined taste, and modest team. Basarte reported the incident to Viceroy Güemes. Echeverz González fled to the priory of San Agustín and pleaded for church asylum, while offering Basarte "the appropriate satisfaction, mediated by the venerable bishop."[2]

The constant fighting gave Viceroy Güemes an opportunity to interfere. Prodded by a royal mandate to "end the scandals," he ordered Echeverz González to Mexico City and placed him under house arrest in January 1753. The viceroy told the former president to ship out to Spain and stand trial. Some civil judges of the Mexican audiencia disagreed, however. Later, the civil prosecutor at the Council of the Indies sharply criticized Güemes's "shocking verdict" against Echeverz González.[3] Nevertheless, the help came too late. The former president fell seriously ill, went to a hospital, and died on May 5, 1753, in Mexico City.[4]

During Güemes's viceregency, the audiencia of Guadalajara enjoyed significant autonomy in many regards.[5] The *Law of the Indies* stated that the audiencia president, who also served as governor of New Galicia, appointed the alcaldes mayores (district judges) and treasury officials, pending royal confirmation.[6] A church lawyer even claimed that Guadalajara did "not recognize any viceroy in the Indies," setting it apart from other subordinate audiencias in the empire.[7] Nevertheless, the church lawyer exaggerated. The law confirmed, for instance, that Guadalajara's "president and civil judges obey the viceroy of New Spain in everything . . . that concerns government, war, and the treasury."[8]

Güemes used these powers to strengthen his hand in Guadalajara. As miners, merchants, and ministers skirmished over control of the government and the spoils of silver production, Güemes sent inspectors to uncover embezzlements and punish culprits. He also appointed new officials, undercutting President Basarte's heavy hand over the prosperous mining camp of Bolaños, about ninety miles northwest of Guadalajara. Güemes seized the camp and appointed a trusted family member as district judge. The viceroy even suggested disbanding the audiencia of Guadalajara to stop the constant commotions, and he found a ready ear in Madrid. The end of the audiencia seemed near. This chapter explores viceregal influence in New Galicia through the lens of the conflicts over Bolaños and the treasury in Guadalajara.[9]

New Galicia had expanded demographically and economically against this backdrop. Guadalajara led the way from the days of the conquest. In the early seventeenth century, more than one thousand Blacks and Spaniards resided in the city, and about sixty Native households dotted the Analco neighborhood. Mule trains supplied the city with Spanish textiles and wine and delivered vinegar, oil, corn, and fish from the countryside.[10] A deep demographic and economic crisis gripped the kingdom from 1635 to the 1640s. Then, cattle raising and agriculture resurged once more, and mining recovered in the mid-1650s. The population grew palpably. Guadalajara boasted more than eight thousand inhabitants around 1738, and about two hundred thousand people lived in New Galicia by 1742.[11]

The Bolaños Brouhaha and the Audiencia

The booming mining camp of Bolaños became the object of contention as miners pried precious silver from the mountain. Since the early seventeenth century, migrants from central Mexico, including many Natives, trickled into the region. They lived side by side with people whom they usually lumped together as Nayarit Indians. After miners struck the first silver bonanza in 1746, the annual output surged to nearly two million silver pesos in 1753 and peaked at just above that mark in 1756. Smaller pits, such as Santa Rosa de Alburquerque, and ore smelting centers sprang up nearby. The boom continued until 1759 when the output dropped off precipitously. A spectacular revival occurred in 1775, but the mines flooded in 1792 and were abandoned. The population reflected this trend. Fortune hunters hastened to the multiethnic valley after the strikes, and over eleven thousand thronged the district in 1760. By 1772, however, their numbers fell to a fourth, as people departed the depleted mines.[12]

During this rapid expansion, there was little royal oversight over Bolaños, and miners evaded taxation. However, a zealous treasury accountant in Zacatecas—appointed by the first minister, Ensenada—reported that several miners shirked paying the royal fifth on silver. Instead of settling taxes in Zacatecas, the miners hauled their precious metal through the forbidding mountains to Guadalajara. The road there was "more uncomfortable and exposed to robberies" than the one going to Zacatecas, but tax collectors were more lenient in the kingdom's capital. The accountant's report reminded Güemes of the situation and paved the way for a larger reform of the mining camp.[13]

As a result, Güemes sent a commissioner to review tax collection in Bolaños in 1750. The commissioner traveled northwest and found six mines in operation, each with twelve to fifteen pickmen. He estimated that they produced roughly 680,000 silver pesos every year. That number contrasted starkly with the lower tax reports in Zacatecas, depriving the Crown of at least 85,000 pesos in annual taxes. Subsequently, Güemes mandated building a factory in Bolaños to assess output and cast the silver into bars on site. Soon after, the Crown converted the factory into a full-fledged treasury. Its officials tracked production in Bolaños and clamped down on tax evasion. By the end of Güemes's term in 1755, the Bolaños treasury had collected roughly 1,183,925 pesos in taxes.[14]

By taking these steps, Güemes collided with President Basarte and his father-in-law, the powerful Marquis of el Castillo de Aysa. The marquis was a wealthy landholder and miner of the region. He had tightened his grip over New Galicia by buying the interim appointment of president in 1740. The position enabled Castillo de Aysa to befriend Güemes's predecessor and important audiencia judges in Mexico City. Castillo de Aysa even traveled to the colonial capital to pay his compliments to the preceding viceroy, "giving gifts and attention as though they were compatriots," and the viceroy "publicly showed his appreciation, inviting him into his coach and the palace functions."[15]

Castillo de Aysa stepped down in 1745 but continued to expand his influence in New Galicia. The judicial review of office cleared him of wrongdoing, despite several serious charges against him. That allowed him to purchase a second term for 18,750 pesos in 1749. Instead of governing himself, however, he installed his son-in-law, José Basarte, in 1750.[16] Castillo de Aysa did not always play by the rules in Bolaños, either, where he owned shares of two mines and loaned cash to others. Castillo de Aysa operated the meat monopoly in town and sometimes sold rotten fare. According to some locals, he "only slaughters young bulls on his hacienda when he feels like it." He allegedly also dodged the taxman when producing about 1,200,000 silver pesos.[17]

Even the alcalde mayor of Jerez (now Jerez de García Salinas, about one hundred miles northeast of Bolaños) was in cahoots with Castillo de Aysa and President Basarte. The alcalde mayor appointed a deputy in Bolaños, and lawsuits against Castillo de Aysa and Basarte fell on deaf ears. One miner's agent lamented that "the deputy alcalde mayor . . . in Bolaños is by name only, because all he does is carry out the president's orders."[18] Güemes also complained that "the alcalde mayor of Jerez has appointed clients or dependents of the president of the audiencia of Guadalajara or the Marquis of el Castillo de Aysa."[19] Moreover, the deputy alcalde mayor embezzled public funds, failed to supply Bolaños with sufficient grain, and unfairly distributed Indian labor assignments and mercury that was needed for refining silver.[20]

Güemes also fumed that almost twelve thousand people lived in Bolaños without solid streets, public squares, a prison, or a courthouse. There was not even a real church, only a small chapel belonging to a hacienda that ministered to the miners. Bolaños remained in Güemes's view a "confusion, disorder, and gathering of people from everywhere, scammers, absconders from work, wayward people from the entire kingdom, while the mines lack manpower and the miners pay excessive wages ... and I consented to the forced labor draft for Indians, although I would much like to avoid that extreme remedy."[21]

Basarte and the deputy alcalde mayor showed more initiative when they noted the viceroy's attention to the camp. They improved the trail through the Sierra Bolaños in 1752 and connected the town with the La Playa mines downstream. They also ordered the digging of ditches to contain the runoff from the mountains. In addition, the town planned to build additional streets, a granary, and a prison. Locals raised 2,488 pesos, and Basarte vowed to collect additional taxes from landowners. He even suggested separating Bolaños from Jerez and establishing its own corregidor (district judge) with a municipal council.[22]

It was too little, too late, however, and Güemes wrested Bolaños from the audiencia of Guadalajara and the alcalde mayor of Jerez on November 7, 1754. The viceroy carved out a new jurisdiction and appointed a corregidor who received an impressive salary of 2,000 pesos annually. That was more than the official income of any other district judge in New Spain, save that of the corregidor of Mexico City. Ensenada agreed to the substantial change.[23] Güemes selected the attorney Diego José Gorospe Padilla for that position. He belonged to a family from Puebla that was remotely related to Güemes's wife, Antonia Pacheco Padilla. Güemes patronized the family on several occasions and expected loyalty and efficacy in exchange.[24]

Güemes added slyly that he did not really seize any territory from Guadalajara. In fact, the district would revert to Guadalajara within eight to ten years. The audiencia also retained hearing criminal appeals from Bolaños, although it surrendered most civil jurisdiction there.[25] An exchange of letters exemplifies Basarte's loss of sway in the district when Güemes's men took over. Basarte asked the treasurer in Bolaños to write up the machinations of an attorney who had tarnished Basarte's honor. The treasurer replied that he was "most mortified not to be able to comply with your request."[26]

Then it was time to set the boundaries of the district with colonial precision. On February 27, 1755, the usher of the Bolaños treasury rode north to the Native pueblo San Gaspar de Huilacatitlan and handed a letter to the *principales* (nobles). The letter informed them of the upcoming land survey, and they agreed.[27] On April 15, 1755, the surveyors gathered in the main square of Bolaños, their astrolabe and measuring ropes ready to establish five leagues (about thirteen miles) in the four cardinal directions. The surveyors marched north along the Bolaños River to the church of San Gaspar de Huilacatitlan, placing markers along the way. They had lunch at a place called "the Cave" and continued their work until the night. The next day, the surveyors faced upset Indians of the pueblo Atzqueltlan (now Azqueltán), who had not received any notice of the survey and feared the loss of their land. After appeasing the Natives, the surveyors walked through hilly terrain and a canyon until they ran into a large rock formation that they could not climb. At that point, they abandoned the survey half a league short of their goal. The surveyors returned to the main square in Bolaños and walked in the three other cardinal directions. In the end, they assigned mines in the south and a nearby silver smeltery to the district.[28]

Gorospe Padilla caused another stir in Bolaños when he took office in February 1755. The corregidor coaxed the locals to form a militia and inspected the mines to assess their output and tax yield. Gorospe Padilla also supervised the construction of an adit, which is a sloping tunnel that drains water out of mines. Several mine operators split expenses for the adit, but the owners of the top sections objected to their share. They began litigating, since they operated mule-driven lifts to remove water, and much of it ran off into the lower pits anyway. According to rumors, Basarte pulled the strings in that fight. Gorospe Padilla was unfazed, however. He appointed two guards to protect the adit and ensure that no one shaved ore from the pillars in the tunnels. Many miners resented the measures, however, especially since they had to pay the guards' salaries. At that point, Güemes stepped in. He approved charging all miners for the adit but dismissed the guards.[29]

Locals also rumbled about ambitious building plans in Bolaños. Gorospe Padilla rejected the terrain that was set aside for a proposed municipal building as too small and prone to inundation. He instead cast his gaze on a blighted hacienda on the main square. The corregidor canceled a sales contract with a prospective buyer, called for two appraisals, paid the owner, and tore down the hacienda. Soon the council building went up, including an apartment for the corregidor, "a jail, a butchery, storage for grain and corn, which arrive abundantly in the town," and even "an inn for those who occupy the stores and storage with their produce."[30] In addition, a church with two naves rose on the main square with an attached cemetery. Gorospe Padilla still needed more space, although the owner of adjacent properties balked at selling. The corregidor nonetheless sequestered and razed the buildings, containing "a small room where a Black cook is living, and two very small stores and a small house composed of one hall and two tiny rooms."[31] He also convinced a resident to donate a house that was suitable for a hospital. The civil prosecutor in Madrid welcomed the new project, provided the regular orders did not seize control.[32]

Gorospe Padilla also abhorred how many people lived in shacks near the mines. They participated in "forbidden gambling such as playing cards, bowling, and others . . . and especially the women have not given their Easter confessions." Most lived in "grass huts or wooden tile sheds made without order or rule, exposing the mines to voracious fires." The previous year, a blaze had raged among the dwellings and reached the Perla mine, causing damage of 10,000 pesos. In addition, Gorospe Padilla's predecessors had in the past "climbed up to administer justice on the mountain," but the inhabitants "drove them away by pelting stones." Yet Gorospe Padilla nudged the people to abandon the shantytown near the gallery mouth and settle at the river, where they were closer to the authorities.[33] Moreover, treasury officials began charging a liquor tax on the brandy distilled in the area. They collected four pesos per barrel on top of the regular alcabala (sales tax) that was levied on all goods. The tax hike was not popular.[34]

Even the treasury officials, who were beholden to Güemes, began to resent Gorospe Padilla's moves. The officials complained that Gorospe Padilla had moved into the treasurer's home. The treasurer and his family already shared the place with the accountant, but Gorospe Padilla refused to move out as long as the municipal council building was incomplete.[35] In addition, Gorospe Padilla sold the positions of the municipal councilors, and the treasury officials demanded to have ceremonial preference at all public functions. Gorospe Padilla dictated with Güemes's support, however, that the councilors superseded them. The corregidor was making too many enemies in town.[36]

Inspecting the Treasury of Guadalajara

While jousting over Bolaños, Güemes also ordered an inspection of the treasury in Guadalajara to curb embezzlement and raise more money for the

Crown. On March 29, 1749, the Crown ordered a yearly cash cut of all treasuries. The treasury officials in Guadalajara stalled the report about their finances, however, and had not complied by 1751. The officials also suspended remitting their annual excess funds to the central treasury of Mexico City, as was their duty. President Basarte and the civil prosecutor of the audiencia of Guadalajara sided with them, giving colorful excuses. They said that highway robbers near Celaya threatened the safe passage of silver. Yet the rural constables did not report any dangers lurking in that region. In response, Güemes sent ten soldiers to Guadalajara to safeguard the transport of silver to Mexico City.[37]

Güemes also appointed Juan Banfi y Villalobos as interim accountant in 1751 to improve the Guadalajaran treasury. Banfi y Villalobos was primarily selected for being the nephew of Ensenada's chief clerk. Charitable reasons to support the family played a role too, because Banfi y Villalobos had eight siblings.[38] In February 1752, Banfi y Villalobos joined President Basarte in inspecting the treasury building. They opened the vault and found silver bars, minted coins, and pearls worth 166,464 pesos. Basarte then ordered the treasury officials to provide a register of all debtors to the treasury, but the officials alleged that Basarte lacked the authority to do so. After more back and forth, Banfi y Villalobos finally established that the officials had embezzled 230,668 pesos.[39]

At that point, Güemes demanded that the Tribunal of Accounts in Mexico City explain why it had not noticed the disappearance of almost a quarter million pesos in Guadalajara. After all, it was the purpose of the tribunal to scrutinize receipts and glean discrepancies. The tribunal claimed that the treasury officials in Guadalajara had artfully arranged the receipts to disguise fraud. They had also used separate bookkeeping of revenue streams to confuse the tribunal even further. The viceroy was not satisfied and ordered the tribunal to work longer hours to review tax papers.[40]

In addition, Güemes commissioned the accountant Juan José Ortiz to audit the Guadalajaran treasury. Ortiz completed the review on December 20, 1752, and found that 296,600 pesos were amiss, almost 66,000 pesos more than according to the first walk-through. Ortiz blamed both the treasurer and a deceased accountant for the loss. In January 1753, Ortiz sent soldiers to detain the treasurer. The treasurer suspected his arrest, however. He opened the door to his home and, seeing the troops, requested "that they let him eat first, because it was already time, and after withdrawing into his house, he escaped through a secret door and took refuge with the Society of Jesus." As a result, Ortiz confiscated his property.[41]

Ortiz and Güemes had to settle for a compromise with the church. According to Ortiz, the treasurer should restore all missing funds to the Crown, lose his property and office, and suffer "perpetual exile from the Indies."[42] Ortiz wanted to drag out the treasurer from the Jesuit church, but his asylum was a matter of ecclesiastical jurisdiction. Ortiz advised against exacerbating the scandal, "because the bishop publicly vowed to defend the immunity" of the church. Instead, Ortiz and Güemes acknowledged the bishop's authority in that regard, and in exchange Ortiz was allowed to question the treasurer on site.[43] Ortiz recovered much for the Crown. He sold the treasurer's home and other property and called in any outstanding debt. Ortiz also ordered the treasurer's guarantors to cover any malfeasance, in total reducing the Crown's loss to roughly 89,423 pesos. Finally, Güemes stripped the treasurer of his office, because he had embezzled funds with "*dolo* [criminal intent], fraud, and bad faith."[44]

At the same time, Ortiz himself had incurred significant costs during one and a half years of scrutinizing books and interrogating both witnesses and suspects. Concluding the proceedings, Ortiz seized 3,000 pesos from the culprits' property to cover his own expenses. He then returned to Mexico City in May 1754. In the next month, the Tribunal of Accounts in the capital ratified the expenses, awarding him a daily allowance of 12 pesos, akin to previous treasury inspectors. This amounted to a total of about 6,500 pesos, which significantly rewarded Ortiz for loyal work facing powerful and dangerous opposition in Guadalajara. Güemes also expressed his pleasure by naming Ortiz as the chief clerk of the viceregal secretariat.[45] In addition, the viceroy named a replacement for the treasurer in Guadalajara, and the Council of the Indies also approved the outcome. It nevertheless rejected Güemes's suggestion to raise the salaries of the Guadalajaran officials to reduce the temptation of fraud in the future.[46]

Furthermore, just before the scandal in the treasury broke out, the acting civil prosecutor of the Guadalajaran audiencia began investigating the fraudulent sale of mercury. At that time, treasury officials distributed that heavy metal, which allowed miners to process silver from ore. The prosecutor followed up on accusations from 1751 that the treasury officials sold a *quintal* (100 pounds) of mercury for more than 120 pesos, whereas the law fixed the price at 90 pesos. The officials also ignored pleas for mercury from miners, while charging agents or merchants who did not own mines higher prices. That was illegal.[47]

The prosecutor dug out a royal cédula from November 19, 1678, which empowered the president to investigate mercury fraud. The president delegated his authority to the prosecutor, who began interviewing miners and merchants about fraud on December 11, 1751.[48] Some witnesses claimed that they had not paid excessive fees and only added a small tip of about two pesos per quintal. Yet others had clearly paid too much. One miner in Bolaños blamed Banfi y Villalobos for selling him three quintales for "343 pesos in addition to a supplement of 43 pesos." That would have been 116 pesos more than the treasury official should have charged.[49] Another miner concurred "that he contributed an additional 200 pesos at the behest of don Juan Banfi [y Villalobos]."[50]

In April 1752, the attorney working for the viceroy reviewed the prosecutor's inquiry. He found that the treasury officials, including Banfi y Villalobos, had not distributed mercury among miners according to need; instead, they "have charged as much as they could . . . and the testimonies of the witnesses more than sufficiently proved that offense." In their defense, the treasury officials showed a royal cédula from December 29, 1739, allowing them to charge three pesos per quintal as tips, clearly demonstrating their appropriate conduct in this matter. Yet the attorney maintained that later royal orders vitiated the 1739 cédula. For that reason, the treasury officials demanded "in reality bribes," and asking for them or "any insinuation in this matter is criminal and detestable." He concluded by suggesting a suspension of the treasury officials.[51]

The outcome of the inquiry embarrassed Güemes, because Banfi y Villalobos had participated in the shady dealings. Publicizing Banfi y Villalobos's participation had probably been the intent of the prosecutor and the president in the first place. Güemes responded by censuring the Guadalajaran treasurer, who sold mercury at steep markups and was "taking advantage of Banfi y Villalobos's innocence . . . to attain the spoils with impunity." More importantly, Güemes also relieved the Guadalajaran prosecutor of his commission for "being an incompetent judge without any jurisdiction." Only the viceroy as superintendent of the mercury distribution could prosecute the fraudulent sales. The Crown had repeatedly affirmed that arrangement in past years, and Güemes appointed the attorney to further investigate the mercury scheme.[52]

That attorney confirmed the findings of the first inquiry against the treasury officials who favored their friends and demanded bribes from others. According to witnesses, the officials had distributed three hundred quintales in the previous months. They charged an additional ten to twenty pesos per quintal, "which were involuntary because they were inappropriate, demanded, and requested."[53] One witness testified that a miner's agent was among the first to request mercury. Nonetheless, Banfi y Villalobos told him that he was too late, whereas "in reality he was rejected because Banfi [y Villalobos] believed that a miner's agent should not merely contribute the same as the others . . . and it was public talk that for 115 to 125 pesos," the treasury officials sold quintales including tips to the agents.[54]

Assuming conservatively that on average treasury officials charged a 20-peso tip per quintal, they gained a total of 6,000 pesos from selling that batch of mercury. That amount was divided among the officials, handsomely supplementing their salary of 1,500 pesos per year. Similar customs apparently reigned in Zacatecas, where customers paid an additional 15 to 18 pesos per quintal until the 1730s.[55] In April 1753, the chronicler Castro Santa-Anna noted with glee that the viceroy had detained Banfi y Villalobos and marched him to the fortress of Veracruz as a punishment. This was not entirely true, however. While Banfi y Villalobos ceased his interim position in Guadalajara, he must have survived the uproar politically and later obtained employment elsewhere.[56]

The fighting in Guadalajara also solidified the role of the bishop as a mediator. While the prelate had no formal say in treasury or audiencia affairs, he lamented back in 1746 that one respected judge had left for Mexico City. Since then, the ministers continually came to see him to complain about one another, often for "childish" reasons. In addition, the audiencia was understaffed, as only two judges and the prosecutor remained on the bench in 1746. That added to the instability and caused both civil and criminal litigation to move at glacial speed. There were "prisoners in jail for many years, begging to be hanged and put out of their misery from so many years in prison." The prelate concluded that appointing some capable ministers to the audiencia would restore order in New Galicia.[57]

Yet Güemes suggested a more drastic change for the audiencia. He favored eliminating the court altogether. Others had proposed such a major change in the past, but Güemes had backing for his idea in Madrid. In a confidential letter from 1751, Ensenada's chief clerk recalled that the Crown suppressed the audiencia of Panama in that year, "and the same will happen with the audiencia of Guadalajara, if your Excellency draws up the report."[58] Güemes complied the next year, but the government in Madrid hesitated nonetheless. The chief clerk also confided in Güemes that they would find a proper response to Basarte's "insolent answer given to Your Excellency."[59]

New Galicia after Ensenada

The Guadalajaran audiencia survived the onslaught, however, as Güemes faced headwinds after Ensenada's fall in 1754. Basarte saw the opportunity and demanded Bolaños's return to Guadalajara's authority in February 1755. He argued that while robbery and murder reigned elsewhere, during his government, Bolaños always remained "well provisioned with corn and meats . . . the most orderly place of the realm." Then Güemes seized the town and "oppressed the settlers with the *sisa* [wine] tax and other intolerable measures, and he so burdened these unhappy and poor people who have to go about 200 leagues to appeal any injustices . . . although they do not expect any relief for their damages, because they are fully aware of the close family bonds between the vicereine and the corregidor." This time, Basarte painted Güemes as the root of misgovernance, and he succeeded with his complaint.[60]

In October 1755, the civil prosecutor of the Council of the Indies still praised Gorospe Padilla's conduct. Yet the prosecutor questioned the advantages of subordinating Bolaños to Mexico City, when the nearest authorities should govern the province. He continued that

> the viceroy's aim has been to seize the jurisdiction over the mines . . . from the president of Guadalajara. . . . I nevertheless consider it inappropriate that the current president owns parts of the mines, and so does the Marquis of el Castillo de Aysa.[61]

The Crown partially unwound Güemes's reform when Amarillas acceded to the viceregency in 1755. The Crown mandated returning Bolaños to the audiencia of Guadalajara on September 16, 1756, although Amarillas suspended the order temporarily. He dismissed Gorospe Padilla, who had only served half a term, and appointed an interim corregidor in June 1757. That appointment probably tamped down some acrimony in Bolaños. In 1759, the audiencia fully recovered the district while the Crown confirmed Amarillas's appointee.

As a result of Güemes's interference, Bolaños had become a separate district under a corregidor who enjoyed more autonomy from the president than the former deputy alcaldes mayor. Well-paid treasury officials had also arrived to track silver production, monitor the town more closely, and report irregularities. In addition, the camp lost significance when silver output declined after 1759. A brief revival rekindled hopes for growth in the remote mountains, but they soon subsided. Probably as a result, the Castillo de Aysa clan fell on hard times, too. When the marquis died in 1778, his son was unable to pay taxes on inheriting the title, and the marquisate went extinct.[62]

Conclusion

Viceroy Güemes used his ample powers in the kingdom of New Galicia. He ordered an investigation of the untaxed silver streaming out of Bolaños and mandated an inspection of the treasury in Guadalajara to stem embezzlement. How much the financial officials overcharged miners for mercury also came under review. Yet, the Marquis of el Castillo de Aysa and President Basarte opposed Güemes. They defended the kingdom's autonomy while peddling influence and colluding with friends and treasury officials. To an extent, Güemes was able to break that cozy relationship.

To attain his goal, the viceroy relieved Guadalajara of most jurisdiction over Bolaños, carved out a new district, and appointed Gorospe Padilla as corregidor. The new corregidor belonged to a branch of the viceregal family and kicked off several energetic reforms. He built a municipal palace and convinced workers to descend from the mountain to settle in town. He also supported expanding an adit, charged the miners additional fees, and set up a militia. What is more, treasury officials beholden to Güemes arrived in the camp and tightened tax collection on the booming silver production as well as food and liquor consumption. Soon enough, locals grumbled about the new regime, and these were not just Basarte's cronies.

Güemes opened the next front by reviewing the malfeasance of treasury officials in Guadalajara. Basarte protected them to a degree and provided colorful excuses for not sending treasury surpluses to Mexico City. Yet Ensenada's client José Banfi y Villalobos revealed that, instead of any surplus, almost 300,000 silver pesos had gone missing. At that point, Güemes sent a commissioner to audit the treasury, and he determined that additional funds had disappeared. As a result, the treasurer fled to the Jesuit church begging for asylum. Barred from dragging him out, the commissioner confiscated the treasurer's property and called in money from debtors and bondsmen to cover losses. The viceroy removed the treasurer from his post and appointed a successor. Consequently, the financial schemes in the treasury of Guadalajara probably declined.

A separate review of the royal sale of mercury again showed discrepancies. Initially, the prosecutor of Guadalajara heard testimony that the treasury officials overcharged miners and agents for mercury. The incriminated officials included Banfi y Villalobos—to Güemes's great embarrassment. Then an attorney in Mexico City took over the investigation and largely confirmed the findings: the officials overcharged miners by more than 20 pesos per quintal of mercury. Agents who did not own mines and traded the heavy metal paid even higher kickbacks. While the episode's consequences are unclear, the ability of treasury officials to demand sizable supplements probably decreased over time. Banfi y Villalobos's fate after this episode remains in the dark, too. His interim appointment in Guadalajara ended, but he later became a treasury official elsewhere. Despite his failings, Güemes must have looked after him, as the viceroy did for the commissioners.

During these conflicts, President Basarte accused Güemes of authoritarianism for meddling in the affairs of the kingdom. Güemes meanwhile tired of the political haggling with the audiencia and its judicial underperformance. He sought to gain more control and called for the suppression of the entire audiencia. The Crown seriously considered the proposal.

Yet Ensenada fell from power in 1754, and the audiencia recovered its standing as an institution. The local backlash in Bolaños against Gorospe Padilla paved the way for his ouster. The next viceroy appointed a successor, and the district returned to Guadalajara. Güemes's reform was not fully undone, however. The corregidor gained a better salary and had more autonomy from the president than the deputies before him. Diligent treasury officials also continued oversight and reported irregularities to Mexico City. Moreover, there are indications that the infighting in the audiencia of Guadalajara eased up at that time. New judges arrived, and the Marquis of el Castillo de Aysa and his people increasingly lost their grip on power. His offspring fell on hard times as circumstances changed and the output in Bolaños waned.

Historians remind us that imperial centers often stabilized rule in its territories by sending intermediaries "from the homeland—a settler or a functionary"—and relied on their "own social connections to ensure effective collaboration."[63] This chapter shows these strategies at work in New Galicia. For instance, Castillo de Aysa relied on his son-in-law and their allies to withstand the viceroy's onslaught. Nevertheless, the marquis had originally come from Aragon (Spain) as a rather humble immigrant himself. He seized the opportunity when his uncle acceded to the bishopric of Guadalajara in 1714.[64] For his part, Güemes weakened Castillo de Aysa's influence by sending his own commissioners. They collaborated with miners in Bolaños who opposed the marquis's heavy hand. The viceroy awarded his loyal servants and punished wayward treasurers, and by doing so furthered his sway in New Galicia. The continual communications between New Spain and New Galicia forged deep bonds between the two kingdoms. They explain to an extent why New Galicia remained with Mexico after independence, whereas other viceroyalties broke apart along the boundaries of the major jurisdictions. This subject, however, would need further exploration.[65]

CHAPTER 7

Güemes's Endgame
Helping the King and Helping Oneself

Introduction

Juan Francisco Güemes, first Count of Revillagigedo since 1749, relinquished the viceroyalty in 1755. He left in style, parading his wealth through the streets of Mexico City. For the chronicler Castro Santa-Anna, the ostentation on that October 14 was too much. He sniped that "the baggage of the most excellent Lord Viceroy Count of Revillagigedo departed this morning, including more than 200 mules loaded with blankets and carpets, and certainly none of the other viceroys who have governed this kingdom have profited as much as this one."[1] The chronicler and other opponents of the viceroy harped about Güemes's self-serving conduct. Yet this was not unusual. Other important ministers of that time likewise looked after themselves and became rich in the Americas while carrying out royal orders faithfully. Güemes was also loyal to the Crown, as he ruffled feathers in New Spain by taking on powerful corporations and oligarchic entitlements.[2]

The chronicler nonetheless makes a fascinating point, because the fate of many viceroys upon yielding power is unknown. This chapter shows that Güemes and his wife, Antonia Padilla Pacheco, threw a lavish fiesta for their successors in the pueblo of Otumba and remained on a nearby hacienda for two additional months. Then they took the direct route toward Veracruz, avoiding the important cities such as Tlaxcala, which had just staged the receptions for the incoming viceroys. As Güemes left, the *juicio de residencia* (final judicial review) got underway to investigate any malfeasance during his term. Güemes's friends showered attention on the judge of the judicial review, which surely helped to reach a desirable conclusion. Nonetheless, one official sued Güemes for removing him from his position in the alcabala (sales tax) collection. The official won the lawsuit and the verdict stung, but the fallout was limited. The kings continued to advance Güemes to important positions in Spain, including the Council of War. The former viceroy also built a palace in Madrid, where he and his family hobnobbed with the aristocracy.

This chapter discusses these significant episodes of Güemes and the lives of several viceregal allies after he released the reins of colonial Mexico. We do not know much about the viceregal clients after their patrons departed for Spain. Güemes's death in 1766 deprived them of a powerful supporter in Madrid. That year, a new viceroy joined the investigative judge José de Gálvez (1765–1771) in Mexico City. Gálvez and the new viceroy started another round of reforms and expelled the Jesuit order from the viceroyalty. They also attacked several of Güemes's friends for opposing the expulsion. Among them was Ignacio Cevallos, Güemes's trusted adviser. Cevallos and others had originally supported Güemes's policies, and now they were ordered to Spain.[3]

The Departure of the Viceregal Family

In 1754, the Duke of Huéscar and others engineered a palace revolt against the first minister, the Marquis of la Ensenada, in Madrid. The duke convinced the king to exile Ensenada to Granada in Andalusia. Güemes received notice of Ensenada's political fall in January 1755, at the latest. He was greatly disillusioned. Writing to the governor of the Philippines, he attributed "all the handling of this noisy work to the Duke of Huéscar, who is on the cusp of power and appreciation with the kings, while the Marquis of la Ensenada, showing the greatest spiritual serenity, remains in Granada, strolling around and reveling without knowing what he has done."[4] Güemes helped circulate a poem that culminated in casting the position of royal favorite minister as highly desirable and yet volatile. At the beginning, the poem insisted on Ensenada's innocence:

If he had committed a crime the King would not be so merciful: the King knows well that he has not offended him,	Pues si crimen hubiera cometido no procediera el Rey tan apiadado: bien sabe el Rey que en nada le ha ofendido

because he has kept pay and honor.	Quando sueldo y honor le ha reservado
Reviewing the annals of the orb	regístrense del orbe los anales
reveals ministers who, although faithful,	y halláranse ministros que aunque fieles
for unknown celestial causes	por recónditas causas celestiales,
saw their laurels turn to stonecrops.	Vieron vueltos en yedras sus laureles
Instead of rewarding loyalty	que en dar el premio a procederes leales
the stars often show cruelty...	también los astros suelen ser crueles...
Ha! Coveted and fickle station	Ha! Valimiento infiel siempre anhelado
And Ha! Amiss for the sake of the nation.	Y Ha! Sin razon de la razon de estado.[5]

The tone of Güemes's letters to Madrid changed significantly after Ensenada's fall. The viceroy had penned Ensenada affectionate phrases such as "My wife affirms her loyalty and appreciation for Your Lordship, and I declare my unchanging obedience and friendship until my death."[6] Ensenada similarly vowed "immutable friendship" with Güemes and expressed to "Madame my allegiance."[7] When Ensenada used the word "friendship," he implied politely that the viceroy was his peer. While Ensenada was twenty-one years younger than Güemes, he was his patron nonetheless.

After Ensenada's fall, Güemes dropped the emphatic expressions when directing his letters to Julián Arriaga, the new secretary of the Indies. Güemes now concluded with conventional phrases such as "I kiss the hands of Your Lordship, your most dedicated and loyal servant."[8] Güemes also requested to be relieved from office. Arriaga granted his wish in 1755, naming the Marquis of las Amarillas as successor. Güemes had served nine years and four months in New Spain.[9]

The incoming viceroy and his wife embarked in Cádiz for New Spain on August 6, 1755. They landed in Veracruz on September 30 and began their slow ascent toward Mexico City. On October 5, a gentleman of Amarillas's entourage came to the palace to announce the arrival of his patron. As a reward for his services, Güemes gave the gentleman a rich gift, probably worth about 4,000 pesos, that more than covered the gentleman's travel expenses. The next day, Güemes's master of the horse and several ministers left Mexico City, hauling a grand coach with stained-glass windows to make Amarillas's voyage more comfortable. Fifty soldiers of the Santa Hermandad (rural police force) rode along, underlining the occasion's importance. They met the incoming viceroy near Xalapa (Veracruz), the first waystation accessible by coach from Mexico City. At that point, they fell in line with Amarillas's entourage.[10]

Preparations for Güemes's departure were underway at that time. Güemes paid 20,000 pesos to his legal representative to "help with the transportation to Spain" and with an eye on the upcoming judicial review. Güemes also deposited 40,000 pesos into the royal treasury for possible penalties during the judicial review.[11] The captain of the palace guard then visited various corporations in the colonial capital to announce the viceregal departure. The corporations bade farewell to the vicereine and the viceroy at court on October 9. Four days later, Güemes crossed the street to call on the archbishop. Both professed to be touched by their close friendship. The following day, the "vicereine Antonia Padilla, her five daughters, ladies, personal assistants . . . and some women and wives of ministers" departed, along with their extensive belongings. The artillery fired a salute as they rolled out of the palace.[12] Soon after, bells in the churches started ringing. The audiencia ministers, Güemes, and his sons rode off. They traveled to the basilica of Our Lady of Guadalupe, where they prayed and kissed the image of the virgin. At that point, the audiencia ministers returned to the capital, while Güemes and his sons rejoined his wife and daughters in San Cristóbal Ecatepec. They spent the night in the alcalde mayor's residence.[13]

Then they left to meet their successors. On October 16, 1755, Güemes and his family began lodging at the sprawling pulque-producing hacienda San Bartolomé de los Tepetates, also known as "of the viceroys." The estate is located about eight miles northeast of Otumba on the edge of the Valley of Mexico. One of Güemes's rich friends had shortly before acquired the hacienda, which boasted "beautiful rooms and comfort."[14] Meanwhile, the Marquis and the Marquise of las Amarillas emerged from Puebla on November 2 and entered Otumba on November 8. Güemes and Padilla Pacheco joined them that day in the pueblo, throwing a "sumptuous banquet of five courses" worth 8,000 pesos, which was a fifth of a viceregal annual salary.[15]

Such elaborate fiestas were not unusual. An early seventeenth-century viceroy had allegedly "spent almost his entire annual salary during the eight days that he joined" his successor in Otumba.[16] The vicereines, senior clergy, and other dignitaries celebrated with the viceroys. During the occasion, Güemes passed the baton, the symbol of viceregal authority, and his report on the state of colonial Mexico to Amarillas. The halberdier guard also switched sides to escort the incoming viceroy. After nightfall, Güemes and his wife withdrew and returned to the hacienda. The Amarillas family left Otumba the next day. They passed the basilica of Guadalupe on November 10 and took quarters in the palace in Mexico City the same day. Unlike his predecessor, however, Amarillas considerably delayed the official entry in the capital until February 9.[17]

Tragedy soon marked the travels of Güemes, Padilla Pacheco, and their children. They remained for almost two additional months at San Bartolomé de los Tepetates, where she drafted her will in anticipation of the voyage. On December 10, they set out east, spending most nights on haciendas along the way. After staying in Xalapa for almost three months, the family descended to Veracruz and embarked on the vessel *América* on April 9, 1756. They reached Havana in mid-May. The family sailed across the Atlantic Ocean and set foot in Cádiz on August 6, 1756. They used the layover and their following voyage to Madrid to meet with relatives and Ensenada, who was exiled in Granada. While these reunions brought moments of joy, Güemes and Padilla Pacheco bemoaned the passing of their daughter María Francisca in Cádiz that month.

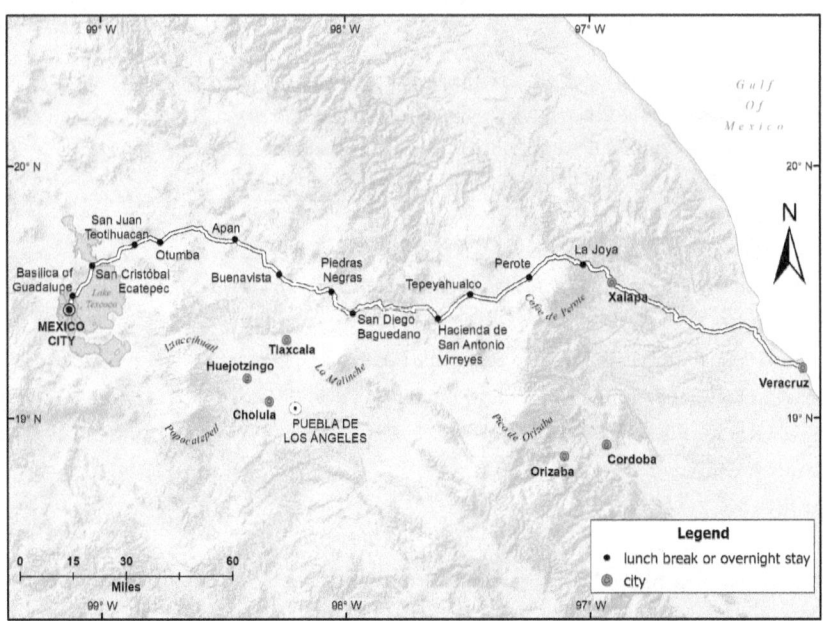

Map 4. Approximate viceregal itinerary from Mexico City to Veracruz. (Designed by Ana Gabriela Arreola Meneses.)

Shortly afterward, on October 11, the former vicereine died, just after returning to Madrid. She was forty-eight years old.[18]

In Spain, the widowed Güemes played an influential role, despite his close ties to the disgraced Ensenada. King Ferdinand appointed Güemes as captain general of Old Castile in 1756. Güemes's stock rose further after Ferdinand's death, when Charles III acceded to the throne in 1759. Charles named Güemes viceroy of Navarre but reversed himself and made him dean of the Council of War in Madrid. Among other achievements, Güemes had impressed the king with the smooth transfer of the Mexico City alcabala tax. The former viceroy became an important adviser, purportedly to the effect that Charles heeded "every proposal concerning America" made by Güemes.[19] The former viceroy, originally from the modest nobility, had gained twenty-two years of overseas experience and moved into the top echelon of government in Madrid.

TABLE 4. Approximate Viceregal Itinerary from Mexico City to Veracruz

ROUTE AND BREAKS	APPROXIMATE MILES
Departure from Mexico City on October 14, 1755, lunch at the Basilica of Guadalupe, arrival at San Cristóbal Ecatepec, overnight stay	15
Departure from San Cristóbal Ecatepec, lunch in San Juan Teotihuacan	21
Arrival at the hacienda San Bartolomé de los Tepetates near Otumba on October 16, departure on December 10	8
Lunch in Apan	21
Overnight stay in Buenavista (now José María Morelos Buenavista, Tlaxcala)	8
Lunch in Piedras Negras	23.5
Overnight stay at the hacienda San Diego Baguedano (Tlaxcala)	10.5
Lunch at the hacienda de San Antonio Virreyes (Jonguito, Puebla)	16
Overnight stay at the hacienda Tepeyahualco (Soto, Puebla)	13
Lunch and overnight stay in Perote	16
Lunch in La Joya	21
Arrival in Xalapa, departure in mid-March 1756	10.5
Arrival in Veracruz on March 23, departure for Spain on April 9	66
Total	about 250

The approximate itinerary draws on second Count of Revillagigedo, *Derrotero en coche para Xalapa y leguas de distancia de sus tornadas*, n.d., n.p. (1794), ACR 413, details may have changed over time; see also Gómez, *Diario curioso*, 104, 123; Castro Santa-Anna, *Diario de sucesos notables*, 5:194; and Güemes to Arriaga, Cádiz, August 6, 1756, no. 168, AGI, México 1506. On Tepeyahualco, see Gerhard, *A Guide to the Historical Geography*, 231.

The End-of-Term Judicial Review

Some colonials griped about Güemes's governance. The satire circulating in New Spain concluded that malfeasance reigned under Güemes, as there was

Much silver and much gold,	Mucha plata, y oro mucho,
and little justice in all,	poca ley en todo ello,
ordinances in droves,	ordenanzas a montones,
yet disorders untold.	Y desordenes sin cuento.[20]

In addition, a former alcalde mayor of Puebla attacked the inordinate wealth of Güemes's personal secretary in 1758. In his view, the secretary had married the daughter of a rich merchant and amassed a fortune of half a million pesos under suspicious circumstances. While Güemes probably favored the merchant on several occasions, the alcalde mayor also settled a score: Güemes had sharply criticized his lackadaisical administration in Puebla in 1752.[21]

Güemes remained faithful to the Crown in contrast with his early-century predecessor Viceroy Duke of Alburquerque (1702–1710). Alburquerque attempted to undermine a reform of the royal mercury distribution, a key metal in refining silver. He also obstructed the alcabala collection in Puebla and stalled the secularization of doctrinas (Native parishes) in the bishopric of Oaxaca. Worse, the duke cashed in on French—and perhaps enemy—ships that sold contraband merchandise in Veracruz. That clandestine business triggered a noisy imbroglio over a marriage between the offspring of two influential families. King Philip V and his ministers finally tired of the duke and relieved him of his duties in 1710, as the critical phase of the War of the Spanish Succession ended. In 1714–1715, the king forced Alburquerque to pay an unheard-of indemnity of roughly 700,000 pesos. This extraordinary sum was explicitly meant to make an example of him so that other viceroys and ministers took note.[22] In a similar move in 1705, the king confiscated one million pesos from the estate of a former Peruvian viceroy, although much cash had already slipped out of royal reach. Subsequent viceroys understood the point. They successfully strengthened royal authority while siphoning off money more subtly.[23]

Clearly, these practices did not coincide with any modern ideal of bureaucrats, although some aspects were moving in that direction. In the early eighteenth century, social connections still mattered greatly when choosing viceroys, and they often trumped professional selection criteria. Viceroys also worked with a vast network of clients and friends who vied for jobs and favors. Viceregal powers were often poorly defined and contested; there was no clear career pattern, and no fixed retirement system yet. Nevertheless, as opposed to many predecessors, Güemes's aptitude mattered when he was selected for the job. He had proven his loyalty and efficacy in military leadership and governance before. As viceroy, he supervised officials, ordered inspections with rigor, and carried out hard-fought reforms, even if he personally opposed them. He differed from predecessors like Alburquerque who saw their appointment mainly as an opportunity to ransack the state.[24]

As a result, the judicial review of his viceregency boded well for Güemes. The Crown appointed a civil judge from Guadalajara for that task. When the civil judge drew near to Mexico City, Ignacio Cevallos and other friends of Güemes welcomed him.[25] According to the chronicler, on December 18, 1756, the civil judge

> arrived in this capital, and because of their friendship, Cevallos left to meet him at [the basilica of] Guadalupe . . . and the Count of San Bartolomé de Xala and his son-in-law arranged a house for him next to the church of the Holy Spirit. . . . The first day, he ate with Cevallos, and San Bartolomé de Xala accompanied them. . . . On December 28, the judge of the judicial review joined . . . other robed magistrates for dinner, and they used the opportunity to pay their compliments and give presents.[26]

Nonetheless, some minor charges surfaced against Güemes in the judicial review. For example, Güemes appointed two officials to assist the warden of Acapulco. They vetted the merchandise on the galleons arriving from the Philippines. The warden could not pay their salaries out of pocket, and the viceroy assigned money from the treasury for the officials. That set an incentive to assess the galleon merchants according to law and curb shady dealings. Nonetheless, Güemes failed to obtain royal approval for withdrawing cash from the royal treasury. In addition, the warden was a viceregal client, and giving him funds to pay the officials smacked of favoritism. Yet the judge of the judicial review shifted the blame away from Güemes and sentenced the warden to reimburse the treasury with 1,209 pesos. The judge then absolved Güemes of all other charges.[27]

The Council of the Indies in Madrid largely agreed with the sentence. The council praised Güemes's success in increasing revenue, especially from the Native tribute and the alcabala administration in Mexico City and Veracruz. Uncovering embezzlement schemes in the treasury of Guadalajara also improved the outlook. As a result, the viceroy had sent a total of 12,697,677 pesos to Spain and 11,256,342 pesos to the Caribbean fortresses during his time at the helm. Concluding its assessment, the council lauded Güemes as the "perfect viceroy."[28]

Yet not all was bliss. A chief clerk of the alcabala administration demanded that Güemes pay his back salary. Güemes had dismissed the chief clerk in 1752 after receiving a damning assessment of his conduct. The chief clerk petitioned the Crown and obtained a royal cédula in the following year to reinstate him, but Güemes suspended the cédula because of his adversary's "lack of respect."[29] The case returned to the Council of the Indies, and Viceroy Amarillas restored the chief clerk to his post in 1757. In the subsequent year, the council rebuked Güemes for disobeying its orders. The council also mandated him to reimburse roughly 7,700 pesos of foregone salary and other income to the chief clerk. Güemes yielded. By this time, Ensenada had fallen from power and no longer shielded Güemes. This lawsuit was also one reason why Güemes and his family took several years to recover Güemes's sizable deposit in Mexico City.[30]

Nonetheless, Güemes had significant cash on hand at the end of his term. As we have seen, besides the deposit for his judicial review, he also gave cash to his legal representative, threw an expensive party in Otumba, and gifted Amarillas's gentleman. In addition, Güemes had 330,000 pesos in his coffers when arriving in Cádiz in 1756. If we add these amounts, he owned about 402,000 pesos just before leaving New Spain, and he may well have stashed away additional funds elsewhere. Meanwhile, Güemes had received an annual salary of 40,000 pesos during his viceregency, which amounts to a total of about 360,000 pesos for his nine years in office (July 1746–October 1755). This meant that he had 42,000 pesos more at his disposal than he had obtained in salary. Güemes could have saved some funds from his previous appointment as captain general of Havana. Yet all viceroys had considerable expenses maintaining family and retainers and traveling to and from New Spain. Güemes noted that he had spent about 20,000 silver pesos from his own pocket just to reach Santiago in Cuba. Therefore, Güemes must have drawn additional income from elsewhere, just like his colleagues. One way was charging for issuing paperwork. A client of Güemes paid a later viceroy 2,000 pesos in 1761 to expedite his appointment papers. This custom was probably pervasive, even during Güemes's time.[31]

When Güemes arrived in Cádiz, he petitioned Arriaga for a tax exemption on his cash, but without much luck. Güemes and his wife negotiated with the secretary of the Indies for almost a month while staying in the port, but Arriaga turned a deaf ear. The secretary argued that the king had taxed other viceroys arriving in Spain with money as well, and setting a precedent in this regard would harm the king's interests.[32]

Despite this setback, Güemes successfully grew his own business upon his return to Madrid. In June 1757, Chinese goods arrived for him in Cádiz, including at least twelve boxes of figurines, silk, and porcelain. Güemes's Flemish agents also imported and marketed sugar and other commodities from Cuba, where he had served as governor. In 1762 alone, Güemes earned 21,000 pesos by selling cochineal, the coveted crimson dye from the Oaxacan highlands. His contacts in the Americas paid off handsomely.[33] A genealogist wrote later that "Güemes was a merchant and speculator to the point that there was no business in which he did not participate." That is exaggerated, but Güemes was shrewd nonetheless. He managed to buy and expand a representative mansion on Mostenses Square in Madrid near the royal palace. He also furnished his daughters with dazzling dowries. Antonia brought 110,000 ducats (151,250 silver pesos) and Juana María 100,000 ducats (137,868 pesos) into their marriages. Güemes provided the means for two other daughters to wed aristocrats, too, and only Francisca Javiera remained unmarried. Güemes could not have paid these substantive sums without additional sources of income.[34]

Unfortunately, we know little else about Güemes's daughters except for the ill-fated marriage of Antonia Güemes Pacheco with the second Count of Bobadilla.[35] They initially seemed a promising match. Güemes had gained a title of nobility, wealth, and influence, whereas the Count of Bobadilla descended from an older lineage. He also hailed from Antequera in Andalusia, the hometown of Antonia's mother. Bobadilla's father served Philip V in the War of the Spanish Succession, when two uncles fell. Philip V created the title as a reward. The pedigree impressed Güemes. His daughter apparently resisted initially but then "submitted to the will of her father" and married Bobadilla on June 26, 1758.[36]

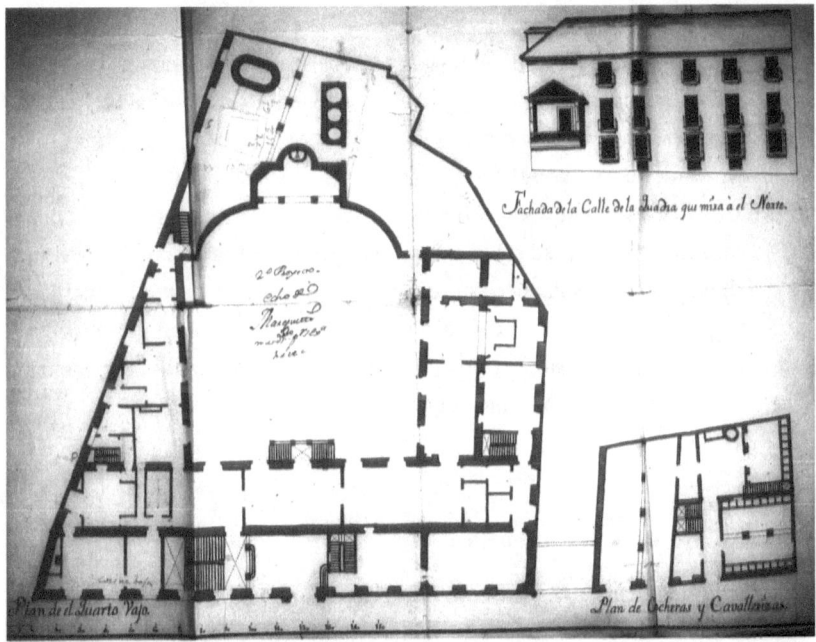

Figure 3. Unknown artist, façade, lower floor, and horse stable of Güemes's palace on Mostenses Square, Madrid. (Source: ACR 464; courtesy of Álvaro Armada and Library of the University of Florida, Gainesville, Department of Special and Area Collections.)

Unbeknown to Güemes, however, Bobadilla had acquired a reputation as a "lad of libertine life." After twenty-two months of married life in Madrid, there were no signs of offspring, and Bobadilla returned to Andalusia to administer his estates, or so he claimed. He also resumed a "certain dalliance with Juana Bilerche, of lowly station." Bobadilla offered his wife 3,000 ducats to stay in Madrid, but she and Güemes insisted on his return. Under these circumstances, the bishop of Málaga exiled Bobadilla from Antequera and ordered him to live in monastic reclusion. No priory accepted him, however, perhaps because of his family's influence. Instead, he continued to go after his business in Antequera.[37]

Bobadilla also sought the help of the archbishop of Toledo to overturn the bishop's mandate, while Güemes Pacheco joined a convent out of "hard necessity." She took her case to the Council of Castile, which "sentenced the Count to supporting her with 3,000 ducats a year . . . in consideration of the 110,000 ducats of dowry that had been given to him." Bobadilla largely ignored the ruling, however. In 1771, Bobadilla took the case to the ecclesiastical court of Madrid demanding a restoration of matrimony, or at least his financial advantages. Güemes Pacheco left the convent in November 1766 to see her dying father in Madrid. She sought a divorce in the ecclesiastical court but was rebuffed. Afterward, the king ordered that the matter be arranged with the pope's consent. The ill-fated story ends here, but since the ambassador to Rome was a friend of Güemes Pacheco's brother Juan Vicente, she probably gained a more favorable settlement. The whole affair started when Güemes obliged his daughter to honor ostensible family interests, although Bobadilla preferred an aristocratic lifestyle without marital fidelity.[38]

The Anti-Governmental Party

Güemes forged lasting ties with colonial Mexicans while in office, although some of them clashed with a later viceroy. Ignacio Cevallos, for example, advised Güemes in the conflict over the alcabala tax in 1753–1754. He became his trusted adviser, and their friendship lasted for decades. Yet Viceroy Marquis of Croix (1766–1771) later accused Cevallos of opposing the expulsion of Jesuits from the kingdom. He removed Cevallos from New Spain in 1768, two years after Güemes's passing. Croix also suspected seven other beneficiaries or friends of Güemes and Cevallos of forming an "anti-governmental party" to obstruct the expulsion. However, this group was originally pro-governmental, because of the suspects' close ties with the former viceroy.[39]

Güemes himself had applauded the arrival of a new first minister, the Marquis of Esquilache, in 1763. Güemes became dean of the Council of War, as Esquilache kicked off another series of trenchant reforms angering powerful corporations and affecting the common people in Spain. For instance, Esquilache prohibited the large hats and long cloaks that men customarily wore in Castile. He aimed at modernizing the dress code and making it harder to conceal unlawful arms. More importantly, the government removed price limits on the grain trade to stimulate supply, but a drought sent prices spiking. From March 21 to 26, 1766, popular and elite groups joined forces and rebelled. The leaders of the Hat and Cloak Revolt demanded a reduction in grain prices, the resignation of Esquilache, and the repeal of the dress code. Güemes participated in the ad hoc council responding to the revolt. While some councilors proposed taking a hard line against the rebels, Güemes and others advocated for compromise. As a result, Charles publicly accepted most demands and pardoned rebellious acts. Fearing for his life, the king escaped from Madrid on the night of March 24. Shortly afterward, Güemes retired from the Council of War. He passed away in Madrid on November 27, 1766.[40]

Subsequently, Charles and his advisers laid the blame for the revolt at the door of the Jesuits and ousted them from the empire on February 27, 1767. Gálvez and Croix carried out the order in New Spain in June, provoking popular uprisings in the Bajío region (northwest of Mexico City). Angry crowds protected the Jesuits, destroyed the despised alcabala collection, and looted stores and armories. The indigenous governor of Pátzcuaro (Michoacán) also demanded obedience from more than one hundred pueblos—reminiscent of the pre-Hispanic kingdom of that region. He called on them to resist the expulsion. Gálvez and the army responded by hanging eighty-five people, including the indigenous governor, severely whipping seventy-three, and sending nearly eight hundred people to jail or exile.[41]

Viceroy Croix also accused sixteen respected residents in Mexico City of subverting the government. He suggested deporting both the criminal and the civil prosecutor of the audiencia for publishing a pamphlet against the order's destruction. The viceroy also jailed three alleged conspirators and shipped them to Spain, with unpleasant layovers in the muggy dungeons of Veracruz and Havana. Yet Croix feared a backlash and opted to deal gently with the remaining suspects, including Cevallos, by then archdeacon of the cathedral. The king called them to Spain under the pretense of promoting them to better positions.[42]

Five of the sixteen suspects had significantly benefited from Güemes's patronage, and three were Cevallos's kin or friends. They tended to be relatively recent arrivals with connections to the Jesuits. Besides Cevallos, for example, Güemes had appointed one suspect as superintendent of the mint in Mexico City and recommended him for a position on the Council of the Indies. Güemes had also named another suspect as official of the viceregal secretariat.[43] At least five suspects had also spent considerable time outside of the kingdom of New Spain in Guatemala or Yucatán. They relied on the viceroy for their social advance.[44] Some of Güemes's and Cevallos's former collaborators had attended Jesuit schools, received the order's support, or declared their pro-Jesuit view in another way. Cevallos himself graduated from Jesuit schools in Guatemala, while one criminal judge had obtained his position in 1751 with the help of the former royal confessor. At that time, the Jesuit provincial of New Spain favored the appointment, because he considered the criminal judge's father a great benefactor of the order. Güemes agreed.[45]

The government in Madrid lacked sufficient evidence to convict most deportees, who profusely declared their fealty. The Crown promoted several of them to coveted positions in the peninsula. Cevallos, for example, became a canon at the cathedral of Seville, where he expired as dean of the chapter in 1784. In addition, the civil prosecutor of the audiencia joined the chancellery of Granada. He was later promoted to the Council of Castile, not coincidentally a few days shy of Gálvez's death.[46]

Conclusion

This chapter has examined important vignettes of Güemes's life after he resigned from the viceregency. He, Padilla Pacheco, and their seven children said goodbye to Mexico City in 1755. They threw a lavish fiesta for their successors in Otumba and stayed two additional months on a nearby hacienda. Then the family traveled toward the coast. They bypassed the cities of Tlaxcala and Puebla, which had just received their successors in great spectacles. The family embarked in Veracruz and reached Spain. At that time, the judicial review began investigating Güemes's conduct in office. He had amassed a substantial amount of cash during his time in office. Nonetheless, the judge of the review dismissed the charges against the former viceroy. Only one official continued his quest and sued in Madrid. The Council of the Indies ordered Güemes to pay him 7,700 pesos in back salary. Güemes suffered a stinging rebuke, because his patron Ensenada had fallen from power in 1754 and could no longer protect him. Notwithstanding this reverse, Güemes advanced to important positions in Madrid and crowned his career by joining the Council of War in 1763. He gave substantial dowries for most daughters to wed aristocrats, although Güemes nudged Antonia Güemes Pacheco into an unhappy marriage.

Politics shifted in Madrid at that time. In 1763, King Charles III appointed Esquilache as his first minister and unleashed José de Gálvez's judicial investigation of New Spain in 1765. Güemes passed away the following year. Viceroy Croix and Gálvez subsequently accused sixteen residents in Mexico City of opposing the Jesuit expulsion and forming an "anti-governmental party." Five of them had been beneficiaries of Güemes's patronage, including the superintendent of the Mint, while three were closely tied to Cevallos. They leaned toward the Jesuits, which mirrored to an extent the political coalition of Ensenada in Madrid, where the Society of Jesus played an outsize role. In 1768, Croix ordered six suspects to Spain. Scholars have ignored that they originally formed part of a pro-governmental party working with the former viceroy and Cevallos. If Güemes had been alive, their fate would probably have looked different.

CONCLUSION

Bourbon Brawn and Brain

GÜEMES, A HARD-NOSED MILITARY officer from northern Spain, set out to shape colonial Mexico. He undercut the entitlements of powerful corporations and intensified royal rule. Friends and clients backed his efforts. Above all, Güemes pruned the power of the religious orders, such as the Franciscans and the Dominicans. He also seized the profitable alcabala tax from the consulado (merchant guild) and diverted a rising revenue flow into the royal treasury. In addition, the viceroy sent inspectors to rein in embezzlements in the kingdom of New Galicia and seized the burgeoning silver mines of Bolaños from the audiencia (high court) of Guadalajara. He even threatened to shut down the audiencia altogether. Here was Bourbon muscle on display, and well before the reforms of Charles III (1759–1788).

First Minister Ensenada and Güemes significantly reduced the number of doctrinas, which were the parishes of the regular orders serving Natives. In 1749, Ensenada mandated turning them over to the diocesan clergy under the supervision of the archbishop of Mexico. In 1753, he went a step further. The first minister convinced the king to issue a sweeping cédula that secularized the whole of Spanish America. Güemes faithfully carried out the instructions. He usually denied an order's request to approve a regular clergyman for a vacant doctrina and instead asked the bishop to install a diocesan priest. The new priest then appeared with the alcalde mayor and, at least sometimes, armed guards to evict the friars from the doctrina. Many in the orders and the regional elites resisted bitterly, and the bishop of Michoacán delayed the process in his diocese. Dozens of Natives in San Bartolomé Capulhuac also rallied against the expulsion of the Augustinians. Yet the Natives of the neighboring pueblo, Santiago Tianguistenco, sallied forth. They backed the alcalde mayor, his deputy, and the seculars, and evicted the order in a noisy ruckus. In most other places, Natives accepted the arrival of the secular priests, which helped dispel concerns about rural unrest. From 1749 to 1755, the religious orders lost 109 doctrinas to the diocesan church, many more than historians have assumed. Güemes and Ensenada also delayed or terminated new foundations of regular priories in the cities. Even the austere Discalced Carmelites had to wait until Ensenada's departure from Madrid to complete their projects. Finally, the secular church succumbed to more state control, too. Güemes tightened the collection of vacated cathedral salaries and traced the royal share of the tithe more closely, despite considerable opposition.

In addition, Ensenada mandated the end of the consulado's administration of the alcabala tax of Mexico City. Güemes carried out the plan by forging a coalition with several immigrants to Mexico City. The Spanish fleet merchants also applauded the move after bickering for years with the consulado over tax charges. Most others in Mexico City accepted the Crown's right to levy the tax, since they had not fared better during the previous administration. Meanwhile, the consulado, the municipal council of Mexico City, and some friars complained acrimoniously. They pressured courtiers in Mexico City and Madrid to reverse the reform. Güemes even anticipated a revolt at the tax gates, but his fears were unfounded, and the transition went ahead without violence. After the takeover, royal revenue almost doubled in 1754. When the Crown lowered the alcabala rate from 8 to 6 percent in June 1756, proceeds tumbled by 39 percent. Nonetheless, income rebounded in 1759, probably owing to a more consistent collection and economic growth.

The viceroy presided over more competitive alcabala auctions in Veracruz, too. Rivaling groups of merchants bid up the price until Juan Bautista Belaunzarán—probably a straw man of the Crown—made an ambitious offer and carried the day. He tightened the collection and gathered more cash. Yet he could not meet his ambitious goals, as merchants probed loopholes of the stringent tax administration. While Belaunzarán's plan failed, royal officials registered higher revenue and continued to do so after they recovered the tax farm from him.

Moreover, Güemes used his ample powers in the northwestern kingdom of New Galicia. His inspectors uncovered embezzlements of nearly 300,000 silver pesos in the treasury of Guadalajara. Both President Basarte and the audiencia of that city had tolerated the malfeasance, and they even actively hampered the investigations. The viceroy then dismissed one accountant and replaced him with an interim appointee. Güemes also harnessed local discontent to wrest the mining camp Bolaños from New Galicia and install treasury officials and a loyal corregidor (district judge)—a distant relative of his wife. As the conflict with the audiencia escalated, Güemes even suggested abolishing the institution. He found a ready ear in Madrid.

Ensenada appreciated Güemes's loyalty and often heeded the viceroy's advice. For example, Güemes opposed Ensenada's idea of establishing a royal monopoly on tobacco and the coveted dyestuff cochineal in New Spain. Ensenada dropped both proposals and installed the tobacco monopoly in Peru only. The first minister also considerably raised Güemes's annual salary to 40,000 pesos. That sent a signal of approval and served as an incentive to govern well at a time when viceroys were losing clandestine opportunities to enrich themselves. Güemes knew that he had better prospects for additional appointments in Spain if he conducted himself according to expectations.

Güemes exemplified a shift away from the high-born viceroys of the seventeenth and early eighteenth centuries. He looked back to a successful military career and usually carried out royal orders with aplomb. In comparison, one of his precursors, the Duke of Alburquerque (1702–1710), actively sabotaged Crown policies. The duke undermined the royal distribution of mercury to refine silver from the mines, hampered a more efficient alcabala tax collection in Puebla, and stalled secularizations in Oaxaca. What is more, he took significant bribes for tolerating contraband commerce with Spanish and French ships and even ran his own illegal trade on the side. When he returned to Spain, the Crown sentenced Alburquerque to an unprecedented indemnity of roughly 700,000 silver pesos, mostly for his transgressions in contraband trade. In contrast, Güemes's viceregency was a time of probity and aggressive reforms.

Beginning his work as viceroy, Güemes entered six cities of New Spain in grand rituals that hewed closely to those of his predecessors. He followed a path of meaning that reminisced the Spanish Conquista and the medieval homages to the kings, which in turn drew on the triumphal marches of the Roman legions and Jesus's arrival in Jerusalem on Palm Sunday. After leaving Veracruz, Güemes rode into Tlaxcala, Puebla, two other cities, and Mexico

City like a victorious captain on horseback. The rituals stood out from the ordinary and transformed an important officer into the king's representative overseas. A whopping crowd flocked to cheer the incoming viceroy and approve the accession. While the king had appointed the viceroy before his arrival in New Spain, the public acclamations sealed the viceroy's pact with his vassals and buttressed legitimacy. That mattered, because the public could well withhold attendance and cheers.

Yet harbingers of change were in the air. While dozens of clients accompanied early eighteenth-century viceroys on their voyage, only twenty retainers came with the Marquis of Casafuerte in 1722. In 1746, an even smaller retinue appeared. Güemes, his wife Antonia Padilla Pacheco, eight children, and perhaps a handful of Spanish and Cuban clients departed Cuba for Veracruz, a striking difference from the early-century entourages. Güemes was also among the first to take the helm of a viceregency after serving as governor elsewhere in the Americas. Nevertheless, Güemes's successor, Amarillas, brought a more sizable retinue in contrast, because his aristocratic wife, Luisa María del Rosario Ahumada, was entitled to her own coterie. The next viceroy again came with a few companions in 1760. He skipped the festive receptions in the cities altogether and rode directly from Veracruz to the viceregal palace. Modesty mostly reigned afterward. During the eighteenth century, then, viceregal entries declined in ostentation, although with some fluctuations.

What is more, despite the scholarly focus on the great rituals, much conduct at the viceregal court did not rise to that level. Many gestures were merely ritualized, that is, standardized, repetitive, and meaningful, such as greeting people in the street. Most viceregal audiences were also largely ritualized, as visitors came to exchange formulaic pleasantries. Nonetheless, the Marquise of las Amarillas broke the pattern in one instance in 1755. She graced the Inquisition with special attention by conversing about her travails in reaching Mexico City. Viceroy Fuenclara also took a few steps toward his visitors to indicate favor on a rare occasion. In addition, the audiences changed slightly in other respects. For example, the Inquisition brought its insignia of power when meeting with a new dignitary for the first time but dispensed with the tokens in the following meetings. Other behavior in the palace was informal, too. Viceroys Fuenclara and Güemes both played cards into the late night and dined with friends and clients, for instance. Güemes and his family also relaxed in the casual atmosphere of a friend's hacienda, where he and his sons went hunting. One of his predecessors indulged himself in San Ángel, south of Mexico City. What is more, Güemes was tardy at least twice when the Inquisition ministers came calling. Despite this demeanor, Güemes did not tolerate truancy in others. He detained members of the municipal council and other corporations on several occasions. These members had shirked the frequent and onerous religious processions. While these individuals absconded or tarried, their corporations continued to display great sensitivity for their public standing in society.

Viceregal trappings of royalty notwithstanding, colonial Mexicans well recognized the difference between the viceroy as the representative of the royal persona and the king himself. The *Law of the Indies*, published in 1680, commanded the viceroy to seek approval from Madrid for important changes. Viceroys were not usually of royal blood, and they rarely if ever received ambassadors of other sovereigns. They could not ennoble commoners or appoint and remove audiencia judges. The audiencia instead regularly reviewed and rejected mandates of viceroys in the eighteenth century, sometimes to the latter's great chagrin. In addition, the necessity of lavishly representing the king declined, as the Crown fostered a sense of moderation, oversight, and imperial cohesion. Since the late seventeenth century at the latest, viceroys rejected the portable canopy that covered them, because it had evolved into a symbol of royal authority. The power of viceregal patronage also starkly declined in that period. During the eighteenth century, the appointment patterns of viceroys changed, as career officers replaced the aristocratic courtiers of the past. These officers distinguished themselves by bravery, diligence, and political ties with leading ministers in Madrid rather than by high birth. Güemes fit this mold. He came from humble nobility and rose to the top with the support of Ensenada and others.

After stepping down from his office in mid-October 1755, Güemes, Pacheco Padilla, and their seven children (one had died) left Mexico City. A long train of mules, carts, and coaches loaded with riches rumbled out of the palace, trotting toward the hacienda "of the viceroys" near Otumba. Güemes and Pacheco Padilla threw a prodigal party in the pueblo for their successors, the Marquis and Marquise of las Amarillas. After the fiesta, the Güemes family remained at the hacienda until December. Later they traveled directly to Xalapa, skirting the cities that had just received their successors. The family descended to

Veracruz in March 1756 and arrived in Cádiz, Spain, on August 6. At roughly the same time, the judicial review of his term in Mexico City cleared Güemes from wrongdoing, although one official sued him in Madrid for removal from his position in the alcabala administration. The Council of the Indies agreed and ordered Güemes to reimburse the official's back salary of about 7,700 pesos. That was a stinging rejoinder for the former viceroy.

Güemes also accepted gifts and perks that would raise eyebrows for government officials nowadays. The viceroy had about 402,000 pesos in his possession shortly before leaving colonial Mexico, which was more than the combined salary that he drew during his time in viceregal office. How is it possible that he owned so much cash, when he had maintained family, retainers, and others at court? Güemes must have had significant additional income besides his salary to support his lifestyle. The viceroy probably demanded money for issuing papers to royal appointees and took gifts expressing appreciation. This was common practice at the time, and there are no complaints against him in this regard. In addition, Güemes was a successful entrepreneur. After returning to Spain, he relied on his contacts in the Americas to import cochineal and other luxury goods. Maybe he even traded during his viceregal term, although we do not know this. That additional revenue furnished his daughters with considerable dowries and built a representative palace in Madrid.

In Spain, his patron Ensenada began losing political control when his collaborator and rival, the secretary of state José Carvajal, died on April 8, 1754. The king and the queen listened to the murmurings of the opposition about Ensenada's subterfuges, and they dismissed him from office on July 20, 1754. A period of political thew ended. The successor, Ricardo Wall, charted a more cautious and conservative course, while keeping distance from France. He moved the empire closer to Habsburg Austria, Portugal, and Great Britain to reduce tensions in Italy and the Americas. Wall was nobody's stooge, however, and continued ordering covert operations against British settlers in Central America. Wall and Julián Arriaga, the new secretary of the Indies, also safeguarded the privileges of corporations to enhance stability and social harmony within the empire. Arriaga and the Marquis of las Amarillas dispelled some acrimony by easing up on the religious orders in New Spain. They allowed the friars to retain some important priories and their churches, even when secular priests began ministering to the faithful in that doctrina. For a while at least, the Crown expected Natives to build new churches in these districts. Amarillas also suggested ordaining more priests with Native language skills and generally dialed back the acculturation of Natives.

Other initiatives pointed in a similar direction. The audiencia of Guadalajara survived Güemes's onslaught and recovered jurisdiction over Bolaños. Despite the setback, Güemes had attained meaningful change, because the treasury officials and the corregidor of Bolaños retained autonomy from the president and the audiencia. Viceroy Amarillas also lowered the alcabala tax rate in Mexico City from 8 to 6 percent and ended taxing sales within the city. This change benefited most residents of the city. Nevertheless, Arriaga also gave a nod to the consulados of Mexico City and Cádiz by reinstating the stodgy fleet shuttling between Andalusia and Veracruz every two or three years. Arriaga suppressed the registered ships, causing higher prices for residents of colonial Mexico. The consulado of Mexico City celebrated the change, although it never recovered the profitable alcabala administration, showing the limits of the colonial consensus over finances.

After Ferdinand's passing, Charles III acceded to the throne in 1759 and ushered in a new cycle of reforms. The king appointed Güemes as dean of the Council of War, while José de Gálvez launched a judicial investigation of New Spain in 1765. Gálvez and a new viceroy exacted more revenue and imposed militia service. They also expelled the Jesuits in 1767. Gálvez violently put down the ensuing protests, and the viceroy accused sixteen ministers in Mexico City of forming an "anti-governmental party." They included Ignacio Cevallos, Güemes's most trusted financial adviser, and seven other beneficiaries of Güemes or relatives and friends of Cevallos. The viceroy ordered six of them to Spain. Scholars have overlooked that these residents originally formed a pro-governmental group that had supported Güemes's reforms. Other viceroys also shunned the clients of their precursors for promotions, but deporting them for political reasons was a different matter.

Scholars have traditionally argued that Gálvez's stint in New Spain and his term as secretary of the Indies (1776–1787) triggered the Bourbon Reforms by assaulting Creole autonomy in the Americas.[1] Since then, historians have departed from this view by opening the lens backward in time. The Marquis of la Ensenada has emerged as an important actor who reduced entitlements, raised revenue, and rebuilt the navy.[2] Allan Kuethe and Kenneth Andrien add that even before, the government broke the power of the consulado of Cádiz, monopolized tobacco sales in Cuba, and carved out a new viceroyalty in South America. The two scholars also highlight the subsequent failures of Gálvez, whose tax policies triggered the riots in New Spain in 1767 and the great Native revolts in the Andes (1780–1782).[3]

That ongoing discussion has cast light on the manifold aims and results of various reform episodes of the eighteenth and early nineteenth centuries. Because of this great diversity, it is now hard to say what the term "Bourbon Reforms" should mean, and when they began or ended.[4] In particular, the quest for a precise date when a Spanish prince kissed the empire awake is a lost cause. In my view, the empire never slept, and energetic queens of the late seventeenth century, such as Mariana of Austria (1634–1696), actively advanced controversial policies. She employed capable royal favorite ministers for her purposes. These favorite ministers slowly evolved into the more formalized role of first ministers over time. They and their rulers forged political coalitions according to convictions and political expediency. The cycles of reform straddled the dynastic divide of 1700, and Ensenada and Güemes implemented yet another cycle of substantive change.[5]

The viceroys of Spanish America have intrigued generations of scholars. Many of them originally studied governance by reviewing the execution of royal mandates by one or several viceroys.[6] More recently, historians have added nuance by positing that lavish rituals expressed local and royal aims, and that vicereines created the court in Mexico City.[7] Academics also underline the geographical limitations on early viceroys, who later gained substantial leeway in carrying out policies. In addition, patronage over retainers declined from the late seventeenth century onward, as career officers largely replaced aristocrats as viceroys. These important scholarly advances have helped show that Güemes served the Crown more loyally and with less bombast than his predecessors.[8]

The study of institutions such as the viceroy has also come a long way. Scholars no longer merely review petrified structures that closely mirrored the royal law. Instead, they now understand institutions as forms of stabilizing social relationships beyond a particular moment. Institutions are in flux, and actors continuously re-create them. The viceroys, for instance, regularly retired after some years of service. They drew down their assistants, and much of their personal imprint on the court dissolved. Viceroys also creatively interpreted the law or tabled orders from Madrid. They found subterfuges, designed their own solutions, and helped themselves to cash and gifts. Viceroys sometimes ignored and more often communicated with their social environment. In most cases, they relied on collaborators in Madrid, at the viceregal court or other authorities in New Spain, and among the people "on the street."[9] These people had their own agenda when they assisted the viceroy, and they shaped colonial governance by following that agenda. This perspective illustrates the fragmented and negotiated character of the early modern state. Any reform needed local support to an extent, and state development resulted from both bottom-up and top-down processes, often with unintended consequences.[10]

In addition, viceregal power in the first half of the eighteenth century did not decline across the board, although this study only permits tentative conclusions. Clearly, the viceregal entry in the six cities yielded to a staging of royal power, the court in Mexico City shrank in size and importance, and viceregal patronage ebbed to a low. The audiencia also challenged the ample jurisdiction of viceroys, and grim military officers replaced high-born nobles. Yet whereas grandeur receded, viceroys also oversaw burgeoning bureaucracies with more employees. Güemes took control of the alcabala collection in Mexico City in 1753–1754, for example, which included supervising eighty-seven royal officials. Güemes also expanded his control over the remaining financial administration in 1747 and 1751, although he remained subject to judicial review of the audiencia. These two events buttress the view that the viceroys increasingly became senior administrators rather than munificent aristocrats.[11]

On a final note, this book shows that the Spanish empire did not simply cascade in importance from the center in Madrid toward its overseas possessions. Instead, the empire consisted of important core kingdoms such as New Spain with its own viceregal court that wielded jurisdiction over other territories such as New Galicia. Both New Spain and New Galicia shared sovereignty with the Crown by upholding their traditions, autonomies, and cultural diversity. Güemes and other viceroys intensified—and not necessarily centralized—royal rule in these territories. Sometimes change came in leaps and bounds and sometimes as an ongoing process over a stretch of time. Güemes carried out important reforms with considerable speed, at a time when the viceroyalty remained firmly anchored in the polycentric Spanish empire.[12]

Measures and Weights

ducado de plata (silver ducat) = 1.375 silver pesos
marco (mark) = 8.5 silver pesos
peso = 8 reales de plata or tomines
real = 12 granos or 34 maravedís

arroba = 25 pounds
fardo = about 150 pounds
quintal = 100 pounds

legua = one league. The Castilian league measured 2.6 miles / 4,223 meters, although leagues varied regionally.
vara = one yard
pie = one foot, one-third of a vara

Dramatis Personae

Amarillas, Marquis of las, Agustín Ahumada y Villalón. Viceroy Amarillas succeeded Güemes in 1755 and died of a stroke in Cuernavaca in 1760.

Amarillas, second Marquise of las, Luisa María del Rosario Ahumada y Vera. She was the daughter of Francisco Pablo Ahumada y Mendoza and Catalina Vera y Leyva. Doña Luisa inherited the title from her father and married her cousin and future viceroy, who became marquis by virtue of the marriage. She also wrote a travel diary. Her young son Agustín died on March 1, 1756, in Mexico City, and her husband passed away in 1760. She then returned to Spain, probably accompanied by her ladies-in-waiting, remarried, and died on December 10, 1791.[1]

Arriaga, Julián. Arriaga served as governor of Venezuela and became intendant of the navy and president of the House of Trade in 1751. He weathered Ensenada's downfall in 1754 and succeeded him as secretary of the Indies. Arriaga held the office for twenty-two years, building a reputation as a moderately conservative administrator with ties to the consulados of Cádiz and Mexico City.

Banfi y Parrilla, José. The *oficial mayor* (chief clerk) of the secretary of the Indies was on good terms with Güemes. He fell into disgrace when his patron Ensenada was arrested in 1754. Nonetheless, Banfi y Parrilla returned to the court in 1760 and became councilor of the Indies in 1762, passing away on August 20, 1776.

Banfi y Villalobos, Juan. The nephew of chief clerk José Banfi y Parrilla, Banfi y Villalobos served as interim accountant of the Guadalajara treasury.

Barroeta y Barrenechea, Juan Crisóstomo (1708–before 1765). Barroeta was born in La Rioja, Spain, and considered himself *montañés* like Güemes. His parents were Benito Joaquín de Barroeta and María Ángel de Barrenechea. He migrated to New Spain to do business and married María Ignacia Rodríguez de Vargas y Monterde y Antillón. In 1728, Barroeta bought the appointment for the *alcaldía mayor* of Miahuatlan, which he served until 1733. On June 2, 1740, he purchased an appointment as regent of the Tribunal of Accounts with an annual salary of 5,000 pesos. Güemes usually opposed such sales of appointments. In 1748, the viceroy underlined Barroeta's poor health and lack of experience. Their relationship improved considerably, however, perhaps helped by the ordination of Barroeta's brother Pedro Antonio de Barroeta y Ángel as archbishop of Lima (1751–1757). In 1752, Güemes praised the regent as impartial and diligent and recommended him as one of the two Mexican non-lawyers to the Council of the Indies. Barroeta advised Güemes on appointing royal officials and assisted in the fight over the Mexico City alcabala. Güemes also named Barroeta's subordinate, the *contador ordenador* (accountant) Juan José Ortiz, as *pesquisidor* (inspector) of the Guadalajara treasury. Ortiz restored 200,000 pesos to that treasury. After Güemes's departure, the regent pleaded with his patron to support his promotion in 1761. Barroeta remained in contact with Güemes's clients in New Spain, being "happy that [Tomás] Vélez [Cachupín] attained the government of New Mexico."[2] Viceroy Marquis of Croix recommended Barroeta posthumously in 1768.[3]

Basarte, José. The son-in-law of the Marquis of el Castillo de Aysa served as president of the audiencia of Guadalajara and governor and captain general of New Galicia from 1750 to 1758.

Belaunzarán, Juan Bautista (1702–June 14, 1762). The merchant purchased the appointment as governor of New Vizcaya from 1733 to 1738 and supplied the thriving mining city of San Felipe Real in Chihuahua with goods. In 1747, civil judge Domingo Trespalacios and the viceroy dismissed several accusations against Belaunzarán and merely assigned a penalty of 500 pesos for owning a store while serving as governor. Later, Güemes objected to Belaunzarán's administration of the Veracruz alcabala, although Belaunzarán probably acted as Ensenada's straw man. Belaunzarán became an ally of Güemes over time. In

1760, Belaunzarán asked Güemes, by then dean of the Council of War in Madrid, for help with a 5,000 peso loan that the Crown had not repaid. Güemes assured Belaunzarán of the "particular affection" that he "always had for your lordship."[4] Doña Ignacia Margarita Rodríguez de Vargas y Monterde y Antillón, Belaunzarán's wife, reported her husband's passing to Güemes on June 14, 1762, "not doubting that your Excellency will keep him in your prayers because of the friendship that you both professed."[5] Their son with the same name continued corresponding with Güemes.[6]

Campillo y Cossío, José. He served as first minister of the monarchy (1741–1743) before Ensenada. One member of his team authored the influential pamphlet *New System*.

Carvajal y Lancáster, José de. The grandee from Cáceres became a colleague and rival of Ensenada. Carvajal joined the Council of the Indies in 1738 and the *cámara* of the Indies (patronage committee) in 1740. He served as interim governor of the council from 1742 to 1744 and as governor from 1748. After 1746, he heard the affairs of all councils and served as secretary of state, that is, foreign affairs. Carvajal passed away on April 8, 1754.

Castillo de Aysa, Marquis of el; Francisco de Aysa Gastón. Born in 1696 in Sesa, Aragon, he joined his uncle and future bishop of Guadalajara, Manuel de Mimbela, in New Galicia in 1713 and obtained a title of nobility in 1727. He became a miner and money lender and served as president of the Guadalajaran audiencia (1738–1743). Castillo de Aysa later purchased the appointment for that position for his son-in-law José Basarte (1750–1758).[7]

Cevallos Villagutierre, Dr. Ignacio Felipe (1710–1784). Cevallos was probably Güemes's most trusted adviser. He was born in Santiago de Guatemala to María Josefa Uría and Manuel Cevallos Villagutierre, alcalde mayor of Sonsonate (El Salvador). Both were immigrants from Béjar near Salamanca in León (Spain). Cevallos was also a nephew of Alonso Cevallos Villagutierre, former audiencia president of Santiago de Guatemala (1702–October 27, 1703) and audiencia president of Guadalajara (1679–1702). Ignacio Cevallos attended a Jesuit colegio in Guatemala and studied at the University of Mexico, where he was a fellow of the colegio mayor of Santa María de Todos Santos. He became a *medio racionero* (lower prebendary) at the Cathedral of Mexico City. He then traveled to Spain to obtain a canonry in 1746 and returned in 1747. The archbishop appointed him in 1749 as *juez visitador de testamentos, capellanías, y obras pias* (inspector of estates and pious works). Güemes recommended him to the Crown in 1747, and Cevallos became treasurer of the cathedral in 1750. Viceroy Croix deported Cevallos to Spain in 1768, where he died as dean of the chapter of Seville in 1784.[8]

Ensenada, Marquis of la; Zenón de Somodevilla. Born 1702 in Alesanco, Logroño, he became first minister in 1743 and Güemes's patron. Ensenada fell from power in 1754 and lived in exile in Granada and Puerto de Santa María until May 1760, when he returned to Madrid. After the Hat and Cloak Revolt against Prime Minister Esquilache, Charles III exiled Ensenada to Medina del Campo in 1766, where he died in 1781.

Gálvez, José de. Gálvez reviewed New Spain as *visitador general* (investigative judge) (1765–1771) and introduced provincial intendants in New Spain as secretary of the Indies (1776–1787).

Gómez de Parada Valdez y Mendoza, Juan Leandro. A native of Guadalajara, he became bishop of Yucatán in 1716 and of Guatemala in 1728. He served as bishop of his hometown from 1736 until 1751.

Huéscar, Duke of, Fernando de Silva Álvarez de Toledo. The duke orchestrated Ensenada's downfall in 1754 and briefly served as president of the Council of the Indies. In 1755, he assumed the title of Duke of Alba after his mother had passed away.

Martínez de Aguirre, Jacinto. The wealthy merchant and alcabala tax farmer of Puebla joined Güemes's ritual family. He owned the hacienda in San Agustín de las Cuevas south of Mexico City, where Güemes and his family frequently relaxed, and the hacienda "de los Tepetates" near Otumba, where many viceroys rested on their way to or from the coast.

Núñez de Villavicencio, Pedro (1698–?). He was born in Mexico City into a wealthy family of Andalusian descent. His mother was Antonia de la Peña, and his father, Juan Núñez de Villavicencio, served as corregidor of Mexico City. In about 1746, the Count of Fuenclara appointed Pedro Núñez de Villavicencio as interim accountant of the royal tribute collection. In 1748, Güemes praised Núñez de Villavicencio's "zeal and application" for the Crown[9] and promoted him to superintendent of the mint, an appointment that the king confirmed. Güemes considered him one of the two non-lawyers who merited promotion to the Council of the Indies. In 1748, the viceroy also recommended his relative Juan Núñez de Villavicencio for his work as *canciller* (chancellor or clerk who wields the royal seal) of the audiencia for a prebendary in Mexico City or Puebla. The close relationship with Núñez de Villavicencio continued after Güemes's return to Spain. In 1761, Núñez de Villavicencio reported about the many deaths and illnesses in his family, which left many impoverished, and requested support for his son's applications for positions.[10]

Padilla Pacheco Aguayo, Antonia Ceferina Paula. She was born in 1708 to María Rosa de Aguayo and Francisco Elías de Padilla Guardiola, elite residents of Antequera in Andalusia. Her grandfather had been a civil judge in Granada and Seville. She married Güemes on December 26, 1733, in the Church of San Sebastián of Antequera when she was twenty-five years old and Güemes fifty-two. Doña Antonia accompanied Güemes to Cuba, where she gave birth to eight children. She served as vicereine in Mexico City and passed away on October 11, 1756, when she was forty-eight, shortly after returning to Madrid.

Rivadeneira y Barrientos, Antonio. The civil prosecutor bought his appointment for 13,000 pesos in 1748. He joined Viceroy Amarillas aboard his ship traversing the ocean in 1755 and put the diary of the Marquise of las Amarillas into verse.[11]

Rubio y Salinas, Manuel José. Rubio y Salinas was appointed archbishop of Mexico in 1747 and arrived in Mexico in 1749. He secularized many regular doctrinas (parishes among Natives) and expanded the number of parochial schools instructing Native children in Spanish.

San Bartolomé de Xala, Count of, Manuel Rodríguez Sáenz Pedroso. He was one of the richest merchants in Mexico City and gained a fortune by importing cacao from Venezuela. He also produced pulque in great quantities, including on the hacienda of Xala (now Mexico State). San Bartolomé de Xala served as Mexico City's alcalde ordinario in 1754, as the consulado's consul in 1739–1740, and as prior in 1759. His daughter married Güemes's secretary, while Güemes's oldest son godfathered their child.

Vélez Cachupín, Tomás. Tomasico (little Tomás), as Güemes called his relative, came from an established noble family in Laredo, Cantabria. His relative Manuel Antonio Vélez Cachupín owned an entailed estate, albeit mortgaged. Vélez Cachupín traveled with Güemes to Cuba and New Spain as his master of the horse. The viceroy named him interim captain general of New Mexico, for which he received royal confirmation on April 6, 1749, and served until 1750 or 1751. Vélez Cachupín returned to Spain with Güemes in 1755 and obtained an additional appointment for the same position. On July 12, 1761, he was back in Mexico City. Civil prosecutor Antonio Rivadeneira twice called on Vélez Cachupín at that time, wishing to "register how much he loved his Excellency," that is, Güemes.[12] The consulado merchant José González Calderón loaned Vélez Cachupín money for his travels to New Mexico. The former master of the horse was cash strapped, because the Spanish merchants did not accept his *libranzas* (payment orders). Vélez Cachupín visited Viceroy Marquis of Cruillas and the vicereine. They received him coolly, despite their common regional background, and "reluctantly" accepted a gift of 2,000 pesos to expedite appointment papers.[13] Vélez Cachupín left Mexico City toward the end of September and began his second term as captain general in Santa Fe in early 1762.[14]

Vizarrón y Eguiarreta, Juan Antonio. Vizarrón y Eguiarreta served as archbishop of Mexico until his death in April 1747.

Wall, Ricardo. Wall replaced Ensenada as first minister in 1754 and stepped down in 1763.

Güemes's Relations with the Audiencia Ministers
CIVIL JUDGES

Andreu y Ferraz, Antonio. He was born in Aragon after 1700 and obtained a doctorate in civil law at the University of Huesca. Andreu y Ferraz never married. He became civil judge of the audiencia of Guatemala in 1735, rose to criminal judge on the Mexican audiencia in 1738, and civil prosecutor in 1748. In 1752, Güemes quarreled with him over the conquest of New Santander. In 1754, Andreu y Ferraz asked the Crown to reprimand the viceroy for appointing an alcalde mayor without putting up the required deposit. In 1753, Güemes recommended Andreu y Ferraz for a promotion to civil judge. Andreu y Ferraz advanced to the position in 1754, although it had already been filled. Güemes described him as devout and diligent and considered him best suited for promotion to the Council of the Indies, perhaps to rid himself of the "excessively scrupulous" minister.[15] Ensenada also considered him trustworthy. On March 22, 1758, the Crown allowed the judge to return to Spain.[16]

Bedoya y Osorio, Pedro. He was born in Belmonte, Cuenca, Spain, and obtained a licentiate, probably from the University of Salamanca. He took the position of civil prosecutor of the Mexican audiencia in 1737. In 1747, the viceroy and the Council of the Indies recommended Bedoya y Osorio's retirement, and the king agreed. In 1748, the Council of the Indies sentenced him to a stinging fine of 6,000 pesos. He had wrongfully prosecuted mint officials in Mexico City for tinkering with the weight and content of coins. Bedoya y Osorio then retired in the same year with half pay. In 1750, the prosecutor of the Council of the Indies reviewed a quarrel between Bedoya and Güemes over jurisdiction of the Tabasco alcabalas. Güemes labeled him "reasonably literate and quite practical in the general affairs of this realm."[17] In 1754, Bedoya y Osorio traveled to Spain to recover his salary after the 6,000 peso fine against him had been struck down. He died in 1757.[18]

Dávila de Madrid, Fernando. Dávila de Madrid was born in Vallecas, Spain, in about 1687 and obtained a licentiate in canon law from the University of Alcalá. The king named Dávila de Madrid as prosecutor in Guadalajara in 1721 and civil judge of Mexico in 1739. Güemes praised his maturity, "integrity, and learning" but also considered him "so petty perplex and scrupulous in the smallest bits and pieces of any matter that major difficulties have arisen." In addition, the judge was "capricious, and on occasion extravagant in his way of thinking."[19] In 1747, Güemes nonetheless wrote a glowing recommendation of Dávila's son Fernando, whom he deemed "knowledgeable, competent, and very dedicated to his studies."[20] The Crown also pondered a prebendary for

Dávila's son Ignacio, while his daughters joined the religious orders. The judge retired in 1764 and died before 1768.[21]

Echávarri y Ugarte Elcorobarrutia, Francisco Antonio. Echávarri was Güemes's enemy on the bench. He was born in 1701 in Vitoria, Basque Country, and received his licentiate in law from the University of Alcalá. In 1735, the king appointed Echávarri as civil judge of Mexico. In 1743, Echávarri won a quarrel with colleague Domingo Valcárcel Formento over seniority. Echávarri defied a 1739 royal prohibition to marry in his district by wedding the well-connected Bárbara Rita de Tamayo from Oaxaca. He then became Viceroy Duke of la Conquista's judge advocate, and Viceroy Count of Fuenclara also praised him in 1743. However, when the judge began visiting Juana Josefa de Echagaray, who lived estranged from her husband, relations soured with Fuenclara, the civil judges, and merchant Jacinto Martínez de Aguirre. Claims also surfaced that Echávarri took advantage of the mines in Zacatecas and Sombrerete. In 1748, Güemes called him "haughty and very ambitious for commissions and jurisdiction, and he always will impinge on the power of the viceroy when he can."[22] Güemes differed with Echávarri on the directorship of the duchy of Atlixco and reprimanded him for shady operations as *juez conservador* (conservator) of the marquisate of the valley of Oaxaca. Nonetheless, Echávarri had broad support at the court in Madrid, as the royal confessor was his "staunch protector,"[23] and the Duchess of Alba asked him to look after her mining rights in New Spain. Echávarri owned well-furnished houses in the city, in San Ángel, and in San Agustín de las Cuevas. The king promoted Echávarri to the chancelleries of Granada or Valladolid to dispel conflicts in Mexico City, but Echávarri declined. He retired from the bench in 1769 with half pay and joined the Council of the Indies in 1770, probably as an honorary appointment. He died April 16, 1774.[24]

Fernández de Madrid, Luis Manuel. He was born around 1685 in Toledo and graduated from the University of Alcalá with a licentiate in 1710. He served as civil judge of Guatemala beginning in 1725 and married María Rodríguez y Rivas y Velasco of Quito (Ecuador), daughter of the audiencia president. They had ten children. In 1738, Fernández de Madrid advanced to criminal judge of Mexico and became civil judge. Güemes thought that he lacked judgment and was easily influenced by his friends. Nonetheless, after the judge's passing on October 16,

1750, the viceroy requested a pension for the widow and supported the promotion of his son Diego Francisco to criminal judge in Mexico in 1752. Another son, Luis, studied theology at the Colegio of San Ildefonso, Mexico City.[25]

López de Adán y González, Francisco. Born in Algete, Madrid, he received a doctorate from the University of Ávila. The king appointed him for a supernumerary position on the Mexican bench in 1735 and converted this into a full position in 1738. López de Adán also joined the order of Santiago. Güemes considered him honorable but without much talent and somewhat childish. The civil judge suffered from frequent rheumatism and died in Mexico City on August 27, 1760.[26]

Malo de Villavicencio, Félix. Malo de Villavicencio was born in 1720 in Guadalajara, New Galicia, where his father, Pedro de Malo de Villavicencio, served as civil judge. His father later rose to civil judge of Mexico and became an enemy of Judge Echávarri. The younger Malo de Villavicencio attended the Universities of Mexico and Seville. In 1742, Félix purchased an appointment to succeed his father's position, which he took after April 22, 1747. He became a knight of Calatrava. He also married María Hurtado de Mendoza, a relative of the Mariscal de Castilla, a nobleman who married Malo de Villavicencio's sister. Malo de Villavicencio built on his father's friendship with civil judges José Rodríguez del Toro and Domingo Valcárcel, among others. Güemes decried his "limited talent without the ability to offset that defect," as he "appears like an old man or someone who is habitually sick," and denied his aptitude for the Council of the Indies.[27] The judge retired in 1773, joined the ecclesiastical chapter of Puebla, and died on May 6, 1787.[28]

Padilla y Córdoba, Pedro. Born near Madrid in roughly 1699, Padilla y Córdoba received bachelor's degrees in civil and canon law from the University of Mexico in 1716. He initially worked alongside his patron, Bishop Nicolás Carlos Gómez de Cervantes, until the Crown appointed him as civil judge of Mexico in 1739. Güemes applauded his virtuous and "very pure customs," although he felt that the judge was too conceited.[29] In Güemes's opinion, he would be more suited as a bishop than a councilor at the royal court, a view shared to an extent by Archbishop Rubio y Salinas. Padilla y Córdoba spoke well of Güemes in the judicial review and died around 1763.[30]

Rodríguez de Gómez de Albuerne, Juan, Marquis of Altamira. Born on May 6, 1696, in Larmuño, Oviedo, Spain, Rodríguez de Gómez received a bachelor's degree from the University of Alcalá in 1713. The king named him civil judge of Guadalajara in 1726 and civil judge of Mexico in December 1738. He served as judge advocate from 1742 and as superintendent of the royal mercury monopoly from 1744. Rodríguez de Gómez married Luisa Pérez de Tagle, the fourth Marquise of Altamira and daughter of a wealthy silver merchant. Their daughter María Cecilia married civil judge Domingo Trespalacios around 1751. Despite these social connections, Güemes considered Rodríguez de Gómez to be "one of the most merited ministers of this audiencia, and useful and necessary as judge advocate." He died on September 14, 1753.[31]

Rodríguez del Toro, José. He was born in Caracas, Venezuela, in 1715 to rich cacao planters. Educated at the University of Salamanca, he purchased an appointment for civil judge of Mexico for 15,000 pesos on May 7, 1741. In 1744, he married Ana María Uribe, daughter of an audiencia judge and heir to a string of haciendas near Tlaxcala. Ana María's brother married Judge Domingo Valcárcel's daughter, and her sisters also married into well-connected families. In 1748, Güemes believed that Rodríguez del Toro's many social "alliances which he acquired notably infringe on administering justice impartially."[32] By 1752, however, Güemes applauded that "his great moderation and orderliness make a good impression."[33] The viceroy recommended Rodríguez del Toro for promotion to the peninsula, although his marriage made it unlikely that he would move. On February 8, 1753, Rodríguez del Toro joined the order of Calatrava, as Güemes's oldest son, Juan Vicente, officiated as godfather. Rodríguez del Toro served as *apoderado* (representative) in the viceroy's judicial review, a task usually given to confidants. In 1755, one Antonio Rodríguez del Toro litigated over alcabala payments on cacao imports, indicating that the family continued the business. The judge died on June 19, 1773, while his widow passed away in 1783, leaving an estate of more than 100,000 pesos.[34]

Trespalacios y Escandón, Domingo. Born just outside Oviedo, Spain, on August 12, 1706, Trespalacios obtained a bachelor's degree in canon law in 1729 from the University of Salamanca. He took the position of civil judge in Mexico on August 7, 1742. Trespalacios and Güemes shared a *montañés* regional background; Güemes considered him virtuous, and "although others may exceed him in intelligence and liveliness, none equals him in work and application."[35] The viceroy recommended promoting Trespalacios to the Council of the Indies. In addition, Trespalacios served as judge superintendent of the municipal council's budget, judge of the royal drainage project, judge of the *media anata* (appointment tax), and protector of the basilica of Guadalupe. Güemes also appointed him to supervise the expansion of the cathedral *sagrario*, although the church opposed any supervision of its work. Trespalacios obtained a marriage license in 1741. In 1757, he married María Cecilia Rodríguez de Albuerne, daughter of Luisa Pérez de Tagle, fourth Marquise of Altamira, and Judge Juan Rodríguez Gómez de Albuerne. After María Cecilia's death, Trespalacios married Francisca Antonio de Escandón y Enríquez. On December 22, 1762, the king named Trespalacios councilor of the Indies. Güemes's allies Valcárcel, Núñez de Villavicencio, and the Count of San Bartolomé de Xala vouched for Trespalacios in the judicial review of 1766. The judicial review struck down a complaint against Trespalacios for denying an interest payment in a pulque auction and levying a wrongful penalty of 500 pesos. Trespalacios advanced to the cámara of the Indies in 1767, and the Council of the Indies upheld the judicial review sentence in 1771. He died on February 5, 1777.[36]

Valcárcel Formento y Vaquerizo, Domingo. Valcárcel was born in Granada, Spain, in 1702 and obtained a doctorate from the University of Alcalá. He became criminal prosecutor of Mexico in 1728 and civil judge in 1736. He married Ana María Altamirano Velasco y Gorraez, daughter of the Count of Santiago of Calimaya, one of the wealthiest landholders of the central region. Valcárcel's daughter married the son of Judge Joaquín Uribe, who inherited much land in Tlaxcala. Valcárcel formed with his fellow colegial Pedro Malo de Villavicencio (despite their quarrel over seniority) a network that included several treasury officials and the Marquis of Santa Fe de Guardiola, a relative of Güemes's wife and longtime corregidor of Mexico City. In 1748, Güemes attacked Valcárcel's "amor propio" (vanity) and his extensive local friendships.[37] A hostile hacendado even fumed that Valcárcel's "arrogance controls all the residents of the realm, and he even dominates the ministers of the audiencia, his companions, through his family relations."³⁸ By the early 1750s, however, Güemes had assigned him several commissions and recommended his son for a prebendary in the cathedral. Valcárcel's vast connections and support mattered for Güemes when tackling the alcabala collection. The viceroy finally called on Valcárcel to defend him in the judicial review, which was a task usually reserved for confidants. In exchange, Güemes probably advocated for him when the king named Valcárcel honorary councilor of the Indies in 1756 and promoted him to the council in 1761, although Valcárcel declined. The judge died in 1783.³⁹

CRIMINAL JUDGES

Chinchilla y Hinestrosa, Manuel de. He was born in Málaga, Spain, in about 1706 and received a bachelor's degree in canon law from the University of Granada in 1726 and Salamanca in 1733. The king appointed him criminal judge of Mexico City in 1737 and admitted him to the order of Calatrava in 1738. In the early 1740s, Viceroy Fuenclara commissioned Chinchilla to supervise the Indian tribute but relieved him for proposing impractical solutions. The king also denied a license to marry a local in 1737, which perhaps contributed to his gambling and inappropriate lifestyle, as Güemes saw it. In 1744, Chinchilla y Hinestrosa claimed that María Josefa "Chepa" was his niece. She was also the wife of merchant Manuel Cosuela, a viceregal ally. Güemes nevertheless believed that Chinchilla lacked the independence that his office required and considered him prematurely aged. After his death on February 8, 1750, his brother, the Marquis of Chinchilla, inherited the estate.⁴⁰

Fernández de Madrid, Diego Francisco. He was born in about 1726 in Guatemala City, where his father, Luis Manuel Fernández de Madrid, served on the audiencia. Diego Fernández de Madrid obtained degrees in philosophy and canon law from the University of Mexico in 1745–1749. The king appointed him with Güemes's support as supernumerary criminal judge of Mexico in 1751, after the passing of his father. He joined the court in 1752, became civil judge in 1774, and died on February 13, 1784.⁴¹

Mesia de la Cerda, José. He was born in Jaén, Spain, in about 1696 and received a bachelor's degree in canon law from the University of Granada. In 1724, he became civil judge of Guadalajara, where he married María Urrutia, the sister of a supernumerary civil judge Fernando Urrutia. In 1731, the Crown censured both Mesia de la Cerda and Urrutia for gambling. Shortly afterward on November 29, 1733, the king ordered Mesia de la Cerda to the Mexican audiencia as criminal judge, where he also served as judge advocate in 1744. In 1748, Güemes called him "boisterous, vain, and satisfied with himself" for seeking to curb viceregal jurisdiction over the treasury and the *acordada* (summary court). Güemes suggested "employing this dean and minister of the criminal chamber elsewhere outside this realm."[42] The judge also took attorney Francisco Javier Gamboa under his wings. In 1752, however, Güemes penned that Mesia de la Cerda was learned, honest, and judicious, but he did not think that the minister would assume a post at the Council of the Indies, because of his elderly wife and bad health. He died in 1760.[43]

Mosquera y Pimentel Quintanilla, Luis, Marquis of Aranda. He was born in Pontevedra, Spain, in 1719, and received bachelor's degrees in civil and canon law from the University of Salamanca. Mosquera became criminal prosecutor of the audiencia of Mexico in 1749 and civil prosecutor in 1755. Güemes recommended him for a position on the Council of the Indies. Mosquera in exchange vouched for the viceroy in the judicial review. Mosquera disliked New Spain. After the death of his father in 1760, he returned to Spain to serve as prosecutor of the Council of the Indies for New Spain in 1761. Judge Echávarri absolved him in the judicial review of 1764. Several viceregal friends, such as Barroeta and the Count of San Bartolomé de Xala testified in Mosquera's favor. The Crown promoted Mosquera to councilor of the Indies before he retired in 1774 with half salary. He died on April 29, 1778.[44]

Orozco Manrique de Lara, Francisco. The king dismissed him from the audiencia of Guatemala in 1747, where he had served since 1724. In 1751, he became supernumerary criminal judge in Mexico. Güemes never mentioned him, although the judge was still sitting in 1755.[45]

Rojas y Abreu, Antonio. He was born in Tenerife, the Canary Islands, on

June 12, 1703, and completed a bachelor's degree in canon law at the Universities of Granada and Salamanca. The king appointed him prosecutor of the Santo Domingo audiencia in 1734, and he became criminal prosecutor of Mexico on April 5, 1742. In 1745, the Crown punished him for challenging the viceregal review of acordada rulings. In 1753, he also admitted to investing in silver mining in Pachuca and Atotonilco el Chico despite legal prohibitions. He claimed that he needed money to support his wife and seven children. The king disregarded his request for promotion to supernumerary civil judge that year. Worse, Rojas y Abreu misacted as executor of Judge José Fernández de Veytia, whose late father had owned 800,000 pesos. According to Rojas y Abreu, three Jesuits convinced the father on his deathbed to write up a note leaving half the estate to the Crown and the other half to the church. His son, however, hid the note in his clothes for "being avaricious," as Rojas y Abreu saw it.[46] Then, prosecutor Pedro Bedoya y Osorio assessed the estate's value and found only 121,000 pesos, of which 26,000 pesos were owed to the superintendency of alcabalas. Fernández de Veytia's heirs blamed Rojas y Abreu for squandering the estate, and Güemes humiliated him in public, causing the Council of the Indies to request a report. Güemes thought the judge was rather uneducated and even less capable than Felipe Tineo. He retired in 1773.[47]

Santaella y Melgarejo Ladrón de Guevara, Ambrosio Eugenio. He was born in 1716 in Mexico City as the son of Judge Ambrosio Tomás Santaella y Melgarejo and obtained degrees in civil and canon law from the University of Mexico. Santaella y Melgarejo practiced law at the audiencia and married Ana Lobero Sancia. They moved to Spain, where he secured an appointment as supernumerary criminal judge of Mexico for a payment of 17,500 pesos in 1742. Güemes considered Santaella y Melgarejo judicious and industrious, and the criminal judge praised Güemes's diligence: "His Excellency has always fulfilled his duty even on the day after the death of his daughter" Josefa Cayetana in 1749.[48] In 1764, the Crown promoted him to civil judge.[49]

Tineo, Felipe. Born in Madrid in the 1680s, Tineo served as a salaried attorney at the audiencia of Zaragoza before becoming protector of the Indians in New Spain in 1728. After suppressing the office, the king named Tineo supernumerary criminal judge of Mexico. Both Güemes and the Council of the Indies held him in low regard. He died on November 3, 1753.[50]

Glossary

adit. A tunnel that drains water out of mines.

alcabala. A sales or excise tax.

alcalde de crimen. A criminal judge of the audiencia.

alcalde mayor. A district judge of the first instance, akin to a corregidor. Alcaldes mayores also carried out royal orders, commanded the militia, and collected tribute, the *alcabala*, and other taxes.

alcalde ordinario. A municipal magistrate.

alguacil. A constable or patrolman.

alguacil mayor. A chief constable.

asesor letrado. The legal adviser of the viceroy.

audiencia. The high court in Mexico City and Guadalajara, which mostly ruled on appellate cases.

auto. A decree or public act of a colonial authority.

bando. Public notice.

billete. A viceregal request for somebody to carry out something, which was more informal and softly worded than a decree or order.

caballerizo. The master of the horse or equerry.

cabildo. The *cabildo civil* was a municipal council, and the *cabildo eclesiástico* (or in the archdiocese, the *cabildo metropolitano*) was the ecclesiastical chapter; that is, the governing body composed of canons and other prebends.

cámara of the Indies. The committee of the Council of the Indies that suggested candidates for office.

Casa de Contratación. The House of Trade in Seville, which supervised traffic with the Spanish Americas.

Casta. A person of mixed ethnic ancestry.

cédula. A royal communication ordering or announcing some action.

colegial mayor. A university graduate who resided in a *colegio mayor*.

colegio. An entry-level university and theological seminary.

colegio mayor. An exclusive residence hall or confraternity tied to a university. In Mexico, there was the colegio mayor of Santa María de Todos Santos. In Spain, the colegios mayores were associated with the foremost universities of Salamanca, Valladolid, and Alcalá.

consul. A senior minister of the *consulado* who acted as judge and administrator.

consulado. A merchant guild; there were consulados in Mexico City and Lima, while the consulado of Seville moved to Cádiz in 1717.

consulta. A written legal consultation.

corregidor. A district judge akin to an alcalde mayor.

Cortes. The assembly of the Estates in Spain; the representatives of the aristocracy, the clergy, and the cities.

Council of the Indies. The council in Madrid that heard appeals to litigation from Spanish America and advised the king on American affairs.

Creole. A person of Spanish descent born in the Americas.

despacho. A dispatch or communication, usually from the Crown.

doctrina. A parish administered by friars to convert Natives to Christianity.

escribano. A scribe and notary.

fiscal. A prosecutor. The *fiscal de lo civil* of the audiencia handled civil matters, while the *fiscal del crimen* presented criminal causes. The Council of the Indies had fiscales for New Spain and Peru, while the fiscal of the Inquisition dealt with criminal law of the church.

hacendado. A large landowner.

hidalguía. The lower nobility.

informe. A report.

intendente. An intendant; a supervisor or provincial governor.

juez comisario. A commissioner who investigates malfeasance.

juicio de residencia. The judicial review of a minister's tenure.

junta. An ad-hoc council.

ladino. In the colonial period, this word was often used to refer to an astute and Spanish-speaking Native.

mayordomo. A lord steward of the royal and viceregal court.

montañés. The people from the mountainous region between Santander and Burgos in northern Spain.

New Spain. Colonial Mexico.

oficial mayor. A chief clerk; for example, of the secretary of the Indies.

oidor. A civil judge of the audiencia.

palio. A portable canopy reserved for kings in the eighteenth century.

parecer. A legal opinion usually provided by a lawyer.

principal. Here, an indigenous noble.

prior. The elected president of the consulado; also the head of a priory of the regular orders.

provincial. Head of a province of a regular order.

pueblo. A Native polity.

real acuerdo. A committee discussing major decisions formed by the viceroy, the civil judges, and the civil prosecutor of the audiencia.

real cédula. See *cédula*.

relación de méritos. A colonial résumé.

residencia. See *juicio de residencia*.

ruego y encargo. "I request and commission," a royal or viceregal prompt for the church to do something.

sala civil. The civil chamber composed of the civil judges and civil prosecutor of the audiencia adjudicating noncriminal cases.

sala de justicia. A chamber or committee of the Council of the Indies that heard judicial appeals.

sala del crimen. The criminal chamber of the audiencia.

visita. A judicial investigation.

visitador general. An investigative judge with broad powers to conduct a *visita general*.

visita general. A broad judicial investigation covering several institutions or an entire kingdom.

Notes

Note on Terms
1. *Law of the Indies*, book 2, title 15, law 3, considered Yucatán and Florida as part of the kingdom of New Spain, but these regions achieved varying forms of autonomy in the eighteenth century.

Introduction
1. Paz, *Posdata*, 154. Cañeque, *The King's Living Image*, 1–3, traces this widespread view, pointing especially to Zapatist criticism of Mexican presidents. According to Hanke, *Guía de las fuentes en Hispanoamérica*, 10, the French scholar Georges Desdevises Du Dézert already viewed viceroys as "true satraps in the oriental style." For in-depth historiographical discussions, see this volume's chapter endnotes and conclusion.
2. Vargas Llosa in an interview with Olivier Guez, "Das System Chávez."
3. Ramos Ávalos, "La democracia pendiente"; and Saldaña, "PAN adelanta en el Senado."
4. Kuethe and Andrien, *The Spanish Atlantic World*, 3–4, 33–39, 115–18.
5. Latasa Vassallo, "Juan Francisco de Güemes y Horcasitas."
6. *Oficial mayor* (chief clerk) José Banfi y Parrilla to Güemes, Madrid, September 4, 1751, Archivo de los Condes de Revillagigedo, Library of the University of Florida, Gainesville, Florida, Department of Special and Area Collections (hereinafter ACR), microfilm reel number 388; on cochineal, see Güemes to Ensenada, Mexico City, April 10, 1752, ACR 354.
7. Historians of Latin America have long analyzed intermediaries and social networks created by patronage, family, business contracts, and other factors. They have departed from determinist views as actors joined, straddled, or left networks; see, for example, Becerra Jiménez, "Redes sociales," 109–50; Castellano and Dedieu, *Réseaux, familles et pouvoirs*; Bertrand, "Clientélisme et pouvoir"; Bertrand, "Del actor a la red," 23–41; Lamikiz, "Social Capital, Networks and Trust," 39–61; Hespanha, "Les autre raisons de la politique," 67–86; and Polo y La Borda, "Don Mauro's Letters," esp. 568–71. One of the earliest practitioners is Schwartz, *Sovereignty and Society*.

8. Curcio-Nagy, *The Great Festivals*, 70–83, argues for the decline of viceregal entries.
9. The Library of the University of Florida, Gainesville, microfilmed the Archivo de los Condes de Revillagigedo years ago. Valle Menéndez, *Juan Francisco de Güemes*, consulted the family archive in Madrid with significant help from Pilar Latasa Vassallo, while Rubio Mañé, *El virreinato*, 1:vi–vii, reviewed the repository in the 1940s, focusing on the second Count of Revillagigedo; see also Rubio Mañé, "Llegada a México," 1–14.
10. Castro Santa-Anna, *Diario de sucesos notables*, vols. 4–6; García Panes y Abellán, *Diario particular*; and Ahumada y Vera, *Diario de viaje*.
11. Many scholars agree now that the Bourbon Reforms were in fact a multifaceted process that stretched over an extended period; see, for instance, Calvo, "Ciencia, cultura y política," loc. 1161, Kindle; and García Ayluardo, "Re-formar la Iglesia," loc. 3980, 4291, Kindle. Pearce, *The Origins of Bourbon Reform*, 7–14, discusses current research.

Chapter 1

1. Latasa Vassallo, "Juan Francisco de Güemes y Horcasitas"; Valle Menéndez, *Juan Francisco de Güemes*, 25–27, 33–49; and Figueroa y Melgar, *Estudio histórico*, 69–71.
2. Kamen, *Philip V of Spain*, 18–19, 26, 31–33, 51, 108–9; Escudero, "El gobierno central," 103; and Castro Monsalve, "Las secretarías," 194–95, 198–99. On the consulado's transfer, see Kuethe, "La Casa de Contratación," 205–18. According to Castejón, "Un *cursus honorum*," 433–37, councilors with American experience joined the Council of the Indies earlier and in greater numbers than scholars thought. In addition, the continuity from Habsburg to Bourbon is far from a settled argument; please see this volume's conclusion. Martínez Millán, "La articulación," 53, holds that since the reign of Philip II (1556–1598), king and advisers crafted policy while the councils ruled on judicial conflicts.
3. Abad León, *El marqués de la Ensenada*, 1:53–63; Gómez Urdáñez, *El proyecto reformista*, 60–66; Stein and Stein, *Silver, Trade, and War*, 236; Kamen, *Philip V of Spain*, 124–25, 245; and Peralta Ruiz, *Patrones, clientes y amigos*, 21. On the Basque people, see also Guerrero Elecalde, "El 'partido vizcaíno,'" 85–100.
4. Cited in Kuethe and Andrien, *The Spanish Atlantic World*, 105, also 143–45; and Latasa Vassallo, "Juan Francisco de Güemes y Horcasitas."
5. Gómez Urdáñez, "Carvajal y Ensenada," 68; Gómez Urdáñez, *Fernando VI*, 85; and Castellano, *Gobierno y poder*, 154. Téllez Alarcia, "Guerra y regalismo," 1079, argues that Ensenada relied on Jesuits and graduates of the *colegios mayores* (exclusive residence halls) associated with the foremost Spanish universities of

Salamanca, Valladolid, and Alcalá. On the royal confessor Francisco Rávago y Noriega, see Escamilla González, "Los confesores reales," 234, 241–47.

6. All quotations in this paragraph in José Benito Zarauz to Güemes, Laredo (Spain), June 18, 1743, ACR 394.

7. Cited in Castellano, *Gobierno y poder*, 141.

8. Cited in Gómez Urdáñez, "Carvajal y Ensenada," 68.

9. Title of appointment as governor, Buen Retiro, January 27, 1748, Archivo General de Indias, Gobierno—Audiencia de México (hereinafter AGI, México) 383.

10. Gómez Urdáñez, *Fernando VI*, 50–54; and Voltes, *La vida y la época*, 99–100, point to the Ensenada-Carvajal dichotomy.

11. Cited in Walter, "Exkurs: Wirtschaftlicher Liberalismus," 792, also 790–93.

12. Bonney, "Early Modern Theories," 195–98; Macías Delgado, "Miguel Antonio de la Gándara," 175–82; and Muhlack, "Physiokratismus," 472–77.

13. Campillo y Cosío, *Nuevo sistema*, 15, 70.

14. Campillo y Cosío, *Nuevo sistema*, 15–25, 31–47, 55–73, 115–21, 126–28, 138–40, 200 (the last pagination is faulty in the print). On this issue, see also Duve, *Sonderrecht*, 202–3, 273–74; Bernecker and Pietschmann, *Geschichte Spaniens*, 194–208; and Owensby, "Between Justice and Economics," 152–56.

15. Martínez Nava, "El Tribunal del Santo Oficio," 285, 292; and Campillo y Cosío, *Nuevo sistema*, 43–56. Scholars discuss the government of José de Campillo y Cossío (1741–1743) and his authorship of *New System*. Stein and Stein, *Silver, Trade, and War*, 209, argue that "Campillo's life had spanned the first four decades of Bourbon Spain and the inconsequential record of failed initiatives in pursuing a model of economic growth." Kuethe and Andrien, *The Spanish Atlantic World*, 4, however, maintain that Campillo y Cossío was "Spain's most influential eighteenth-century political thinker," who broke the grip of the Seville oligarchy. See also Kuethe, "La desregulación comercial," 273; and Lynch, *Bourbon Spain*, 97. Navarro García, "El falso Campillo," 5–14, doubts Campillo y Cossío's authorship, attributing it instead to an anonymous author tied to Bernardo Ward, because the second half of his *Proyecto economico* is almost identical with *New System*.

16. Juan and Ulloa, *Discourse and Political Reflections*, 218, also 148–56, 172.

17. Ward, *Proyecto economico*, xiii; Ward drafted his work after returning from his review of poorhouses in Europe (1750–1754). The manuscript was published following his death in 1762; see Castellano, "Bernardo Ward," 185–200.

18. "Noticias particulares y reservadas," Madrid, July 28, 1746, AGI, México 610. According to *Law of the Indies*, book 7, title 4, law 5, King Philip II ordered the deportation of the Roma in 1580.

19. Ensenada, "puntos de gobierno," in Rodríguez Villa, *Don Cenon de Somodevilla*, 164. The author of *Nuevo Sistema*, 263, suggested the Roma's deportation to the Orinoco River.

20. *Real cédula* (royal communication), San Lorenzo, October 30, 1745, Archivo Municipal de Atlixco (hereinafter AMA), 2006, box 6, exp. 4, fols. 21–21v; see also the royal order published by Ginés de Hermosa y Espejo, Seville, 1749, AMA, 2006, box 6, exp. 4, fol. 25. See Gómez Alfaro, *The Great Gypsy Round-Up*, 11, 14, 20, 25–26, 34, 53, 73, 113–14.

21. Bonney, "Early Modern Theories," 173–76; Pieper, *La Real Hacienda*, 62–63, 82–83; and Llombart Rosa, "El pensamiento económico," 16–17. Lynch, *Bourbon Spain*, 102–6, gives 10 and 8 percent tax rates on property and personal income in Aragon; see also Kamen, *Philip V of Spain*, 117–19. According to Dedieu, "Dinastía y élites de poder," 390–91, the Nueva Planta strengthened the first ministers' patronage rights in Catalonia.

22. Cited in Rodríguez Villa, *Don Cenon de Somodevilla*, 90.

23. Llombart Rosa, "El pensamiento económico," 16–18; according to Llombart Rosa, the author Miguel de Zavala y Auñón also suggested a removal of price caps on grain, because higher prices spurred producers to grow more and alleviate shortages, but this remained a hot-button issue. See also Gómez Urdáñez, *El proyecto reformista*, 180–88; Pieper, *La Real Hacienda*, 62–63; and Zavala y Auñón, *Representación al Rey Nuestro Señor D. Phelipe V*.

24. Gómez Urdáñez, *El proyecto reformista*, 180, 185–88; Ruiz Torres, *Reformismo e Ilustración*, 278–79; Lynch, *Bourbon Spain*, 102–6; Pieper, *La Real Hacienda*, 80–82; and Kamen, *Philip V of Spain*, 117–19.

25. Draft of Ensenada's letter to Güemes, Aranjuez, May 24, 1748, AGI, México 1506, no. 41. 1.

26. Ensenada, *Representación dirigida por el Marqués de Ensenada á Fernando VI sobre el estado del Real Erario y sistema y método para lo futuro*, Aranjuez, April 16, 1747, in Rodríguez Villa, *Don Cenon de Somodevilla*; and Gómez Urdáñez, *Fernando VI*, 180–81. Stein and Stein, *Silver, Trade, and War*, 239, maintain that Ensenada favored the royal textile factory in Guadalajara, Spain, whereas Carvajal supported manufactures in Extremadura and León and small-scale enterprises in Brihuega and Seville; Helguera Quijada, "Un empeño fallido de reindustrialización," 222–23, points to additional royal enterprises.

27. Ensenada, *Representación*, Madrid, 1751, in Rodríguez Villa, *Don Cenon de Somodevilla*, 126.

28. Carvajal y Lancáster, *Testamento político*, 13–20; Delgado Barrado, *El proyecto político de Carvajal*, 29; and Gómez Urdáñez, *Fernando VI*, 51–52. See also Gómez Molleda, "El pensamiento de Carvajal," 117–37.

29. Pearce, *The Origins of Bourbon Reform*, 11, 127, 132–33; and Stein and Stein, *Silver, Trade, and War*, 236, 241–50. Nonetheless, Baskes, *Staying Afloat*, 6–7, 277, argues now that the Atlantic convoy system contained "supply volatility" and risks, while competition among merchants prevented price gouging. Note that the Treaty of Aix-la-Chapelle concluded the War of the Austrian Succession, which had begun in 1740.

30. Ensenada, *Representación*, Aranjuez, June 18, 1747, in Rodríguez Villa, *Don Cenon de Somodevilla*, 63; Pearce, *The Origins of Bourbon Reform*, 148; Klein, *The American Finances*, 73–74; Burkholder, *Spaniards in the Colonial Empire*, esp. 74, 83, 97; and Rosenmüller, *Corruption and Justice*, 116–20.

31. Anonymous author, *Papeles del Duende de Mexico*, n.d., Instituto Nacional de Antropología e Historia Library (hereinafter INAH), Colección Antigua (CA), microfilm roll 55, fol. 86.

32. C. Walker, "The Upper Classes," 53–82; Pearce, *The Origins of Bourbon Reform*, 145–51; Eissa-Barroso, "Having Served in the Troops," 330–32, 355–56; and Eissa-Barroso, "Las capitanías generales," 138–39. Güemes to Arriaga, Mexico City, March 10, 1755, ACR 455; royal order issued by Ensenada to Güemes, Madrid, February 5, 1754, AGI, México 1352; and Güemes to Arriaga, Mexico City, March 10, 1755, AGI, México 1352. Note that according to king to Casafuerte, Seville, March 14, 1732, Archivo General de la Nación (Mexico City) (hereinafter AGN), Reales Cédulas Originales (RCO) 51, exp. 14, fols. 70–72v; Güemes to Ensenada, Mexico City, June 4, 1752, ACR 347; and Del Río, "La inestable capital," 17–20, 25, Virrey Casafuerte had already appointed a governor for Sinaloa in 1732.

33. López-Cordón Cortezo, "Servicios y favores," 233; Kamen, *Philip V of Spain*, 250; and Sarrablo Aguareles, *El conde de Fuenclara*, 2:254–55, 261–65.

34. All quotations in this paragraph in the draft of Pedro Navarro to Ensenada (?), n.d., AGN, Inquisición 1328, exp. 6, fols. 248–249v.

35. Ensenada, *Representación*, Aranjuez, June 18, 1747, in Rodríguez Villa, *Don Cenon de Somodevilla*, 126. See also Güemes to Ensenada, Havana, April 29, 1746, AGI, México 1506, no. 4; royal *despacho* (dispatch), Buen Retiro, June 21, 1745, AGI, México 1506, no. 1; and appointment title, Aranjuez, June 21, 1745, AGI, México 1506, no. 2. On the salary, see Report of the Tribunal of Accounts, Mexico City, November 15, 1780, Biblioteca Nacional de México (hereinafter BNM), Fondo Reservado (FR), manuscrito 439 (1376). According to Güemes to king, Mexico City, February 24, 1747, AGI, México 1506, no. 26, the salary had been raised for Fuenclara; and the royal cédula, Buen Retiro, July 10, 1747, AGI, México 1506, no. 26.1, confirmed this amount for Güemes, too. See also Güemes to Ensenada, Mexico City, July 2, 1748, ACR 399; Rubio Mañé, *El virreinato*, 1:212; and *Law of the Indies*, book 3, title 3, law 72. Solórzano y Pereyra, *Política Indiana*, book 5, chap. 2, para. 14, stressed the importance of appropriate salaries, and so did Pierre Grégoire de Toulouse, *De republica libri sex et viginti*, book 2, chap. 6, para. 18, in 1609, recommending that "the judges' salaries be sufficient, and the customary fee assessment be taken from them."

36. Ferdinand VI to Güemes, Buen Retiro, December 4, 1748, ACR 374; note signed by the Duke of Arión, n.p., April 18, 1750, Archivo del Real Palacio (Madrid) (hereinafter ARP) 482, fol. 28; Alonso Muñoz to Marquis of Villafranca, Buen Retiro, April 14, 1750, ARP 1341, fol. 14; Alonso Muñoz to Güemes,

Buen Retiro, April 14, 1750, AGN, RCO 70, exp. 59; and royal title, Buen Retiro, August 12, 1749, AGI, México 384. The royal title is also published in Valle Menéndez, *Juan Francisco de Güemes*, 796.

37. Cabildo session, Mexico City, July 20, 1753, in Francisco del Barrio Lorenzot, *Compendio de los libros capitulares de la Muy Noble Insigne, y Muy Leal Ciudad de Mexico (1743–1765)*, Archivo Histórico de la Ciudad de México (hereinafter AHCM), Ayuntamiento, Actas del Cabildo 438A, vol. 5, fol. 76, referring to the *junta de policía*.

38. Sessions of the cabildo on April 6, April 13, and September 7, 1747, AHCM, Ayuntamiento, Actas del Cabildo 438A, fols. 40–41, 43v–44, referring to the *mayordomo* (steward).

39. Gómez Urdáñez, "Carvajal y Ensenada," 67, sees a union between Carvajal and Bragança because of their Portuguese origins, while Castellano, *Gobierno y poder*, 133–54, stresses their disagreements. On Carvajal's network, see Ozanam, *Les diplomates espagnols*, 34, who argues that the Duke of Huéscar, Ricardo Wall, and Cardinal Portocarrero advanced a political project, while later factions such as the Aragonese Party coalesced around personal, family, and regional ties; see also Ozanam, *La diplomacia de Fernando VI*, 9. According to Gómez Gómez, "La nueva tramitación de los negocios," 220–21, after July 22, 1746, the Council of the Indies had to send all royal cédulas through the "via reservada," which meant that Ensenada reviewed them before publication.

40. Molina Cortón, *Reformismo y neutralidad*, 434–67. Gómes Urdáñez, *Fernando VI*, 113, 118, denies that British ambassador Benjamin Keene possessed evidence against Ensenada, but Téllez Alarcia, *D. Ricardo Wall: Aut Caesar aut nullus*, 180–90, shows that Keene obtained mandates to Spanish American authorities to harass British settlers; see also Baudot Monroy, *La defensa del Imperio*, 414–16. Téllez Alarcia, "Guerra y regalismo," 1053–54, casts doubt on the chief role of Ambassador Keene in the conspiracy; on the lack of scholarship on Wall, see Téllez Alarcia, "Richard Wall: Light and Shade," 123–36. The classical account is in Lynch, *Bourbon Spain*, 182–85, drawing on Lodge, *The Private Correspondence of Sir Benjamin Keene*, xix–xx, also 38n1.

41. Christoph Migazzi to Maria Theresa, Madrid, August 19, 1754, Österreichisches Staatsarchiv, Haus-, Hof- und Staatsarchiv, Staatenabteilung Spanien, Diplomatische Korrespondenz (1754.05–1754.12), box 85, folder 2, no. 35, fols. 47v–48.

42. Ambassador Duke of Duras to Rouillé, Aranjuez, July 27, 1754, Archives du Ministère des Affaires Étrangères, Correspóndance Politique, Espagne (hereinafter AMAE, CPE), 514, fol. 414; see also fols. 409r–413v; and Duras to Rouillé, Aranjuez, August 14, 1754, AMAE, CPE 514, fols. 462v–464.

43. Duras to Rouillé, July 27, 1754, AMAE, CPE 514, fol. 430; see also fols. 408–429. Note that Castro Monsalve, "Las secretarías," 212, 213–14, views Wall's term as the beginning of "enlightened politics, markedly regalist, anti-Jesuit,

and anti-colegial [graduates of a privileged study hall], characteristic of the reign of Charles III"; while Alcaraz Gómez, *Jesuitas y reformismo*, 647–48, is critical of Queen Barbara of Bragança, the Duke of Huéscar, and Keene, who masterminded the conspiracy against Ensenada. The scholar argues that Wall's cabinet consisted of "individuals of lesser stature" with their "openly declared and unmitigated hate towards the Society of Jesus." See also Burkholder, *Biographical Dictionary of Councilors of the Indies*, xxxiv.

44. Güemes to Arriaga, Mexico City, March 6, 1755, AGI, México 1506, no. 156; royal cédula, Buen Retiro, April 3, 1755, AGI, México 1506, no. 156.1; Güemes to Arriaga, Mexico City, March 6, 1755, AGI, México 1506, no. 157; and Güemes to Arriaga, Mexico City, March 15, 1755, ACR 455. See also Kuethe, "La desregulación comercial," 268–92; Kuethe, "El fin del monopolio," 52–53; and Stein and Stein, *Silver, Trade, and War*, 196–98, 256. On Arriaga, see Baudot Monroy, "Orígenes familiares," 181. According to Alcaraz Gómez, *Jesuitas y reformismo*, 697, Sebastián de Eslava succeeded as secretary of war and the Count of Valparaíso as secretary of the navy.

Chapter 2

1. Using the diaries covering the 1755 procession poses a challenge for examining Güemes's entry, yet García Panes y Abellán, *Diario particular*, 67, 69, claims that he recorded Amarillas's entry "in accordance with that of all his predecessors." While the difference between Güemes's and Amarillas's entry was probably minor, García Panes overstates the case in comparison with earlier viceroys. See also Ahumada y Vera, *Diario de viaje*. García Panes, *Diario particular*, 68–69, holds that the civil prosecutor, Antonio Rivadeneira y Barrientos, wrote Ahumada y Vera's diary, while Llanos, "Introduction to *Diario de viaje*," 15–19, argues that the prosecutor merely put the content in verse.
2. Lista de la familia (embarkation list), Cádiz, May 27, 1789, AGI, Casa de la Contratación (Contratación) 5533, N. 3, R. 8; Gómez, *Diario curioso*, 5; and Moreno Cebrián, "La vida cotidiana," 117, also 126–34.
3. Morales Martínez, "Antes de la fiesta," 470–73, 489, referring to Viceroy Marquis of el Risco.
4. Memoria de las cosas, cited in Morales Martínez, "Antes de la fiesta," 489.
5. Morales Martínez, "Antes de la fiesta," 471–75.
6. Büschges, "Del criado al valido," 162. Le Roux, "La maison du roi," 16–21, provides a snapshot of French court offices.
7. Philip V to Jean-Baptiste Ducas, Madrid, May 8, 1702, AGI, México 610; see also Bertrand, *Grandeur et misères*, 210. According to Viceroy Duke of Linares's (1710–1716) Memoria de la familia (embarkation list), Cádiz, July 25, 1710, AGI, Contratación 5465, N. 2, R. 107; and the royal decree on margin of consulta of

the Council of the Indies, n.p., March 31, 1710, AGI, México 610, the Duke of Linares brought forty-one clients and no slaves in 1710. On his taking office, Linares to king, Mexico City, January 6, 1711, AGI, México 483; and Alburquerque to king, Mexico City, January 5, 1711, AGI, México 485. Escamilla González, "La corte," 374, 394–95, pinpoints the viceregal court's decline to Linares, when a "caste of bureaucrats" appeared; Escamilla González, "Permanence and Change," 230–33, argues that viceroys and empire simultaneously lost legitimacy. Escamilla González and Moreno Gamboa, "El Duque de Linares," 181–83, convincingly foreground Linares as the first Bourbon "soldier-viceroy." Valero's embarkation list, Cádiz, March 10, 1716, AGI, Contratación 5469, N. 2, R. 10, fols. 10–11; see also note *Aquí la familia*, n.d., which lists seventy travelers including Valero; title of appointment, Buen Retiro, November 22, 1715, reprised in appointment title, Cádiz, May 3, 1716, AGI, Contratación 5469, N. 2, R. 10, fols. 1–2; and José Sánchez and Francisco Leri, Nómina de los . . . Presidentes, n.p., 1716, AGI, Escribanía de Cámara de Justicia (Escribanía) 278A.

8. Casafuerte's embarkation list, Cádiz, June 16, 1722, AGI, Contratación 5472, N. 2, R. 5, fols. 7r–8v. On Casafuerte's background, see Eissa-Barroso, "The Honor of the Spanish Nation," 51; and Rubio Mañé, *El virreinato*, 1:267.

9. According to Patiño to Francisco de Varas y Valdés, Madrid, December 10, 1733; and license to embark, Cádiz, January 8, 1734, AGI, Contratación 5481, N. 2, R. 23, fols. 9–11r, Joaquín Horcasitas y Güemes, Bartolomé Novia, Tomás Vélez Cachupín, and Alfonso Antonio Gómez Bárcena joined Güemes in traveling to Cuba. Joaquín Horcasitas y Güemes died fighting pirates near Cuba, while Novia is unaccounted for in New Spain; see Order of the Commissioner and Chief Naval Accountancy, Cádiz, January 3, 1734, AGI, Contratación 1463; Güemes to Ensenada, Havana, April 29, 1746, AGI, México 1506, no. 4; royal *despacho*, Buen Retiro, June 21, 1745, AGI, México 1506, no. 1; and appointment title, Aranjuez, June 21, 1745, AGI, México 1506, no. 2. See also Valle Menéndez, *Juan Francisco de Güemes*, 65.

10. Embarkation list, Cádiz, July 23, 1755, AGI, Contratación 5497, N. 2, R. 14, fols. 15–16. On Amarillas, see Baeza Martín, "Agustín de Ahumada y Villalón." Rubial García, "Las virreinas novohispanas," 5, points out that three other viceroys also obtained their titles by marriage.

11. Castro Santa-Anna, *Diario de sucesos notables*, 5:167; according to 5:232, Amarillas's son died on March 1, 1756, in Mexico City. See also Pietschmann, "Diego García Panes," 203, 222, 231.

12. Francisco Cajigal de la Vega's *auto* (order), Cádiz, September 28, 1737, AGI, Contratación 5483, N. 2, R. 27 fols. 7–8; Croix's embarkation list, Madrid, March 5, 1766, AGI, Contratación 5509, N. 3, R. 15, fols. 1–3; note at margins from April 9, 1766, AGI, Contratación 5509, N. 3, R. 15, fol. 3; Martín de Mayorga's embarkation list, San Lorenzo, November 20, 1772; royal order, El Pardo, February 10, 1773, the two preceding documents in AGI, Contratación 5518, N. 2, R. 7,

fols. 3, 5; and Antonio María Bucareli y Ursúa's embarkation list, San Lorenzo, November 12, 1765, AGI, Contratación 5508, N. 1, R. 72, fols. 3-5.
13. Ramos, *Identity, Ritual, and Power*, 44; and Stollberg-Rilinger, *Rituale*, 106-8.
14. Büschges, "Urban Public Festivals," 115, 118; and Gonzalbo Aizpuru, "El virreinato," 196. See also Valenzuela Márquez, "La recepción pública," 512; and for a later period, Morelli, "La publicación," 177-218.
15. Güemes to Ensenada, Mexico City, July 10, 1746, AGI, México 1506, no. 7; García Panes y Abellán, *Diario particular*, 73-75; Ahumada y Vera, *Diario de viaje*, 37-38; and Rubio Mañé, *El virreinato*, 1:117.
16. Session of the *cabildo* (municipal council) of Mexico City, Mexico City, May 25, 1746; Güemes to cabildo, Veracruz, June 6, 1746; and cabildo to Güemes, Mexico City, June 13, 1746, all three documents in AHCM, Ayuntamiento, Cédulas y Reales Órdenes 2977, exp. 76, fols. 3-4, 9, 11-11v. According to cabildo session, May 25, 1746, AHCM, Ayuntamiento, Cédulas y Reales Órdenes 2977, exp. 76, fols. 3-4, the cabildo began organizing the viceregal entry and dinner receptions at that point. See also Inquisitor Pedro Anselmo Sánchez de Tagle's order, Mexico City, May 25, 1746; Güemes to Inquisition, Veracruz, June 6, 1746; Güemes's edict, n.d.; and Sánchez de Tagle to Güemes, Mexico City, June 14, 1746, the four preceding documents in AGN, Inquisición 889, fols. 51-51v, 53-53v, 55, 56-56v. Güemes's dispatch, Mexico City, July 9, 1755, AGN, General de Parte (GdP) 41, exp. 76.
17. Ahumada y Vera, *Diario de viaje*, 38-41; and García Panes y Abellán, *Diario particular*, 85-90.
18. Güemes to Sánchez de Tagle, Tlaxcala, June 22, 1746, AGN, Inquisición 889, fol. 57; and Berndt León Mariscal, "Discursos," 235-37.
19. García Panes y Abellán, *Diario particular*, 98; see also Ahumada y Vera, *Diario de viaje*, 44-46.
20. Gonzalbo Aizpuru, "El virreinato," 197-98.
21. Drawing on Stollberg-Rilinger, *Rituale*, 41, 97. Schreffler, *The Art of Allegiance*, 101, argues that the ritual itself constituted the bond of vassalage.
22. Castro Santa-Anna, *Diario de sucesos notables*, 5:169, reports on provincials welcoming Amarillas. See also García Panes y Abellán, *Diario particular*, 96-99; Berndt León Mariscal, "Discursos," 239-41; Ramos, *Identity, Ritual, and Power*, 48-50; and Rubio Mañé, *El virreinato*, 1:118.
23. García Panes y Abellán, *Diario particular*, 100-102; Berndt León Mariscal, "Discursos," 242; and Ramos, *Identity, Ritual, and Power*, 46, 56, 59-60. On the decline of Tlaxcala, see Cuadriello, *The Glories*, 82-83.
24. García Panes y Abellán, *Diario particular*, 103-5, shows that Cholula and Huejotzingo were, in fact, cities; confirmed by Gerhard, *A Guide to the Historical Geography*, 116, 142; and Rubio Mañé, *El virreinato*, 1:118. On Veracruz, Tlaxcala, and Puebla, see Cañeque, *The King's Living Image*, 123.
25. On the dates, see Güemes to Ensenada, Mexico City, July 10, 1746, AGI,

México 1506, no. 7; Gerónimo del Campo Marin to Inquisition, Mexico City, October 17, 1710, AGN, Inquisición 740, exp. 4, fol. 70; and Inquisition order, Mexico City, October 1710, AGN, Inquisición 740, exp. 4, fol. 70–70v; identical orders were issued in 1722, 1740, 1746, and 1755. See also García Panes y Abellán, *Diario particular*, 105–6; Ajofrín, *Diario del viaje*, 186; Vera, *Itinerario parroquial*, 125–26; Sigüenza y Góngora, *Teatro de virtudes*; Rubio Mañé, *El virreinato*, 1:117–19, 128, 137, 146–48, 191, 195–96; and Sarrablo Aguareles, *El conde de Fuenclara*, 2:51–52. For a discussion of the battle at Otumba, see Daniel, "Tactical Factors," 189–92. Viceroys Duke of Linares (1717), Marquis of Casafuerte (1734), Duke of la Conquista (1741), and Marquis of las Amarillas (1760) died in New Spain. They were older by the time they took office, because they were primarily appointed for their distinguished careers rather than their high birth.

26. García Panes y Abellán, *Diario particular*, 106–7. Colonials often spelled San Cristóbal Ecatepec as San Xptoval, leaning on Greek letters.

27. Agustín González Ramírez de Zarate, certification, Mexico City, November 7, 1742, AGN, Inquisición 889, fol. 26; Gómez, *Diario curioso*, 5, 104, 122; and Rubio Mañé, *El virreinato*, 1:148, 167, 183, 196.

28. Drawing on Ahumada y Vera, *Diario de viaje*, 54–55, 62. On the entry date, diligence of Inquisition secretary Agustín Antonio Castrillo y Collantes, Mexico City, July 11, 1746, AGN, Inquisición 889, fol. 64; and Güemes to Ensenada, Mexico City, July 10, 1746, AGI, México 1506, no. 7. On hats, see Cañeque, *The King's Living Image*, 141.

29. See, e.g., the viceregal decree seen in the cabildo civil session on September 17, 1749, in Barrio Lorenzot, *Compendio de los libros capitulares*, AHCM, Ayuntamiento, Actas del Cabildo 438A, vol. 5, fol. 57v; Güemes to king, Mexico City, July 22, 1751, AGI, México 1348; and *auto* (decree) by Eugenio de las Peñas Río, Mexico City, June 19, 1924, AGN, Inquisición 810, fol. 473–473v.

30. *Law of the Indies*, book 3, title 3, law 19. Solórzano y Pereyra, *Política Indiana*, book 5, chap. 12, paras. 47–48, gives a brief history of the palio. On Archbishop Juan Antonio Vizarrón y Eguiarreta using the palio in 1731, which Viceroy Casafuerte opposed, see Güemes to king, Mexico City, May 15, 1749, AGI, México 1346, referring to royal cédula, San Lorenzo, October 30, 1748. Escamilla González, "Permanence and Change," 220, shows that the palio covered earlier viceroys walking into churches. For Ramos, *Identity, Ritual, and Power*, 48–50; and Ramos, "Succession and Death," 202, the palio became an exclusive royal prerogative in 1701; see also Jorzick, *Herrschaftssymbolik*, 41; and Rubio Mañé, *El virreinato*, 1:126, 146, 162, 165. According to Berndt León Mariscal, "Discursos," 228, 251, Amarillas also rejected the palio. Rivera, *Diario curioso*, 96, notes that Bishop-Viceroy Juan de Ortega y Montañes visited the Profesa Church on March 14, 1696, and "rejected the palio under which they wanted to receive him." While Cañeque, "Imaging the Spanish Empire," 41, argues that "the palio under which the viceroy processed . . . was a quintessential marker of royalty," Mues Orts, "El

'entierro fingido,'" 31n37, also 21, holds that the use of the palio distinguished king from viceroy.

31. Ramos, *Identity, Ritual, and Power*, 45, 51; Curcio-Nagy, *The Great Festivals*, 82; and Rubio Mañé, *El virreinato*, 1:132–33. Valenzuela Márquez, "La recepción pública," 512n35, argues that Chile's governor refused swearing to uphold privileges in 1709 as part of Bourbon reformism.

32. García Panes y Abellán, *Diario particular*, 110–11; and Ahumada y Vera, *Diario de viaje*, 66–67.

33. García Panes y Abellán, *Diario particular*, 110–11; Ahumada y Vera, *Diario de viaje*, 67–68; and Castro Santa-Anna, *Diario de sucesos notables*, 5:221–22. Cortés's palace is now the Monte de Piedad; see also viceregal decree, Mexico City, October 13, 1746; and cabildo civil session, Mexico City, October 29, 1746, both documents in Barrio Lorenzot, *Compendio de los libros capitulares*, AHCM, Ayuntamiento, Actas del Cabildo 438A, vol. 5, fol. 33. On Amarillas's arch, see Morales Folguera, *Cultura simbólica*, 133; see also Sigüenza y Góngora, *Teatro de virtudes*, 22. Arrom, *La Güera Rodríguez*, 116–17, shows that Emperor Iturbide marched on San Francisco Street past the Profesa Church in 1821.

34. Kodres, "Magic of Presence," 192, argues for heroization in the Baltics. This cannot be fully transferred to New Spain, since Atlas was not a hero per se; Curcio-Nagy, "Sor Juana Inés de la Cruz," 356, 361. See Sigüenza y Góngora, *Teatro de virtudes*, 5, on the notable arch from 1680, produced by the erudite Sigüenza y Góngora, which depicted twelve Aztec rulers; see also Calvo, "El rey y sus Indias," 445; and Mínguez Cornelles, "Jeroglíficos para un Imperio," 65. On Charles III and IV, see Morales Folguera, "El fin de una época," 533–42; and Serrano Martín, "La lealtad triunfante," 26–27. According to Alberro, "Las cuatro partes del mundo," 147–62, the entries also representaron America, Asia, Africa, and Europe. According to Bois, "Le roi, l'armée et la cour," 174, the French king appeared in similar imagery. C. E. Martin, *Governance and Society*, 97–120, denies counter-theater in colonial festivals of Chihuahua. According to Gonzalbo Aizpuru, "El virreinato," 199, Viceroy Linares was asked to attract loyal vassals just as Jupiter attracted Ganymedes, equating the viceroy with Jupiter. On a Spanish version of Neptune in Naples, see Dombrowski, "Eine maritime Renaissance," 211–15. Panofsky, *Studies in Iconology*, 149, analyzes allegories; while Zucker, "Iconography," 372–75, summarizes scholarly criticisms of excessive iconography.

35. Referring to Francisco Aguiar y Seixas, see Gonzalbo Aizpuru, "El virreinato," 197–200.

36. Rodríguez de Arispe, *Representacion panegyrica*, para. 5. The author and the ecclesiastical chapter probably financed the publication of the pamphlet to commemorate its contribution to the viceregal entry, although a record of the arch's images is lost.

37. Rodríguez de Arispe, *Representacion panegyrica*, para. 9; and Rodríguez de

Arispe, *Alegorico symulacro del célebre Príncipe Atlante*, para. 9. On "fear of God," see Garriga, "Crimen corruptionis," 23–24.

38. Rodríguez de Arispe, *Representacion panegyrica*, para. 8. A brief discussion of Güemes's arch is provided by Morales Folguera, *Cultura simbólica*, 132–33; Mínguez [Cornelles], "Héroes clásicos," 66–67, renders a painting of Philip V as Hercules dressed in the hide of the lion of Nemea. See also Ramos and Escamilla González, "Sucesión y renovación," 393.

39. Calderón de la Barca, *Fieras afemina amor*. Calderón de la Barca wrote the play between 1669 and 1674, and the 1749 manuscript shows its lasting popularity. For a general interpretation of the play, see Vélez-Sainz, "Anatomía áulica," 3–11.

40. Rodríguez de Arispe, *Representacion panegyrica*, para. 8.

41. Rodríguez de Arispe, *Representacion panegyrica*, para. 1 is titled "He greets with gentle harmony," and para. 2 claims that "Venus displays her beauty." Note that Hesperia also referred to Italy, the site of some of Güemes's important military exploits.

42. Rodríguez de Arispe, *Alegorico symulacro*, para. 5. See also Güemes to Ensenada, Mexico City, July 10, 1746, AGI, México 1506, no. 7; and Sarrablo Aguareles, *El conde de Fuenclara*, 2:51–52.

43. García Panes y Abellán, *Diario particular*, 110–11; and Ahumada y Vera, *Diario de viaje*, 68–70. See also Gómez, *Diario curioso*, 8.

44. Pérez Samper, "El poder del símbolo," 379–93; see also Pérez Samper, "La llegada de Carlos III," 35–36.

45. Solórzano y Pereyra, *Política Indiana*, book 4, chap. 2, para. 1; and Stollberg-Rilinger, *Rituale*, 34.

46. Jorzick, *Herrschaftssymbolik*, 78–79, 81–83, 154; and Calvo, "El rey y sus Indias," 427–83.

47. Kodres, "Magic of Presence," 192. Cañeque, "Imagining the Spanish Empire," 35, 38, argues that kings experienced "political deification" because the "assimilation of the monarch to God endowed him with a majesty and power as incomprehensible to the human mind as God's majesty and power." The king then transferred some sacredness to viceroys who ruled in their stead; see also Cañeque, *The King's Living Image*, 30–32.

48. Sigüenza y Góngora, *Teatro de virtudes*, 3, 5–6, considers viceroys as princes, for instance, when he opposes triumphal arches celebrating the death of many enemies, because "we have always experienced princes who have governed us in unbloody ways" (2). The author, in using the term "god," refers to mythology; for instance, he states that "this God Conso or Neptun was the son of Isis" (14). On mirrors, see Covarrubias Orozco, *Emblemas morales*, 182, 269; and Mínguez Cornelles, "Imperium reflexum," 325–52.

49. Farnesius Eburonis, *De Simulacro*, 11, in the original "Nam quid est princeps, nisis aut viva dei imago, aut veluti quidam terrenus deus?" The French jurist Farnesius Eburonis (Henri du Four) passed away in Pavia, Italy, in 1613.

50. Pietschmann, *Las reformas borbónicas*, 66; Pietschmann, "La corte virreinal," 483; and Calvo, "El rey y sus Indias," 451. Ramos, *Identity, Ritual, and Power*, 65, sees the viceroy as the king's "simulacrum"; see also Cañeque, "Imagining the Spanish Empire," 30–31.
51. Sariñana y Cuenca, *Llanto del occidente*, fol. 22.
52. Royal cédula to Valero, Tudela, May 22, 1719, AGN, RCO 40, exp. 65, fols. 136–37; *Law of the Indies*, book 3, title 3, law 67; and Escamilla González, "La corte," 374. For the hand kiss, see Gómez, *Diario curioso*, 63.
53. Solórzano y Pereyra, *Política Indiana*, book 5, chap. 12, paras. 3–6, 15, 37, 40. See also *Law of the Indies*, book 3, title 3, laws 12, 36; royal cédula, Madrid, February 2, 1716, in Konetzke, *Colección de documentos*, vol. 3, tome 1, 122–23; and García-Gallo, "La legislación indiana," 99–139. According to Dombrowski, "Eine maritime Renaissance," 195, 201, an early sixteenth-century viceroy in Naples proclaimed himself as "most illustrious prince" and "upholder of justice." According to Martínez Millán, "La articulación," 46, the viceroy of Sicily claimed in 1558 that the viceroys formed "a single body with the king." This throws into relief the difference with eighteenth-century Mexican viceroys. Note that Güemes suspended a civil judge of the audiencia of Guadalajara in 1751, but the Crown reinstated that minister three years later. This remained a rare move, however; see royal cédula signed by Ensenada to Güemes, San Lorenzo, November 19, 1749, Real Academia de la Historia 9-9-4, 1759, fol. 528; and royal order signed by José de Goyeneche, Buen Retiro, December 23, 1754, AGI, Gobierno—Audiencia de Guadalajara (hereinafter AGI, Guadalajara) 89.
54. Marquis of Valero to king, Mexico City, November 29, 1720, AGI, México 480, referring to an *alcalde ordinario*.
55. Seijas y Lobera, *Gobierno militar*, 216; see also *Law of the Indies*, book 3, title 3, law 51; Rivero Rodríguez, *La edad de oro*, 245–46; and Rosenmüller, *Corruption and Justice*, 134–37. See Sáez-Arance, "La Corte de los Habsburgos," 7–8; and Asch, "Introduction: Court and Household," 18–25, on centralizing patronage networks at the royal court.
56. Morales Folguera, *Cultura simbólica*, 138–39.
57. García Panes y Abellán, *Diario particular*, 68, 70.
58. Rivero Rodríguez, *La edad de oro*, 237; and Büschges, "Del criado al valido," 163–64. Gil Pujol, "Una cultura cortesana," 235, emphasizes restrictions on viceroys. Only the viceroyalty of Navarre continued into the eighteenth century.
59. *Law of the Indies*, book 3, title 3, law 19. See Rubio Mañé, *El virreinato*, 1:134, 138–39, 141, 146, 164, referring to the Duke of Escalona's entry; and see Ramos, *Identity, Ritual, and Power*, xxx–xxxi, 59–64, on expensive entries, especially that of the Count of Montezuma, whose fifty-six days' stay in Puebla cost 18,000 pesos.
60. Cabildo session, May 25, 1746; AHCM, Ayuntamiento, Cédulas y Reales Órdenes 2977, exp. 76, fols. 3–4; see also cabildo civil session, Mexico City,

August 7, 1755, in Barrio Lorenzot, *Compendio de los libros capitulares*, AHCM, Ayuntamiento, Actas del Cabildo 438A, vol. 5, fol. 85. Mues Orts, "El 'entierro fingido,'" 23, claims that Archbishop-Viceroy Vizarrón's modest entry merely included four days of bullfights.

61. Castro Santa-Anna, *Diario de sucesos notables*, 5:175, 181–83; and Rubio Mañé, *El virreinato*, 1:183.

62. *Real acuerdo* (meeting of viceroy with civil judges and prosecutor) to king, March 9, 1756, AGI, México 544; and *parecer* (legal opinion) of the fiscal (prosecutor) of the Council of the Indies, Madrid, August 20, 1757, AGI, México 544.

63. Juan de Carvajal Cardona, certification, n.d., Puebla, AGI, México 544, folder Año de 1755 Testimonios; and notification, Tlaxcala, May 19, 1747, AGI, México 544. Puebla claimed only paying for a letter to the viceroy, although Berndt León Mariscal, "Discursos," 229, notes an eighteenth-century royal order forbidding Puebla to spend more than 3,000 pesos on entries.

64. *Real acuerdo* to king, March 9, 1756, AGI, México 544; and royal order, Madrid, December 11, 1760, AHCM, Ayuntamiento, Historia, Juras y Funerales de Reyes 2282, fols. 141v–142.

65. Based on Gonzalbo Aizpuru, "El virreinato," 205–6; Larkin, *The Very Nature of God*, 13–14; and Melvin, *Building Colonial Cities*, 8.

66. García Panes y Abellán, *Diario particular*, 113–15; Gómez, *Diario curioso*, 5, 104; Pietschmann, "Diego García Panes," 218–21, referring to the Marquis of Croix; and Morales Folguera, *Cultura simbólica*, 146–50.

67. Robles, *Diario de sucesos notables*, 232; Gómez, *Diario curioso*, 5, 114; López Álvarez, *Poder, lujo y conflicto*, 87–93, 126; and Escamilla González, "La corte," 379. According to Sariñana y Cuenca, *Llanto del occidente*, fol. 26v, ecclesiastical canons owned four-in-hands. See also Recio Mir, "Alamedas, paseos y carruajes," 528–34. Curcio-Nagy, *The Great Festivals*, 80, argues that viceregal entries on horseback ended after 1722, while for García Panes y Abellán, *Diario particular*, 116–17, 118–21, Matías de Gálvez was the last to ride on horseback, in 1783.

68. Gómez, *Diario curioso*, 10; and Berndt León Mariscal, "Between Monarchic and Local Identity," 55–72. On accessions in Quito, see Büschges, "Urban Public Festivals," 114–31.

Chapter 3

1. Castrillo y Collantes, certification, Mexico City, November 13, 1755, AGN, Inquisición 889, fol. 113.

2. Based on Stollberg-Rilinger, *Maria Theresia*, 318–20. According to Lisón Tolosano, "Referencia y autoreferencia," even courtiers were temporarily at

variance. The first minister Olivares (served 1621–1643), for instance, interrupted the "strict hierarchical vocabulary" of a public victory procession in 1638 when he immersed himself in the delighted crowd and drew his hat, a gesture that he did not even perform for the king.

3. Pérez Samper, "La mesa real," 206, also 208, argues that the "life of the court, from the king to the last of the servants, was carefully and meticulously governed by court etiquette, which in the case of the Habsburgs was the most severe, rigorous, and ceremonious in the world," while the Bourbon kings began relaxing protocol. Escamilla González, "La corte," 374, maintains that a "rigorous 'etiquette' or court protocol governed the life of this court," which is true for many aspects. Escamilla González, "Permanence and Change," 226–30, provides fascinating nuance; see also Stollberg-Rilinger, *Maria Theresia*, 51–53.

4. Winterling, "Der Fürstenhof," 33–35; Gómez Urdáñez, *Fernando VI*, 71, 74–75; and Stollberg-Rilinger, *Maria Theresia*, 369.

5. Drawing on Stollberg-Rilinger, "Comunicación simbólica," 45–46; and Stollberg-Rilinger, *Rituale*, 9–11, 36, 47. Following her, I use the terms "ceremonies," "public spectacles," and "rites" as synonymous with rituals. Gonzalbo Aizpuru, "Las fiestas del pasado," 180, notes that fiestas separated the exceptional from the mundane. Herzog, *Upholding Justice*, 8, holds convincingly that "routine activities" often mattered more than lavish rituals.

6. Geertz, *The Interpretation of Cultures*; Ramos, *Identity, Ritual, and Power*, xx, xviii–xix, xxvi–xxvii; and Ramos, "Succession and Death," 187–88, 214. Curcio-Nagy, *The Great Festivals*, 3–9, argues for entertainment and "social control" by elites; see also Büschges, "Ceremonial Demarcations," 106; and Kodres, "Magic of Presence," 202.

7. *Siete partidas*, book 2, title 9, law 27; see Maqueda Abreu, "La corte española del Barroco," 131.

8. Gómez Urdáñez, *Fernando VI*, 45–46, 65, 74–75, 131, 138.

9. Gómez Urdáñez, *Fernando VI*, 71, 74–75.

10. The viceregal court appears in Sariñana y Cuenca, *Llanto del occidente*, fol. 16; see also Rubial García, "Las virreinas novohispanas," 3–44; Büschges, "La corte virreinal," 131–40; Premo, "Half Real," 14–15; Escamilla González, "La corte," 387; Pietschmann, *Las reformas borbónicas*, 67; Pietschmann, "La corte virreinal;" and Semboloni Capitani, *La construcción de la autoridad virreinal*. Rubio Mañé's classic *El virreinato*, 1:215–84, examines court gossip and socializing; on viceregal patronage, see Latasa Vassallo, "La casa del obispo-virrey Palafox," 210–228; and Rosenmüller, *Patrons, Partisans, and Palace Intrigues*, 33–35.

11. See, for example, Castro Santa-Anna, *Diario de sucesos notables*, 5:199.

12. *Bando* (public notice) of Antonio Bonilla, Mexico City, December 2, 1789, ACR 344; there is little evidence how these petitions to the viceroys actually

worked. See also Castrillo y Collantes, certification, Mexico City, December 24, 1753, AGN, Inquisición 889, fols. 96–97.

13. Castro Santa-Anna, *Diario de sucesos notables*, 4:53.
14. Büschges, "Ceremonial Demarcations," 103.
15. Rosenmüller, *Corruption and Justice*, 199.
16. Sariñana y Cuenca, *Llanto del occidente*, fol. 19; see also Curiel, "Mourning Rites," 37–38.
17. All quotations in this paragraph are in Sariñana y Cuenca, *Llanto del occidente*, fols. 18–19.
18. King to Linares, Madrid, September 27, 1713, AGN, RCO 36, exp. 61; Linares to king, Mexico City, December 15, 1712, AGI, México 484; royal officials to king, Mexico City, November 15, 1712, AGI, México 484; and parecer of the prosecutor of the Council of the Indies, Madrid, June 15, 1713, AGI, México 484. On Naples, see Büschges, "Ceremonial Demarcations," 102.
19. González Ramírez de Zarate, certification, Mexico City, December 24, 1743, AGN, Inquisición 889, fols. 43v–44.
20. Castrillo y Collantes, certification, Mexico City, December 24, 1746, AGN, Inquisición 889, fol. 74v. According to Jorzick, *Herrschaftssymbolik*, 41, 45–46, Charles V drew on the Burgundian ritual that built on Roman precursors.
21. González Ramírez de Zarate, certification, Mexico City, December 24, 1743, AGN, Inquisición 889, fols. 43v–44.
22. Castrillo y Collantes, certification, Mexico City, July 11, 1746, AGN, Inquisición 889, fol. 64–64v; see also certification of Castrillo y Collantes, Mexico City, July 12, 1747, AGN, Inquisición 889, fol. 70. Rubio Mañé, "Llegada a México," 1–14, published the certifications on Güemes's arrival.
23. Castrillo y Collantes, certification, Mexico City, July 11, 1746, AGN, Inquisición 889, fol. 65–65v.
24. Castrillo y Collantes, certification, Mexico City, July 12, 1747, AGN, Inquisición 889, fol. 70–70v. This could have been a tradition, since Fuenclara had also invited the inquisitors to the Coliseum; see González Ramírez de Zarate, certification, Mexico City, November 7, 1742, AGN, Inquisición 889, fol. 26v.
25. Castrillo y Collantes, certification, Mexico City, July 12, 1747, AGN, Inquisición 889, fol. 70v.
26. Castrillo y Collantes, certification, Mexico City, July 12, 1747, AGN, Inquisición 889, fol. 70–70v.
27. See Rawlings, *The Spanish Inquisition*, 135–37, on the decline of the Holy Office.
28. González Ramírez de Zarate, certification, Mexico City, November 7, 1742, AGN, Inquisición 889, fol. 26v. Sariñana y Cuenca, *Llanto del occidente*, fols. 23–24, noted in 1660 that taking four to six steps away from the chair was "customary on other occasions."
29. González Ramírez de Zarate, certification, Mexico City, December 24,

1743, AGN, Inquisición 889, fol. 43; Castrillo y Collantes, certification, Mexico City, December 24, 1746, AGN, Inquisición 889, fols. 74–75; Castrillo y Collantes, certification, Mexico City, December 23, 1747, AGN, Inquisición 889, fol. 79v–80; and Castrillo y Collantes, certification, Mexico City, December 24, 1753, AGN, Inquisición 889, fols. 96–97; while also drawing on González Ramírez de Zarate, certification, Mexico City, December 22, 1742, AGN, Inquisición 889, fols. 32–33; González Ramírez de Zarate, certification, December 24, 1742, AGN, Inquisición 889, fols. 34–35; González Ramírez de Zarate, certification, Mexico City, December 22, 1743, AGN, Inquisición 889, fol. 42; González Ramírez de Zarate, certification, Mexico City, December 24, 1744, AGN, Inquisición 889, fols. 47–48; Castrillo y Collantes, certification, Mexico City, December 24, 1745, AGN, Inquisición 889, fols. 49–50; Castrillo y Collantes, certification, Mexico City, December 24, 1749, AGN, Inquisición 889, fol. 82–82v; Castrillo y Collantes, certification, Mexico City, December 24, 1750, AGN, Inquisición 889, fols. 84–85; José de Oveso Rávago, certification, Mexico City, December 24, 1751, AGN, Inquisición 889, fols. 86–87; and Castrillo y Collantes, certification, Mexico City, December 23, 1752, AGN, Inquisición 889, fols. 92–93.

30. Draft of Pedro Navarro de Isla to Ensenada (¿), n.d., AGN, Inquisición 1328, exp. 6, fol. 248; see also Ensenada to Pedro Navarro de Isla, Aranjuez, May 25, 1744, AGN, Inquisición 1328, fols. 238–239v; parecer of the prosecutor, Madrid, May 16, 1749, AGI, Escribanía 245A, folder Papeles pertenecientes a la Residencia de . . . Fuenclara, fols. 25–27 (letters of elided Spanish words are rendered in italics); and testimony of witnesses, Mexico City, October 14–17, 1748, AGI, Escribanía 245A, folder 7, fols. 14–65. The legal foundation is in *Law of the Indies*, book 7, title 2, laws 1–3.

31. Testimony by Pablo Antonio Pérez, guardian of Franciscan friary, Mexico City, February 18, 1757, AGI, Escribanía 246B, fol. 528; see also testimony of criminal judge Ambrosio Eugenio Santaella y Melgarejo, Mexico City, January 18, 1757, AGI, Escribanía 246B, fol. 55v; and José de Cárdenas, AGI, Escribanía 246B, fols. 483v–484v. On elite homes, see Güemes's bando, Mexico City, April 6, 1747, AGN, Bandos 4, exp. 1.

32. Consulta of the Council of the Indies, Madrid, May 29, 1750, AGI, México 385.

33. Castro Santa-Anna, *Diario de sucesos notables*, 4:66.

34. Pérez Samper, "La mesa real," 206–9; and López-Cordón Cortezo, "Servicios y favores," 223–24.

35. Pérez Samper, "La mesa real," 211–14.

36. Morales Martínez, "Antes de la fiesta," 471–72.

37. Rubio Mañé, *El virreinato*, 1:162. Rubial García, "Las virreinas novohispanas," 13–14, argues that the "vicereine was absent at the reception ceremonies . . . and the public festivals where the viceroy acted as a figure of power"; see also Pietschmann, "La corte virreinal," 496.

38. Castro Santa-Anna, *Diario de sucesos notables*, 4:250.
39. Castro Santa-Anna, *Diario de sucesos notables*, 5:36, 136, 147; see also Escamilla González, "Permanence and Change," 222.
40. Castro Santa-Anna, *Diario de sucesos notables*, 4:239.
41. Castro Santa-Ana, *Diario de sucesos notables*, 5:171; see also Rubial García, "Las virreinas novohispanas," 29. Montes González, "La 'jaula,'" 244, points to the long clerical opposition to the vicereine's gallery.
42. Castro Santa-Anna, *Diario de sucesos notables*, 4:174; royal order, Buen Retiro, December 4, 1748, ACR 476; Güemes to Ensenada, Mexico City, December 13, 1750, ACR 401; Güemes to Ensenada, San Agustín, June 25, 1752, ACR 357; and Escamilla González, "La corte," 383. On the daughters, see Figueroa y Melgar, *Estudio histórico*, 73–74.
43. Güemes to Ensenada, Mexico City, September 19, 1753, AGI, México 1506, no. 134; and Güemes to Ensenada, Mexico City, July 1, 1754, AGI, México 1506, no. 147. See also Rosenmüller, *Corruption and Justice*, 185.
44. Castro Santa-Anna, *Diario de sucesos notables*, 5:7–8; see also Escamilla González, "La corte," 387.
45. Güemes to king, July 10, 1751, ACR 388.
46. Felix de Sandoval to Luis de Bárcena, Mexico City, March 22, 1755, AGN, Inquisición 889, fols. 103–103v; see also Descalzo Lorenzo, "El arte de vestir," 197–200.
47. Güemes to Jesuit Provincial Juan Antonio Baltasar, San Ángel, August 19, 1752, ACR 344; see also Baltasar to Güemes, Mexico City, August 16, 1752, ACR 344; and *Law of the Indies*, book 2, title 16, laws 48–50.
48. Castro Santa-Anna, *Diario de sucesos notables*, 4:9, also 39, noting the visit of Ignacio Cevallos and the Count of San Bartolomé de Xala.
49. *Papeleta de Mexico de 30 de Abril 1756*, n.p., ACR 360. According to Castro Santa-Anna, *Diario de sucesos notables*, 5:197, the archbishop often spent several days in his country house in Tacubaya. See also Escamilla González and Moreno Gamboa, "El Duque de Linares," 159–61; and Rubial García, "Las virreinas novohispanas," 19–20. On boat rides, see Rosenmüller, *Patrons, Partisans, and Palace Intrigues*, 46.
50. On lacking deference, see Escamilla González, "Permanence and Change," 229; and Rubio Mañé, *El virreinato*, 2:30–31.
51. Güemes to king, Mexico City, July 8, 1751, AGI, México 1348.
52. *Law of the Indies*, book 3, title 15, law 6.
53. Argument by Cañeque, *The King's Living Image*, 141–42.
54. Castro Santa-Anna, *Diario de sucesos notables*, 4:53.
55. *Law of the Indies*, book 3, title 15, laws 1, 3, 6–7, 25–27, 30, 33. According to king to audiencia, San Lorenzo, July 23, 1735, BNM, FR, manuscritos 437, exp. 198, fols. 433–34, both viceroy and archbishop sat on a throne with canopy in the basilica of Guadalupe, while according to Büschges, "Ceremonial Demarcations,"

109–10, the Crown rejected that right for the archbishop of Valencia (Spain) in 1621. See also Montes González, "La 'jaula,'" 244.
56. Stollberg-Rilinger, *Rituale*, 209.
57. Cabildo session on January 8 and 15, 1749, in Barrio Lorenzot, *Compendio de los libros capitulares*, AHCM, Ayuntamiento, Actas del Cabildo 438, vol. 5, fol. 53.
58. Consulado, *Instruzion relativa a todos los puntos y negozios del Consulado, Para Govierno de los Señores Diputados*, Mexico City, June 8, 1755, AGN (hereinafter *Instruzion relativa*), Archivo Histórico de Hacienda (hereinafter AHH) 635, exp. 8, fol. 38–38v.
59. Viceregal decree, n.d., read in cabildo session on July 14, 1750, AHCM, Ayuntamiento, Actas del Cabildo 75A, fol. 25; and Ramos, *Identity, Ritual, and Power*, vi–vii. See also Stollberg-Rilinger, *Rituale*, 209–10.
60. Autos of Fermín Echeverz González, Guadalajara, June 2, 1747, AGI, Guadalajara 106, fols. 17–18, 50. According to Francisco Porres Baranda, Memoria de las personas, n.d. (Guadalajara, 1747), Archivo Municipal de Guadalajara, Actas del Cabildo, AC6/1747, antiguo paquete (old box classification) 1, leg. 74, fols. 1–2, the municipal council instructed seventy-nine people to attend Ferdinand's accession, but some absented nonetheless; see also Büschges, "Ceremonial Demarcations," 111–12.
61. Viceregal decree, n.d., read in cabildo session on July 14, 1750, AHCM, Ayuntamiento, Actas del Cabildo 75A, fol. 25; see also viceregal decree, Mexico City, July 13, 1750, AHCM, Ayuntamiento, Actas del Cabildo 75A, fol. 24v. According to extraordinary cabildo session, Mexico City, February 11, 1760, AHCM, Ayuntamiento, Actas del Cabildo 81A, fol. 8–8v, the municipal council threatened any minister with a fine of four pesos for failing to attend King Charles III's accession.
62. Viceregal decree, January 18, 1747, in Barrio Lorenzot, *Compendio de los libros capitulares*, AHCM, Ayuntamiento, Actas del Cabildo 438, fol. 37; and cabildo sessions, Mexico City, May 13 and August 9, 1748, AHCM, Ayuntamiento, Actas del Cabildo 438A, fols. 48v–50. See also notoriety, Mexico City, October 18, 1748, AHCM, Ayuntamiento, Actas del Cabildo 73A, fol. 45.
63. Castro Santa-Anna, *Diario de sucesos notables*, 4:219.
64. Quotation in cabildo session, Mexico City, September 6, 1754, AHCM, Ayuntamiento, Actas del Cabildo 79A, fol. 21. See also vote of José Francisco de Cuevas y Aguirre, cabildo session, Mexico City, September 30, 1754, AHCM, Ayuntamiento, Actas del Cabildo 79A, fol. 24–24v; viceregal decree, Mexico City, September 2, 1754, AHCM, Ayuntamiento, Actas del Cabildo 79A, fol. 22; Güemes to cabildo, Mexico City, February 25 and March 16, 1754; cabildo sessions, Mexico City, March 1, March 5, and March 18, 1754, the five preceding documents AHCM, Ayuntamiento, Actas del Cabildo 79A, fols. 10–12; and Castro Santa-Anna, *Diario de sucesos notables*, 5:32.
65. Cañeque, *The King's Living Image*, 119, on authoritarian seventeenth-century viceroys.

66. Gómez, *Diario curioso*, 63, also 5, 10, 19, 41, 58.
67. Rosenmüller, *Corruption and Justice*, 177–78, 229.
68. Güemes to Ensenada, Mexico City, May 24, 1752, AGI, México 1349.
69. Garzarón's *reconocimiento* (inspection), Mexico City, April 13, 1717, AGI, Escribanía 278A, folder 8, fols. 150–51; and royal cédula to Linares, Madrid, November 28, 1714, AGN, RCO 36, exp. 150, fols. 416–17; based on *Law of the Indies*, book 2, title 15, laws 20–21, also book 2, title 16, law 6. Güemes to Ensenada, Mexico City, May 24, 1752, AGI, México 1349; see also Sarrablo Aguareles, *El conde de Fuenclara*, 2:189–91. On the real acuerdo, royal cédula, Madrid, October 8, 1689, in Konetzke, *Colección de documentos*, vol. 2, tome 2, 815.
70. Oath of José Díaz de Celis as interim royal official before the *semanero*, Mexico City, December 17, 1750, AGI, Escribanía 246A, folder 1, fol. 210v; real acuerdo's order, Mexico City, February 11, 1724, AGI, México 492, fols. 41–43; and Herzog, *Upholding Justice*, 46, on Quito.
71. *Law of the Indies*, book 8, title 1, law 4.
72. Parecer of the prosecutor, Madrid, April 8, 1755; consulta of the Council of the Indies, Madrid, August 29, 1755; and royal decree, n.d., the three preceding documents in AGI, México 385; see also Bertrand, *Grandeur et misères*, 121.
73. "Constituciones de el arzobispado," chap. 18, 21–24; on the *fiestas de precepto* (accepted holidays), see also Perujo and Pérez Angulo, *Diccionario de ciencias eclesiásticas*, 550–51; and Gonzalbo Aizpuru, "Las fiestas novohispanas," 44–45.
74. Viceregal decree, Mexico City, July 13, 1750, AHCM, Ayuntamiento, Actas del Cabildo 75A, fol. 24v; and Castro Santa-Anna, *Diario de sucesos notables*, 4:51, referring to December 4, 1754. According to *Law of the Indies*, book 3, title 15, law 6, the audiencia accompanied the viceroy to mass on "the first days of the three Easter days and those of Corpus Christi, the Assumption of Our Lady, and Praying to the Church, and on other holiday occasions." See also Gonzalbo Aizpuru, "Las fiestas del pasado," 180; and Gonzalbo Aizpuru, "El virreinato," 192–93. According to Herzog, *Upholding Justice*, 44, the audiencia of Quito observed similar holidays.
75. Audiencia to king, Guadalajara, July 11, 1748; see also parecer of the civil prosecutor, Guadalajara, April 6, 1748; and king to audiencia of Guadalajara, Aranjuez, June 23, 1747, the three preceding documents in AGI, Guadalajara 106. According to *Law of the Indies*, book 2, title 15, law 18; and royal cédula, Madrid, October 8, 1689, in Konetzke, *Colección de documentos*, vol. 2, tome 2, 815, the late seventeenth-century audiencia of Lima (Peru) took many additional "court holidays that the viceregal piousness introduced," when the Crown reissued orders to follow the schedule of the Council of the Indies.
76. Manuel de la Sierra, certification, Guadalajara, April 25, 1748, AGI, Guadalajara 106, including the quotations in this paragraph. Ramos, "Celebrating the Patriarch(s)," 74–76, notes that Saint Joseph protected Puebla from lightning.

According to the "Constituciones de el arzobispado," 23, the first Mexican provincial council claimed the same; see also Voekel, *Alone before God*, 54.

77. On the staff of authority, see González Ramírez de Zarate, certification, Mexico City, December 24, 1743, AGN, Inquisición 889, fols. 43v–44.

Chapter 4

1. Taylor, *Magistrates of the Sacred*, 126–30; Rubial García, "Las órdenes mendicantes," 215–37; Armas Medina, "Evolución histórica," 101–29; *Canons and Decrees of . . . Trent*, session 25, chaps. 6, 11; *Law of the Indies*, book 1, title 15, laws 1, 3, 6; and Güemes to king, n.d. (1749), ACR 395.
2. The viceregal decree, Mexico City, November 10, 1750, AGI, México 2712, ordered secularizing San Sebastián in Mexico City, Santa Cruz, Santa Ana Tianguistenco, San Bartolomé Capulhuac, and Octupan. Güemes to king, draft, n.d. (1749), ACR 395; Carlos de Figueroa, certification, n.d., Latin American Library at Tulane University, New Orleans, Viceregal and Ecclesiastical Manuscript Collection (hereinafter VEMC) 8, exp. 52, fol. 222; and Manuel Caravantes to Arriola, Actopan, November 17, 1750, AGI, México 2712. Augustín Zapata was the interim priest, his vicar was Anastasio de Santa María, and the vicar in the neighboring pueblo Xalatlaco, Manuel Verdugo, served as ecclesiastical judge. Pride in their priory could be one reason for the response; see Melvin, *Building Colonial Cities*, 4. Taylor, ". . . de corazón pequeño y ánimo apocado," 288, notes the presence of outsiders in San Bartolomé Capulhuac, and while the pueblo spoke Nahuatl, Otomí, and Spanish, there was no linguistic conflict at that time; see also Vera, *Itinerario parroquial*, 12.
3. Carlos de Figueroa, certification, n.d., VEMC 8, exp. 52, fol. 222.
4. According to *media anata* (a tax of half an annual salary) payment, August 12, 1748, AGN, AHH 1058, exp. 1, Juan José Colina served as alcalde mayor of Metepec from January 1, 1748, to December 9, 1750. Valle Menéndez, *Juan Francisco de Güemes*, 450, argues that Colina is a last name from Cantabria. According to Amarillas to Arriaga, Mexico City, March 13, 1756, AGI, México 516, Güemes issued a decree on August 11, 1755, to conjoin Santiago Tianguistenco with the *alcaldía mayor* (district of an alcalde mayor) of Tenango del Valle, while Gerhard, *A Guide to the Historical Geography*, 272, points out that San Bartolomé Capulhuac switched from Metepec to Tenango del Valle in 1762. Both pueblos belonged to the alcaldía mayor of Metepec before these changes.
5. Testimony of José Meninde, Mexico City, November 26, 1750, VEMC 8, exp. 52, fol. 177–177v.
6. Inventory of alcalde mayor Juan José Colina, and the ecclesiastical judge Manuel Verdugo, San Bartolomé Capulhuac, November 14, 1750, AGI, México 2712, fol. 41–41v.

7. Information of Antonio González, Juan Marqués, and Antonio Quezada, Santiago Tianguistenco, December 5, 1750, VEMC 8, exp. 52, fols. 184–187v.
8. Defense of Francisco Velarde, Mexico City, n.d. (probably December 7, 1750), VEMC 8, exp. 52, fols. 196–214v.
9. Viceregal decree, Mexico City, November 18, 1750, AGI, México 2712, fols. 50–51; and precept of Francisco Arriola, provincial of Santísimo Nombre de Jesús, Mexico City, November 21, 1750, VEMC 8, exp. 52, fol. 171–171v. The prior's name was Ignacio Fernández de Vela.
10. Confession of Fernández de Vela, Mexico City, November 26, 1750, VEMC 8, exp. 52, fol. 174.
11. Confession of Francisco Velarde on behalf of Fernández de Vela, Mexico City, n.d., VEMC 8, exp. 52, fols. 202–203v.
12. Confession of Fernández de Vela, Mexico City, November 26, 1750, VEMC 8, exp. 52, fols. 174v–175v; the original reads "illud quod differetur non aufertur."
13. The quotations in this paragraph are from confession of Fernández de Vela, Mexico City, November 26, 1750, VEMC 8, exp. 52, fol. 175–175v.
14. Sentence of Provincial Francisco Arriola, January 3, 1751, VEMC 8, exp. 52, fols. 225–26. On guilt, see Lárraga, *Promptuario de la theologia moral*, 343; and Avilés, *Regla de S. Agustín*, 282–83.
15. Güemes's *ruego y encargo* (request), Mexico City, February 17, 1751; and Arriola to Güemes, Mexico City, January 3, 1751, both in VEMC 45, exp 39.
16. Castro Santa-Anna, *Diario de sucesos notables*, 5:8.
17. See, e.g., Manuel Hidalgo, *promotor fiscal* (chief lawyer) of the diocese of Oaxaca, to king, Antequera (now the city of Oaxaca), September 11, 1704, AGI, México 881; see also royal cédula, Madrid, November 24, 1705, AGN, RCO 32, exp. 202, fols. 463–465r; and Güemes's report to king, n.d. (probably July 9, 1753), AGI, México 2712. See also Belanger, "Secularization and the Laity," 79; Melvin, *Building Colonial Cities*, 26; Pérez Puente, "La creación de las cátedras públicas," 65; Rosenmüller, *Patrons, Partisans, and Palace Intrigues*, 137–39; Álvarez de Toledo, *Politics and Reform*, 74; Piho, *La secularización de las parroquias*, 20, 140–41; Escamilla González, *José Patricio Fernández de Uribe*, 14; Luna Moreno, "Alternativa en el siglo XVIII," 360; Rubial García, "Las órdenes mendicantes," 227; Taylor, *Magistrates of the Sacred*, 85; and Cortés Peña, *La política religiosa de Carlos III*.
18. Anonymous author, *Primera parte. El Duende de Mexico da la bienvenida al Excelentísimo Señor Virrey*, n.d. (1755), INAH, CA, microfilm roll 56, fol. 83. Campillo y Cosío, *Nuevo sistema*, 43–47.
19. *Representaciones hechas* by the archbishops of Mexico and Lima to Carvajal, San Lorenzo, November 30, 1748, Archivo Histórico del Arzobispado de México (Mexico City) (hereinafter AHAM), box 104 CL, book 3; and Carvajal to archbishop designate of Mexico, Buen Retiro, January 2, 1749, AHAM, box 104 CL, book 3. Kuethe and Andrien, *The Spanish Atlantic World*, 178, emphasize the importance of the November junta.

20. Consulta, Madrid, March 28, 1749, AGI, México 2712. On the meeting, see Aguirre, "La secularización de doctrinas," 500–505; Andrien, "The Coming of Enlightened Reform," 184; and Sánchez Bella, *Iglesia y Estado*, 121; on the junta (meeting) compositions, see Fayard, *Les membres du Conseil de Castille*, 132, 165, 227, 234; Burkholder, *Biographical Dictionary of Councilors of the Indies*, 7, 41–42, 68–69, 103; Castellano, *Gobierno y poder*, 135–41; Gómez Urdáñez, "Carvajal y Ensenada," 65–92; and Fonck, "Les confesseurs jésuites," 94, 108. Brading, *Church and State*, 63, sees Carvajal as a driving force in secularization; while Alcaraz Gómez, *Jesuitas y reformismo*, 372–78, views the royal confessor, Francisco Rávago y Noriega (1747–1755), as the principal negotiator with Rome. According to Barrientos Grandón, *Guía prosopográfica*, 102–3, the Marquis of la Regalía, Antonio José Álvarez de Abreu, councilor of the Indies, championed Rávago's tough course against the regulars; see also Luque Taaván, "Antonio José Álvarez de Abreu."
21. Royal cédula, Buen Retiro, October 4, 1749, AGN, RCO 69, exp. 104; royal cédula to archbishops of Lima, Mexico City, and Santa Fe, Buen Retiro, October 4, 1749, AGI, México 2712; Cardinal Portocarrero to Rávago, Rome, August 9, 1751, AGI, México 2712; and papal bull, November 6, 1751, AGI, México 2712.
22. Royal cédula, Buen Retiro, February 1, 1753, AGN, RCO 73, exp. 13, fols. 35–38v; ruegos y encargos of Güemes to the bishops of Puebla (Tlaxcala), Oaxaca (Antequera), and Michoacán (Valladolid), Mexico City, February 18, 1754; and Güemes to Ensenada, Mexico City, October 12, 1754, the four preceding documents in AGI, México 2713. See also Sánchez Bella, *Iglesia y Estado*, 135; and Castellano, *Gobierno y poder*, 151–53.
23. Royal cédula, Buen Retiro, October 4, 1749, AGN, RCO 69, exp. 104.
24. Güemes to Ensenada, Mexico City, October 31, 1747, ACR 404.
25. Güemes to José Banfi y Parrilla, Mexico City, May 12, 1751, ACR 404. Kuethe and Andrien, *The Spanish Atlantic World*, 179–93, analyze the Peruvian reactions.
26. *Memoria de las veinte y dos misiones cedidas por la compañía de Jesús a la mitra de Durango a fin del año de 1753*, attached to Juan Antonio Baltasar to Güemes, Mexico City, March 7, 1750, AGN, Historia 20, exp. 8, fols. 63–65v; and Güemes to Ensenada, Mexico City, December 6, 1751, AGI, México 1851. In detail, Deeds, *Defiance and Deference*, 132–34, 154–77; see also Borges Morán, *Religiosos*, 231–36.
27. Royal cédula, Buen Retiro, October 4, 1749, AGN, RCO 69, exp. 103; royal cédula, signed by Ensenada to Güemes, Madrid, October 6, 1752, AGN, RCO 72, exp. 135, fols. 383–84; and royal cédula, Buen Retiro, February 1, 1753, AGN, RCO 73, exp. 13, fols. 35–38v. The governor's exchange with the Guatemalan archbishop during May 12–14, 1755, VEMC 28, exp. 3, fols. 1–9; and Güemes to Amarillas, Mexico City, October 8, 1755, ACR 395.
28. The two doctrinas in the capital were San Sebastián Atzacoalco (Arrabal), which owned estates, according to Francisco Arriola to Güemes, Mexico City,

November 19, 1750, AGI, México 2712; and Santa Cruz Cuauhcotzinco (Soledad). See also Pérez Puente, "La creación de las cátedras públicas," 57n38.

29. Auto of Miguel de Carmona y Godoy, n.p., January 17, 1753, AGI, México 2712; and Güemes's instructions to Gorospe Padilla, Mexico City, November 28, 1754, in Torre Villar, *Instrucciones*, 853–61. This includes Santiago Chimaltitlan in Bolaños in the diocese of Guadalajara, which was temporarily under viceregal purview. Rosenmüller, "La 'langosta que arruina,'" 48–50, lists the secularized doctrinas of that period.

30. Güemes to José Banfi y Parrilla, Mexico, May 12, 1751, ACR 404. On the appointment process, see Diego Ortiz de Parada to king, n.p., Fall 1752, AGI, México 2712; and Güemes's instructions to Amarillas, Mexico City, October 8, Torre Villar, *Instrucciones*, 830. See also archbishop to viceroy, Mexico City, December 11, 1751, AGI, México 2712; Güemes's reply, Mexico City, December 12, 1751, AGI, México 2712; and Güemes to bishop of Michoacán, Mexico City, July 17, 1753, VEMC 12, exp. 4, fols. 7–10. On close collaboration, see Aguirre, "La secularización de doctrinas," 499.

31. Quotation in Manuel José Rubio y Salinas to Ensenada, Mexico City, February 10, 1752, AGI, México 2712. On the Mexican archbishop's appointment, see king to pope, Buen Retiro, December 21, 1747; and royal decree attached to consulta of the *cámara* of the Indies (patronage committee), July 5, 1747, the last two documents in AGI, México 439. On the bishop of Puebla, see Salazar Andreu, "Domingo Pantaleón Álvarez de Abreu," 253.

32. Martín Elizacoechea to king, Valladolid, October 21, 1751, AGI, México 2712. See also, for instance, ruego y encargo to bishop, Mexico City, October 29, 1753, ACR 395. On Michoacán and Bishop Elizacoechea (served 1745–1756), see García del Ser and Imízcoz, "El alto clero vasco," 135, 154–56; Mazín Gómez, *El cabildo catedral*, 306; and Brading, *Church and State*, 72. The bishop of Oaxaca in the 1720s was Ángel de Maldonado; see royal cédula, Madrid, November 24, 1705, AGN, RCO 32, exp. 202, fols. 463–465r; Güemes's report to king, n.d. (probably July 9, 1753), AGI, México 2712; and Buenaventura Blanco y Elguero to king, Antequera, April 19, 1756, ACR 395. The *procurador general* (legal representative) of the Dominican province claimed in November 1753 that 230 regulars had been displaced; n.d., AGI, México 2712; and Rosenmüller, *Patrons, Partisans, and Palace Intrigues*, 137–39. Jaramillo Magaña, *Hacia una iglesia*, 14–17, argues that parts of the secular church fought state restrictions in other respects.

33. According to Güemes to Ensenada, Mexico City, July 8, 1753, AGI, México 2712, the Guadalajaran bishop advanced secularization, although Taylor, "Los pueblos indígenas," 139, argues that later "exemptions were made." See also "Estado que tuvo esta Provincia de Santiago de Xalisco hasta el año de 1750," in Rueda, *Descripciones franciscanas*, 122–24; and Torre Curiel, *Vicarios en entredicho*, 167.

34. Certification of Salvador Cabañas, January 14, 1754, INAH, Fondo Franciscano (FF) 139, fols. 237v–238.
35. Francisco Solula Rosa, Inventory, 1763, INAH, FF 139, fol. 3, also fols. 25, 29. See also Güemes to bishop of Michoacán, Mexico City, July 17, 1753, VEMC 12, exp. 4, fols. 11v–12; Güemes's report to king, Mexico City, n.d. (probably July 9, 1753), AGI, México 2712; Ocaranza, *Capítulos de la historia franciscana*, 494; and Castro Santa-Anna, *Diario de sucesos notables*, 4:1.
36. Consulta of the junta, Madrid, March 28, 1749, AGI, México 2713. On other houses, see Sánchez Villa-Señor, *Theatro americano*, 1:34; and *Canons and Decrees of... Trent*, session 25, chaps. 2–3.
37. *Law of the Indies*, book 1, title 2, laws 19–20.
38. Report of Güemes to king, n.d. (probably July 9, 1753), AGI, México 2712; and Francisco Solula Rosa, *cuadernos inventariales*, 1763, INAH, FF 139, fol. 2.
39. Report of Güemes to king, n.d. (probably July 9, 1753), AGI, México 2712.
40. Viceregal decree, Mexico City, November 10, 1750, AGI, México 2712. Güemes's view became the basis for the royal cédula dated June 23, 1757; see Alcaraz Gómez, *Jesuitas y reformismo*, 377–78.
41. Consulta of Francisco Ximénez Caro to Rubio y Salinas, Mexico City, June 26, 1753, AGI, México 2712; and Güemes to bishop of Michoacán, Mexico City, July 17, 1753, VEMC 12, exp. 4, fols. 11v–12. On special laws for social groups, see Duve, *Sonderrecht*, 202–3, 273–74; on private property in churches and pueblos, see Lockhart, *The Nahuas after the Conquest*, 229. I differ somewhat from O'Hara, *A Flock Divided*, 102–5, who sees Güemes's reports as the "detached observation of an administrator" seeking to de-Indianize the doctrinas.
42. José Espinosa to archbishop, Tochimilco, December 22, 1751, AGI, México 2712.
43. Based on Silva Prada, "Impacto de la migración urbana," 77–109; and Sánchez Santiró, "El nuevo orden parroquial," 63–64, 76–77, 86–88. O'Hara, "Stone, Mortar, and Memory," 672, shows that in 1793, 26 percent of the parishioners considered themselves Indians in the "integrated" parish of San Pablo. See also Gonzalbo Aizpuru, *Historia de la educación*, 243, esp. note 56.
44. Confession, n.p., August 11, 1753, VEMC 16, exp. 12, fols. 4–5; see also the confessions by the *regidor primero* (senior councilmember) and constable of Atlatlauca and others, August 11–13, 1753, VEMC 16, exp. 12, fols. 1v–16. On the linguistic failings of priests, see *Opusculos varios de diversas materias... trabajados por... Francisco Larrea, del Orden de Predicadores... Años de 1751 y 1752*, AHAM, box 48, book 2, fol. 14. According to Gerhard, *A Guide to the Historical Geography*, 102–6, Ozumba and Atlatlauca belonged to the alcaldía mayor of Chalco.
45. Confession, August 13, 1753, VEMC 16, exp. 12, fols. 13v, 15–15v, probably referring to the barrio Texcalpan in Tlayacapan (Morelos).
46. Confession, August 13, 1753, VEMC 16, exp. 12, fols. 15v–16.

47. Petition of Juan Baptista de Bolde, vicar of Santa María Ozumba, VEMC 16, exp. 12, fol. 2. Note that according to VEMC 16, exp. 12, fol. 1v, the deputy alcalde mayor took the testimonies because the notary of Santa María Ozumba was absent; Taylor, *Magistrates of the Sacred*, 506–18, notes that the alcaldías mayores of Cuernavaca and Cuautla saw repeated Native conflicts.

48. Testimonies, Santiago Tianguistenco, December 5–7, 1750, all documents in VEMC 8, exp. 52, fols. 180–88.

49. Certification, deputy alcalde mayor, June 16, 1734, San Bartolomé Tepetitlan, INAH, FF 140, fols. 1–12. On the background, Sánchez Bella, *Iglesia y Estado*, 121–29.

50. Certification of notary Salvador Cabañas, January 14, 1754, INAH, FF 139, fol. 237.

51. Anonymous, n.d., *Reverente satisfacción*, AGN, Inquisición 945, exp. 23, fol. 149, referring to San Agustín Huexutla (Huejutla de Reyes, Hidalgo).

52. Certification of deputy alcalde mayor, Texcoco, June 16, 1734, INAH, FF 140, fols. 43–45. According to Rubial García, *Una monarquía criolla*, 20, seventeenth-century observers criticized the Augustinians as a "monarchy."

53. Taylor, *Magistrates of the Sacred*, 506, 516.

54. Güemes's report to king, Mexico City, n.d. (probably July 9, 1753), AGI, México 2712.

55. Güemes to Amarillas, Mexico City, October 8, 1755, in Torre Villar, *Instrucciones*, 844–45; original in ACR 395.

56. Lockhart, *The Nahuas after the Conquest*, 208–9; and Sánchez Santiró, "El nuevo orden parroquial," 81. Aguirre, "La secularización de doctrinas," 489–90, suggests that between 1673 and 1740, the number of doctrinas declined, yet the religious still administered 50 percent more pastoral assignments than the seculars.

57. *Reverente satisfacción*, AGN, Inquisición 945, exp. 23, fol. 162v.

58. *Reverente satisfacción*, AGN, Inquisición 945, exp. 23, fols. 139, 162, 149v.

59. Castro Santa-Anna, *Diario de sucesos notables*, 4:133–34.

60. Cabildo to king, Mexico City, July 27, 1753, AGI, México 2712. The cabildos of Querétaro, San Felipe, Salvatierra, and León asked the king to return the doctrina; see auto, Bolaños, January 17, 1753; testimonies taken by the corregidor, Querétaro, October 13, 1751, no. 3; cabildo to king, Querétaro, January 1, 1751, no. 6; parecer of the Dominican prior, Querétaro, October 20, 1751; cabildo of San Felipe to king, October 29 and November 13, 1751; cabildo of León to king, November 17, 1751; cabildo of Salvatierra to king, November 20, 1751; testimony, September 5, 1737; Francisco Antonio de Rivera to Juan Antonio Abasolo, n.d.; Diego Ortiz de Parada to king, 1752, all documents in AGI, México 2712. On elites and cabildos, see Pazos Pazos, *El ayuntamiento*, 380–83.

61. The Franciscan José de Isla of San Gabriel de Xacopan called on Native authorities to ensure that parishioners in San Juan Bautista de Xichu attended

church; see testimony, Tacuba, November 12, 1749, INAH, FF 109, fol. 230. See also Felipe de Velasco to Güemes, Mexico City, April 3, 1751, AGN, Bienes Nacionales (BN) 396, exp. 16, fols. 3–4; viceregal ruego y encargo to archbishop, Mexico City, May 19, 1751, AGN, BN 396, exp. 16, fols. 4–6; archbishop to viceroy, May 22, 1751, AGN, BN 396, exp. 16, fol. 2–2v; Rubial García, *Una monarquía criolla*, 24–25; and Taylor, *Magistrates of the Sacred*, 86.

62. Notoriety of Prior Diego de los Cobos, Mexico City, January 22, 1620, AGN, BN 741, exp. 15. The Mixtecs and Zapotecs were mostly administered by the Dominicans, while Metztitlan (Hidalgo) was Augustinian territory.

63. Viceregal decree, Mexico City, May 12, 1753, ACR 395; see also Castro Santa-Anna, *Diario de sucesos notables*, 4:119.

64. Castro Santa-Anna, *Diario de sucesos notables*, 4:120–21.

65. Viceregal decree, Mexico City, May 12, 1753, ACR 395; notoriety by notary Antonio de Mesa, Mexico City, May 23, 1753, AGI, México 2712; and Güemes's report to king, Mexico City, n.d. (probably July 9, 1753), AGI, México 2712. See also Silva Prada, "Impacto de la migración urbana," 80–83; Lockhart, *The Nahuas after the Conquest*, 220; and O'Hara, "Stone, Mortar, and Memory," 653–54. Perhaps the sodality of Spaniards was the same as the "Creole nation" that had resisted the chapel in the 1670s.

66. Royal cédula signed by Ensenada to Güemes, Madrid, July 22, 1746, AGN, RCO 66, exp. 51; and king to viceroys, presidents, audiencias, and governors of Peru and New Spain, Segovia, May 15, 1717, AGN, RCO 38, exp. 18, fols. 45–46, referencing a royal cédula to audiencia of Quito, April 24, 1703. Melvin, *Building Colonial Cities*, 3, argues for "a time of expansion and prosperity for the mendicants, [and] when populations of friars increased, new houses were founded in cities," see also 7–8, 41–46; and Rex Galindo, *To Sin No More*, 30, 39–40.

67. On San Felipe Neri, see Güemes to king, Mexico City, August 16, 1748; chapter to Güemes, June 28, 1748; parecer of the prosecutor, Madrid, July 1, 1749; consulta of the Council of the Indies, Madrid, July 22, 1749, all four documents in AGI, México 514; and Güemes to Ignacio Goyeneche, Mexico City, October 6, 1753, AGI, México 1351. The prosecutor of the Council of the Indies also approved the expansion of the theological seminary attached to the cathedral, according to Güemes to king, Mexico City, May 15, 1749; and parecer of the prosecutor, Madrid, June 3, 1750, both documents in AGI, México 513; and cabildo session, Mexico City, June 26, 1753, AHCM, Ayuntamiento, Actas del Cabildo 78, fol. 20. In addition, the Jesuits counted on their excellent ties to the court in Madrid to build a college in León (Guanajuato) and obtain a permit for a seminary in Pátzcuaro; see royal order, Buen Retiro, December 8, 1747, AGI, México 439; Güemes to king, July 20, 1748, Mexico City, AGI, México 513; Provincial Juan Antonio Baltasar to Güemes, n.d.; Güemes to king, Mexico City, February 4, 1752, April 22, 1752, and May 15, 1752, the four preceding documents in ACR 374; and royal cédula, San Lorenzo, November 7, 1752, AGN, RCO 72, exp. 166, fols. 458–62.

68. On the Franciscan third order, see royal order, Buen Retiro, February 24, 1750, AGI México 442; on Valladolid, see Miguel Anselmo Alderete to king, Valladolid, December 22, 1747, VEMC 74, exp. 11. Rex Galindo, *To Sin No More*, 204–5; and Melvin, *Building Colonial Cities*, 31, show that internal divisions hampered foundations. According to the testimony of Manuel de la Canal, Mexico City, January 19, 1757, AGI, Escribanía 246B, fol. 64, Güemes opposed a house in San Miguel el Grande. Chowning, *Rebellious Nuns*, 25, 27, 32–34, analyzes the conflict between relaxed and strict observance in the Purísima Concepción convent there after 1756.

69. Consulta of the Council of the Indies, Madrid, September 6, 1751, with the king's resolution noted in the margins, n.d., AGI, México 443; see also Arricivita, *Crónica seráfica y apostólica del colegio de Propaganda Fide*, 431–37; and Espinosa, *Chronica apostolica y seraphica de todos los colegios de Propaganda Fide*, 524–26.

70. Güemes to Ensenada, San Agustín de las Cuevas, July 1, 1752, ACR 357.

71. Güemes to Arriaga, Mexico City, n.d. (March 1755), ACR 455; see also Gómez Parada to king, Guadalajara, November 2, 1750; and consulta of the Council of the Indies, Madrid, July 28, 1753, and August 13, 1755, the three preceding documents in AGI, Guadalajara 82. See also Taylor, *Magistrates of the Sacred*, 193. Ensenada also rejected a Priory of the Sacred Heart of Jesus in Mexico City in 1751, although the royal cédula, September 24, 1754, referenced in mandate (auto) of the real acuerdo, Mexico City, July 19, 1752, AGN, Historia 113, fol. 410–410v, gave the green light; see also mandate of the real acuerdo, Mexico City, September 5, 1748, AGN, Historia 113, fols. 274v–275; and consulta of the Council of the Indies and royal decree on its margins, Council of the Indies, Madrid, May 20, 1751, AGI, México 385. Núñez de Haro y Peralto, *Descripción del arzobispado*, 42–43, provides a description of that house. Audiencia to king, Mexico City, December 23, 1752, AGI, México 543A, denied a request from Mother María Ignacia de Azlor y Echeverri for a house of the Sisters of the Company of Mary.

72. According to a note by the prior Pablo de la Concepción, December 9, 1756, ACR 485, Padilla Pacheco gave 16,500 *reales de vellón* to the priory; see also Martínez Rosales, "La provincia de San Alberto," 471–74, 488–95; and Borges Morán, *Religiosos*, 205–9.

73. Community of the Discalced Carmelites to king, Valladolid, December 31, 1747; see also prior and priory of San Juan de Dios to king, January 5, 1748; and priory of Santa Catarina de Siena to king, January 10, 1748, all in VEMC 74, exp. 11; consultas of the Council of the Indies, Madrid, February 28, 1746, and November 23, 1746; and consulta of September 13, 1746 and attached royal order, all in AGI, México 438, referring to proposed houses in Guadalajara, San Luis Potosí, Valladolid, Tehuacan de las Granadas (Puebla), and Puebla. See also king to Fuenclara, Aranjuez, May 18, 1746, AGN, RCO 66, exp. 33; Güemes to Ensenada, Mexico City, April 12, 1747, AGI, México 1506, no. 32; Güemes to Ensenada, San Agustín de las Cuevas, July 1, 1752, ACR 357; and Güemes to Ensenada, Mexico

City, October 31, 1747, ACR 404. According to *Law of the Indies*, book 1, title 3, law 1, bishop and viceroy could veto any foundation. Güemes to king, n.d., AGI, México 1352, wrote that he complied with the royal cédula of March 6, 1754, to help the Discalced Carmelites relocate their convent from Santa Fe to Santo Desierto (now Desierto de los Leones on the outskirts of Mexico City) with an annual royal subsidy of 12,000 pesos. See also Sánchez Villa-Señor, *Theatro americano*, 1:244–45, 350, 2:205–6; and Borges Morán, *Religiosos*, 203.

74. Güemes to Ensenada, Mexico City, December 6, 1751, AGI, México 1851; and Güemes to Ensenada, San Agustín de las Cuevas, July 1, 1752, ACR 357.
75. Güemes to Ensenada, San Agustín de las Cuevas, July 1, 1752, ACR 357.
76. Meeting report, Madrid, December 21, 1752, AGI, México 1851.
77. Royal cédula, April 22, 1753, referenced in Manuel José Rubio y Salinas to king, July 3, 1754, AGI, México 807; Castro Santa-Anna, *Diario de sucesos notables*, 5:53–55; and Melvin, *Building Colonial Cities*, 66–67.
78. Royal cédula to cabildo, Buen Retiro, February 10, 1748, AHCM, Ayuntamiento, Cédulas y Reales Órdenes 2977, exp. 78, fols. 1–6; and royal cédula to cabildo, Buen Retiro, September 15, 1748, AHCM, Ayuntamiento, Cédulas y Reales Órdenes 2977, exp. 78, fols. 7–9. According to royal cédula to captain general of New Galicia, October 19, 1756, AHCM, Ayuntamiento, Cédulas y Reales Órdenes 2977, exp. 78, fol. 30; royal cédula to abbot and ecclesiastical chapter, Aranjuez, June 12, 1774, AHCM, Ayuntamiento, Cédulas y Reales Órdenes 2977, exp. 78, fols. 36–37v; and royal cédula to abbot and ecclesiastical chapter, San Ildefonso, September 7, 1774, AHCM, Ayuntamiento, Cédulas y Reales Órdenes 2977, exp. 78, fols. 38–39, the king later ordered that at least seven of the prebendaries should teach a Native language.
79. Ruego y encargo of Alburquerque to dean and chapter of Mexico, Mexico City, May 23, 1709, AGN, BN 636, exp. 4; royal cédula to municipal council, Aranjuez, May 27, 1749, AHCM, Ayuntamiento, Cédulas y Reales Órdenes 2977, exp. 78, fols. 10–19v; and *Colegiata de Nuestra Señora de Guadalupe de Mexico: Extracto sacado de los papeles originales*, n.d., VEMC 52, exp. 18. On finding money, see Güemes to Ensenada, September 25, 1748, ACR 476.
80. Castro Santa-Anna, *Diario de sucesos notables*, 4:92–93.
81. Cited in Alcaraz Gómez, *Jesuitas y reformismo*, 506, also 506–23.
82. Lynch, *Bourbon Spain*, 187–89; Téllez Alarcia, "Guerra y regalismo," 1075–78; Hermann, *L'église d'Espagne*, 127–38; Castañeda Delgado and Marchena Fernánde, *La jerarquía de la iglesia*, 155; and Taylor, *Magistrates of the Sacred*, 15.
83. Miguel Francisco de Herrera to Inquisition and archbishop, Veracruz, August 5, 1753, AGN, Inquisición 935, exp. 7, fols. 393, 397–98, citing "All power is given to me in heaven and on earth" (Matthew 28:18), "I acknowledge my fault, and my sin is ever before me" (Psalms 51:3–4), and "I absolve you of your sins" (the absolution in the confessional).
84. Güemes to dean of the ecclesiastical chapter, Mexico City, October 8, 1750,

Archivo del Cabildo de la Catedral de México (hereinafter ACCM), Actas del Cabildo Eclesiástico 40, fols. 126v–127, referring to his *billetes* (notes prompting some action) from 1747 and 1748; and dean to Güemes, Mexico City, October 13, 1750, drawing on a report of accountant José de Mier, Mexico City, August 20, 1748, both documents in ACCM, Actas del Cabildo Eclesiástico 40, fols. 127v–129v.

85. Session of the ecclesiastical chapter, Mexico City, October 9, 1750, ACCM, Actas del Cabildo Eclesiástico 40, fol. 125–125v. See also archbishop to Güemes, Mexico City, October 17, 1746, AHAM, box 63, exp. 4; royal cédula to dean and ecclesiastical chapter, Buen Retiro, March 19, 1750; royal cédula to Archbishop Rubio y Salinas, Buen Retiro, March 19, 1750; Güemes's billete to chapter, Mexico City, September 28, 1750; reply of the chapter, Mexico City, October 1, 1750; and archbishop to Güemes, October 1, 1750, Mexico City, the five preceding documents in ACCM, Actas del Cabildo Eclesiástico 40, fols. 120v–121, 124–124v. On the blank order, see session of the ecclesiastical chapter, Guadalajara, November 11, 1750, Archivo Histórico del Arzobispado de Guadalajara (hereinafter AHAG), Capitular XI desde 1746 hasta 1759, fol. 76v.

86. Güemes to José Banfi y Parrilla, Mexico City, May 12, 1751, ACR 404.

87. Nicolás García to the maestro general José de la Vallina, Aranjuez, June 7, 1754, INAH, FF 139, fols. 257–257v; see also Castro Santa-Anna, *Diario de sucesos notables*, 4:133–34. The Franciscans represented the province of Santo Evangelio in central New Spain, while the *oficial mayor* was José Banfi y Parrilla; see also Álvarez Icaza Longoria, *La secularización de doctrinas*, 111.

88. Gómez Urdáñez, *Fernando VI*, 100–114.

89. Royal cédula, Aránjuez, June 23, 1757, VEMC 12, exp. 4, fols. 25–29; Amarillas to bishop of Michoacán, Mexico City, November 30, 1757, VEMC 12, exp. 4, fols. 36–37, 40v–41; instruction to Amarillas, Madrid, n.d. (1755), AGI, México 2712; and Taylor, "Los pueblos indígenas," 139. Saldaña Solís, "El inicio de la secularización de las doctrinas," 122–25, argues convincingly for a period of "conciliación," taking into account that according to the minutes of Amarillas, Mexico City, January 8, 1756, AGN, Templos y Conventos vol. 15, exp. 1, fol. 5, the king ordered Amarillas to secularize the Franciscan doctrinas Cuernavaca and Calimaya, and the Augustine doctrina Culhuacan, because their priest had passed away. He should also "remove the priests of Chapantongo and Chilquautlan of this order and Otumba of that [Franciscan] order, and those of Yauhtepec and Cuauhtepec of Santo Domingo, although they have not fallen vacant due to the passing or renunciation of their priests." According to Ynventario, INAH, FF 139, fols. 80–86, at least six Franciscan doctrinas were secularized between 1755 and 1766.

90. The local perspective remains innovative; see, for example, Schroeder and Poole, *Religion in New Spain*.

91. Abad Pérez, *Los Franciscanos*, 142–43; and Medina, *Los Dominicos*, 95.

According to royal cédula, Madrid, July 15, 1797, AHAG, Serie Franciscanos, Secularización de doctrinas, fols. 1–3, the Franciscans still had twelve doctrinas in the bishopric of Guadalajara in 1797 and subsequently lost all but three of them.
92. Taylor, *Magistrates of the Sacred*, 14, argues for a "far reaching, if disjointed" program, taking twenty-six doctrinas during 1751–1756 and another series from 1772 to 1776, and the friars lost a total of fifty doctrinas during the second half of the century; see also 15, 83–86, 506–10; and Taylor, "Los pueblos indígenas," 138–39. Brading, *Church and State*, 63, emphasizes Ensenada's leading role in secularization, while for Álvarez Icaza Longoria, *La secularización de doctrinas*, 111, Carvajal's death "did not result at all in abandoning the project." Tanck de Estrada, *Pueblos de indios*, 161–68, perceptively argues that secularizations slowed down in the last years of Archbishop Rubio y Salinas; Rubial García, "Las órdenes mendicantes," 227, shows that Viceroys Marquis of las Amarillas (1755–1760) and Marquis of Cruillas (1760–1766) slowed down secularization. Gerhard, *A Guide to the Historical Geography*, 104, 246, 248, notes many examples of secularizations in this period; see also Mazín Gómez, *El cabildo catedral*; and Morales, "Secularización de doctrinas," 465–95. Menegus Bornemann, Morales, and Mazín Gómez, *La secularización de las doctrinas*, focus largely on the sixteenth and early seventeenth centuries. Andrien, "The Coming of Enlightened Reform," 187, 194–95, 198, 200, argues for a steady progress of secularization, which Viceroy Count of Superunda (1745–1761) continued after 1757 in Peru. Kuethe and Andrien, *The Spanish Atlantic World*, 184, maintain that the period 1756–1758 saw substantial secularizations in Lima; see also Pearce, *The Origins of Bourbon Reform*, 163–64; and Cortés Peña, *La política religiosa de Carlos III*. On the dates of secularization in New Spain, see del Valle Menéndez, *Juan Francisco de Güemes*, 421, 630.
93. Royal cédula, Buen Retiro, February 18, 1753, AGN, RCO 73, exp. 17, fol. 47; Güemes's instruction to bishop of Michoacán, Mexico City, July 17, 1753, VEMC 12, exp. 4, fol. 10v; Brading, *Church and State*, 77; and Belanger, "Secularization and the Laity," 78–93.

Chapter 5

1. The quotation in the chapter title is in Güemes to Álvarez de Toledo Lobato, Mexico City, July 4, 1755, ACR 347. The Bible, an important source of inspiration for colonial Mexicans, often lumps tax farmers together with other sinners; see, e.g., Matthew 9:10: "Now it happened, as Jesus sat at the table in the house, that behold, many tax collectors and sinners came and sat down with Him and His disciples."
2. Valle Pavón, "El consulado de comerciantes," 16–17, argues for a recovery of consulado power in the late colonial period. See also Valle Pavón, *Donativos*,

144; and Sánchez Santiró, "La hacienda reformada," 143–78. These scholars focus mostly on the period after 1753–1754.

3. Pearce, *The Origins of Bourbon Reform*, 14, also 150, asserts that determined ministers heightened royal control in overseas realms; while Cardim et al., introduction to *Polycentric Monarchies*, 5, argue that negotiations among Crown, territories, or corporations created legitimacy. Grafe and Irigoin, "A Stakeholder Empire," 613, 629; see also Irigoin and Grafe, "Bargaining for Absolutism," 173–209, underline the necessary consensus for financial reforms, as colonial elites "expected a return on their investment," and "relations between crown and subject were based on mutual rights and duties that had a price tag to them." Kuethe and Andrien, *The Spanish Atlantic World*, 241–42, 247, 251, show that Governor Count of Ricla (1763–1766) negotiated with the elites in Havana to raise the alcabala from 2 to 6 percent and revamp export tariffs in exchange for commercial liberalization. Grieco, *The Politics of Giving*, 5–11, contends that donations to the Crown were "bargaining devices" including for popular classes rather than "extractive mechanisms" (30). On negotiations, see Muthoo, "A Non-Technical Introduction," 147–62; and C. J. Martin, "Negotiating Political Agreements," 9–11.

4. Arias, "Building Fiscal Capacity," 662–93, argues insightfully that elites in strategic and vulnerable places such as Havana in the mid-1760s agreed to deprivatize tax collections to enhance the city's protection and curb nonpaying free riders. Yet the networks in Veracruz did not promise to improve the city's defenses, and Mexico City was safer from foreign attacks than elsewhere. Serrano Hernández, "Building an Empire," 478, shows that the viceroyalty shipped much of its tax revenue to the Spanish Caribbean and increasingly the Philippines to reinforce fortresses and construct warships, as Spain was not the exclusive recipient of transmittances. According to Sánchez Durán, "Interacciones," 86–100, the hard-fought alcabala auction in Castile served both bidder and Crown, while Bertrand, *Grandeur et misères*, 334–43, analyzes a comparable fight over the Puebla alcabala after 1695.

5. Marichal, *Bankruptcy of Empire*, 5–6, also 1–15, 55. Kuethe, "La desregulación comercial," 274–75; and Kuethe and Andrien, *The Spanish Atlantic World*, 252, claim that the Crown did not collect alcabalas in Veracruz before José de Gálvez's *visita* (judicial investigation).

6. Referring to Viceroys Marquis of Cerralvo (1624–1635) and Marquis of Cadereita (1635–1640); see consulado to Güemes, Mexico City, November 26, 1753, AGN, AHH 550, exp. 54; consulado to Güemes, Mexico City, November, n.d., 1753, AGN, AHH 129, exp. 1; and cabildo of Mexico City to king, December 22, 1753, AGI, México 2093. See also Serrano Hernández, "Building an Empire," 343–62; Álvarez de Toledo, *Politics and Reform*, 48–49; Valle Pavón, "Ocultación," 323–24, 336; and Valle Pavón, "El consulado de comerciantes," 62–64, 71. Older works include Pastor, "La alcabala como fuente," 1–16; Elliott, *The Count-Duke of Olivares*, 244–77, 486–95; Smith, "Sales Taxes in New Spain," 2; and *Law of the Indies*, book 8, title 13, law 14.

7. Serrano Hernández, "Building an Empire," 335, 340, 476–79, sees the Unión de Armas project to spread the tax burden among the empire as a "moderate success" (479); while Bertrand, *Grandeur et misères*, 333–35; and Valle Pavón, "El consulado de comerciantes," 89–90, 96–101, also argue for important changes during the period. These arguments dispel the older tenet of imperial stagnation or decline in the late seventeenth century.

8. Consulado to Güemes, Mexico City, November, n.d., 1753, AGN, AHH 129, exp. 1; and royal order, Madrid, December 3, 1707, AGI, México 402. See also royal cédula to Casafuerte, Madrid, November 28, 1722, AGN, RCO 43, exp. 74, fols. 268–69; and draft of *servicios del consulado*, n.d., AGN, AHH 640, exp. 44. Valle Pavón, "El consulado de comerciantes," 105–7, emphasizes that the Crown utilized private offers to force a raise in proceeds.

9. Güemes, *Reglamento para la administración y cobranza de los reales derechos de alcabalas* . . . Mexico City, September 26, 1753 (hereinafter *Reglamento de alcabalas*), Biblioteca Nacional de España (hereinafter BNE), manuscritos 10358, 476, vol. 4, 2, fols. 25–26; royal cédula to cabildo, Buen Retiro, August 6, 1746, AHCM, Ayuntamiento, Cédulas y Reales Órdenes 2977, exp. 77, fol. 1; and king to Casafuerte, Madrid, November 28, 1722, AGN, RCO 43, exp. 74, fol. 268–69. On the loans, draft of *servicios del consulado*, n.d., AGN, AHH 640, exp. 44.

10. Ensenada to Güemes, Madrid, October 7, 1747, AGN, RCO 67, exp. 114, fols. 338–39; consulado to king, Mexico City, March 1, 1754, AGI, México 2093; and consulado to king, Mexico City, January 4, 1753, AGI, México 2501. On such meetings, see also Serrano Hernández, "Building an Empire," 330; Escamilla González, "Urgencia militar," 245–53; Valle Pavón, "El consulado de comerciantes," 130; Valle Pavón, *Donativos*, 26; Stein and Stein, *Silver, Trade, and War*, 197, 207; and Fonseca and Urrutia, *Historia general*, 2:29–30.

11. According to *Pliego de condiciones*, attached to consulado to Pedro Cristóbal de Reinoso y Mendoza, Mexico City, April 20, 1734, AGN, Indiferente Virreinal 5470, exp. 33, fols. 5v, 22. The area included the alcaldías mayores of Texcoco, Chiconautla, Tlalnepantla, Coyoacan, San Agustín de las Cuevas, Xochimilco, Iztapalapa, Mexicalcingo including Venta Nueva, Chalco, Tlalmanalco, Coatepec, Cuautitlan, Tepotzotlan, San Juan Teotihuacan, Zumpango, Tula, Otumba, and the fair in Xalapa (Veracruz); certification of Baltasar García de Mendieta, Mexico City, January 2, 1754, AGN, AHH 640, exp. 44. On mounted guards, see Valle Pavón, "Ocultación," 325–26.

12. *Pliego de condiciones*, attached to consulado to Pedro Cristóbal de Reinoso y Mendoza, Mexico City, April 20, 1734, AGN, Indiferente Virreinal 5470, exp. 33, fol. 22–22v.

13. Güemes to king, Mexico City, October 22, 1753, AGI, México 2093; see also *Pliego de condiciones*, attached to consulado to Pedro Cristóbal de Reinoso y Mendoza, Mexico City, April 20, 1734, AGN, Indiferente Virreinal 5470, exp. 33, fol. 22–22v. On exempt clergy, see *Law of the Indies*, book 8, title 13, law 17.

14. See, e.g., Güemes to Ensenada, Mexico City, October 31, 1747, ACR 404.
15. Güemes to king, Mexico City, October 22, 1753, AGI, México 2093. Manuel Álvarez de Toledo Lobato to Güemes, Madrid, January 31, 1755, ACR 347, also thanked Güemes for his efforts "in favor of . . . the consulado"; see also Stein and Stein, *Silver, Trade, and War*, 244.
16. Güemes, *Reglamento de alcabalas*, fols. 23–24; Güemes to king, Mexico City, October 20, 1751, AGI, México 2093; and Güemes to king, Mexico City, October 22, 1753, AGI, México 2093.
17. Güemes to king, Mexico City, October 20, 1751, AGI, México 2093; see also *Pliego de condiciones*, attached to consulado to Pedro Cristóbal de Reinoso y Mendoza, Mexico City, April 20, 1734, AGN, Indiferente Virreinal 5470, exp. 33, fol. 13–14v; and *Law of the Indies*, book 8, title 13, law 24. According to Ventura Beleña, *Recopilación sumaria*, 1:87, the royal cédula from September 5, 1735, stipulated that inheritance that "can be easily divided" was exempt, whereas indivisible property paid alcabala.
18. Güemes to king, Mexico City, October 22, 1753, AGI, México 2093.
19. Güemes's instructions to Amarillas, Mexico City, October 8, 1755, in Torre Villar, *Instrucciones*, 819; although the original or draft in AGI, México 1506, no. 167a, is dated November 28, 1754.
20. Valle Pavón, *Donativos*, 29–31; see also Valle Pavón, "Los excedentes," 969–1016.
21. Consulado to king, Mexico City, December 31, 1753, AGN, AHH 635, exp. 3; *Pliego de condiciones*, attached to consulado to Pedro Cristóbal de Reinoso y Mendoza, Mexico City, April 20, 1734, AGN, Indiferente Virreinal 5470, exp. 33, fol. 5v; consulado to Güemes, Mexico City, November 26, 1753, AGN, AHH 550, exp. 54; and prior and consuls to king, Mexico City, January 4, 1753, AGI, México 2501. See also Güemes, *Reglamento de alcabalas*, fols. 25–26. Stein and Stein, *Silver, Trade, and War*, 244, show that the fleet merchants did not always sell in Xalapa as required but elsewhere, causing strife with the consulado.
22. The value of the pulque monopoly dropped from 128,000 to 105,500 pesos at that time; see consulado, *Instruzion relativa*, AHH 635, exp. 8; and Juan Antonio Baltasar to Francisco Rávago y Noriega, Mexico City, n.d. (probably January 1753), AGI, México 2501. Voekel, "Peeing on the Palace," 187, counts 1,600 pulque taverns at the end of the century.
23. Güemes to Ensenada, Mexico City, December 18, 1752; see also minutes of Ensenada to Güemes, Aranjuez, June 23, 1752; Pedro Carranza to king, Madrid, August 31, 1752; Ensenada to Güemes, Madrid, October 2, 1752; Güemes to king, Mexico City, October 22, 1753; and consulado to king, Mexico City, March 1, 1754, all documents in AGI, México 2093. On Belaunzarán, see Valle Pavón, "El consulado de comerciantes," 135–36. On credit and the reputation of merchants, see Lamikiz, *Trade and Trust*, 9–14.
24. Güemes's proclamation, Mexico City, September 26, 1753, AGN, Bandos 4,

exp. 36; see also minutes of Ensenada to Güemes, Aranjuez, June 23, 1752, AGI, México 2093; and Valle Pavón, "El consulado de comerciantes," 137–38.

25. Güemes's proclamation, Mexico City, September 26, 1753, AGN, Bandos 4, exp. 36; Ensenada to Güemes, October 2, 1752; Güemes to king, Mexico City, October 22, 1753; Güemes's Ordenanza, Mexico City, September 26, 1753; and Güemes to Ensenada, Mexico City, December 8, 1753, the four preceding documents in AGI, México 2093.

26. Consulta of the Council of the Indies on José Honoro de Soto y Amate, Madrid, July 12, 1748, AGI, México 1121; and Güemes to Ensenada, Mexico City, December 8, 1753, AGI, México 2093.

27. Fonseca and Urrutia, *Historia general*, 2:52. According to the testimony of Isabel Pérez, Isla de Santa María, July 21, 1720, AGI, Contratación 5470, N. 2, R. 56; Güemes to Ensenada, Mexico City, September 25, 1748, AGI, México 1849; *Lista de los Sugetos nombrados*, n.d., AGI, México 2093; and Güemes's decree, Mexico City, December 23, 1753, AGI Escribanía 246C, book 9, fols. 183–184v; Superintendent José del Mazo Calderón was possibly a relative of the *oficial mayor* Juan Francisco del Mazo Calderón and originally served as interim accountant of the treasury. Meanwhile, according to Güemes to Ensenada, December 8, 1753, AGI, México 2093; testimony of Joaquín de Uria, Mexico City, February 18, 1757, and testimony of Mateo Arcipreste Sáenz de Santa María, Mexico City, February 18, 1757, the two preceding documents in AGI, Escribanía 246B, fols. 567–71, 578–83, the consulado had previously employed the accountants Mateo Arcipreste Sáenz de Santa María and Joaquín de Uria. According to report, Cádiz, October 27, 1752, AGI, Contratación 5494, N. 1, R. 38, the senior accountant Francisco Trelles was originally a resident of Veracruz who had traveled from Spain to New Spain.

28. Güemes's *Instrucción secreta, que ha de obserbar Don Joseph del Mazo Calderon Superintendente Administrador de las Reales Alcabalas deesta Ciudad* (hereinafter *Instrucción secreta*), Mexico City, October 8, 1753, AGI, México 2093.

29. Güemes's *Instrucción secreta*; Güemes's proclamation, Mexico City, September 26, 1753, AGN, Bandos 4, exp. 36, fols. 216–218v; and Fonseca and Urrutia, *Historia general*, 2:58.

30. Güemes to king, January 15, 1754, AGI, México 2093; see also Juan Antonio Baltasar to Rávago, Mexico City, n.d. (probably January 1753); prior and consuls to Rávago, Mexico City, January 4, 1753, and March 1754, the three previous documents in AGI, México 2501. On the resistance of the secular clergy in Puebla, see Bertrand, *Grandeur et misères*, 339–42.

31. Güemes to Ensenada, December 8, 1753, AGI, México 2093.

32. Order of prior and consuls, November 12, 1753; and estimate by architects Manuel Álvarez and Lorenzo Rodríguez, Mexico City, November 16–26, 1753, both documents in AGN, AHH 640, exp. 45. According to Güemes to Ensenada, Mexico City, October 12, 1754, AGI, México 2501; and consulado, *Instruzion*

relativa, fol. 7, the consulado was expected to instead draw on the *avería*—a 0.6 percent tax on Spanish imports.

33. Sessions of the cabildo, October 29, November 28, and December 22, 1753, AHCM, Ayuntamiento, Actas del Cabildo 78A, fols. 31–32, 38v–40, 42; and cabildo to king, December 22, 1753, AGI, México 2093. According to Priestley, *José de Gálvez*, 343–44, colonial Mexicans prized *nieve* (ice) from the volcanoes as a delicacy and bought it for roughly one real per pound. In addition, tanners and artisans bought *cordobanés* (leather hides) from a warehouse in Mexico City under a loose monopoly, and the lessee paid some one thousand pesos to the Crown.

34. Prior and consuls to Güemes, November 27, 1754, AGN, AHH 635, exp 5.

35. Consulado to Güemes, Mexico City, November (?) 1753, AGN, AHH 129, exp. 1; see also Castro Santa-Anna, *Diario de sucesos notables*, 4:190.

36. Draft of consulado (probably) to king, n.d., AGN, AHH 635, exp. 9.

37. Güemes's decree, Mexico City, December 2, 1753, AGN, AHH 635, exp. 5.

38. Minutes of Ensenada to Güemes, Aranjuez, June 23, 1752, AGI, México 2093; Pedro de Uriarte and José González Calderón to consulado, Mexico City, June 25, 1755, AGN, AHH 550, exp. 53, fols. 1–2; petition of merchants to viceroy, Mexico City, April 30, 1755; and Güemes's decree, Mexico City, June 3, 1755, the two preceding documents in AGN, AHH 550, exp. 53.

39. Billete of prior and consuls, Mexico City, June 26, 1755, AGN, AHH 550, exp. 53, fols. 3–4v; see also Castro Santa-Anna, *Diario de sucesos notables*, 5:126; consulado to Güemes, Mexico City, April 9, 1755; and Antonio Andreu y Ferraz to Güemes, Mexico City, April 10, 1755, the two preceding documents in AGN, Civil 1332, exp. 1, fols. 1–2. On restraint, see draft of a consulado letter, n.d., AGN, AHH 550, exp. 53. One representative was the famous lawyer Francisco Javier Gamboa; see *relación de méritos* (colonial résumé) of Francisco Javier Gamboa, Madrid, February 1, 1757, AGI, Gobierno—Indiferente General (hereinafter AGI, Indiferente) 157, N. 6, 1, fols. 1–3v. Albi, *Gamboa's World*, 2, argues in a major study that Gamboa was not a subaltern but a mediator between Spanish and Mexican societies.

40. The senior consul was Juan Castañiza, while Domingo Trespalacios served as the cabildo's *superintendente y conservador de proprios y rentas* (budget superintendent). Council member Miguel Díaz was a relative of Trespalacios and opposed sending an agent, and so did Juan Antonio Huramán and Francisco Antonio Casuso; extraordinary sessions on May 21, 26, and 31, and June 11 and 14, 1755, AHCM, Ayuntamiento, Actas del Cabildo 79A, fols. 52–72; see also Barrio Lorenzot, *Compendio de los libros capitulares*, n.d., AHCM, Ayuntamiento, Actas del Cabildo 438A, fols. 83–85.

41. Castro Santa-Anna, *Diario de sucesos notables*, 4:119.

42. *Instrucción secreta*, AGI, México 2093.

43. Fleet deputies to king, Mexico City, December 7, 1747, AGI, México 2501.

See also Güemes to Ensenada, Mexico City, October 15, 1754, AGI, México 2501. According to Lamikiz, *Trade and Trust*, 92, about sixty fleet merchants associated with the Cádiz consulado lived in Mexico City in 1755; see also Pearce, *British Trade*, 8; Kuethe, "El fin del monopolio," 38–40; Pérez-Mallaína Bueno, *Política naval española*, 202–28; Lynch, *Bourbon Spain*, 148; G. Walker, *Spanish Politics*, 10–15; and Klaveren, *Europäische Wirtschaftsgeschichte*, 172–74.

44. Güemes to Ensenada, July 31, 1751, n.p., AGI, México 2501.

45. Fleet deputies to king, Mexico City, December 7, 1747; see also king to Francisco Fernández Molinillo, Buen Retiro, January 3, 1748; Güemes to Ensenada, Mexico City, July 31, 1751; Güemes to (probably) Ensenada, Mexico City, July 2, 1751; Arriaga (at that time president of the House of Trade) to Ensenada, Madrid, March 16, 1752; and (probably) Ensenada to Güemes, Aranjuez, April 22, 1752, the six preceding documents in AGI, México 2501.

46. Güemes's proclamation, Mexico City, September 26, 1753, AGN, Bandos 4, exp. 36, fols. 216–218v.

47. Güemes to king, Madrid, October 3, 1756, ACR 393; see also Fonseca and Urrutia, *Historia general*, 2:58. See the litany of complaints against the fleet merchants in consulado, *Instruzion relativa*.

48. Consulta of the cámara of the Indies, Madrid, February 17, 1746, with the king's resolution attached, AGI, México 438; (probably) Ensenada to Rubalcava, Madrid, October 10, 1747, and Francisco de Varas y Valdés to Ensenada, Cádiz, November 13, 1747, both documents in AGI, México 1849; title of appointment, Buen Retiro, March 14, 1750, AGI, México 442; archbishop Manuel Rubio y Salinas to king, Mexico City, November 28, 1749, AGI, México 807; and relación de méritos of Cevallos, n.d., AGI, Indiferente 224, N. 82. On the appointment of Rubio y Salinas, see king to pope, Buen Retiro, December 21, 1747, AGI, México 439; license to travel, Cádiz, May 23, 1749, AGI, Contratación 5490, N. 1, R 24; summary of Güemes's recommendation of Cevallos, Mexico City, July 16, 1749, AGI, Indiferente 224, N. 82; and reply of the prosecutor of the Council of the Indies, Madrid, May 19, 1754, AGI, México 516. See also royal cédula to Güemes, Aranjuez, May 12, 1751, AGN, RCO 71, exp. 122, fol. 363, naming Cevallos as *comisario apostólico juez executor* (judge commissioner) of the Santa Cruzada. According to Pearce, *The Origins of Bourbon Reform*, 160, the Peruvian Viceroy Count of Superunda similarly trusted José Herboso, treasurer of Lima's ecclesiastical chapter, who originally came from the La Plata region of Argentina. It cannot be ascertained here to which degree these treasurers differed from seventeenth-century viceregal *validos* (favorite ministers). According to Büschges, "Del criado al valido," 164–81, viceregal validos assisted with government and patronage, although two were tried and punished for undue patronage—unlike Cevallos.

49. José Banfi y Parrilla to Güemes, Madrid, September 4, 1751, ACR 388, referring to Confessor Francisco Rávago y Noriega.

50. On the alcabala, see Valle Pavón, "El consulado de comerciantes," 16–17; and Sánchez Santiró, "La hacienda reformada," 143–78.

51. Consulado to king, Mexico City, March 1, 1754, AGI, México 2093; see also cabildo to king, December 22, 1753, AGI, México 2093.

52. Anonymous author, *Papeles del Duende de Mexico*, n.d., INAH, CA, microfilm roll 55, fol. 86–86v.

53. Consulado to king, Mexico City, March 1, 1754, AGI, México 2093. See also consulado, *Instruzion relativa*, fol. 45. The regent was Juan Crisóstomo Barroeta y Barrenechea (Barroeta for short), who backed Güemes in the juicio de residencia; testimony, Mexico City, January 17, 1757, AGI, Escribanía 246B, fol. 27v; see the letters of Barroeta to Güemes, Mexico City, June 23, 1761, and July 1, 1761, ACR 404; and consulado to Manuel Álvarez de Toledo, Mexico City, March 11, 1754, AGI, México 2501. See also testimony of Manuel Cosuela, Mexico City, September 12, 1750, AGI, Escribanía 217A, book 2, fol. 9. According to Sanchiz and Conde Díaz Rubín, "La Familia Monterde y Antillón," 99–100, 115–16, María Ignacia Rodríguez de Vargas y Monterde y Antillón was married to Juan Crisóstomo Barroeta and her sister Ignacia Margarita to Juan Bautista Belaunzarán, while María Josefa wed Manuel Cosuela.

54. Güemes's report to Ensenada, Mexico City, January 30, 1748, AGI, México 1506, no. 40; see also Ensenada to Inquisitor Pedro Navarro, Aranjuez, May 25, 1744, AGN, Inquisición 1328, exp. 6, fol. 239.

55. Güemes to Ensenada, Mexico City, January 23, 1752, AGI, México 1506, no. 109.

56. Kuethe and Andrien, *The Spanish Atlantic World*, 162–65. Manuel Rodríguez Sáenz Pedrozo married Josefa Soria Villaroel y Berduzco and obtained the title of Count of San Bartolomé de Xala in 1749. He also invested in mining companies in Pachuca and Real del Monte, according to Couturier, *The Silver King*, 70; Ladd, *The Mexican Nobility*, 199; Tutino, "Creole Mexico," 64; and Castro Santa-Anna, *Diario de sucesos notables*, 4:35. On San Bartolomé de Xala's family ties, see Valle Pavón, "Relaciones de negocios," 117–41; and Velasco Mendizábal, "Un riojano entre vascos y montañeses," 123–59. Romero de Terreros, *Una casa del siglo XVIII*, analyzes San Bartolomé de Xala's palace in Mexico City on today's Venustiano Carranza Street.

57. Castro Santa-Anna, *Diario de sucesos notables*, 4:58–59.

58. Castro Santa-Anna, *Diario de sucesos notables*, 4:33; see also 5:83. Viceroy Fuenclara appointed Castro Santa-Anna to the alcaldía mayor of Zimapan in 1744 and two years later to the alcaldía mayor of Chalco and Tlalmanalco. Castro Santa-Anna delivered his oath in the real acuerdo on August 21, 1746. He initially saw his prospects of promotions dimmed under Güemes. His father also worked as an accountant for the alcabala during the consulado administration, and they were related to important colonial families. That shaped Castro Santa-Anna's critical view of Güemes's reformist policies. Yet the real acuerdo proposed him for a

prebendary in 1748, and the king appointed him instead for the alcaldía mayor of Tacuba in that year. As a result, Castro Santa-Anna later moderated his acrimony towards Güemes; see real acuerdo to king, August 31, 1748, AGI, México 542; certification of alcaldes mayores, n.d. (probably Mexico City, 1748), AGI, Escribanía 245A, book 1; certification of alcaldes mayores, n.d. (probably Mexico City, February 1757), AGI, Escribanía 246A, book 1, fol. 153v; and testimony of Juan Antonio Casas Novas, Mexico City, July 12, 1748, AGI, Indiferente 152, N. 2.

59. Extraordinary and ordinary cabildo sessions, Mexico City, March 1 and September 30, 1754, AHCM, Ayuntamiento, Actas del Cabildo 79A, fols. 10–10v, 24–24v. According to extraordinary sessions of the cabildo, Mexico City, May 21, 26, and 31, and June 11 and 14, 1755, AHCM, Ayuntamiento, Actas del Cabildo 79A, fols. 52–72; and Barrio Lorenzot, *Compendio de los libros capitulares*, n.d., AHCM, Ayuntamiento, Actas del Cabildo 438A, fols. 77v, 83–85, Bartolomé de Xala became alcalde ordinario in 1754, and the council also divided over sending a representative to Madrid, which Güemes denied.

60. Güemes to Cevallos, Madrid, December 7, 1762, ACR 388; see also Güemes to Cevallos, February 9, 1762; and Cevallos to Güemes, Madrid, April 5, 1763, both letters in ACR 404; and letters of Cevallos to Güemes, Mexico City, May 4, 1762, April 12, 1763, and April 30, 1763, and Güemes to Cevallos, Madrid, October 9, 1763, all letters in ACR 396. See also Belaunzarán to Güemes, Mexico City, July 13, 1761, ACR 344; Manuel Cosuela to Güemes, Mexico City, December 2, 1761, ACR 387; and Güemes to Manuel Cosuela, Madrid, April 5, 1763, ACR 388.

61. Güemes to Juan Bautista Belaunzarán, Madrid, July 1, 1763, ACR 387; and Belaunzarán to Güemes, Mexico City, December 1, 1764, ACR 387. According to Sanchiz and Conde Díaz Rubín, "La Familia Monterde y Antillón," 102, Juan Bautista Belaunzarán died in Mexico City on June 14, 1762. Juan Vicente Güemes Horcasitas y Padilla, later second Count of Revillagigedo, had officiated as godfather at the induction of the merchant Jacinto Martínez de Aguirre to the military order of Calatrava on July 20, 1754, although he was thirty-two years younger than the merchant. According to Valle Menéndez, *Juan Francisco de Güemes*, 328, Juan Vicente was born on April 20, 1736, in Havana. Jacinto Martínez de Aguirre declared in his testimony, Mexico City, January 3, 1743, AGN, Historia 120, exp. 13, that he was forty years old. According to AGN, BN 53, exp. 14, Martínez de Aguirre paid over 13,000 pesos for three priest stipends in 1738, and according to depósito irregular of the consulado, Mexico City, February 18, 1743, AGN, Judicial 21, exp. 67, fols. 116v–118; royal cédula to audiencia, San Ildefonso, August 15, 1742, AGN, RCO 62, exp. 57, fols. 170–179v; Castro Santa-Anna, *Diario de sucesos notables*, 5:15; and Güemes to Arriaga, Mexico City, October 20, 1755, ACR 404, Martínez de Aguirre served as alcalde ordinario (magistrate) of the Mexico City cabildo and as consul in 1743, and supplied the Windward Squadron by viceregal commission. On his son, see Juan Martínez de Astiz to Güemes, Mexico City, April 20, 1763; and Manuel de

Rivas Cacho to Güemes, Mexico City, April 27, 1763, both preceding documents in ACR 396. According to copy of decree of Viceroy Marquis of Cruillas, n.p., September 17, 1762; and copy of the representation of Cruillas to Arriaga, Mexico City, April 9, 1763, both preceding documents in ACR 396, Cruillas delayed the end of Martínez de Aguirre's pulque business and supported the merchant's petition to retain the business.

62. Manuel Álvarez de Toledo Lobato to Güemes, Madrid, January 31, 1755, ACR 347. According to Fayard, *Les membres du Conseil de Castille*, 239, 436, Álvarez de Toledo Lobato was probably related to Manuel Joaquín Álvarez de Toledo, Count of Oropesa, who served as first minister and president of the Council of Castile in the late seventeenth century.

63. The two previous quotations are in Güemes to Álvarez de Toledo Lobato, Mexico City, July 4, 1755, ACR 347.

64. Güemes, *Reglamento de alcabalas*, fol. 43. See also Valle Pavón, "El consulado de comerciantes," 140–41.

65. Amarillas's decree, Mexico City, November 3, 1756; and (probably) Amarillas's decree, Mexico City, July 19, 1756, both documents in AGN, AHH 550, exp. 53; and cabildo to king, March 23, 1756, AGI, México 2094.

66. Consulado to Viceroy Amarillas, Mexico City, September 13, 1756, AGN, AHH 550, exp. 53.

67. Arriaga to consulado, Madrid, December 8, 1756, AGN, Indiferente Virreinal 5036, exp. 13, fols. 1–2v; and Amarillas's decree, Mexico City, January 3, 1757, AGN, Indiferente Virreinal 4832, exp. 97. See also consulado draft, n.d. (after July 19, 1756), AGN, AHH 550, exp. 53.

68. Stein and Stein, *Silver, Trade, and War*, 197; and Pearce, *The Origins of Bourbon Reforms*, 168–69.

69. Sentence of the *sala de justicia* (judicial chamber) of the Council of the Indies, Madrid, March 13, 1758, AGI, México 1506, no. 171a, confirms the 800,000 pesos yield. Tutino, *Making a New World*, 19–21, argues for growth in the eighteenth-century Bajío, although "deepening predations" began in the 1770s; TePaske, "General Tendencies," 320–26, analyzes rapid expansion in trade, mining, and agriculture in the period 1740–1775, driven partially by population growth. Sánchez Santiró, *Corte de caja*, 14, 22, notes that the Crown legalized the *repartimiento de mercancías* (the illegal but tolerated trade of district judges with Indians) in 1751, which added to revenue. Pearce, *The Origins of Bourbon Reforms*, 153, argues for a 47 percent rise in alcabala receipts in Peru after the legalization of the repartimiento de mercancías, and the Count of Superunda even claimed a 60 percent rise. According to Moreno Cebrián, *El corregidor de Indios*, 740, however, revenue rose slowly.

70. Güemes to king, October 22, 1753, AGI, México 2093; see also certification of Manuel González de la Serna, Mexico City, July 7, 1753, AGI, México 2093.

71. According to Güemes, *Reglamento de alcabalas*; and report of the Tribunal

of Accounts, Mexico City, November 15, 1780, BNM, FR, manuscritos 439, fols. 333v–334, an alcabala accountant earned 3,000 pesos, which was 243 pesos more than an accountant on the tribunal of accounts.

72. *Noticias particulares*, Madrid, July 28, 1746, AGI, México 610.

73. Güemes to Ensenada, Mexico City, January 2, 1747, AGI, México 1506, no. 14. The viceroy also corrected the notaries' excessive fees for issuing tax contracts; see Güemes to king, July 31, 1747, ACR 421.

74. Francisco Siscara and José Camino to king, Veracruz, January 18 and October 13, 1728, attached to Patiño to Marquis of Casafuerte, Puerto de Santa María, Wednesday, July 20, 1729, AGN, RCO 48, exp. 43, fols. 106–108; report titled *papel de peinado Valenzuela que Su Excelencia mandó se tubiese presente*, Mexico City, March 15, 1759, ACR 379 (hereinafter *papel de peinado*; probably referring to Nicolás Peinado, a Mexico City mint official).

75. *Súplica* (appeal) of city, residents, and commerce of Veracruz to king, n.d. (1750), AGI, Escribanía 217A, pt. 3, fols. 35–36v; parecer of the prosecutor, Madrid, February 30, 1751, AGI, Escribanía 217A, pt. 3, fol. 61v; and Güemes to Ensenada, Mexico City, September 15, 1751, ACR 354.

76. The *alférez real* (standard bearer), the *depositario general* (treasurer), and the *alcalde provincial* (magistrate) opposed giving power of attorney; see súplica of Belaunzarán to king, n.p., n.d. (1750), AGI, Escribanía 217A, pt. 3, fols. 6–7v; and súplica of city, residents, and commerce of Veracruz to king, n.d. (1750), AGI, Escribanía 217A, pt. 3, fol. 37–37v.

77. Parecer of the prosecutor, Madrid, February 30, 1751; sentence of the Council of the Indies' judicial chamber consisting of José Cornejo y Ibarra, Gerónimo de Sola y Fuente, and Juan Vázquez de Agüero, Madrid, November 3, 1751; Belaunzarán to Ensenada, Mexico City, April 12, 1750; and Ensenada's decree, Madrid, January 18, 1751, the four preceding documents in AGI, Escribanía 217A, pt. 3, fols. 1, 42, 61–65; and consulta of the Council of the Indies, Madrid, May 26, 1751, AGI, México 385.

78. Güemes to Ensenada, Mexico City, September 19, 1754; and Güemes to Ensenada, Mexico City, June 22, 1754, both documents in ACR 354. Valle Pavón, "Antagonismo," 116, shows that this discussion over the tax rate continued into the 1790s.

79. Güemes to Ensenada, June 22, 1754, Mexico City, ACR 354.

80. *Papel de peinado*, ACR 379; Arriaga to Güemes, Buen Retiro, May 16, 1757; and Güemes to Arriaga, Madrid, May 26, 1757, the last two documents in ACR 395. Juan Bautista Belaunzarán to Güemes, Mexico City, July 13, 1761, ACR 344.

81. Güemes to Belaunzarán, Madrid, July 1, 1763, ACR 387; and Belaunzarán to Güemes, Mexico City, December 1, 1764, ACR 387.

82. Scholars argue that the later eighteenth-century reforms inaugurated the efficient tax state. Marichal, *Bankruptcy of Empire*, 5–6, for instance, maintains in his excellent book that the late Habsburg tax levy in New Spain was "singularly

ineffectual," and Crown coercion then created a centralized and efficient "fiscal submetropolis" that flushed the empire with cash after 1760; see also 1–15, 55. Marichal, "Rethinking Negotiation," 217, emphasizes the "relative stability of tax rates" in New Spain, "where the alcabala remained at 6 percent for over 150 years from 1630 to 1780." Meanwhile, Pearce, *The Origins of Bourbon Reform*, 7–14, argues that reforms started before the 1760s.

83. Irigoyen and Grafe, "Bargaining for Absolutism," 179–82, hold that opposition prevented the Crown from changing tax collections, despite growing reformist fervor in the eighteenth century.

84. Güemes to king, Madrid, October 3, 1756, ACR 393.

85. My argument differs somewhat from Serrano Hernández, "Building an Empire," 335, 340–41, quotation on 341, that the Crown pitted corporate bodies against one another and "sought support from the local elites so that the majority of the population would perceive the new rules as issued from a consensus." According to Güemes's instruction to Amarillas, Mexico City, October 8, 1755, in Torre Villar, *Instrucciones*, 811, Mexico City's consulado opposed registered ships.

86. Güemes, *Reglamento de alcabalas*, fol. 45; and Güemes to Arriaga, Madrid, May 26, 1757, ACR 395.

87. Sánchez Santiró, "La hacienda reformada," 143–44, 165–68; see also Brading, *Miners and Merchants*, 52. In the case of Veracruz, it is hard to distinguish between tax farmers and local communities, as Sánchez Santiró does, because both claimed to represent the common good. According to Kessler, "Enforcing Virtue," 73–75, 104, 117, French merchants often claimed that Christian charitable ideals guided their actions.

Chapter 6

1. Manuel de la Sierra to Ambrosio Eugenio Santaella y Melgarejo, n.d., Archivo Histórico Nacional (Madrid, hereinafter AHN), Consejos 21003, folder Superior Gobierno 1753, Testimonies, fols. 104–105v; see also Santaella y Melgarejo's decree, Guadalajara, June 19, 1752, AHN, Consejos 21003, folder Superior Gobierno 1753, Testimonies, fol. 106; auto of Echeverz González, n.d., n.p., AHN, Consejos 21003, folder Superior Gobierno 1753, Testimonies, fol. 116; and Santaella y Melgarejo to king, Mexico City, March 17, 1753, AHN, Consejos 21003, folder Superior Gobierno 1753, Testimonies, fols. 127–128v.

2. Parecer of the prosecutor of the Council of the Indies, Madrid, n.d. (November 1753), AHN, Consejos 21003, fols. 93–94v; and Castro Santa-Anna, *Diario de sucesos notables*, 4:74–75. Echeverz González quoted Miguel de Cervantes, who reads in the original, "el que no está hecho a bragas, las costuras le hacen llagas."

3. Parecer of the prosecutor of the Council of the Indies, Madrid, n.d. (November 1753), AHN, Consejos 21003, fols. 93–94v.

4. Güemes to king, Mexico City, June 30, 1753, AHN, Consejos 21003, fols. 129–130; Güemes to king, n.d. (probably April 1753), AHN, Consejos 21003, fols. 87–92; and Castro Santa-Anna, *Diario de sucesos notables*, 4:74–75. See also Ambrosio Eugenio Santaella y Melgarejo to king, Mexico City, June 15, 1753, AHN, Consejos 21003, fols. 132–133v.

5. Mota y Escobar, *Descripción geográfica*, 43.

6. *Law of the Indies*, book 3, title 2, law 1; see also Parry, *La audiencia de Nueva Galicia*, 190–93, 203–5, 213–15, 245–47; Diego-Fernández Sotelo, "Fiscales, oidores, presidentes," 23–40; Garriga, "Concepción y aparatos de la justicia," 40–41, 55; and Muro Romero, *Las Presidencias-Gobernaciones*, 57–71.

7. Villarroel, *Govierno eclesiastico-pacifico*, 420. Herzog, "La presencia ausente," 819–26, shows that witnesses in Quito (now Ecuador) testified on the conduct of Peruvian viceroys during the judicial reviews, while, for instance, *Sumaria Secreta* of Juan de Ortega y Montañes, AGI, Escribanía 233A, folder 2; and *Sumaria y Pesquisa Secreta* of Güemes, AGI, Escribanía 246B, demonstrate that Guadalajarans did not testify on Mexican viceroys.

8. *Law of the Indies*, book 2, title 15, law 52, similarly law 47. According to Mota Padilla, *Historia del reino de Nueva Galicia*, 261–62, the Guadalajara president appointed all district judges, save Zacatecas, and the audiencia controlled the royal treasury for a short period after 1607, before reverting to the viceroys. According to Bertrand, *Grandeur et misères*, 92, a royal cédula from May 1692 stated that the "superintendence of the treasury is the exclusive charge of the viceroy of New Spain," ignoring the objections of the Guadalajara audiencia. Note that according to Güemes to Ensenada, Mexico City, June 26, 1748, AGI, México 1506, no. 45; and Güemes to Ensenada, Mexico City, May 27, 1751, AGI, México 1506, no. 95, Güemes labeled Guadalajara's government as "presidential" as opposed to the "pretorial" or fully autonomous audiencia of Guatemala.

9. Becerra Jiménez and Regalado Pinedo, "La consolidación de una capital," 463–65, argue insightfully that "Mexico City rarely dared to interfere in the internal affairs of the kingdom of New Galicia. Guadalajara had become . . . almost as important as the viceregal capital . . . in its political determination, economic dynamics, and judicial patronage power." See also Parry, *La audiencia de Nueva Galicia*, 245–47; Diego-Fernández Sotelo, Introduction to *La Nueva Galicia en el ocaso del imperio español*, xxxi–xxxiv; and Diego-Fernández Sotelo, "Las reales audiencias indianas," 21–68. Compare with the fractured audiencia of Santo Domingo as discussed in Eagle, "Beard-Pulling," 467–93.

10. Mota y Escobar, *Descripción geográfica*, 46–50; on Mota y Escobar, see Moreno and Murià, *De mediados del siglo XVI a finales del siglo XVIII*, 456–57.

11. Becerra Jiménez and Regalado Pinedo, "Tierras, minas y crecimiento demográfico," 444–49; Oliver Sánchez, "La evolución de la población," 611–21; and Regalado Pinedo, *L'Ouest mexicain*, 275.

12. Carbajal López, *La población en Bolaños*, 35–38, 103–24, 237–41; Carbajal

López, *La minería en Bolaños*, 14, 41–42, 46–53; Stangl, "¿Provincias y partidos?," 169–73; López Miramontes, *Las minas de Nueva España*, 12–13; and López Miramontes, "El establecimiento del real de minas de Bolaños," 408–36. Brading, "La minería de la plata en el siglo XVIII," 319, lists 1736 as the founding date of Bolaños, see also 323–25. Miranda, *El tributo indígena*, 261–62, shows that authorities often offered tribute exemptions to Natives who submitted to colonial rule. Valle Menéndez, *Juan Francisco de Güemes*, 482–88, summarizes the conflict in Bolaños. According to José Martínez de Lisarraga to viceroy, Mexico City, January 21, 1765, AGN, Minería 138, fols. 32–56v, five of the six mines were called la Perla, la Castellana, Montañesa, Zapopan, and la Conquista. For recent studies on mining, see Lane, *Silver City*; Couturier, *The Silver King*.

13. No author (probably José Díaz de Celis), Reparos que se manifestan, n.p., n.d.; see also Díaz de Celis to Güemes, Zimapan, October 20, 1748; and Díaz de Celis to Güemes, Mexico City, July 17, 1750, the three preceding documents in ACR 378; and king to Güemes, Buen Retiro, August 6, 1746, AGI, México 438. According to relación de méritos of Díaz de Celis, Madrid, October 7, 1739, AGI, Indiferente 148, N. 94, 1, fols. 1–2, Ensenada was serving as navy commissioner when he issued Díaz de Celis two certificates of good conduct. According to information by Díaz de Celis, Cádiz, June 31, 1742, AGI, Contratación 5485, N. 1, R. 27, fol. 4v, Díaz de Celis came originally from Santillán, near Burgos, and Ensenada appointed him treasurer in Zacatecas. Finally, according to testimony of Juan Crisóstomo Barroeta, Mexico City, January 17, 1757, and testimony of Manuel Cosuela, both documents in AGI, Escribanía 246B, fol. 27v, 150; list of appointments, AGI, Escribanía 246A, folder 1, 1757, fol. 210v; and Güemes to Ensenada, Mexico City, September 24, 1748, ACR 401, Güemes appointed Díaz de Celis as interim accountant of the Mexico City treasury on December 17, 1750, after serving on the 1748 commission in Zimapan to uncover embezzlements; see also Valle Menéndez, *Juan Francisco de Güemes*, 486.

14. Güemes to king, Mexico City, July 15, 1750, ACR 378. The *juez comisario* (commissioner) was Fernando González del Campillo; see royal decree, September 4, 1753, referenced in summary attached to consulta of the Council of the Indies, n.d., AGI, Guadalajara 107. Pedro Toral Valdés became treasurer, according to Güemes's report to Amarillas on Bolaños, Mexico City, October 2, 1755, in Torre Villar, *Instrucciones*, 862; see also summary of royal decree, attached to reply of the prosecutor of the Council of the Indies, Madrid, October 25, 1755, AGI, Guadalajara 89; and Güemes to Arriaga, Mexico City, April 12, 1755, AGI, Guadalajara 89. According to report of Joaquín Antonio Cortillas and Santiago Abad, Mexico City, September 12, 1757, AGI, Escribanía 246A, folder 5, fols. 5–12, the treasury had gathered 1,230,002 pesos.

15. Bishop to Triviño, Guadalajara, March 13, 1746, AGI, Guadalajara 106, referring to Viceroy Fuenclara.

16. Castillo de Aysa paid an additional 6,250 pesos to the Crown to install

Basarte; see royal provision to civil judge Domingo Valcárcel, Madrid, December 27, 1746, AGI, Escribanía 402B; instruction to Valcárcel by prosecutor José Borrull, Madrid, December 17, 1746, AGI, Escribanía 402B; Valcárcel to king, Guadalajara, December 3, 1746, AGI, Escribanía 393, pt. 5a, fols. 14–23v; sentence of the judicial chamber of the Council of the Indies, Madrid, July 23, 1749, AGI, Escribanía 393, pt. 5a, fols. 9–12v; and title of appointment, Buen Retiro, March 13, 1750, AGI, Guadalajara 82.

17. Quotation in Juan Atanasio Cervantes's letter to Antonio de Mier, agent of Diego Mijares, n.d., AGI, Guadalajara 115, exp. 1, folder testimonies; see also consulta of the Council of the Indies to Triviño, Madrid, December 17, 1743, AGI, Escribanía 402A; and bishop to Triviño, Guadalajara, March 13, 1746, AGI, Guadalajara 106. Mota Padilla, *Historia del reino de Nueva Galicia*, 497, praised Castillo de Aysa for improving public security and the water supply.

18. Cervantes's letter to Mier, agent of Mijares, n.d., AGI, Guadalajara 115, exp. 1, folder testimonies.

19. Güemes to Arriaga, Mexico City, April 12, 1755, ACR 455.

20. Three letters by Juan Atanasio de Cervantes to Antonio de Mier, agent of Diego Mijares, n.d., AGI, Guadalajara 115, exp. 1, folder testimonies; instruction to Diego Gorospe Padilla, in Torre Villar, *Instrucciones*, 853–54; and Carbajal López, *La minería en Bolaños*, 75–76. According to Pedro Malo de Villavicencio's decree, Mexico City, October 23, 1741, AGN, GdP 33, exp. 110, the captain protector of Natives also quarreled with the deputy alcalde mayor.

21. Güemes to Arriaga, Mexico City, April 12, 1755, ACR 455; see also title, Mexico City, November 7, 1754, AGN, Provincias Internas 129, fol. 172. Francisco Echazarreta and his brothers-in-law José Arribarrojo, Juan Francisco de Feria, Francisco Brena, and Diego Mijares worked as miners in Bolaños and provided Güemes with ammunition against Castillo de Aysa and Basarte, although in Güemes's report to Amarillas on Bolaños, Mexico City, October 2, 1755, in Torre Villar, *Instrucciones*, 863–64, the viceroy sharply criticized Arribarrojo. According to López Miramontes, *Las minas de Nueva España*, 14–15, 23–27, Francisco Javier Uribarren and José García Malavear also wrote reports about Bolaños, which Güemes had requested for the royal mining cabinet.

22. Deputy alcalde mayor Juan Rodríguez Landeros to Basarte, Bolaños, April 21, 1752; and presidential decree, Guadalajara, April 22, 1752, both documents in AGI, Guadalajara 107, folder 1752, testimonies, fols. 37–39; deputy alcalde mayor to Basarte, Bolaños, May 4, 1752, AGI, Guadalajara 107, folder 1753, Testimonies, fol. 50–50v; and Basarte to king, Guadalajara, February 25, 1755, AGI, Guadalajara 89.

23. Title, Mexico City, November 7, 1754, AGN, Provincias Internas 129, fols. 176–83; Güemes's decree, Mexico City, November 7, 1754, in Torre Villar, *Instrucciones*, 851; Juan Zarascua's certification of Güemes's appointment of December 9, 1754, AGI, Escribanía 246A, folder 1, fol. 161; and Castro Santa-Anna, *Diario de*

sucesos notables, 5:71. See also Figueroa y Melgar, *Estudio histórico*, 74; and Ladd, *The Mexican Nobility*, 198.

24. Rosenmüller, "Friends, Followers, Countrymen," 55–57.

25. Güemes to Arriaga, Mexico City, April 12, 1755, ACR 455; and Güemes's decree, Mexico City, November 7, 1754, in Torre Villar, *Instrucciones*, 850–51.

26. Pedro Toral Valdés to Basarte, Bolaños, February 6, 1755, AGI, Guadalajara 89.

27. *Obedecimiento* (show of obedience) by Alcalde Xacinto Ortiz and *alguacil mayor* (chief constable) José Antonio for the community expressed to Juan de la Cruz, San Gaspar de Huilacatitlan, February 27, 1755; see also treasury officials to captain protector Juan Antonio Romualdo Fernández Córdova, Bolaños, February 8, 1755; and Fernández Córdova to *hijos justiciales* (children in justice) of Chimaltitlan, Colotitlan, February 15, 1755, all three documents in Biblioteca Pública del Estado de Jalisco, Archivo de la Real Audiencia de Guadalajara (hereinafter BPEJ-ARAG), ramo civil, box 59, exp. 5, fols. 20–21, 23–23v, 28.

28. Güemes's decree, Mexico City, February 13, 1755, BPEJ-ARAG, ramo civil, box 59, exp. 5, fol. 30–30v; and land survey signed by José de Saucedo y Aguas, San Antonio de Bolaños, April 15, 1755, BPEJ-ARAG, ramo civil, box 59, exp. 5, fols. 36–37.

29. Viceregal decree, Mexico City, September 4, 1755, AGN, GdP 41, exp. 90; viceregal decree, hacienda de los Tepetates, October 27, 1755, AGN, GdP 41, exp. 99; *Instrucción militar*, Mexico City, November 28, 1754, in Torre Villar, *Instrucciones*, 860–61; and Carbajal López, *La minería en Bolaños*, 86. On date of taking office, treasury officials to Güemes, Bolaños, February 15, 1755, BPEJ-ARAG, ramo civil, box 59, exp. 5, fol. 49.

30. Viceregal decree, Mexico City, August 11, 1755, AGN, GdP 41, exp. 87, according to which the hacienda owner was Francisco Javier Uribarren, who had opposed Castillo de Aysa.

31. Report of (probably) Güemes's legal adviser, Mexico City, August 6, 1755; see also Gorospe Padilla to Güemes, Bolaños, July 18, 1755, both documents in AGN, Indiferente Virreinal 2711, exp. 6, fols. 21–23v; viceregal decree, Mexico City, August 11, 1755, AGN, GdP 41, exp. 86; and Amarillas's decree, Mexico City, December 24, 1755, AGN, GdP 41, exp. 101.

32. Amarillas to king, Mexico City, October 26, 1756; parecer of the fiscal of the Council of the Indies, Madrid, July 8, 1757; and consulta of the Council of the Indies, Madrid, July 14, 1757, the three previous documents in Archivo Dávila Garibi, Guadalajara, microfilm roll 100 (taken originally from AGI, Guadalajara 89).

33. Viceregal decree, Mexico City, August 6, 1755, AGN, GdP 41, exp. 85.

34. Three viceregal decrees, Mexico City, July 4, 1755, AGN, GdP 41, exp. 73, 74, 83; and Güemes's report to Amarillas on Bolaños, Mexico City, October 2, 1755, in Torre Villar, *Instrucciones*, 863–64.

35. Pedro Toral Valdés to Amarillas, Bolaños, February 14, 1756, AGN, Indiferente Virreinal 2711, exp. 6, fols. 24–26v.
36. Diego Rangel y Viezma to Güemes, n.d.; and Güemes's decree, Mexico City, July 30, 1755, both documents in AGN, Indiferente Virreinal 2711, exp. 6, fols. 17–18v.
37. Royal cédula, Madrid, March 29, 1749, AGN, RCO 69, exp. 43; Güemes to king, Mexico City, February 18, 1752, ACR 354; and Güemes to king, Mexico City, March 24, 1753, ACR 412.
38. Güemes to José Banfi y Parrilla, Mexico City, May 12, 1751, ACR 404; Güemes to Ensenada, Mexico City, February 8, 1753, ACR 412 (also in AGI, México 1350); Güemes to Banfi y Parrilla, October 6, 1751, ACR 464; royal order to embark to Banfi y Villalobos signed by Ensenada, Madrid, August 16, 1745; and Alexo Gutiérrez de Rubalcava's dispatch to embark, Cádiz, November 21, 1746, both preceding documents in AGI, Contratación 5488, N. 3, R. 34, fols. 1–1v, 3. According to Gómez Gómez, *Actores del documento*, 80–81, 125, 177, José Banfi y Parrilla came from a Milanese family residing in Spain and joined the secretary of the Indies in 1732 during José Patiño's term as first minister. He fell from office on July 21, 1754, after Ensenada's arrest, but returned to court in 1760.
39. Basarte's report, Guadalajara, February 11, 1752, testimony, AGI, Guadalajara 89, fols. 6v–7v; and Güemes to king, Mexico City, September 21, 1754, AGI, Guadalajara 89. The Guadalajaran treasurer was Manuel Cuevas.
40. Güemes to king, Mexico City, February 6, 1753, AGI, Guadalajara 89; and Bertrand, *Grandeur et misères*, 121.
41. Castro Santa-Anna, *Diario de sucesos notables*, 4:78, also 52; see also Güemes to king, Mexico City, September 21, 1754, AGI, Guadalajara 89. Juan José Ortiz's title was *juez comisario*.
42. Fiscal of the Council of the Indies, Madrid, October 17, 1755, AGI, Guadalajara 89.
43. Fiscal of the Council of the Indies, Madrid, October 17, 1755; and Güemes to king, Mexico City, September 21, 1754, the two previous documents in AGI, Guadalajara 89. According to ecclesiastical chapter session, Guadalajara, February 20, 1753, referencing papal bull, Rome, December 20, 1751, and royal cédula, Buen Retiro, March 5, 1752, AHAG, Capitular XI desde 1746 hasta 1759, fol. 120v; and royal cédula to Cardinal Portocarrero, Buen Retiro, September 16, 1751, AGI, Guadalajara 82, the Franciscan fray Francisco de San Buenaventura Tejada y Díez de Velasco served as bishop of Guadalajara beginning in 1751.
44. Güemes to king, Mexico City, September 21, 1754, AGI, Guadalajara 89; and inventory of Ortiz, n.d., AGI, Guadalajara 89.
45. Ortiz to Güemes, Mexico City, May 25, 1754; report of the Tribunal of Account's *mesa de memoria* (archive), Mexico City, June 19, 1754; and tribunal's report, June 19, 1754, all three preceding documents in AGI, Guadalajara 89; see also Castro Santa-Anna, *Diario de sucesos notables*, 4:75.

46. Castro Santa-Anna, *Diario de sucesos notables*, 4:94; Güemes to king, March 24, 1753, ACR 412; parecer of the fiscal of the Council of the Indies, Madrid, October 17, 1755; and consulta of the Council of the Indies, February 13, 1756, the two preceding documents in AGI, Guadalajara 89. According to these documents, the new official was Juan Antonio Gutiérrez Herrera.

47. Francisco Javier Uribarren to Tomás Ortiz de Landazuri, Guadalajara, November 6, 1751, AGI, Guadalajara 89, testimonies, fols. 13–14.

48. Reply of prosecutor José Manuel de la Garza Falcón, Guadalajara, November 8, 1751, AGI, Guadalajara 89, testimonies, fol. 14; royal cédula to Alonso Cevallos Villagutierre, Madrid, November 19, 1678, AGI, Guadalajara 89, testimonies, fol. 13–13v; Francisco López Portillo to Güemes, Guadalajara, April 23, 1752, AGI, Guadalajara 89, testimonies, fols. 9v–11v; Basarte to Güemes, Guadalajara, April 5, 1752, AGI, Guadalajara 89, testimonies, fol. 12–12v; and Güemes to king, Mexico City, February 6, 1753, AGI, Guadalajara 89.

49. Testimony of Pedro Avila, Bolaños, January 10, 1752, AGI, Guadalajara 89, testimonies, fol. 45; see also testimony of Clemente Bernal, Guadalajara, December 11, 1751, and January 26, 1752, AGI, Guadalajara 89, testimonies, fols. 19v–20v, 39v.

50. Rodríguez Gallardo to Marquis of Altamira, Mexico City, April 28, 1752, AGI, Guadalajara 89, testimonies, fol. 62–62v.

51. Rodríguez Gallardo to Marquis of Altamira, Mexico City, April 28, 1752, AGI, Guadalajara 89, testimony, fols. 59, 61–64.

52. Güemes to king, Mexico City, February 6, 1753, AGI, Guadalajara 89.

53. Testimony of Eugenio Francisco de Castro, Guadalajara, October 26, 1752, AGI, Guadalajara 89, testimony, fol. 83v.

54. Testimony of Miguel del Pulgar, Guadalajara, October 27, 1752, AGI, Guadalajara 89, folder Testimonio . . . contra ofiziales reales, fol. 85.

55. Langue, *Los señores de Zacatecas*, 79–80. According to Bertrand, *Grandeur et misères*, 29–31, the treasury officials also negotiated *regalías* (tips) on royal *libranzas* (payment orders comparable to checks), depending on the social standing of the petitioner and the time of issuance, and they usually amounted from a third to a half of the original amount.

56. Castro Santa-Anna, *Diario de sucesos notables*, 4:113. On Banfi y Villalobos, see Langue, "Trabajadores y formas de trabajo," 488–89.

57. Bishop of Guadalajara Juan Gómez de Parada to Fernando Triviño, Guadalajara, March 13, 1746, AGI, Guadalajara 106; this letter was cited extensively in parecer of the fiscal, Madrid, June 30, 1749, AGI, Guadalajara 106. For the composition of the audiencia, see *Law of the Indies* book 2, title 15, law 7.

58. José Banfi y Parrilla to Güemes, Madrid, September 4, 1751, ACR 388.

59. José Banfi y Parrilla to Güemes, Madrid, September 4, 1751, ACR 388; see also Güemes to Ensenada, Mexico City, April 2, 1754, ACR 354; and Güemes to Ensenada, Mexico City, May 24, 1752, AGI, México 1349, although I have not found

his report written on April 2, 1752. Seijas y Lobera, *Gobierno militar*, 268, called for dissolving the Guadalajara audiencia; Juan and Ulloa, *Discourse and Political Reflections*, 258, criticized the audiencia of Panama. See also Burkholder and Chandler, *From Impotence to Authority*, 41; and Navarro García, *Don José de Gálvez*, 92–93.

60. Basarte to king, Guadalajara, February 25, 1755, AGI, Guadalajara 89.

61. Parecer of the fiscal of the Council of the Indies, Madrid, October 25, 1755, AGI, Guadalajara 89.

62. Royal cédula to Amarillas, Buen Retiro, September 16, 1756; two dictamenes of the fiscal of the audiencia Marquis of Aranda, Mexico City, September 25, 1758, and February 26, 1759; and Corregidor Agustín Benites to Amarillas, Bolaños, December 14, 1758, all four documents in BPEJ-ARAG, civil, box 59, exp. 5, fols. 68–71v, 76–77, 83–85v; king to Amarillas, Madrid, December 31, 1759, AGN, RCO 79, exp. 30, fol. 3; Arriaga to Amarillas, Madrid, June 11, 1757, AGN, RCO 77, exp. 68, fol. 163-163v; and Cajigal to Receptor Toribio Gómez de Tagle, Mexico City, July 3, 1760, AGN, GdP 42, exp. 327, fol. 310–310v. Garibay, "Biografía del Marqués del Castillo de Aysa," traces the decline of Castillo de Aysa's family.

63. Burbank and Cooper, "The Empire Effect," 241.

64. Felices de la Fuente, *Condes, marqueses y duques*, 95–96.

65. This observation on the viceroyalty of New Spain differs from the South American experience, where, as Puente Brunke, "El virreinato peruano," 83–97, reminds us, the audiencias primarily governed the territory and shaped the transition to independence.

Chapter 7

1. Castro Santa-Anna, *Diario de sucesos notables*, 5:170.

2. Sala y Vila, "Una corona bien vale," 17–150; and Moreno Cebrián, "Acumulación y blanqueo," 266–69, study viceregal wealth acquisition beyond the official salary; see chapter 2 of this book for viceregal entourages.

3. Vázquez Varela, "La corte virreinal," 175–214; Vázquez Varela, "Jorge de Villalonga's Entourage," 111–26; and Vázquez Varela, "Redes de patronazgo," 135–47. Vázquez Varela, *"De la primera sangre de este reino,"* argues that no viceregal clients remained in New Granada, having scant access to lucrative office.

4. Güemes to Pedro Manuel de Arandia, governor of the Philippines (1752–1759), Mexico City, March 17, 1755, ACR 485.

5. Anonymous author, couplet titled "Dejame pluma que con rudo canto," attached to Güemes to Arandia, Mexico City, March 17, 1755, ACR 485.

6. Güemes to Ensenada, Mexico City, February 21, 1747, AGI, México 1506, no. 25, reads: "Mi Muger renueva a Vuestra Merced los recursos de su reconocimiento y estimación; y yo la invariable fineza y amistad con que soy de Vuestra Merced todo hasta morir." See Rosenmüller, "Friends, Followers, Countrymen,"

54–55. Pearce, "Minister and Viceroy," 478–79, shows a similar relation between Ensenada and the Peruvian viceroy.

7. Ensenada to Güemes, Buen Retiro, August 14, 1748, AGI, México 1506, no. 41.2, reads: "A Madama mis rendimientos... Quedo de Vuestra Merced con inmutable amistad."

8. Güemes to Arriaga, Mexico City, April 12, 1755, AGI, Guadalajara 95.

9. Council of the Indies notary Antonio de Salazar, Madrid, March 13, 1758, AGI, México 1506, no. 171a.

10. Castro Santa-Anna, *Diario de sucesos notables*, 5:167–72; Amarillas to Arriaga, Mexico City, November 30, 1755, AGN, Correspondencia de virreyes, 1.a serie, 1, exp. 36; Amarillas to Arriaga, February 18, 1756, ACR 354; and Ahumada y Vera, *Diario de viaje*, 33–53. On the approximate value of the headband, see audiencia's receipt of royal cédula to Viceroy Berenguer de Marquina, Mexico City, July 21, 1802, AGN, Real Audiencia 4, exp. 8, fols. 75–78, which prohibited giving awards to gentlemen. On the coach, see Berndt León Mariscal, "Discursos," 233.

11. Quotation in Castro Santa-Anna, *Diario de sucesos notables*, 5:157; on the deposit, royal order, San Lorenzo, October 29, 1747, AGI, México 439.

12. Castro Santa-Anna, *Diario de sucesos notables*, 5:171.

13. Castro Santa-Anna, *Diario de sucesos notables*, 5:169–72.

14. Castro Santa-Anna, *Diario de sucesos notables*, 5:173; see also Ajofrín, *Diario del viaje*, 184. On the hacienda, see Armella de Aspe, *San Bartolomé de los Tepetates*, 50–54. Amarillas to Arriaga, Mexico City, November 30, 1755, AGN, Correspondencia de virreyes, 1.a serie, 1, exp. 36; and Amarillas to Arriaga, February 18, 1756, ACR 354. On Jacinto Martínez de Aguirre's acquisition, see contract, Mexico City, January 15, 1749, AGN, Tierras 3353, exp. 43. Tepetate is a volcanic rock frequently used in construction.

15. Castro Santa-Anna, *Diario de sucesos notables*, 5:180–81, also 174, 177; see also Ahumada y Vera, *Diario de viaje*, 53.

16. Andrés Cavo, cited in Rubio Mañé, *El virreinato*, 1:137, also 210; and *Law of the Indies*, book 3, title 3, law 72. The early seventeenth-century viceregal salary amounted to 27,573 pesos.

17. Ahumada y Vera, *Diario de viaje*, 53–56; Castro Santa-Anna, *Diario de sucesos notables*, 5:173, 175, 181–85, 220; and García Panes y Abellán, *Diario particular*, 105–6. According to Amarillas to Arriaga, Mexico City, November 30, 1755, AGN, Correspondencia de virreyes, 1a serie, 1, exp. 36, Amarillas traveled from Veracruz to Mexico City in one and a half months. Amarillas to Arriaga, Mexico City, November 30, 1755, AGI 1352; and Güemes's instructions to Amarillas, Mexico City, October 8, 1754, in Torre Villar, *Instrucciones*, 795–837. See also Ramos, *Identity, Ritual, and Power*, 44.

18. Castro Santa-Anna, *Diario de sucesos notables*, 5:194, 200, 243, 248. See also Güemes to Arriaga, Cádiz, August 6, 1756, AGI, México 1506, no. 168; Arriaga

to Güemes, Madrid, August 10, 1756, AGI, México 1506, no. 168.1; Arriaga to Güemes, Madrid, August 24, 1756, AGI, México 1506, no. 169.1; Güemes to Arriaga, Cádiz, September 1, 1756, AGI, México 1506, no. 170; and Valle Menéndez, *Juan Francisco de Güemes*, 648. According to Gómez Urdáñez, *Fernando VI*, 114, Ensenada remained exiled in Granada until September 1757, when he moved to Puerto de Santa María outside of Cádiz.

19. The French consul general Abbé Béliardi to Nicolas-René Berryer, cited in Stein and Stein, *Apogee of Empire*, 13. For example, Güemes recommended audiencia ministers Luis Mosquera y Pimentel and Domingo Trespalacios y Escandón for positions on the Council of the Indies (see the appendix), and according to Castejón, "Un *cursus honorum*," 440, Charles III promoted them later as the first two councilors with American experience. See also, e.g., Eslava's order to Güemes to convene a meeting to discuss cannon calibers, Buen Retiro, May 9, 1757, ACR 395; and Eissa-Barroso, "Politics, Political Culture, and Policy Making," 246n229.

20. Anonymous author, *Primera parte. El Duende de Mexico da la bienvenida al Excelentísimo Señor Virrey*, n.d., INAH, CA, microfilm roll 56, fol. 81–81v.

21. Francisco Bastán y Cárdenas, Marquis of Viso-Alegre, to king, Mexico City, October 3, 1758, AGI, México 1853, referring to secretary Alfonso Antonio Gómez Bárcena and the merchant Count of San Bartolomé de Xala. According to Felices de la Fuente, *Condes, marqueses y duques*, 306, Viso-Alegre's title was established in 1711, before Güemes's title. Such friction of alcaldes mayores with viceroys was not unusual. According to royal cédula to Fuenclara, San Lorenzo, November 13, 1745, Konetzke, *Colección de documentos*, vol. 3, tome 1, 237, Fuenclara denied Viso-Alegre's predecessor Miguel Román de Castilla y Lugo the use of a stagecoach with "two coachmen and four mules." Güemes's criticism of Viso-Alegre is in Güemes to Arriaga, Mexico City, March 10, 1755, AGI, México 1352. Bravo Lira, "Régimen virreinal," 404; and Arnold, *Bureaucracy and Bureaucrats*, 25–30, argue that the viceregal secretary became an independent office in 1742 with the appointment of Francisco Fernández Molinillo, who drew a notable salary of 3,000 pesos. Nonetheless, Alfonso Antonio Gómez Bárcena defied this process, as he traveled with Güemes to Cuba to serve as his personal secretary. Ensenada pondered naming another independent viceregal secretary but yielded to Güemes's wishes to appoint Gómez Bárcena, albeit without salary. A fully independent office with permanent salaried officials emerged only after Güemes's term; see king to Council of the Indies or Triviño, Aranjuez, April 23, 1742, AGI, México 383; embarkation papers, AGI, Contratación 5481, N. 2, R. 23, fol. 11r.; Güemes to Ensenada, October 24, 1752, AGI, México 1506, no. 120; and Ensenada to Güemes, San Lorenzo, October 22, 1753, AGI, México 1506, no. 120.2.

22. Rosenmüller, *Patrons, Partisans, and Palace Intrigues*, 154–56. On Alburquerque's conflict with the consulado, see also Escamilla González, "La nueva alianza," 41–63; and Valle Pavón, "El respaldo económico," 941–63.

23. Moreno Cebrián, "Acumulación y blanqueo," 266–76, shows that Peruvian

viceroy Marquis of Castelfuerte (1734–1736) accepted around 790,000 pesos in gifts. See Sala y Vila, "Una corona bien vale," 39, on Viceroy Count of Monclova.
24. Ertman, *Birth of the Leviathan*, 9–34, sees Latin Europe predominantly as a form of patrimonial absolutism and reserves bureaucratic absolutism for other states. For Weber, *Economy and Society*, 220–23, the ideal typical bureaucrats have well-defined jurisdictions in hierarchical and depoliticized offices, receive a salary usually with retirement benefits, and rarely work in additional occupations. They advance in careers according to supervised performance and seniority rather than owning their offices. Weber pointed out that these ideal types never existed historically. They certainly do not apply to Güemes or most other viceroys. Costa, "Patronage and Bribery," 23–59, views the important sixteenth-century Viceroy Count of Villar of Peru as a combination of Weberian patrimonial and bureaucratic rule; see also Osterhammel, "The Imperial Viceroy," 15–18.
25. According to Güemes to Arriaga, Mexico City, June 12, 1755, ACR 455; Güemes to Arriaga, Mexico City, June 14, 1755, ACR 455; Güemes to Ensenada, Mexico City, January 30, 1748, AGI, México 1506, no. 40; Güemes to Ensenada, Mexico City, January 23, 1752, AGI, México 1506, no. 109; and Güemes's instruction to Amarillas, Mexico City, November 28, 1754, AGI, México 1506, no. 167a, Güemes gave Judge Domingo Valcárcel Formento y Vaquerizo several commissions by the early 1750s, appointed him *auditor de guerra* (judge advocate), and recommended his son for a prebendary in the Cathedral of Mexico City. The viceroy called on Valcárcel to defend him in the juicio de residencia, an important task given to reliable friends.
26. *Papeleta de México de 25 Noviembre 1756 hasta 9 de Enero 1757*, ACR 360; see also royal cédula, Aránjuez, July 6, 1755, AGI, Escribanía 246 A, book 1, fols. 1–3; charge against Güemes, 1757, AGI, Escribanía 246A, book 5, fols. 1–3; rebuttal by Baltasar Rodríguez Medrano, Mexico City, AGI, Escribanía 246A, book 5, fols. 27–28v; and sentence by Galindo, Mexico City, June 6, 1757, AGI, Escribanía 246A, book 5, fols. 34–50v.
27. Barroeta to Güemes, Mexico City, June 23, 1761, ACR 404; and sentence of the Council of the Indies, Madrid, March 13, 1758, AGI, Escribanía 1194. The *guarda mayor* (treasury official) in Acapulco drew 1,502 pesos a year. The *Law of the Indies* outlined the juicio de residencia procedure in book 5, title 14.
28. Sentence of the Council of the Indies, Madrid, March 13, 1758, AGI, Escribanía 1194, fols. 1–5, quotation in fol. 4 (a copy of the sentence is also in AGI, México 1506, no. 171a).
29. José Ortiz de Saracho on behalf of Güemes to king, Madrid, May 11, 1758, AGI, Escribanía 246C, folder 28, Demanda puesta por don Diego Álvarez, fol. 22.
30. Consulta of the Council of the Indies, Madrid, October 17, 1760, AGI, Escribanía 246C, folder 28, Demanda puesta por don Diego Álvarez, fol. 35; royal cédula, Buen Retiro, August 28, 1753, AGI, Escribanía 246C, folder 28, fols. 4–8; Manuel Antonio Alejo Manzano, attorney of Diego Álvarez, to king, Madrid,

April 7, 1758, AGI, Escribanía 246C, folder 28, fols. 10–20; sentence of the judicial chamber of the Council of the Indies, Madrid, September 15, 1758, AGI, Escribanía 246C, folder 28, fols. 27–28; and Güemes to king, Mexico City, September 12, 1754, AGI, México 1352. Taking office by Álvarez, Mexico City, December 23, 1755, AGI, Escribanía 246C, book 9, fols. 72v–74; and testimonies against Álvarez, Mexico City, March 18–28, 1754, AGI, Escribanía 246C, book 9, fols. 161–77; and Güemes's decree, Mexico City, December 23, 1753, fols. 183–84. According to king to Count of Güemes, Buen Retiro, 1780, drawing on Güemes's communications from February 4, 1759, and October 7, 1760, AGI, México 1506, no. 172.1, Güemes's son Antonio María forewent the deposit in exchange for not paying the *lanza* (tax) on his title of nobility.

31. Tomás Vélez Cachupín to Güemes, Mexico City, September 23, 1761, ACR 388. For instance, the consulta of the Council of the Indies, October 30, 1719, AGI, México 379, charged Viceroy Duke of Linares (1710–1716) a 6,000 peso fine for expediting these papers and selling office appointments.

32. Güemes to Arriaga, Cádiz, August 18, 1756, AGI, México 1506, no. 169; Arriaga to Güemes, Madrid, August 24, 1756, AGI, México 1506, no. 169.1; and Güemes to Arriaga, Cádiz, September 1, 1756, AGI, México 1506, no. 170. For the salary, see Güemes to Ensenada, Mexico City, July 12, 1746, ACR 374 (one copy in ACR 476); and report of the Tribunal of Accounts, Mexico City, November 15, 1780, BNM, FR, manuscritos 439, fols. 333–39. See also Valle Menéndez, *Juan Francisco de Güemes*, 66.

33. *Nota de los Caxones . . . pertenezientes al Conde de Güemes*, attached to Manuel Díaz Saravia to Güemes, Cádiz, June 15, 1757, ACR 464; Güemes to Manuel Díaz Sarabia, Madrid, August 2, 1757, ACR 427; Gerónimo de la Maza Alvarado to Güemes, Cádiz, June 1, 1762, and June 25, 1762; and Güemes to Maza Alvarado, Madrid, February 7, 1763, the three preceding documents in ACR 347; and Castro Santa-Anna, *Diario de sucesos notables*, 5:173.

34. According to Figueroa y Melgar, *Estudio histórico*, 72, quotation on 73, Juana María married Francisco de Paula de Tovar, Count of Cancelada. See also Valle Menéndez, *Juan Francisco de Güemes*, 331. Mostenses Square draws its name from its former Premonstratensian Priory.

35. We know more about the lives of Güemes's sons. The second Count of Revillagigedo, viceroy of colonial Mexico (1789–1794), eclipses his father Güemes in the popular imagination today, although the municipal council stridently opposed his vanity and authoritarianism; see Meißner, *Eine Elite im Umbruch*, 104–7, 116; and Miranda Pacheco, "El juicio de residencia al virrey Revillagigedo," 49–50, 64–65. Ozanam, *Les diplomates espagnols*, 289–91, 365, relates that Güemes's second son, Antonio María Güemes Pacheco Padilla, baptized in Havana on July 16, 1742, and later Count of Güemes, served as envoy to Sweden from 1780, ambassador to Prussia from 1785, and councilor of state from 1795. He married María Muñoz Jofre Loaysa y Salcedo in 1790. He became third Count of

Revillagigedo in 1799 and passed away in Madrid on April 2, 1804. Álvaro María de Navia Osorio de Güemes, the son of Güemes's daughter Francisca, was born in 1771. He worked as an interpreter in the Turin embassy during the Napoleonic Wars, whereupon his mother had to bail him out of debtor's prison.

36. Anonymous author (possibly one of Antonia's siblings), *Extracto instructivo de lo acaecido con el Conde de la Bobadilla*, n.d., ACR 411 (hereinafter *Extracto instructivo*). See also *Representación ó Memorial dado á Su Majestad por Don Luis María de Narvaez, Argote y Guzmán, Conde de Bobadilla; pretendiendo los honores de Grande de España*, AHN, Sección Nobleza (Toledo), Valencia, folder C.1, D. 7; Vilar y Pascual, *Diccionario histórico, genealógico, y heráldico*, 300; and García Carraffa and García Carraffa, *Diccionario heráldico y genealógico*, vol. 59, 56–57.

37. Anonymous author, *Extracto instructivo*, including the quotations in this paragraph.

38. Anonymous author, *Extracto instructivo*. The Count of Floridablanca served as ambassador to Rome (1772–1776) and was titled on November 7, 1773, so the source must have been written after that date; see Díaz-Trechuelo y López-Spínola, "Juan Vicente de Güemes Pacheco"; and Vallejo García-Hevia, "José Moñino y Redondo."

39. Navarro García, "Destrucción de la oposición política"; and Brading, *Miners and Merchants*, 39. See also Brading, *Church and State*, 4–5, 12–16; and Andrés-Gallego, *El motín de Esquilache*, 600–603. On Cevallos, see chapter 5 of this volume.

40. Note on the back of an invitation by the Marquise of Fuente Pelayo, AHN, Sección Nobleza (Toledo), Torrelaguna, folder C. 442, D. 36, records Güemes's death; see also Valle Menéndez, *Juan Francisco de Güemes*, 421, 630. Güemes to Cevallos, Madrid, October 9, 1763, ACR 396, reported on Ricardo Wall's resignation. Stein and Stein, *Apogee of Empire*, 83–107, point to the leaders of the Council of Castile and its governor, the bishop of Cartagena, Diego de Rojas y Contreras, and other privileged factions who overthrew Esquilache with popular support; see also Kuethe and Andrien, *The Spanish Atlantic World*, 262–66, 272–73. López García, *El motín contra Esquilache*, 13–14, 237–39, emphasizes popular political agency, especially of salaried "criados, construction workers, and servants" while downplaying palace politics. Andrés-Gallego, *El motín de Esquilache*, explains the revolt as elite machinations against Esquilache's program.

41. Castro Gutiérrez, *Nueva ley y nuevo rey*, 97, 115–208, 262–75, argues that no "sector of colonial society" (110) supported Gálvez, because he offered little in return for new taxes and other imposiciones; see also Tanck de Estrada and Marichal, "¿Reino o colonia?," 313–14, 340; Kuethe and Andrien, *The Spanish Atlantic World*, 251–52, 269–71, 275–78; and Navarro García, "Destrucción de la oposición política," 14. Zepeda Cortés, "José's Secrets," offers new research on Gálvez.

42. According to Navarro García, "Destrucción de la oposición política," 3–4, 7, 10–14; and Brading, *Miners and Merchants*, 39, one civil judge withdrew into a monastery for his advanced age, while two were allowed to remain in New Spain for illness. See also Tanck de Estrada and Marichal, "¿Reino o colonia?," 315; and Farriss, *La corona y el clero*, 125.

43. On Martín Aspiroz, see Castro Santa-Anna, *Diario de sucesos notables*, 5:147; and Valle Menéndez, *Juan Francisco de Güemes*, 561. On Pedro Núñez de Villavicencio, see Güemes to Núñez de Villavicencio, Mexico City, March 8, 1761, ACR 404; Güemes to Núñez de Villavicencio, Madrid, July 1, 1763, ACR 387; relación de méritos, AGI, Indiferente 148, N. 58; and testimony of Barroeta, January 17, 1757, AGI, Escribanía 246B, fol. 27v. See also Tanck de Estrada, "El rector desterrado," 181–88.

44. Except for Pedro Núñez de Villavicencio, scion of an established Creole family; see Sanchiz and Conde Díaz Rubín, *Historia genealógica*, 207. Historians have also discussed discrimination against Creoles; see Brading, *Mito y profecía*, 80–88; Lavallé, *Las promesas ambiguas*; and Burkholder and Chandler, *From Impotence to Authority*, 83–115. Pietschmann, "Antecedentes políticos de México," 23–24, 43, argues that Charles III opposed monopolies and oligarchic power structures rather than oppressing Creoles, while Castejón, "Un cursus honorum," 451, denies Gálvez's anti-Creole bias in appointing audiencia ministers.

45. Escamilla González, "Los confesores reales," 241–42.

46. The civil prosecutor was Juan Antonio Velarde y Cienfuegos. According to Urrutia, *Descripción histórico-artística*, 15; Salazar Mir, *Los expedientes de limpieza de sangre*, 94–95; and García Melero, "Realizaciones arquitectónicas," 260, Cevallos may have served as dean of the cathedral in Cádiz before going to Seville; see also *Diccionario Biográfico Español*, "Ignacio de Ceballos Villagutierre"; and Zahino Peñafort, "El criollo mexicano," 120n28. According to Arriaga to Marquis of el Real Tesoro, San Ildefonso, August 13, 1773, AGI, Contratación 5518, N. 1, R. 63, fol. 1, Ignacio Negreiros y Herrera returned to Mexico City in 1773 to resume his work as the accountant of the Tribunal of Accounts. On Gamboa, see Bucareli to Arriaga, Mexico City, November 26, 1772, AGN, Correspondencia de virreyes 5, exp. 1, fols. 405–6; Branciforte to Llaguno, Mexico City, August 29, 1794, AGN, Correspondencia de virreyes 179, fol. 32–32v; Otero, "Apuntes," 365; Albi, *Gamboa's World*, 109–15; and Burkholder and Chandler, *Biographical Dictionary of Audiencia Ministers*, 346–47.

Conclusion

1. Marichal, *Bankruptcy of Empire*, 6, argues that the tax collection in New Spain was "singularly ineffectual" before 1760. Stein and Stein, *Apogee of Empire*,

viii, also deny radical change in the first half of the century. Stein and Stein, *Silver, Trade, and War*, 232, add that "by 1740 . . . the burden of the Habsburg legacy had reasserted itself. The worst of Spain's eighteenth-century crises seemed to have subsided in somnolent stagnation," and on page 266, they observe that the "inability of a carefully selected leading minister to carry out a policy of even moderate change . . . was symbolized by the failed enterprise of Ensenada"; see also 263–66. I disagree with Stein and Stein's point. Lamikiz, *Trade and Trust*, 14, acknowledges Ensenada's reforms while proposing that Charles III "gave added vigor" to modernization. Zepeda Cortés, "Trumped by Politics," 549–50, views Pedro Antonio de Cossío's treasury superintendence (1780–1783) as one of the "boldest governance experiments conducted during the Bourbon era." Paquette, *Enlightenment, Governance, and Reform*, 2, also stresses the changes of the later century. Escamilla González, *José Patricio Fernández de Uribe*, 39–40, underlines Gálvez's Augean task. Lempérière, *Entre Dieu et le roi*, 63–70, 310–11, denies that the Bourbon Reforms created a modern state, given that absolutism and corporate society had already coexisted since the late Middle Ages. McFarlane, *Colombia before Independence*, doubts the effectiveness of reforms at the regional level. Pérez Herrero, "Economía y poder," 27–29, maintains that the reforms aimed at a recentralization of the monarchy and improving tax collection. Cruz, *Gentlemen, Bourgeois, and Revolutionaries*, 3–15, emphasizes Spain's political but not social transformation in the second half of the eighteenth century. Classical scholarship on the Bourbon Reforms includes Brading, *Miners and Merchants*, 33–96; Brading, "La monarquía católica," 39, sees the Bourbon Reforms as the origin of independence. See also Arnold, *Bureaucracy and Bureaucrats*; Burkholder and Chandler, *From Impotence to Authority*; Tutino, "Creole Mexico," v–vii; and Barbier, *Reform and Politics*, 5, 7–9.

2. Lynch, "El reformismo borbónico," 40, 45; Lynch, *Bourbon Spain*, 164; and Castro Gutiérrez, *Nueva ley y nuevo rey*, 96–97, 264–75. Gómez Urdáñez, *Fernando VI*, 81, 105, maintains that the monarchy boasted more than eighty-five warships and reached "the fullness of Spanish enlightened despotism" (144) by 1754; Pieper, *La Real Hacienda*, 12, 62–64, 80–82, shows that Ensenada successfully revamped the financial administration, which remained unchanged under Charles III. Bouhrass, "La administración virreinal," thoroughly synthesizes the period.

3. Kuethe and Andrien, *The Spanish Atlantic World*, 3–6, 25, 348–50.

4. Calvo, "Ciencia, cultura y política," loc. 1161, Kindle; García Ayluardo, "Reformar la Iglesia," loc. 3980, 4291, Kindle; and Bertrand, *Grandeur et misères*, 291, 325, underscore the "long durée" of reforms including stringent *visitas generales* that ended with the arrival of provincial intendants in 1787. For Pearce, *The Origins of Bourbon Reform*, 7–14, 152–69, any distinction between the first and second half of the century is now obsolescent, without disputing the latter's more far-ranging aims. Eissa-Barroso, *The Spanish Monarchy*, 10, maintains that the

reforms of the early century were "no more vigorous, far-reaching, or 'colonial'" than the later ones. Navarro García, "El reformismo borbónico," 496, points to the reforms throughout the eighteenth century. Lane, *Silver City*, 2–4, makes the case for successful tax reforms in early eighteenth-century Potosí (now Bolivia).

5. Storrs, *The Resilience of the Spanish Monarchy*, 10–14, argues for Spanish vitality in the late seventeenth century; see also Rosenmüller, *Corruption and Justice*, 134–42. On the imagined transition from the allegedly spent Charles II to the fertile and warlike Bourbon Philip V, see Ramos and Escamilla González, "Sucesión y renovación," 384–85, 402–3.

6. See, for instance, Calderón Quijano, *Los virreyes de Nueva España en el reinado de Carlos III*; Calderón Quijano, *Los virreyes de Nueva España en el reinado de Carlos IV*; Haddick, "The Administration of Viceroy Iturrigaray"; and Jones, "New Spain and the Viceregency."

7. Ramos, *Identity, Ritual, and Power*; Curcio-Nagy, *The Great Festivals*; and Gonzalbo Aizpuru, "Las fiestas del pasado," 177–81. Morales Folguera, *Cultura simbólica*, analyzes the visual culture of exequies and viceregal entries. Büschges, "Del criado al valido," 157–81; and Büschges, "La corte virreinal," 131–40, observes the aristocratic character of viceregal courts in Italy and Spain compared to the court in Mexico. Important are also Escamilla González, "Permanence and Change"; Escamilla González, "La corte"; Cañeque, *The King's Living Image*; and Rubial García, "Las virreinas novohispanas," 3–44.

8. Semboloni Capitani, *La construcción de la autoridad virreinal*; and Pearce, "Minister and Viceroy," 478, based on his book *The Origins of Bourbon Reform*. On the changing social profile of viceroys, see Eissa-Barroso, "Of Experience, Zeal, and Selflessness," 317–45. Yalí Román, "Sobre alcaldías mayores," 28–30; and Pietschmann, "Alcaldes Mayores, Corregidores und Subdelegados," 188, throw light on declining viceregal patronage over alcaldes mayores in the 1970s; see also Rosenmüller, *Corruption and Justice*, 123–52.

9. Based on Stollberg-Rilinger, *Rituale*, 39; and Ramírez, "Institutions of the Spanish American Empire," 121.

10. Holenstein, "Introduction: Empowering Interactions," 1–31; on negotiated politics, see MacKay, *The Limits of Royal Authority*.

11. Real cédula signed by Ensenada to Güemes, Buen Retiro, August 27, 1747, AGN, RCO 67, exp. 76, fols. 273–279; and real cédula, Ensenada to Güemes, Aranjuez, June 30, 1751, AGN, RCO 71, exp. 150, fols. 547–552v. On the trend toward greater administration, see Pietschmann, "Antecedentes políticos de México," 49–60.

12. Münkler, *Empires*, viii, 4–11, makes the cascading argument; see also Cardim, "Political Status and Identity," 101–16. Cardim et al., introduction to *Polycentric Monarchies*, 3–8, argue that all parts of the empire thought of themselves as centers; Yun Casalilla, "Introducción: Entre el imperio colonial," 11–13, emphasizes relations among kingdoms; Calvo, "Trayectorias de luz y de sombra," 493–94,

argues for Guadalajara's midlevel position in an empire of courts and leading cities; and Pietschmann, "Diego García Panes," 211–33, points to the antagonistic eighteenth-century projects of a composite empire versus a hierarchical nation-state composed of individuals. See also Benton, *A Search for Sovereignty*, 1–31, 280; Benton, "Introduction: Law and Empire in Global Perspective," 1092–100; and Burbank and Cooper, "The Empire Effect," 241–42. MacLachlan, *Imperialism and the Origins*, 1, maintains that Madrid attempted "to harness the latest technology and organize resources and markets," including of "Indo-Mexico"; and Paquette, *The European Seaborne Empires*, 4, 18, emphasizes "coercive violence," political asymmetry, and collaboration as principles of empires. For Kamen, *Empire: How Spain Became a World Power*, 491, empires were "transnational organizations that aimed to mobilize the resources . . . a broad network of connections."

Dramatis Personae

1. Ahumada y Vera, *Diario de viaje*; see also Castro Santa-Anna, *Diario de sucesos notables*, 5:167.
2. Barroeta to Güemes, Mexico City, June 23 and July 1, 1761, both letters in ACR 404.
3. Güemes's report to Ensenada, Mexico City, January 30, 1748, AGI, México 1506, no. 40; Güemes to Ensenada, Mexico City, January 23, 1752, AGI, México 1506, no. 109; Güemes to Arriaga, Mexico City, September 28, 1755, ACR 401; Barroeta to Güemes, Mexico City, June 23 and July 1, 1761, ACR 404; Barroeta's testimony, Mexico City, January 17, 1757, AGI, Escribanía 246B, fol. 27v; Croix to Arriaga, Mexico City, December 31, 1768, AGN, Correspondencia de virreyes 13, fols. 57–58; and Sanchiz and Conde Díaz Rubín, "La Familia Monterde y Antillón," 115.
4. Güemes to Belaunzarán, Madrid, July 1, 1763, ACR 387.
5. Ignacia Margarita Rodríguez de Vargas y Monterde y Antillón to Güemes, Mexico City, April 19, 1763, ACR 342A.
6. Güemes to Ensenada, Mexico City, June 22, 1754, ACR 354; Belaunzarán's son to Güemes, December 1, 1764, ACR 387; dictamen of the fiscal of the Council of the Indies, Madrid, February 30, 1751, and sentence, sala de justicia, Madrid, November 3, 1751, AGI, Escribanía 217A; consulta of the Council of the Indies, Madrid, May 13, 1738, AGI, Guadalajara 186; audiencia of Guadalajara to king, July 10, 1739, AGI, Guadalajara 186; royal despacho by Fernando Triviño to Güemes; Buen Retiro, January 31, 1747, AGI, Guadalajara 89; Güemes to king, Mexico City, July 16, 1748, AGI, Guadalajara 89; Güemes to king, Mexico City, April 8, 1752, ACR 374; audiencia sentence, Guadalajara, August 14, 1752, AGI, Escribanía 394, folder Año de 1752; testimonio de los autos, fols. 450v, 457;

community of Chihuahua to king, n.d., AGI, Guadalajara 186; consulta, Council of the Indies, Madrid, December 6, 1746, AGI, Guadalajara 186; Güemes to Belaunzarán, Madrid, July 1, 1763, ACR 387; and Belaunzarán to Güemes, Mexico City, December 1, 1764, ACR 387.
7. Felices de la Fuente, *Condes, marqueses y duques*, 95–96.
8. Castro Santa-Anna, *Diario de sucesos notables*, 4:58; José Banfi y Parrilla to Güemes, Madrid, September 4, 1751, ACR 388; Güemes to Cevallos, February 9, 1762, ACR 404; Cevallos to Güemes, Madrid, April 5, 1763, ACR 404; Güemes to Ensenada, Mexico City, January 23, 1752, AGI, México 1506, no. 109; real cedula signed by José de Veytia Linage, Madrid, November 19, 1678, AGI, Guadalajara 89; archbishop to king, Mexico City, November 28, 1749, AGI, México 807; and appointment title, Buen Retiro, March 14, 1750, AGI, México 442. I am grateful for genealogist Udo Grub's communications on Cevallos.
9. Güemes to Ensenada, Mexico City, September 19, 1748, ACR 395.
10. Güemes to Ensenada, Mexico City, September 14, 1748, and September 19, 1748, ACR 395; Núñez de Villavicencio to Güemes, Mexico City, March 8, 1761, ACR 404; and Güemes to Núñez de Villavicencio, Madrid, July 1, 1763, ACR 387.
11. King to Güemes, Buen Retiro, February 20, 1748, AGI, Guadalajara 82.
12. Vélez Cachupín to Güemes, Mexico City, July 15, 1761, ACR 388.
13. Vélez Cachupín to Güemes, Mexico City, September 23, 1761, ACR 388.
14. *Fundamentos que manifiestan la antiguedad*, n.d., ACR 348; letters of Manuel Antonio Vélez Cachupín to Güemes, Castro Urdiales, March 11, 1765, and Bilbao, May 30, 1768, ACR 347; Tomás Vélez Cachupín to Güemes, Mexico City, July 15, 1761, and September 23, 1761; and Güemes to Vélez Cachupín, Madrid, April 5, 1763, the three preceding letters in ACR 388; Güemes to king, May 16, 1752, ACR 374; appointment title for Antonio Herrero, Buen Retiro, December 13, 1749, AGI, Guadalajara 82; and Ebright and Hendricks, *The Witches of Abiquiu*, 82, 288.
15. Güemes to Arriaga, September 28, 1755, ACR 401.
16. King to Andreu, Madrid, March 22, 1758, AGN, Correspondencia de diversas autoridades 3, exp. 66, fol. 144; Güemes to Ensenada, Mexico City, January 30, 1748, AGI, México 1506, no. 40; Güemes to Ensenada, Mexico City, January 23, 1752, AGI, México 1506, no. 109; relación de méritos, AGI, Indiferente 146, N. 106, fols. 1–3; Ensenada to Andreu, Aranjuez, May 25, 1744, AGN, Inquisición 1328, exp. 6, fols. 243–244v; Valle Menéndez, *Juan Francisco de Güemes*, 400–403; Burkholder and Chandler, *Biographical Dictionary of Audiencia Ministers* (hereinafter BC),18; and Hamnett, *The Mexican Bureaucracy* (hereinafter Hamnett), 25.
17. Güemes to Ensenada, Mexico City, January 23, 1752, AGI, México 1506, no. 109.
18. Güemes to king, April 3, 1747, AGI, México 1341; Güemes to Ensenada, Mexico City, January 30, 1748, AGI, México 1506, no. 40; real cédula, Buen Retiro, September 29, 1748, AGN, RCO 68, 33, fols. 129–136; Güemes to king, May 18, 1750, AGI, México 1346; Bedoya y Osorio to Crown, Guadalajara, April 30, 1754, AGI, México 1852; and BC, 41.

19. Güemes to Ensenada, Mexico City, January 23, 1752, AGI, México 1506, no. 109.
20. Güemes to king, Mexico City, April 5, 1747, AGI, Mexico 5427.
21. Real cédula to archbishop, Buen Retiro, October 4, 1746, AHAM, caja 63, exp. 4; Güemes to Ensenada, Mexico City, January 30, 1748, AGI, México 1506, no. 40; and BC, 98–99.
22. Güemes's report to king, January 30, 1748, AGI, México 1506, no. 40.
23. José Banfi y Parrilla to Güemes, Madrid, September 4, 1751, ACR 388.
24. License to embark, November 12, 1735, AGI, Contratación 5482, N. 1, R. 69; taking of office, January 13, 1741, AGN, Indiferente Virreinal 2387, exp. 27; Güemes to king, Mexico City, March 22, 1748, AGI, México 1344; Ensenada to Güemes, Madrid, January 22, 1749, AGN, RCO 69, fol. 33; consulta of the Council of the Indies, Madrid, June 30, 1751, AGI, México 385; Güemes to king, March 22, 1748, AGI, México 1851; consulta of the Council of the Indies, May 17, 1751, AGI, México 694B; Güemes to Ensenada, Mexico City, January 23, 1752, AGI, México 1506, no. 109; Duke of Alba and Duke of el Arco to king, 1754, AGI, México 1852; Echávarri to king, n.d., VEMC 74, exp. 17; Langue, "Mineros y poder," first paragraph; Hamnett, 14; BC, 104; and Burkholder, *Biographical Dictionary of Councilors of the Indies*, 36–37.
25. Güemes to Ensenada, Mexico City, January 30, 1748, AGI, México 1506, no. 40; Güemes to king, Mexico City, November 3, 1750, ACR 396; Güemes to king, Mexico City, November 3, 1750, AGI, México 544; Güemes to Ensenada, Mexico City, January 23, 1752, AGI, México 1506, no. 109; relación de méritos, Madrid, January 14, 1756, AGI, Indiferente 156, N. 2, 1; and BC, 116–17.
26. Relación de méritos, Madrid, June 25, 1738, AGI, Indiferente 148, N. 44, 1, fols. 1–4; Güemes to Ensenada, Mexico City, January 30, 1748, AGI, México 1506, no. 40; Güemes to Ensenada, Mexico City, January 23, 1752, AGI, México 1506, no. 109; and BC, 182–83.
27. Güemes to Ensenada, Mexico City, January 23, 1752, AGI, México 1506, no. 109.
28. License to embark, Cádiz, March 4, 1745, AGI, Contratación 5487, N. 1, R. 29; Joaquín José Vázquez y Morales to Juan Antonio Valenciano, Madrid, August 14, 1750, AGI, México 534A; consulta of the cámara of the Indies, Madrid, July 17, 1751, AGI, México 443; title of appointment, Aranjuez, May 14, 1751, AGI, México 443; Hamnett, 20, 24; and BC, 195–97.
29. Güemes to Ensenada, Mexico City, January 23, 1752, AGI, México 1506, no. 109.
30. Rubio y Salinas to king, Mexico City, August 2, 1755, AGI, México 807; Güemes to Ensenada, Mexico City, January 30, 1748, AGI, México 1506, no. 40; and testimony of Padilla y Córdoba, Mexico City, January 17, 1757, AGI, Escribanía 246B, fol. 14v.
31. Güemes to Ensenada, Mexico City, January 23, 1752, AGI, México 1506, no.

109; see also Güemes's report to Ensenada, Mexico City, January 30, 1748, AGI, México 1506, no. 40; consulta of the Council of the Indies, Madrid, February 4, 1751, AGI, México 385; and BC, 296.

32. Güemes's report to Ensenada, Mexico City, January 30, 1748, AGI, México 1506, no. 40.

33. Güemes to Ensenada, Mexico City, January 23, 1752, AGI, México 1506, no. 109.

34. Evaluation of inheritance, Mexico City, November 11, 1783, AGN, Intestados 294, exp. 3, fols. 85–135; Castro Santa-Anna, *Diario de sucesos notables*, 4:87–88; and Hamnett, 14.

35. Güemes to Ensenada, Mexico City, January 23, 1752, AGI, México 1506, no. 109.

36. Consulta of the Council of the Indies, Madrid, May 9, 1737, AGI, Escribanía 1060; Güemes to Ensenada, Mexico City, January 30, 1748, AGI, México 1506, no. 40; parecer of the fiscal of the Council of the Indies, Madrid, January 22, 1751, AGI, México 543A; Güemes to king, Mexico City, December 18, 1752, AGI, México 516; Güemes to king, Mexico City, December 18, 1752, AGI, México 1349; Güemes to king, Mexico City, June 12, 1755, ACR 455; sentence of the sala de justicia of the Council of the Indies, Madrid, March 11, 1771, AHN, Consejos 21461, exp. 7, fols. 34–35; BC, 331; and Burkholder, *Biographical Dictionary of Councilors of the Indies*, 122–23.

37. Güemes to Ensenada, Mexico City, January 30, 1748, AGI, México 1506, no. 40.

38. Melchor de los Cameros Morato, Uruapan, July 10, 1749, AGI, México 1850.

39. Güemes to Ensenada, Mexico City, January 23, 1752, AGI, México 1506, no. 109; Güemes to Arriaga, Mexico City, June 12, 1755, ACR 455; Güemes to Arriaga, Mexico City, June 14, 1755, ACR 455; Barroeta y Barrenechea to Güemes, Mexico City, July 1, 1761, ACR 404; BC, 339–40; Burkholder, *Biographical Dictionary of Councilors of the Indies*, 129–30; Tutino, "Creole Mexico," 100, 143; Valle Menéndez, *Juan Francisco de Güemes*, 430; Velázquez, *El Marques de Altamira*, 25–26; and Bertrand, "Clientélisme et pouvoir," 147–48. The visitador general was Pedro Domingo de Contreras.

40. Güemes to Ensenada, Mexico City, January 30, 1748, AGI, México 1506, no. 40; Güemes to king, Mexico City, May 18, 1750, AGI, México 515; power of attorney, Mexico City, 1770, AGI, Contratación 5662, N. 6, 1, fols. 8–10v, 11–11v; heirs to Casa de Contratación, Málaga, February 21, 1761, AGI, Contratación 5662, N. 6, 1, fols. 19–24; and BC, 96–97.

41. Güemes to king, Mexico City, April 5, 1747, AGI, México 542; Güemes to king, Mexico City, November 3, 1750, AGI, México 544; consulta of the cámara of the Indies, Madrid, July 17, 1751, AGI, México 443; appointment title, Aranjuez, May 14, 1751, AGI, México 443; Güemes to Ensenada, Mexico City, January 23, 1752, AGI, México 1506, no. 109; and BC, 116.

42. Güemes to Ensenada, Mexico City, January 30, 1748, AGI, México 1506, no. 40.

43. Güemes to Ensenada, Mexico City, January 23, 1752, AGI, México 1506, no. 109; relación de méritos, Granada, November 5, 1721, AGI, Indiferente 140, N. 85, 1, 4; Hamnett, 15; and BC, 212, 334–35.

44. License to embark, October 5, 1748, AGI, Contratación 5489, N. 1, R. 22; relación de méritos, Salamanca, June 9, 1747, AGI, Indiferente 151, N. 11, fols. 1–2; Güemes to king, Mexico City, June 30, 1753, AGI, México 516; testimony of Mosquera, Mexico City, 1757, AGI, Escribanía 246B, fol. 304; Echávarri to king, Mexico City, December 15, 1764; and fiscal Salazar to king, Madrid, May 10, 1765, both preceding documents in AHN, Consejos 21460, exp. 7, bk. 1, fols. 1–7v; Hamnett, 25; BC, 226; and Burkholder, *Biographical Dictionary of Councilors of the Indies*, 83–84.

45. Consulta of the Council of the Indies, Madrid, April 29, 1755, AGI, México 1122; and BC, 242–43.

46 Güemes to king, Mexico City, June 8, 1755, ACR 354.

47. Güemes to king, Mexico City, May 18, 1750, AGI, México 1346; Güemes to king, San Agustín, December 14, 1752, ACR 357; Rojas y Abreu to king, Mexico City, October 26, 1752, AGI, México 1657; three letters of Rojas y Abreu to Ensenada, Mexico City, February 6, 1753, June 30, 1753, and October 23, 1753, AGI, México 1657; relación de méritos, 1731, extended in 1761, AGI, Indiferente 145, N. 20; BC, 298–99; and Hamnett, 25.

48. Testimony of Santaella y Melgarejo, Mexico City, January 18, 1757, AGI, Escribanía 246B, fol. 47v.

49. Güemes to king, April 3, 1747, AGI, México 1341; Güemes to Ensenada, Mexico City, January 23, 1752, AGI, México 1506, no. 109; relación de méritos of his son Antonio, n.d., n.p., AGI, Indiferente 158, N. 28, 1, fols. 1–3; Hamnett, 25; and BC, 314–15.

50. Güemes to Ensenada, Mexico City, January 23, 1752, AGI, México 1506, no. 109; and BC, 528.

Bibliography

Archival Sources
MEXICO

Archivo Dávila Garibi, Guadalajara
    Microfilm roll 100
Archivo del Cabildo de la Catedral de México (ACCM)
    Actas del Cabildo Eclesiástico 40
Archivo General de la Nación (AGN)
    Archivo Histórico de Hacienda (AHH) 129, 550, 635, 640, 1058
    Bandos 4
    Bienes Nacionales (BN) 53, 396, 636, 741
    Civil 1332
    Correspondencia de diversas autoridades 3
    Correspondencia de virreyes, 1.a serie, 1, 5, 13, 179
    General de Parte (GdP) 33, 41, 42
    Historia 20, 113, 120
    Indiferente Virreinal 2387, 2711, 4832, 5036, 5470
    Inquisición 740, 810, 889, 935, 945, 1328
    Intestados 294
    Judicial 21
    Minería 138
    Provincias Internas 129
    Real Audiencia 4
    Reales Cédulas Originales (RCO) 32, 36, 38, 40, 43, 48, 51, 62, 66–73, 77, 79
    Templos y Conventos 15
    Tierras 3353
Archivo Histórico de la Ciudad de México (AHCM)
(Formerly the Archivo Histórico del Distrito Federal [AHDF])
    Ayuntamiento, Actas del Cabildo 73A, 75A, 78, 78A, 79A, 438A
    Ayuntamiento, Cédulas y Reales Órdenes 2977
    Ayuntamiento, Historia, Juras y Funerales de Reyes 2282
Archivo Histórico del Arzobispado de Guadalajara (AHAG)
    Capitular XI desde 1746 hasta 1759
    Serie Franciscanos, Secularización de doctrinas
Archivo Histórico del Arzobispado de México (AHAM)
    Box 48, 63, 104

Archivo Municipal de Atlixco (Puebla State) (AMA)
    2006, box 6
Archivo Municipal de Guadalajara
    Actas del Cabildo, AC6/1747 antiguo paquete (box according to old classification) 1, folder 74
Biblioteca Nacional de México (BNM)
    Fondo Reservado (FR), manuscritos 437, 439, 455, 604, 1392
Biblioteca Pública del Estado de Jalisco (BPEJ)
    Archivo de la Real Audiencia de Guadalajara (ARAG), ramo civil, box 59
Instituto Nacional de Antropología e Historia (INAH) Library
    Colección Antigua (CA), microfilm roll 56
    Fondo Franciscano (FF) 109, 139–40

SPAIN

Archivo del Real Palacio (ARP), Madrid, box 482, 1341
Archivo General de Indias (AGI)
    Casa de la Contratación (Contratación) 1463, 5465, 5469, 5470, 5472, 5481, 5482, 5483, 5485, 5487–5490, 5494, 5497, 5508, 5509, 5518, 5533, 5662
    Escribanía de Cámara de Justicia (Escribanía) 217A, 233A, 245A, 246A–C, 278A, 393, 394, 402A–B, 1060, 1194
    Gobierno—Audiencia de Guadalajara (Guadalajara) 82, 89, 106, 107, 115, 186
    Gobierno—Audiencia de México (México) 379, 383–85, 402, 438, 439, 442, 443, 480, 483–85, 492, 513, 516, 534A, 542, 543A, 544, 610, 694B, 807, 881, 1121, 1122, 1341, 1344, 1346, 1348–52, 1506, 1657, 1849, 1850–53, 2093, 2094, 2501, 2712, 2713, 5427
    Gobierno—Indiferente General (Indiferente) 140, 145, 146, 148, 151, 152, 156–58, 224
Archivo Histórico Nacional (AHN), Madrid
    Consejos 21003, 21460, 21461
    Sección Nobleza, Toledo
    Valencia, folder 1, D. 7
    Torrelaguna, folder 442, D. 36
Biblioteca Nacional de España (BNE), Madrid
    Reglamento para la administración y cobranza de los reales derechos de alcabalas, unión de armas y armada de Barlovento, dispuesto y mandado observar por D. Juan Francisco Güemes y Horcasitas, Conde de Revillagigedo, Virrey de Nueva España, Mexico City, September 26, 1753, edited by the second Count of Revillagigedo (*Reglamento de alcabalas*), manuscritos 10358, 476, vol. IV
Real Academia de la Historia (RAH), Madrid
    9-9-4

USA

Library of the University of Florida, Department of Special and Area Collections, Gainesville, Florida
 Archivo de los Condes de Revillagigedo (ACR), microfilm reels no. 342A, 344, 347, 348, 354, 357, 360, 374, 376, 378, 379, 387, 388, 393–96, 399, 401, 409, 413, 421, 427, 434, 455, 464, 476, 485
Latin American Library at Tulane University, New Orleans
 Viceregal and Ecclesiastical Manuscript Collection (VEMC), boxes 8, 12, 16, 28, 45, 52, 74

AUSTRIA

Österreichisches Staatsarchiv, Haus-, Hof- und Staatsarchiv, Staatenabteilung Spanien, Vienna
Diplomatische Korrespondenz (1754.05–1754.12), box 85

FRANCE

Archives du Ministère des Affaires Étrangères (AMAE), Paris
 Correspóndance Politique, Espagne (CPE), vol. 514

Primary Sources

Ahumada y Vera, Luisa María del Rosario, Marquesa de las Amarillas. *Diario de viaje de Cádiz a México*. Edited by Clara Ramírez and Claudia Llanos. Mexico City: Universidad Nacional Autónoma de México, 2016.

Ajofrín, Francisco de. *Diario del viaje que por orden de la Sagrada Congregación de Propaganda Fide hizo a la América Septentrional en el siglo XVIII el p[adre] fray Francisco de Ajofrín*. Edited by Vicente Castañeda y Alcover. Madrid: Real Academia de la Historia, 1959.

Arricivita, Juan Domingo. *Crónica seráfica y apostólica del colegio de Propaganda Fide de la Santa Cruz de Querétaro en la Nueva España . . .* Mexico City: Don Felipe de Zúñiga y Ontiveros, 1792.

Avilés, Francisco de, ed. *Regla de S. Agustín y constituciones de su religion, compendiadas, y traducidas de Latin en Castellano . . .* Madrid: Juan Sanz, 1719.

Calderón de la Barca, Pedro. *Fieras afemina amor*. Barcelona: Antonio de Cavallería, 1667; Alicante, Spain: Biblioteca Virtual Miguel de Cervantes, 2001. http://www.cervantesvirtual.com/nd/ark:/59851/bmcf7699.

———. *Fieras afemina amor*. Madrid: Ayuntamiento, 1749; Alicante, Spain: Biblioteca Virtual Miguel de Cervantes, 2013. http://www.cervantesvirtual.com/nd/ark:/59851/bmcxw4s1.

Campillo y Cosío, José. *Nuevo sistema de gobierno económico para la América: Con los males y daños que le causa el que hoy tiene, de los que participa copiosamente España; y remedios universales para que la primera tenga considerables ventajas, y la segunda mayores intereses*. Madrid: Imprenta de Benito Cano, 1789.

Canons and Decrees of the Sacred and Oecumenical Council of Trent. Edited and translated by J. Waterworth. London: Dolman, 1848. https://history.hanover.edu/texts/trent.html.

Carvajal y Lancáster, José de. *Testamento político o idea de un govierno católico (1745)*. Edited by José Miguel Delgado Barrado. Córdoba: Servicio de Publicaciones, Universidad de Córdoba, 1999.

Castro Santa-Anna, José Manuel de. *Diario de sucesos notables: Documentos para la historia de Méjico*. Vols. 4–6. Mexico City: Imprenta de Juan R. Navarro, 1854.

"Constituciones de el arzobispado y provincia de la muy insigne y muy leal ciudad de Tenochtitlan, México, de la Nueva España, concilio primer." In *Concilios provinciales mexicanos: Época colonial*, edited by María del Pilar Martínez López-Cano and Francisco Javier Cervantes Bello, 1–102. Mexico City: Universidad Nacional Autónoma de México, Instituto de Investigaciones Históricas, 2004. http://www.historicas.unam.mx/publicaciones/%obpublicadigital/libros/concilios/concilios_index.html.

Covarrubias Orozco, Sebastian de. *Emblemas morales de Don Sebastian de Covarrubias Orozco, Capellan del Rey N.S. Maestrescuela, y Canonigo de Cuenca, Consultor del Santo Oficio: Dirigidas a Don Francisco Gómez de Sandoval y Roxas, Duque de Lerma . . .* Madrid: Luis Sanchez, 1610.

Espinosa, Isidro Félix de. *Chronica apostolica y seraphica de todos los colegios de Propaganda Fide de esta Nueva-España de Missioneros Franciscanos Obseruantes . . .* Mexico City: Viuda de D. Joseph Bernardo de Hogal, 1746.

Farnesius Eburonis, Henricus. *De Simulacro Reip[ublicae] sive de Imaginibus Politicae et Oeconomicæ virtutis. Panegyrici libri IIII. absoluti. In quibus quam imperii faciem adumbrent quaedam illustrium familiarum insignia: apologi: emblemata: fabulae: adagia: hieroglyphica: breviter ostenditur. Huc accedunt mores: leges: ritus antiquorum: synonyma virtutum: paradoxa disputantium: exemplorum testimonia, ac denique orationes pro arte imperandi quinque.* Papiae [Pavia]: Andrea Vianai, 1593.

Fonseca, Fabián de, and Carlos de Urrutia. *Historia general de real hacienda, escrita por D. Fabian de Fonseca y D. Carlos de Urrutia, por orden del virey, conde de Revillagigedo: Obra hasta ahora inedita y que se imprime con permiso del supremo gobierno*. 6 vols. Mexico City: V. G. Torres, 1845–1853.

García Panes y Abellán, Diego. *Diario particular del camino que sigue un virrey de México desde su llegada a Veracruz hasta su entrada pública en la capital*. Madrid: Centro de Estudios Históricos de Obras Públicas y Urbanismo, 1994.

Gómez, José. *Diario curioso y cuaderno de las cosas memorables en México durante el gobierno de Revillagigedo (1789–1794)*. Edited by Ignacio González-Polo. Mexico City: Universidad Nacional Autónoma de México, 1986.

Juan, Jorge, and Antonio de Ulloa. *Discourse and Political Reflections on the Kingdoms of Peru: Their Government, Special Regimen of Their Inhabitants, and Abuses* . . . Translated by John J. TePaske and Besse A. Clement. Norman: University of Oklahoma Press, 1978.

Konetzke, Richard, ed. *Colección de documentos para la historia de la formación social de Hispanoamérica, 1493–1810*. 3 vols., 5 tomes. Madrid: Consejo Superior de Investigaciones Científicas, 1953–1962.

Lárraga, Francisco. *Promptuario de la theologia moral: Muy vtil para todos los que han de exponer de co[n]fessores, y para la debida administracion del Santo Sacramento de la Penitencia; Nuevamente reconocido, mejorado, corregido, y añadido por su autor en esta dezimaquarta edición*. Madrid: Manuel Román, 1718.

Law of the Indies. See *Recopilación de leyes de los reynos* . . .

Núñez de Haro y Peralta, Alonso. *Descripción del arzobispado de México de 1793 y el informe reservado del arzobispo de México de 1797: Núñez de Haro y Peralta*. Edited by Margarita Menegus Bornemann. Mexico City: Universidad Nacional Autónoma de México, Centro de Estudios sobre la Universidad, 2005.

Pierre Grégoire de Toulouse. *De republica libri sex et viginti: Antea en duos distincti tomos, nunc vno concise & artificiose comprehensi*. 3rd ed. Frankfurt: Typis Matthæi Kempfferi, sumpt[i]bus Philippi Jacobi Fischeri, 1642.

Recopilación de leyes de los reynos de las Indias mandada imprimir y publicar por la Magestad Católica del Rey Don Carlos II. Nuestro Señor . . . 1741. Facsimile. Madrid: Consejo de la Hispanidad, 1953. www.leyes.congreso.gob.pe/leyes_indias.aspx.

Rivera, Juan Antonio. *Diario curioso de México*. Vol. 8 of *Documentos para la historia de México*. Mexico City: Antigua Imprenta de la Voz de la Religión, 1854.

Robles, Antonio de. *Diario de sucesos notables*. Edited by Antonio Castro Leal. Mexico City: Editorial Porrúa, 1946.

Rodríguez de Arispe, Pedro José. *Alegorico symulacro del célebre Príncipe Atlante, que en la sumptuosa Montéa de un Triumphal Arco* . . . Mexico City: Viuda de D. Joseph Bernardo de Hogal, 1746. Biblioteca Nacional de México, FR 604.

———. *Representacion panegyrica*. Mexico City: Viuda de D. Joseph Bernardo de Hogal, 1746. Biblioteca Nacional de México, FR 604.

Rueda, Laura, ed. *Descripciones franciscanas de la Provincia de Santiago de Xalisco, siglo XVIII*. Zapopan: El Colegio de Jalisco, 1996.

Sánchez Villa-Señor, José Antonio. *Theatro americano: Descripción general de los reynos, y provincias de la Nueva-España, y sus jurisdicciones; Dedicala al rey nuestro señor el señor D. Fernando VI, monarcha de las Españas*. 3 vols. Mexico City: Viuda de D. Joseph Bernardo de Hogal, 1748. Facsimile, Mexico City: Editora Nacional, 1952.

Sariñana y Cuenca, Isidro. *Llanto del occidente en el ocaso del mas claro sol de* las Españas: Funebres demostraciones, que hizo, pyra real, que erigio en las exequias del rey N. Señor D. Felipe IIII, el Grande... Mexico City: Viuda de Bernardo Calderón, 1666.

Seijas y Lobera, Francisco de. *Gobierno militar y político del reino imperial de la Nueva España (1702)*. Edited by Pablo Emilio Pérez-Mallaína Bueno. Mexico City: Universidad Nacional Autónoma de México, 1986.

Siete partidas del rey don Alfonso el Sabio: Cotejados con varios códices antiguos, por la Real Academia de la Historia. Vol. 2, parts 2 and 3. Madrid: Imprenta Real, 1807.

Sigüenza y Góngora, Carlos. *Teatro de virtudes políticas que constituyen a un príncipe: Advertidas en los monarcas antiguos del Mexicano Imperio, con cuyas efigies se hermoseó el Arco triunfal que la... Ciudad de México erigió para... recibimiento del... Virrey Conde de Paredes, Marqués de La Laguna*. Mexico City: Viuda de Bernardo Calderón, 1680. Biblioteca Virtual Miguel de Cervantes, www.cervantesvirtual.com.

Solórzano y Pereyra, Juan. *Politica Indiana... Dividia en seis libros, en los quales con gran distinción, y estudio se trata, y resuelve todo lo tocante al Descubrimiento, Descripcion, Adquisicion, y Retencion de las mesmas Indias... (1648)*. Amberes [Antwerp]: Henrico y Cornelio Verdussen, 1703.

Torre Villar, Ernesto de la, ed. *Instrucciones y memorias de los virreyes novohispanos*. Vol. 2. Mexico City: Editorial Porrúa, 1991.

Ventura Beleña, Eusebio, ed. *Recopilación sumaria de todos los autos acordados...* 2 vols. Mexico City: Don Felipe de Zúñiga y Ontiveros, 1787.

Vera, Fortino Hipólito. *Itinerario parroquial del arzobispado de Mexico: Reseña historica, geografica y estadistica, de las parroquias del mismo arzobispado; Apendices erecciones parroquiales de México y Puebla y Santuario del Sacromonte (1880)*. Facsimile. Mexico City: Biblioteca Enciclopédica del Estado de México, 1981.

Villarroel, Gaspar de. *Govierno eclesiastico-pacifico y union de los dos cuchillos pontificio y regio (1657)*. Vol. 2. Madrid: Antonio Marín, 1738.

Ward, Bernardo. *Proyecto economico en que se proponen varias providencias, dirigidas á promover los intereses de España, con los medios y fondos necesarios para su planificación*. Madrid: Joaquín Ibarra, 1779.

Zavala y Auñón, Miguel de. *Representación al Rey Nuestro Señor D. Phelipe V... dirigida al mas seguro aumento del Real Erario y conseguir la felicidad, mayor alivio, riqueza y abundancia de su Monarquía...* N.p.: probably self-published, 1732.

Secondary Sources

Abad León, Felipe. *El marqués de la Ensenada, su vida y su obra*. 2 vols. Madrid: Editorial Naval, 1985.

Abad Pérez, Antolín. *Los Franciscanos en América*. Madrid: Editorial MAPFRE, 1992.
Aguirre, Rodolfo. "La secularización de doctrinas en el arzobispado de México: Realidades indianas y razones políticas, 1700–1749." *Hispania Sacra* 60, no. 122 (2008): 487–505.
Alberro, Solange. "Las cuatro partes del mundo en las fiestas virreinales peruanas y novohispanas." In *Passeurs, mediadores culturales y agentes de la primera globalización en el mundo ibérico, siglos XVI–XIX*, edited by Scarlett O'Phelan Godoy and Carmen Salazar-Soler, 147–62. Lima: Pontificia Universidad Católica del Perú, 2005.
Albi, Christopher. *Gamboa's World: Justice, Silver Mining, and Imperial Reform in New Spain*. Albuquerque: University of New Mexico Press, 2021.
Alcaraz Gómez, José F. *Jesuitas y reformismo: El padre Francisco de Rávago (1747–1755)*. Valencia: Facultad de Teología San Vicente Ferrer, 1995.
Álvarez de Toledo, Cayetana. *Politics and Reform in Spain and Viceregal Mexico: The Life and Thought of Juan de Palafox, 1600–1659*. Oxford: Clarendon Press, 2004.
Álvarez Icaza Longoria, María Teresa. *La secularización de doctrinas y misiones en el arzobispado de México, 1749–1789*. Mexico City: Universidad Nacional Autónoma de México, 2015.
Andrés-Gallego, José. *El motín de Esquilache, América y Europa*. Madrid: Editorial MAPFRE; Consejo Superior de Investigaciones Científicas, 2003.
Andrien, Kenneth J. "The Coming of Enlightened Reform in Bourbon Peru: Secularization of the *Doctrinas de indios*, 1746–1773." In *Enlightened Reform in Southern Europe and Its Atlantic Colonies, c. 1750–1830*, edited by Gabriel B. Paquette, 183–202. Farnham, Surrey, England: Ashgate Publishing, 2009.
Arias, Luz Marina. "Building Fiscal Capacity in Colonial Mexico: From Fragmentation to Centralization." *Journal of Economic History* 73, no. 3 (September 2013): 662–93.
Armas Medina, Fernando de. "Evolución histórica de las doctrinas de indios." *Anuario de Estudios Americanos* 9 (1952): 101–29.
Armella de Aspe, Virginia. *San Bartolomé de los Tepetates: Historia de una hacienda*. Mexico City: Diesel Nacional, 1988.
Arnold, Linda. *Bureaucracy and Bureaucrats in Mexico City, 1742–1835*. Tucson: University of Arizona Press, 1988.
Arrom, Silvia Marina. *La Güera Rodríguez: The Life and Legends of a Mexican Independence Heroine*. Oakland: University of California Press, 2021.
Asch, Ronald G. "Introduction: Court and Household from the Fifteenth to the Seventeenth Centuries." In *Princes, Patronage and the Nobility: The Court at the Beginning of the Modern Age, c. 1450–1650*, edited by Ronald G. Asch and Adolf M. Birke. Oxford: Oxford University Press, 1991.
Baeza Martín, Ascensión. "Agustín de Ahumada y Villalón." Real Academia de la Historia, *Diccionario biográfico electrónico*. https://dbe.rah.es/.

Barbier, Jacques A. *Reform and Politics in Bourbon Chile, 1755–1796*. Ottawa: University of Ottawa Press, 1980.

Barrientos Grandón, Javier. "Guía prosopográfica de la judicatura letrada indiana (1503–1898)." In *Nuevas aportaciones a la historia jurídica de Iberoamérica*, edited by José Andrés-Gallego, 1–1640. Madrid: Fundación Histórica Tavera; Fundación Hernando de Larramendi, 2000. CD-ROM.

Baskes, Jeremy. *Staying Afloat: Risk and Uncertainty in Spanish Atlantic World Trade, 1760–1820*. Stanford, CA: Stanford University Press, 2013.

Baudot Monroy, María. *La defensa del Imperio: Julián de Arriaga en la Armada (1700–1754)*. Madrid: Ministerio de Defensa; Murcia, Spain: Ediciones de la Universidad de Murcia, 2013.

———. "Orígenes familiares y carrera profesional de Julián de Arriaga, Secretario de Estado de Marina e Indias (1700–1776)." *Espacio, Tiempo y Forma*, series IV, *Historia Moderna*, no. 17 (2004): 163–85.

Becerra Jiménez, Celina G. "Redes sociales y oficios de justicia en Indias: Los vínculos de dos alcaldes mayores neogallegos." *Relaciones* 33, no. 132 (Winter 2012): 109–50.

Becerra Jiménez, Celina G., and Aristarco Regalado Pinedo. "La consolidación de una capital: Guadalajara." In *Historia del reino de la Nueva Galicia*, edited by Thomas Calvo and Aristarco Regalado Pinedo, 463–92. Guadalajara: Universidad de Guadalajara, Centro Universitario de Ciencias Sociales y Humanidades, 2016.

———. "Tierras, minas y crecimiento demográfico." In *Historia del reino de la Nueva Galicia*, edited by Thomas Calvo and Aristarco Regalado Pinedo, 435–62. Guadalajara: Universidad de Guadalajara, Centro Universitario de Ciencias Sociales y Humanidades, 2016.

Belanger, Brian Conal. "Secularization and the Laity in Colonial Mexico: Querétaro, 1598–1821." PhD diss., Tulane University, 1990.

Benton, Lauren. "Introduction: Law and Empire in Global Perspective." *American Historical Review* 117, no. 4 (October 2012): 1092–100.

———. *A Search for Sovereignty: Law and Geography in European Empires, 1400–1900*. Cambridge: Cambridge University Press, 2010.

Berndt León Mariscal, Beatriz. "Between Monarchic and Local Identity: An Ephemeral Facade for Charles IV's Proclamation Ceremony in Mexico (1789)." In *Festivals and Daily Life in the Arts of Colonial Latin America, 1492–1850: Papers from the 2012 Mayer Center Symposium at the Denver Art Museum*, edited by Donna Pierce, 55–72. Denver: Mayer Center for Pre-Columbian and Spanish Colonial Art at the Denver Art Museum, 2014.

———. "Discursos de poder en un nuevo dominio: El trayecto del virrey marqués de las Amarillas de Veracruz a Puebla, las fiestas de entrada y el ceremonial político." *Relaciones* 26, no. 101 (Winter 2005): 227–59.

Bernecker, Walther L., and Horst Pietschmann. *Geschichte Spaniens: Von der frühen Neuzeit bis zur Gegenwart*. 4th ed. Stuttgart: Kohlhammer Verlag, 2005.

Bertrand, Michel. "Del actor a la red: Análisis de redes e interdisciplinariedad." In *Actores locales de la nación en la América Latina: Estudios estratégicos*, edited by Evelyne Sánchez, 23–41. Puebla, Mexico: Benemérita Universidad Autónoma de Puebla; Apetatitlán de Antonio Carvajal, Mexico: El Colegio de Tlaxcala, 2011.

———. "Clientélisme et pouvoir en Nouvelle-Espagne." In *Cultures et sociétés, Andes et Méso-Amérique: Mélanges en hommage à Pierre Duviols*, edited by Raquel Thiercelin, vol. 1, 147–59. Aix-en-Provence: Publications de l'Université de Provence, 1992.

———. *Grandeur et misères de l'office: Les officiers de finances de Nouvelle-Espagne, XVIIe–XVIIIe siècles*. Paris: Publications de la Sorbonne, 1999.

Bois, Jean-Pierre. "Le roi, l'armée et la cour au XVIIe siècle." In *Les course d'Espagne et de France au XVIIe siècle: Actas del colloquia celebrado del 26 al 28 de Novembre de 2001 en Madrid*, edited by Chantal Grell and Benoît Pellistrandi, 171–88. Madrid: Casa de Velázquez, 2007.

Bonney, Richard. "Early Modern Theories of State Finance." In *Economic Systems and State Finance*, edited by Richard Bonney, 163–231. Oxford: Clarendon Press, 1995.

Borges Morán, Pedro. *Religiosos en Hispanoamérica*. Madrid: Editorial MAPFRE, 1992.

Bouhrass, Asmaa. "La administración virreinal y el comercio en Nueva España (1740–1765)." PhD diss., Universidad de Sevilla, 1999.

Brading, David A. *Church and State in Bourbon Mexico: The Diocese of Michoacán 1749–1810*. Cambridge: Cambridge University Press, 1994.

———. "La minería de la plata en el siglo XVIII: El caso Bolaños." *Historia Mexicana* 18, no. 3 (January–March 1969): 317–33.

———. *Miners and Merchants in Bourbon Mexico, 1763–1810*. Cambridge: Cambridge University Press, 1971.

———. *Mito y profecía en la historia de México*. Mexico City: Fondo de Cultura Económica, 2004.

———. "La monarquía católica." In *De los imperios a las naciones: Iberoamérica*, edited by Antonio Annino, Luis Castro Leiva, and François-Xavier Guerra, 19–43. Zaragoza, Spain: Ibercaja, Obra Cultural, 1994.

Bravo Lira, Bernardino. "Régimen virreinal: Constantes y variantes de la constitución política en Iberoamérica (siglos XVI al XXI)." In *El gobierno de un mundo: Virreinatos y audiencias en la América hispánica*, edited by Feliciano Barrios Pintado, 375–430. Cuenca, Spain: Ediciones de la Universidad de Castilla–La Mancha, 2004.

Burbank, Jane, and Frederick Cooper, "The Empire Effect." *Public Culture* 24, no. 2 (2012): 239–47.

Burkholder, Mark A. *Biographical Dictionary of Councilors of the Indies, 1717–1808*. Westport, CT: Greenwood Press, 1986.

———. *Spaniards in the Colonial Empire: Creoles vs. Peninsulars?* Chichester, W. Susx., England: Wiley-Blackwell, 2012.
Burkholder, Mark A., and D. S. Chandler. *Biographical Dictionary of Audiencia Ministers in the Americas, 1687–1821.* Westport, CT: Greenwood Press, 1982.
———. *From Impotence to Authority: The Spanish Crown and the American Audiencias, 1687–1808.* Columbia: University of Missouri Press, 1977.
Büschges, Christian. "Ceremonial Demarcations: The Viceregal Court as Space of Political Communication in the Spanish Monarchy (Valencia, Naples, and Mexico, 1621–1635)." In *The Dynastic Centre and the Provinces: Agents and Interactions*, edited by Jeroen Duindam and Sabine Dabringhaus, 94–113. Leiden: Brill, 2014.
———. "La corte virreinal en la América hispánica colonial durante la época colonial." In *Actas do XII Congresso Internacional de AHILA, Oporto, 1999*, vol. 2, edited by Eugénio dos Santos, 131–40. Porto, Portugal: Faculdade de Letras, Universidade do Porto; Centro Leonardo Coimbra, 2001.
———. "Del criado al valido: El padronazgo de los virreyes de Nápoles y Nueva España (primera mitad del siglo XVII)." In *Las cortes virreinales de la monarquía española: América e Italia*, edited by Francesca Cantù, 157–81. Rome: Viella Libreria Editrice, 2008.
———. "Urban Public Festivals as Representations and Elements of Social Order in Colonial Ecuador." In *Observation and Communication: The Construction of Realities in the Hispanic World*, edited by Johannes-Michael Scholz and Tamar Herzog, 113–31. Frankfurt: Vittorio Klostermann, 1997.
Calderón Quijano, José Antonio, ed. *Los virreyes de Nueva España en el reinado de Carlos III.* Seville: Escuela de Estudios Hispano-Americanos, 1967.
———, ed. *Los virreyes de Nueva España en el reinado de Carlos IV.* 2 vols. Seville: Escuela de Estudios Hispano-Americanos, 1972.
Calvo, Thomas. "Ciencia, cultura y política." In *Las reformas borbónicas, 1750–1808*, edited by Clara García Ayluardo. Mexico City: Fondo de Cultura Económica, 2010. Kindle.
———. "El rey y sus Indias: Ausencia, distancia y presencia (siglos XVI–XVIII)." In *México en el mundo hispánico*, edited by Óscar Mazín Gómez, vol. 2, 427–83. Zamora: El Colegio de Michoacán, 2000.
———. "Trayectorias de luz y de sombra." In *Historia del reino de la Nueva Galicia*, edited by Thomas Calvo and Aristarco Regalado Pinedo, 493–515. Guadalajara: Universidad de Guadalajara, Centro Universitario de Ciencias Sociales y Humanidades, 2016.
Cañeque, Alejandro. "Imaging the Spanish Empire: The Visual Construction of Imperial Authority in Habsburg New Spain." *Colonial Latin American Review* 19, no. 1 (April 2010): 29–68.
———. *The King's Living Image: The Culture and Politics of Viceregal Power in Colonial Mexico.* London: Routledge, 2004.

Cantù, Francesca, ed. *Las cortes virreinales de la monarquía española: América e Italia*. Rome: Viella Libreria Editrice, 2008.
Carbajal López, David. *La minería en Bolaños, 1748–1810: Ciclos productivos y actores económicos*. Zamora: El Colegio de Michoacán; Guadalajara: Campus Universitario del Norte, Universidad de Guadalajara, 2002.
———. *La población en Bolaños, 1740–1848: Dinámica demográfica, familia y mestizaje*. Zamora: El Colegio de Michoacán, 2008.
Cardim, Pedro. "Political Status and Identity: Debating the Status of American Territories across the Sixteenth and Seventeenth Century Iberian World." *Rechtsgeschichte: Legal History* 24 (2016): 101–16.
Cardim, Pedro, Tamar Herzog, José Javier Ruis Ibáñez, and Gaetano Sabatini. Introduction to *Polycentric Monarchies: How Did Early Modern Spain and Portugal Achieve and Maintain a Global Hegemony?*, edited by Pedro Cardim, Tamar Herzog, José Javier Ruis Ibáñez, and Gaetano Sabatini, 3–8. Eastbourne, E. Susx., England: Sussex Academic Press, 2012.
Castañeda Delgado, Paulino, and Juan Marchena Fernández. *La jerarquía de la iglesia en Indias: El episcopado americano, 1500–1850*. Madrid: Editorial MAPFRE, 1992.
Castejón, Philippe. "Un *cursus honorum* entre dos mundos: Los magistrados borbónicos del gobierno de Indias (1701–1808)." *Colonial Latin American Review* 31, no. 3 (September 2022): 433–59.
Castellano, Juan Luis. "Bernardo Ward." In *Economía y economistas españoles*, vol. 3, *La Ilustración*, edited by Enrique Fuentes Quintana, 185–200. Barcelona: Galaxia Gutenberg, 1999.
———. *Gobierno y poder en la España del siglo XVIII*. Granada: Editorial Universidad de Granada, 2006.
Castellano, Juan Luis, and Jean-Pierre Dedieu, eds. *Réseaux, familles et pouvoirs dans le monde ibérique à la fin de l'Ancien Régime*. Paris: CNRS Éditions, 1998.
Castro Gutiérrez, Felipe. *Nueva ley y nuevo rey: Reformas borbónicas y rebelión popular en Nueva España*. Zamora: El Colegio de Michoacán; Mexico City: Universidad Nacional Autónoma de México, 1996.
Castro Monsalve, Concepción de. "Las secretarías de los consejos, las de estado y del despacho y sus oficiales durante la primera mitad del siglo XVIII." *Hispania* 59, no. 201 (1999): 193–215.
Chowning, Margaret. *Rebellious Nuns: The Troubled History of a Mexican Convent, 1752–1863*. Oxford: Oxford University Press, 2006.
Cortés Peña, Antonio Luis. *La política religiosa de Carlos III y las órdenes mendicantes*. Granada: Editorial Universidad de Granada, 1989.
Costa, Luis Miguel. "Patronage and Bribery in Sixteenth-Century Peru: The Government of Viceroy Conde del Villar and the Visita of Licentiate Alonso Fernández de Bonilla." PhD diss., Florida International University, 2005.
Couturier, Edith Boorstein. *The Silver King: The Remarkable Life of the Count of*

Regla in Colonial Mexico. Albuquerque: University of New Mexico Press, 2003.

Cruz, Jesus. *Gentlemen, Bourgeois, and Revolutionaries: Political Change and Cultural Persistence among the Spanish Dominant Groups, 1750–1850*. Cambridge: Cambridge University Press, 1996.

Cuadriello, Jaime. *The Glories of the Republic of Tlaxcala: Art and Life in Viceregal Mexico*. Translated by Christopher J. Follett. Austin: University of Texas Press, 2011.

Curcio-Nagy, Linda A. *The Great Festivals of Colonial Mexico City: Performing Power and Identity*. Albuquerque: University of New Mexico Press, 2004.

———. "Sor Juana Inés de la Cruz and the 1680 Viceregal Entry of the Marquis de la Laguna into Mexico City." In *Europa Triumphans: Court and Civic Festivals in Early Modern Europe*, edited by J. R. Mulryne, Helen Watanabe-O'Kelly, and Margaret Shewring, vol. 2, 352–57. Aldershot, Hants., England: Ashgate Publishing, 2005.

Curiel, Gustavo. "Mourning Rites, Processions, and Funerary Monument: The Mexico City Inquisition and Funerary Observances for the Death of King Philip IV (1666)." In *Festivals and Daily Life in the Arts of Colonial Latin America, 1492–1850: Papers from the 2012 Mayer Center Symposium at the Denver Art Museum*, edited by Donna Pierce, 31–54. Denver: Mayer Center for Pre-Columbian and Spanish Colonial Art at the Denver Art Museum, 2014.

Daniel, Douglas A. "Tactical Factors in the Spanish Conquest of the Aztecs." *Anthropological Quarterly* 65, no. 4 (October 1992): 187–94.

Dedieu, Jean-Pierre. "Dinastía y élites de poder en el reinado de Felipe V." In *Los Borbones: Dinastía y memoria de nación en la España del siglo XVIII*, edited by Pablo Fernández Albaladejo, 381–420. Madrid: Marcial Pons; Casa de Velázquez, 2002.

Deeds, Susan M. *Defiance and Deference in Mexico's Colonial North: Indians under Spanish Rule in Nueva Vizcaya*. Austin: University of Texas Press, 2003.

Delgado Barrado, José Miguel. *El proyecto político de Carvajal: Pensamiento y reforma en tiempos de Fernando VI*. Madrid: Consejo Superior de Investigaciones Científicas, 2001.

Delgado Barrado, José Miguel, and José Luis Gómez Urdáñez, eds. *Ministros de Fernando VI*. Córdoba: Servicio de Publicaciones, Universidad de Córdoba, 2002.

Del Río, Ignacio. "La inestable capital de la gobernación de Sonora y Sinaloa (1732–1823): Una reseña preliminar." *Estudios de Historia Novohispana*, no. 28 (2009): 17–36.

Descalzo Lorenzo, Amalia. "El arte de vestir en el ceremonial cortesano: Felipe V." In *España festejante: El siglo XVIII*, edited by Margarita Torrione, 197–204. Málaga, Spain: Centro de Ediciones de Diputación de Málaga, 2000.

Díaz-Trechuelo y López-Spínola, María Lourdes. "Juan Vicente de Güemes Pacheco de Padilla y Horcasitas." Real Academia de la Historia, *Diccionario biográfico electrónico*. https://dbe.rah.es/.

Diccionario Biográfico Español. "Ignacio de Ceballos Villagutierre." Real Academia de la Historia, *Diccionario biográfico electrónico*. http://dbe.rah.es/.

Diego-Fernández Sotelo, Rafael. "Fiscales, oidores, presidentes y regentes de la Audiencia de la Nueva Galicia." In *Élites y poder: México y España, siglos XVI al XX*, edited by Águeda Jiménez Pelayo, 23–40. Guadalajara: Universidad de Guadalajara, 2003.

———. Introduction to *La Nueva Galicia en el ocaso del impero español: Los papeles del derecho de la audiencia de la Nueva Galicia del licenciado Juan José Ruiz Moscoso y su agente fiscal y regidor del ayuntamiento de Guadalajara, 1780–1810*, edited by Rafael Diego-Fernández Sotelo and Marina Mantilla Trolle, vol. 1, xiii–lxvii. Zamora: El Colegio de Michoacán; Guadalajara: Universidad de Guadalajara, 2003.

———. "Las reales audiencias indianas como base de la organización político-territorial de la América hispana." In *Convergencias y divergencias: México y Andalucía, siglos XVI–XIX*, edited by Celina G. Becerra Jiménez and Rafael Diego-Fernández Sotelo, 21–68. Guadalajara: Universidad de Guadalajara; Zamora: El Colegio de Michoacán, 2007.

Dombrowski, Damian. "Eine maritime Renaissance: Neapel, das Meer und die Kunst unter Vizekönig Pedro de Toledo." *Wallraf-Richartz-Jahrbuch* 75 (2014): 185–228.

Duve, Thomas. *Sonderrecht in der Frühen Neuzeit: Studien zum ius singulare und den privilegia miserabilium personarum, senum und indorum in Alter und Neuer Welt*. Frankfurt: Vittorio Klostermann, 2008.

Eagle, Marc. "Beard-Pulling and Furniture-Rearranging: Conflict within the Seventeenth-Century Audiencia of Santo Domingo." *The Americas* 68, no. 4 (April 2012): 467–93.

Ebright, Malcolm, and Rick Hendricks. *The Witches of Abiquiu: The Governor, the Priest, the Genizaro Indians, and the Devil*. Albuquerque: University of New Mexico Press, 2006.

Eissa-Barroso, Francisco A. "Las capitanías generales de provincias estratégicas hispanoamericanas durante los reinados de Felipe V: Aproximación al perfil socio-profesional de una institución atlántica." In *Élites, representación y redes atlánticas en la Hispanoamérica moderna*, edited by Francisco A. Eissa-Barroso, Ainara Vázquez Varela, and Silvia Espelt-Bombín, 111–73. Zamora: El Colegio de Michoacán, 2017.

———. "'Having Served in the Troops': The Appointment of Military Officers as Provincial Governors in Early Eighteenth-Century Spanish America, 1700–1746." *Colonial Latin American Historical Review* 18, no. 4 (October 2013): 329–59.

———. "'The Honor of the Spanish Nation': Military Officers, Mediterranean Campaigns and American Government under Felipe V." In *Early Bourbon Spanish*

America: Politics and Society in a Forgotten Era (1700–1759)*, edited by Francisco A. Eissa-Barroso and Ainara Vázquez Varela, 39–60. The Hague: Brill, 2013.

———. "'Of Experience, Zeal, and Selflessness': Military Officers as Viceroys in Early Eighteenth Century Spanish America." *The Americas* 68, no. 3 (January 2012): 317–45.

———. "Politics, Political Culture, and Policy Making: The Reform of Viceregal Rule in the Spanish World under Philip V (1700–1746)." PhD diss., University of Warwick, 2010.

———. *The Spanish Monarchy and the Creation of the Viceroyalty of New Granada (1717–1739): The Politics of Early Bourbon Reform in Spain and Spanish America*. Leiden: Brill, 2016.

Elliott, John H. *The Count-Duke of Olivares: The Statesman in an Age of Decline*. New Haven, CT: Yale University Press, 1986.

Ertman, Thomas. *Birth of the Leviathan: Building States and Regimes in Medieval and Early Modern Europe*. Cambridge: Cambridge University Press, 1997.

Escamilla González, Francisco Iván. "Los confesores reales de España en la época borbónica y su intervención en la política americana de la monarquía: El caso de Francisco de Rávago, SJ, confesor de Fernando VI." In *La dimensión imperial de la Iglesia novohispana*, edited by Francisco Javier Cervantes Bello and María del Pilar Martínez López-Cano, 225–48. Puebla: Benemérita Universidad Autónoma de Puebla, Instituto de Ciencias Sociales y Humanidades "Alfonso Vélez Pliego," 2016.

———. "La corte de los virreyes." In *Historia de la vida cotidiana en México*, vol. 2, *La ciudad barroca*, edited by Antonio Rubial García, 371–406. Mexico City: Fondo de Cultura Económica, 2005.

———. *José Patricio Fernández de Uribe: El cabildo eclesiástico de México ante el Estado Borbónico*. Mexico City: Conaculta, 1999.

———. "La nueva alianza: El Consulado de México y la monarquía borbónica durante la guerra de sucesión." In *Mercaderes, comercio y consulados de Nueva España en el siglo XVIII*, edited by Guillermina del Valle Pavón, 41–63. Mexico City: Instituto Mora, 2003.

———. "Permanence and Change in Mexico City's Viceregal Court, 1535–1821." In *A Companion to Viceregal Mexico City, 1519–1821*, edited by John F. López, 215–36. Leiden: Brill, 2021.

———. "Urgencia militar e imposiciones fiscales: La renta de alcabalas en la Junta de Arbitrios de Real Hacienda de Nueva España, 1744." In *La fiscalidad novohispana en el imperio español: Conceptualizaciones, proyectos y contradicciones*, edited by María del Pilar Martínez López-Cano, Ernest Sánchez Santiró, and Matilde Souto Mantecón, 239–66. Mexico City: Instituto Mora; Universidad Nacional Autónoma de México, Instituto de Investigaciones Históricas, 2015.

Escamilla González, Francisco Iván, and Olivia Moreno Gamboa. "El Duque de

Linares: Innovación devocional en la corte virreinal novohispana a principios del siglo XVIII." In *La construcción de la feligresía: Control, negociación y conflicto en la Iglesia novohispana*, edited by Francisco Javier Cervantes Bello and María del Pilar Martínez López-Cano, 149–83. Puebla, Mexico: Benemérita Universidad Autónoma de Puebla, 2021.

Escudero, José Antonio. "El gobierno central de las Indias: El consejo y la secretaría del despacho." In *El gobierno de un mundo: Virreinatos y audiencias en la América hispánica*, edited by Feliciano Barrios Pintado, 95–118. Cuenca, Spain: Ediciones de la Universidad de Castilla–La Mancha, 2004.

Farriss, Nancy M. *La corona y el clero en el México colonial, 1759–1821: La crisis del privilegio eclesiástico*. Translated by Margarita Bojalil. Mexico City: Fondo de Cultura Económica,1995.

Fayard, Janine. *Les membres du Conseil de Castille à l'époque moderne (1621–1746)*. Geneva: Librairie Droz, 1979.

Felices de la Fuente, María del Mar. *Condes, marqueses y duques: Biografías de nobles titulados durante el reinado de Felipe V*. Madrid: Ediciones Doce Calles; Seville: Junta de Andalucía, 2013.

Figueroa y Melgar, Alfonso de. *Estudio histórico sobre algunas familias españolas*. Vol. 4. Madrid: Escuelas Profesionales del Sagrado Corazón, 1970.

Fonck, Béatrice. "Les confesseurs jésuites des Bourbones d'Espagne au XVIIIe siècle: Approches et perspectives." In *Les Jésuites en Espagne et en Amérique: Jeux et enjeux de pouvoir (XVIe–XVIIIe siècles)*, edited by Annie Molinié, Alexandra Merle, and Araceli Guillaume-Alonso, 83–108. Paris: Presses de l'Université de Paris-Sorbonne, 2007.

García Ayluardo, Clara. "Re-formar la Iglesia." In *Las reformas borbónicas, 1750–1808*, edited by Clara García Ayluardo. Mexico City: Fondo de Cultura Económica, 2010. Kindle.

García Carraffa, Alberto, and Arturo García Carraffa. *Diccionario heráldico y genealógico de apellidos españoles y americanos*. Vol. 59. Madrid: Nueva Imprenta Radio, 1962.

García del Ser, María Victoria, and José María Imízcoz. "El alto clero vasco y navarro en la monarquía hispánica del siglo XVIII: Bases familiares, economía del parentesco y patronazgo." In *La iglesia hispanoamericana, de la colonia a la república*, edited by Rodolfo Aguirre and Lucrecia Enríquez, 125–88. Mexico City: Universidad Nacional Autónoma de México, 2008.

García-Gallo, Concepción. "La legislación indiana de 1630 a 1680 y la Recopilación de 1680." *Anuario de Historia del Derecho Español*, no. 49 (1979): 99–139.

García Melero, José Enrique. "Realizaciones arquitectónicas de la segunda mitad del siglo XVIII en los interiores de las catedrales góticas españolas." *Espacio, Tiempo y Forma*, series VII, *Historia del Arte*, no. 2 (1989): 223–86.

Garibay, Enrique. "Biografía del Marqués del Castillo de Aysa." Unpublished manuscript.

Garriga, Carlos. "Concepción y aparatos de la justicia: Las Reales Audiencias de las Indias." In *Convergencias y divergencias: México y Perú, siglos XVI–XIX*, edited by Lilia V. Oliver Sánchez, 21–72. Guadalajara: Universidad de Guadalajara; Zamora: El Colegio de Michoacán, 2006.

———. "Crimen corruptionis: Justicia y corrupción en la cultura del ius commune (Corona de Castilla, siglos XVI–XVII)." *Revista Complutense de Historia de América*, no. 43 (2017): 21–48.

Geertz, Clifford. *The Interpretation of Cultures: Selected Essays*. New York: Basic Books, 1973.

Gerhard, Peter. *A Guide to the Historical Geography of New Spain*. 2nd ed. Norman: University of Oklahoma Press, 1993.

Gil Pujol, Xavier. "Una cultura cortesana provincial: Patria, comunicación y lenguaje en la Monarquía Hispánica de los Austrias." In *Monarquía, imperio y pueblos en la España moderna: Actas de la IV reunión científica de la Asociación Española de Historia Moderna, Alicante, 27–30 de mayo de 1996*, edited by Pablo Fernández Albadalejo, 225–57. Alicante, Spain: Caja de Ahorros del Mediterráneo, Universidad de Alicante, 1997.

Gómez Alfaro, Antonio. *The Great Gypsy Round-Up, Spain: The General Imprisonment of Gypsies in 1749*. Madrid: Gypsy Research Center, 1991.

Gómez Gómez, Margarita. *Actores del documento: Oficiales, archiveros y escribientes de la Secretaría de Estado y del Despacho Universal de Indias durante el siglo XVIII*. Madrid: Centro de Estudios Políticos y Constitucionales, 2003.

———. "La nueva tramitación de los negocios de Indias en el siglo XVIII: De la 'vía del consejo' a la 'vía reservada.'" In *El gobierno de un mundo: Virreinatos y audiencias en la América hispánica*, edited by Feliciano Barrios Pintado, 203–50. Cuenca, Spain: Ediciones de la Universidad de Castilla–La Mancha, 2004.

Gómez Molleda, María Dolores. "El pensamiento de Carvajal y la política internacional española del siglo XVIII." *Hispania*, no. 58 (1955): 117–37.

Gómez Urdáñez, José Luis. "Carvajal y Ensenada, un binomio político." In *Ministros de Fernando VI*, edited by José Miguel Delgado Barrado and José Luis Gómez Urdáñez, 65–92. Córdoba: Servicio de Publicaciones, Universidad de Córdoba, 2002.

———. *Fernando VI*. Madrid: Arlanza Ediciones, 2001.

———. *El proyecto reformista de Ensenada*. Lleida, Spain: Editorial Milenio, 1996.

Gonzalbo Aizpuru, Pilar. "Las fiestas del pasado." In *La fiesta mexicana*, edited by Enrique Florescano and Bárbara Santana Rocha, vol. 1, 177–81. Mexico City: Fondo de Cultura Económica, 2016.

———. "Las fiestas novohispanas: Espectáculo y ejemplo." *Mexican Studies/Estudios Mexicanos* 9, no. 1 (Winter 1993): 19–45.

———. *Historia de la educación en la época colonial: La educación de los criollos y la vida urbana*. Mexico City: El Colegio de México, 2005.

———. "El virreinato." In *La fiesta mexicana*, edited by Enrique Florescano and

Bárbara Santana Rocha, vol. 1, 191–206. Mexico City: Fondo de Cultura Económica, 2016.

Grafe, Regina, and Alejandra Irigoin. "A Stakeholder Empire: The Political Economy of Spanish Imperial Rule in America." *Economic History Review* 65, no. 2 (May 2012): 609–51.

Grieco, Viviana L. *The Politics of Giving in the Viceroyalty of Rio de la Plata: Donors, Lenders, Subjects, and Citizens*. Albuquerque: University of New Mexico Press, 2014.

Guerrero Elecalde, Rafael. "El 'partido vizcaíno' y los representantes del rey en el extranjero: Redes de poder, clientelismo y política exterior durante el reinado de Felipe V." In *Actas de la VIII Reunión Científica de la Fundación Española de Historia Moderna, Madrid, 2–4 de junio de 2004*, vol. 2, *El equilibrio de los imperios: De Utrecht a Trafalgar*, edited by Agustín Guimerá Ravina and Víctor Peralta Ruiz, 85–100. Madrid: Fundación Española de Historia Moderna, 2005.

Guez, Olivier. "Das System Chávez ähnelt dem Kuba Castros." *Frankfurter Allgemeine Zeitung*, September 19, 2010. https://www.faz.net/aktuell/feuilleton/buecher/autoren/im-gespraech-mario-vargas-llosa-das-system-chavez-aehnelt-dem-kuba-castros-11039772.html.

Guimerá, Agustín, ed. *El reformismo borbónico. Una visión interdisciplinar*. Madrid: Consejo Superior de Investigaciones Científicas; Alianza Editorial, 1998.

Haddick, Jack A. "The Administration of Viceroy Iturrigaray." PhD diss., University of Texas, Austin, 1954.

Hamnett, Brian R. *The Mexican Bureaucracy before the Bourbon Reforms, 1700–1770: A Study in the Limitations of Absolutism*. Institute of Latin American Studies, Occasional Papers 26. Glasgow: University of Glasgow, 1979.

Hanke, Lewis. *Guía de las fuentes en Hispanoamérica para el estudio de la administración virreinal española en México y en el Perú, 1535–1700*. Cologne: Böhlau Verlag, 1976.

Hausberger, Bernd. "Matrikel Consulado." Unpublished manuscript.

Helguera Quijada, Juan. "Un empeño fallido de reindustrialización: Las reales fábricas del siglo XVIII en Castilla y León." In *Instituciones políticas, comportamientos sociales y atraso económico en España (1580–2000): Homenaje a Ángel García Sanz*, edited by Francisco Comín Comín, Ricardo Hernández García, and Javier Moreno Lázaro, 211–246. Salamanca, Spain: Ediciones Universidad de Salamanca, 2017.

Hermann, Christian. *L'église d'Espagne sous le patronage royal (1476–1834): Essai d'ecclésiologie politique*. Madrid: Casa de Velázquez, 1988.

Herzog, Tamar, "La presencia ausente: El virrey desde la perspectiva de las élites locales (Audiencia de Quito, 1670–1747)." In *Monarquía, imperio y pueblo en la España moderna*, edited by Pablo Fernández Albadalejo, 819–26. Alicante, Spain: Universidad de Alicante, 1997.

———. *Upholding Justice: Society, State, and the Penal System in Quito (1650–1750)*. Ann Arbor: University of Michigan Press, 2004.

Hespanha, António Manuel. "Les autres raisons de la politique: L'économie de la grâce." In *Recherche sur l'histoire de l'État dans le monde ibérique, 15e–20e siècle*, edited by Jean-Frédéric Schaub, 67–86. Paris: Presses de l'École Normale Supérieure, 1993.

Holenstein, André. "Introduction: Empowering Interactions; Looking at Statebuilding from Below." In *Empowering Interactions: Political Cultures and the Emergence of the State in Europe, 1300–1900*, edited by Wim Blockmans, André Holenstein, and Jon Mathieu, 1–31. Farnham, Surrey, England: Ashgate, 2009.

Irigoin, Alejandra, and Regina Grafe. "Bargaining for Absolutism: A Spanish Path to Nation-State and Empire Building." *Hispanic American Historical Review* 88, no. 2 (May 2006): 173–209.

Jaramillo Magaña, Juvenal. *Hacia una iglesia beligerante: La gestión episcopal de fray Antonio de San Miguel en Michoacán (1784–1804); Los proyectos ilustrados y las defensas canónicas*. Zamora: El Colegio de Michoacán, 1996.

Jones, Kenneth Warren. "New Spain and the Viceregency of the Marqués de Casafuerte, 1722–1734." PhD diss., University of California, Santa Barbara, 1971.

Jorzick, Regine. *Herrschaftssymbolik und Staat: Die Vermittlung königlicher Herrschaft im Spanien der frühen Neuzeit*. Munich: Oldenbourg, 1998.

Kamen, Henry. *Empire: How Spain Became a World Power, 1492–1763*. New York: HarperCollins, 2003.

———. *Philip V of Spain: The King Who Reigned Twice*. New Haven, CT: Yale University Press, 2001.

Kessler, Amalia D. "Enforcing Virtue: Social Norms and Self-Interest in an Eighteenth-Century Merchant Court." *Law and History Review* 22, no. 1 (Spring 2004): 71–118.

Klaveren, Jacob van. *Europäische Wirtschaftsgeschichte Spaniens im 16. und 17. Jahrhundert*. Stuttgart: Gustav Fischer, 1960.

Klein, Herbert S. *The American Finances of the Spanish Empire: Royal Income and Expenditures in Colonial Mexico, Peru, and Bolivia, 1680–1809*. Albuquerque: University of New Mexico Press, 1998.

Kodres, Krista. "Magic of Presence: The Ceremony of Taking an Oath of Allegiance in 1690 in Tallinn (Reval)." In *Images and Objects in Ritual Practices in Medieval and Early Modern Northern and Central Europe*, edited by Krista Kodres and Anu Mänd, 183–203. Newcastle upon Tyne: Cambridge Scholars Publishing, 2013.

Kuethe, Allan J. "La Casa de Contratación en la época de su traslado a Cádiz." In *La Casa de la Contratación y la navegación entre España y las Indias*, edited by Antonio Acosta Rodríguez, Adolfo González Rodríguez, and Enriqueta Vila Vilar, 205–18. Seville: Universidad de Sevilla; Consejo Superior de Investigaciones Científicas, 2003.

———. "La desregulación comercial y la reforma imperial en la época de Carlos III: Los casos de Nueva España y Cuba." *Historia Mexicana* 41, no. 2 (October–December 1991): 265–92.

———. "El fin del monopolio: Los Borbones y el Consulado andaluz." In *Relaciones de poder y comercio colonial: Nuevas perspectivas*, edited by Enriqueta Vila Vilar and Allan J. Kuethe, 35–66. Seville: Escuela de Estudios Hispano-Americanos, 1999.

Kuethe, Allan J., and Kenneth J. Andrien. *The Spanish Atlantic World in the Eighteenth Century: War and the Bourbon Reforms, 1713–1796*. Cambridge: Cambridge University Press, 2014.

Ladd, Doris M. *The Mexican Nobility at Independence, 1780–1826*. Austin: Institute of Latin American Studies, University of Texas, Austin, 1976.

Lamikiz, Xabier. "Social Capital, Networks and Trust in Early Modern Long-Distance Trade: A Critical Appraisal." In *Merchants and Trade Networks in the Atlantic and the Mediterranean, 1550–1800: Connectors of Commercial Maritime Systems*, edited by Manuel Herrero Sánchez and Klemens Kaps, 39–61. London: Routledge, 2017.

———. *Trade and Trust in the Eighteenth-Century Atlantic World: Spanish Merchants and Their Overseas Networks*. Woodbridge, Suff., England: Boydell and Brewer, 2010.

Lane, Kris. *Potosí: The Silver City That Changed the World*. Oakland: University of California Press, 2019.

Langue, Frédérique. "Mineros y poder en Nueva España: El caso de Zacatecas en vísperas de la Independencia." *Revista de Indias* 51, no. 192 (1991): 327–41.

———. *Los señores de Zacatecas: Una aristocracia minera del siglo XVIII novohispano*. Mexico City: Fondo de Cultura Económica, 1999.

———. "Trabajadores y formas de trabajo." *Historia Mexicana* 40, no. 3 (1991): 463–506.

Larkin, Brian. *The Very Nature of God: Baroque Catholicism and Religious Reform in Bourbon Mexico City*. Albuquerque: University of New Mexico Press, 2010.

Latasa Vassallo, Pilar. "La casa del obispo-virrey Palafox: Familia y patronazgo; Un análisis comparativo con la corte virreinal hispanoamericana." In *Palafox: Iglesia, Cultura y Estado en el siglo XVII*, edited by Ricardo Fernández Gracia, 201–28. Pamplona, Spain: Ediciones Universidad de Navarra, 2001.

———. "Juan Francisco de Güemes y Horcasitas." Real Academia de la Historia, *Diccionario biográfico electrónico*. https://dbe.rah.es/.

Lavallé, Bernard. *Las promesas ambiguas: Ensayos sobre el criollismo colonial en los Andes*. Lima: Pontificia Universidad Católica del Perú; Instituto Riva-Agüero. 1993.

Lempérière, Annick. *Entre Dieu et le roi, la République: Mexico, XVIe–XIXe siècles*. Paris: Les Belles Lettres, 2004.

Le Roux, Nicolas. "La maison du roi sous les premiers Bourbons: Institution sociale et outil politique." In *Les cours d'Espagne et de France au XVIIe siècle: Actas del coloquio celebrado del 26 al 28 de noviembre de 2001 en Madrid*, edited by Chantal Grell and Benoît Pellistrandi, 13–40. Madrid: Casa de Velázquez, 2007.

Lisón Tolosano, Carmelo. "Referencia y autorreferencia en el ritual cortesano." In *Les cours d'Espagne et de France au XVIIe siècle: Actas del coloquio celebrado del 26 al 28 de noviembre de 2001 en Madrid*, edited by Chantal Grell and Benoît Pellistrandi, 3–12. Madrid: Casa de Velázquez, 2007.

Llanos, Claudia. "Introduction to *Diario de viaje*." In *Diario de viaje de Cádiz a México*, by Luisa María del Rosario Ahumada y Vera, Marquesa de las Amarillas, edited by Clara Ramírez and Claudia Llanos, 15–19. Mexico City: Universidad Nacional Autónoma de México, 2016.

Llombart Rosa, Vicent A. "El pensamiento económico de la Ilustración en España (1730–1812)." In *Economía y economistas españoles*, vol. 3, *La Ilustración*, edited by Enrique Fuentes Quintana, 7–89. Barcelona: Galaxia Gutenberg, 1999.

Lockhart, James. *The Nahuas after the Conquest: A Social and Cultural History of the Indians of Central Mexico, Sixteenth through Eighteenth Centuries*. Stanford, CA: Stanford University Press, 1992.

Lodge, Richard, ed. *The Private Correspondence of Sir Benjamin Keene, K. B. (1933)*. Cambridge: Cambridge University Press, 2014.

López Álvarez Alejandro. *Poder, lujo y conflicto en la Corte de los Austrias: Coches, carrozas y sillas de mano, 1550–1700*. Madrid: Ediciones Polifemo, 2007.

López-Cordón Cortezo, María Victoria. "Servicios y favores en la Casa de la Reina." In *El poder del dinero: Ventas de cargo y honores en el Antiguo Régimen*, edited by Francisco Andújar Castillo and María del Mar Felices de la Fuente, 223–44. Madrid: Biblioteca Nueva, 2011.

López García, José Miguel. *El motín contra Esquilache: Crisis y protesta popular en el Madrid del siglo XVIII*. Madrid: Alianza Editorial, 2006.

López Miramontes, Álvaro. "El establecimiento del real de minas de Bolaños." *Historia Mexicana* 23, no. 3 (January–March 1974): 408–36.

———. *Las minas de Nueva España en 1753*. Mexico City: Instituto Nacional de Antropología e Historia, 1975.

Luna Moreno, Carmen de. "Alternativa en el siglo XVIII: Franciscanos de la provincia del Santo Evangelio de México." In *Actas del IV Congreso Internacional sobre los Franciscanos en el Nuevo Mundo (siglo XVIII): Cholula-Puebla del 22 al 27 de Julio de 1991*, 343–71. Madrid: Editorial Deimos, 1991.

Luque Talaván, Miguel. "Antonio José Álvarez de Abreu." Real Academia de la Historia, *Diccionario biográfico electrónico*. https://dbe.rah.es/.

Lynch, John. *Bourbon Spain, 1700–1808*. Oxford: Basil Blackwell, 1989.

———. "El reformismo borbónico e Hispanoamérica." In *El reformismo borbónico: Una visión interdisciplinar*, edited by Agustín Guimerá, 37–60. Madrid: Consejo Superior de Investigaciones Científicas; Alianza Editorial, 1998.

Macías Delgado, Jacinta. "Miguel Antonio de la Gándara." In *Economía y economistas españoles*, vol. 3, *La Ilustración*, edited by Enrique Fuentes Quintana, 175–84. Barcelona: Galaxia Gutenberg, 1999.

MacKay, Ruth. *The Limits of Royal Authority: Resistance and Obedience in Seventeenth-Century Castile*. Cambridge: Cambridge University Press, 1999.

MacLachlan, Colin M. *Imperialism and the Origins of Mexican Culture*. Cambridge, MA: Harvard University Press, 2015.

Maqueda Abreu, Consuelo. "La corte española del Barroco vista por los extranjeros." In *Les cours d'Espagne et de France au XVIIe siècle: Actas del coloquio celebrado del 26 al 28 de noviembre de 2001 en Madrid*, edited by Chantal Grell and Benoît Pellistrandi, 125–48. Madrid: Casa de Velázquez, 2007.

Marichal, Carlos. *Bankruptcy of Empire: Mexican Silver and the Wars between Spain, Britain, and France, 1760–1810*. Cambridge: Cambridge University Press, 2007.

———. "Rethinking Negotiation and Coercion in an Imperial State." *Hispanic American Historical Review* 88, no. 2 (May 2008): 211–18.

Martin, Cathie Jo. "Negotiating Political Agreements." In *Political Negotiation: A Handbook*, edited by Jane Mansbridge and Cathie Jo Martin, 7–34. Washington, DC: Brookings Institution Press, 2015.

Martin, Cheryl English. *Governance and Society in Colonial Mexico: Chihuahua in the Eighteenth Century*. Stanford, CA: Stanford University Press, 1996.

Martínez Millán, José. "La articulación de la monarquía española a través de la Corte: Consejos territoriales y Cortes virreinales en los reinados de Felipe II y Felipe III." In *Las cortes virreinales de la monarquía española: América e Italia*, edited by Francesca Cantù, 39–63. Rome: Viella Libreria Editrice, 2008.

Martínez Nava, Isabel. "El Tribunal del Santo Oficio de Logroño y Don José del Campillo y Cossío." *Berceo* 140 (2000): 275–92.

Martínez Rosales, Alfonso. "La provincia de San Alberto de Indias de Carmelitas Descalzos." *Historia Mexicana* 31, no. 4 (April–June 1982): 471–543.

Mazín Gómez, Óscar. *El cabildo catedral de Valladolid de Michoacán*. Zamora: El Colegio de Michoacán, 1996.

McFarlane, Anthony. *Colombia before Independence: Economy, Society, and Politics under Bourbon Rule*. Cambridge: Cambridge University Press, 1993.

Medina, Miguel Ángel. *Los Dominicos en América: Presencia y actuación de los Dominicos en la América colonial española de los siglos XVI–XIX*. Madrid: Editorial MAPFRE, 1992.

Meißner, Jochen. *Eine Elite im Umbruch: Der Stadtrat von Mexiko zwischen kolonialer Ordnung und unabhängigem Staat, 1761–1821*. Stuttgart: Franz Steiner, 1993.

Melvin, Karen. *Building Colonial Cities of God: Mendicant Orders and Urban Culture in New Spain*. Stanford, CA: Stanford University Press, 2012.

Menegus Bornemann, Margarita, Francisco Morales, and Óscar Mazín Gómez. *La secularización de las doctrinas de indios en la Nueva España: La pugna entre las dos iglesias*. Mexico City: Universidad Nacional Autónoma de México, Instituto de Investigaciones sobre la Universidad y la Educación, 2010.

Mínguez [Cornelles], Víctor. "Héroes clásicos y reyes héroes en el Antiguo Régimen." In *La construcción del héroe en España y México (1789–1847)*, edited by Manuel Chust and Víctor Mínguez, 51–70. Valencia: Publicacions de la Universitat de València, 2003.

Mínguez Cornelles, Víctor. "Imperium reflexum: El espejo como metáfora del poder del Príncipe en la Edad Moderna." In *La visión especular: El espejo como tema y como símbolo*, edited by Ester Alba Pagán, Manuel Albaladejo Vivero, Rafael Gil Salinas, and Sergi Doménech García, 325–52. Madrid: Calambur Editorial, 2018.

———. "Jeroglíficos para un Imperio: La cultura emblemática en el virreinato de la Nueva España." *Quiroga: Revista de Patrimonio Iberoamericano*, no. 11 (January–June 2017): 56–68.

Miranda, José. *El tributo indígena en la Nueva España durante el siglo XVI*. 2nd ed. Mexico City: El Colegio de México, 2005.

Miranda Pacheco, Sergio. "El juicio de residencia al virrey Revillagigedo y los intereses oligárquicos en la ciudad de México." *Estudios de Historia Novohispana*, no. 29 (2003): 49–75.

Molina Cortón, Juan. *Reformismo y neutralidad: José de Carvajal y la diplomacia de la España preilustrada*. Mérida, Spain: Editora Regional de Extremadura, 2003.

Montes González, Francisco. "La 'jaula' de las virreinas: Polémica en torno a un asiento indecoroso en la catedral de México." In *Barroco iberoamericano: Identidades culturales de un imperio*, edited by Carme López Calderón, María de los Ángeles Fernández Valle, and Inmaculada Rodríguez Moya, vol. 1, 231–47. Santiago de Compostela, Spain: Andavira Editora, 2013.

Morales, Francisco. "Secularización de doctrinas: ¿Fin de un modelo evangelizador en la Nueva España?" In *Archivo Ibero-Americano* 52, nos. 205–208 (1992): 465–95.

Morales Folguera, José Miguel. *Cultura simbólica y arte efímero en la Nueva España*. Granada: Junta de Andalucía, 1991.

———. "El fin de una época: Iconografía de la fiesta bajo dos reinados; Carlos III y Carlos IV." In *España festejante: El siglo XVIII*, edited by Margarita Torrione, 533–42. Málaga, Spain: Centro de Ediciones de Diputación de Málaga, 2000.

Morales Martínez, Alfredo José. "Antes de la fiesta: Notas sobre el viaje y recibimiento de los virreyes del Perú." In *Las cortes virreinales de la monarquía española: América e Italia*, edited by Francesca Cantù, 465–92. Rome: Viella Libreria Editrice, 2008.

Morelli, Federica. "La publicación y el juramento de la constitución de Cádiz en Hispanoamérica: Imágenes y valores (1812–1813)." In *Observation and Communication: The Construction of Realities in the Hispanic World*, edited by

Johannes-Michael Scholz and Tamar Herzog, 177–218. Frankfurt: Vittorio Klostermann, 1997.

Moreno, Heriberto, and José María Murià. *De mediados del siglo XVI a finales del siglo XVIII*. Vol. 2 of *Historia general de Jalisco*, edited by José María Murià and Angélica Peregrina. Zapopan: El Colegio de Jalisco, 2015.

Moreno Cebrián, Alfredo. "Acumulación y blanqueo de capitales del Marqués de Castelfuerte (1723–1763)." In *El "Premio" de ser virrey: Los intereses públicos y privados del gobierno virreinal en el Perú de Felipe V*, edited by Alfredo Moreno Cebrián and Nuria Sala y Vila, 151–276. Madrid: Consejo Superior de Investigaciones Científicas, 2004.

——. *El corregidor de Indios y la economía peruana del siglo XVIII: Los repartos forzosos de mercancías*. Madrid: Consejo Superior de Investigaciones Científicas, 1977.

——. "La vida cotidiana en los viajes ultramarinos." In *España y el ultramar hispánico hasta la Ilustración: I Jornadas de historia marítima*, 113–34. Madrid: Instituto de Historia y Cultura Naval, 1989.

Mota Padilla, Matías Ángel de la. *Historia del reino de Nueva Galicia en la América septentrional, 1742*. Facsimile edited by José Parres Arias and José Luis Razo Zaragoza. Mexico City: Instituto Nacional de Antropología e Historia; Guadalajara: Universidad de Guadalajara, 1973.

Mota y Escobar, Alonso de la. *Descripción geográfica de los reinos de Nueva Galicia, Nueva Vizcaya y Nuevo León*. 2nd ed. Mexico City: Editorial Pedro Robredo, 1940.

Mues Orts, Paula. "El 'entierro fingido' del marqués de Casafuerte: Escultura y burla como figuración de la disensión, y medio de intervención." In *Intervenciones y escultura virreinal: Historia e interpretación*, edited by Patricia Díaz Cayeros and Fanny Unikel Santoncini, 13–43. Mexico City: Universidad Nacional Autónoma de México, Instituto de Investigaciones Estéticas, 2022.

Muhlack, Ulrich. "Physiokratismus." In *Lexikon zum aufgeklärten Absolutismus in Europa: Herrscher-Denker-Sachbegriffe*, edited by Helmut Reinalter, 472–77. Vienna: Böhlau Verlag, 2005.

Münkler, Herfried. *Empires: The Logic of World Domination from Ancient Rome to the United States*. Translated by Patrick Camiller. Cambridge: Polity Press, 2007.

Muro Romero, Fernando. *Las Presidencias-Gobernaciones en Indias (siglo XVI)*. Seville: Escuela de Estudios Hispano-Americanos, 1975.

Muthoo, Abhinay. "A Non-Technical Introduction to Bargaining Theory." *World Economics* 1, no. 2 (April–June 2000): 145–66.

Navarro García, Luis. "Destrucción de la oposición política en México por Carlos III." *Naveg@mérica: Revista electrónica editada por la Asociación Española de Americanistas*, no. 1 (2008). https://revistas.um.es/navegamerica/article/view/43991. Originally published in *Anales de la Universidad Hispalense*, no. 24 (1964): 13–34.

———. *Don José de Gálvez y la comandancia general de las provincias internas del norte de Nueva España*. Seville: Consejo Superior de Investigaciones Científicas, 1964.

———. "El falso Campillo y el reformismo borbónico." *Temas Americanistas*, no. 12 (1995): 10–31.

———. "El reformismo borbónico: Proyectos y realidades." In *El gobierno de un mundo: Virreinatos y audiencias en la América hispánica*, edited by Feliciano Barrios Pintado, 489–501. Cuenca, Spain: Ediciones de la Universidad de Castilla–La Mancha, 2004.

Ocaranza, Fernando. *Capítulos de la historia franciscana*. Vol. 1. Mexico City: n.p., 1933.

O'Hara, Matthew D. *A Flock Divided: Race, Religion, and Politics in Mexico, 1749–1857*. Durham, NC: Duke University Press, 2010.

———. "Stone, Mortar, and Memory: Church Construction and Communities in Late Colonial Mexico City." *Hispanic American Historical Review* 86, no. 4 (2006): 647–80.

Oliver Sánchez, Lilia V. "La evolución de la población en el siglo XVIII." In *Historia del reino de la Nueva Galicia*, edited by Thomas Calvo and Aristarco Regalado Pinedo, 611–46. Guadalajara: Universidad de Guadalajara, Centro Universitario de Ciencias Sociales y Humanidades, 2016.

Osterhammel, Jürgen. "The Imperial Viceroy: Reflections on an Historical Type." In *The Dynastic Centre and the Provinces: Agents and Interactions*, edited by Jeroen Duindam and Sabine Dabringhaus, 13–29. Leiden: Brill, 2014.

Owensby, Brian P. "Between Justice and Economics: 'Indians' and Reformism in Eighteenth-Century Spanish Imperial Thought." In *Legal Pluralism and Empires, 1500–1850*, edited by Lauren Benton and Richard J. Ross, 143–70. New York: New York University Press, 2013.

Ozanam, Didier, ed. *La diplomacia de Fernando VI: Correspondencia reservada entre D. José Carvajal y el Duque de Huéscar, 1746–1749*. Madrid: Consejo Superior de Investigaciones Científicas, 1975.

———, ed. *Les diplomates espagnols du XVIIIe siècle: Introduction et répertoire biographique, 1700–1808*. Madrid: Casa de Velázquez; Bordeaux: Maison des Pays Ibériques, 1998.

Panofsky, Erwin. *Studies in Iconology: Humanist Themes in the Art of the Renaissance*. New York: Harper and Row, 1972.

Paquette, Gabriel B., ed. *Enlightened Reform in Southern Europe and Its Atlantic Colonies, c. 1750–1830*. Farnham, Surrey, England: Ashgate Publishing, 2009.

———. *Enlightenment, Governance, and Reform in Spain and Its Empire, 1759–1808*. Basingstoke, Hants., England: Palgrave Macmillan, 2008.

———. *The European Seaborne Empires: From the Thirty Years' War to the Age of Revolutions*. New Haven, CT: Yale University Press, 2019.

Parry, John H. *La audiencia de Nueva Galicia en el siglo XVI: Estudio sobre el gobierno colonial español*. Translated by Rafael Diego Fernández and Eduardo Williams. Zamora: El Colegio de Michoacán; Fideicomiso Teixidor, 1993.

Pastor, Rodolfo. "La alcabala como fuente para la historia económica y social de la Nueva España." *Historia Mexicana* 27, no. 1 (July–September 1977): 1–16.

Paz, Octavio. *Posdata*. 28th ed. Mexico City: Siglo XXI, 2005.

Pazos Pazos, María Luisa. *El ayuntamiento de la ciudad de México en el siglo XVII: Continuidad institucional y cambio social*. Seville: Diputación Provincial de Sevilla, 1999.

Pearce, Adrian J. *British Trade with Spanish America, 1763–1808*. Liverpool: Liverpool University Press, 2007.

———. "Minister and Viceroy, Paisano and Amigo: The Private Correspondence of the Marqués de la Ensenada and the Conde de Superunda, 1745–1749." *The Americas* 73, no. 4 (October 2016): 477–90.

———. *The Origins of Bourbon Reform in Spanish South America, 1700–1763*. New York: Palgrave Macmillan, 2014.

Peralta Ruiz, Víctor. *Patrones, clientes y amigos: El poder burocrático indiano en la España del siglo XVIII*. Madrid: Consejo Superior de Investigaciones Científicas, 2006.

Pérez Herrero, Pedro. "Economía y poder: Revisión historiográfica. El reformismo borbónico y el crecimiento económico en la Nueva España: Revisión de un modelo interpretativo." In *Las reformas borbónicas y el nuevo orden colonial*, edited by José Francisco Román Gutiérrez, 17–50. Mexico City: Instituto Nacional de Antropología e Historia, 2020.

Pérez-Mallaína Bueno, Pablo Emilio. *Política naval española en el Atlántico, 1700–1715*. Seville: Escuela de Estudios Hispano-Americanos, 1982.

Pérez Puente, Leticia. "La creación de las cátedras públicas de lenguas indígenas y la secularización parroquial." *Estudios de Historia Novohispana*, no. 41 (2009): 45–78.

Pérez Samper, María de los Ángeles. "La llegada de Carlos III al trono español." *Nueva revista*, no. 157 (2016): 25–36.

Pérez Samper, María Ángeles. "La mesa real en la corte borbónica española del siglo XVIII." In *España festejante: El siglo XVIII*, edited by Margarita Torrione, 205–18. Málaga, Spain: Centro de Ediciones de Diputación de Málaga, 2000.

———. "El poder del símbolo y el símbolo del poder: Fiestas reales en Madrid al advenimiento al trono de Carlos III." In *Coloquio Internacional Carlos III y su Siglo: Actas*, vol. 2, *Poder y sociedad en la época de Carlos III*, 377–93. Madrid: Universidad Complutense de Madrid, 1990.

Perujo, Niceto Alonso, and Juan Pérez Angulo, eds. *Diccionario de ciencias eclesiásticas*. Barcelona: Librería de Subirana Hermanos, 1885.

Pieper, Renate. *La Real Hacienda bajo Fernando VI y Carlos III (1753–1788): Repercusiones económicas y sociales*. Madrid: Ministerio de Economía y Hacienda, 1992.

Pietschmann, Horst. "Alcaldes Mayores, Corregidores und Subdelegados: Zum Problem der Distriktsbeamtenschaft im Vizekönigreich Neuspanien." *Jahrbuch für Geschichte Lateinamerikas*, no. 9 (1972): 173–270.

———. "Antecedentes políticos de México, 1808: Estado territorial, estado novohispano, crisis política y desorganización constitucional." In *México, 1808–1821: Las ideas y los hombres*, edited by Pilar Gonzalbo Aizpuru and Andrés Lira González, 23–70. Mexico City: El Colegio de México, 2014.

———. "La corte virreinal de México en el siglo XVII en sus dimensiones jurídico-institucionales, sociales y culturales: Aproximación al estado de la investigación." In *La creatividad femenina en el mundo barroco hispánico: María de Zayas, Isabel Rebeca Correa, Sor Juana Inés de la Cruz*, edited by Monika Bosse, Barbara Potthast, and André Stoll, vol. 2, 481–97. Kassel, Germany: Edition Reichenberger, 1999.

———. "Diego García Panes y Joaquín Antonio de Rivadeneira Barrientos, pasajeros en un mismo barco: Reflexiones en torno al México 'imperial' entre 1755 y 1808." In *Un hombre de libros: Homenaje a Ernesto de la Torre Villar*, edited by Alicia Mayer, 203–33. Mexico City: Universidad Nacional Autónoma de México, 2012.

———. *Las reformas borbónicas y el sistema de intendencias en Nueva España*. Mexico City: Fondo de Cultura Económica, 1996.

Piho, Virve. *La secularización de las parroquias en la Nueva España y su repercusión en San Andrés Calpan*. Mexico City: Instituto Nacional de Antropología e Historia, 1981.

Polo y La Borda, Adolfo. "Don Mauro's Letters: The Marquis of Villagarcía and the Imperial Networks of Patronage in Spain." *The Americas* 76, no. 4 (October 2019): 555–83.

Premo, Bianca. "Half Real: Presence and Absence in Mexico's Juzgado General de Naturales." *Law and History Review* 40, no. 3 (August 2022): 1–17.

Priestley, Herbert Ingram. *José de Gálvez: Visitor-General of New Spain (1765–1771)*. Berkeley: University of California Press, 1916.

Puente Brunke, José de la. "El virreinato peruano en el primer siglo XVIII americano (1680–1750): Organización territorial y control administrativo." In *Los virreinatos de Nueva España y del Perú (1680–1740): Un balance historiográfico*, edited by Bernard Lavallé, 83–97. Madrid: Casa de Velázquez, 2019.

Ramírez, Susan Elizabeth. "Institutions of the Spanish American Empire in the Hapsburg Era." In *A Companion to Latin American History*, edited by Thomas H. Holloway, 106–23. Chichester, W. Susx., England: Wiley-Blackwell, 2011.

Ramos, Frances L. "Celebrating the Patriarch(s) of Puebla." In *Festivals and Daily Life in the Arts of Colonial Latin America, 1492–1850: Papers from the 2012 Mayer Center Symposium at the Denver Art Museum*, edited by Donna Pierce, 73–96. Denver: Mayer Center for Pre-Columbian and Spanish Colonial Art at the Denver Art Museum, 2014.

———. *Identity, Ritual, and Power in Colonial Puebla*. Tucson: University of Arizona Press, 2012.

———. "Succession and Death: Royal Ceremonies in Colonial Puebla." *The Americas* 60, no. 2 (October 2003): 185–215.

Ramos, Frances L., and Iván Escamilla González. "Sucesión y renovación del cuerpo de la monarquía: Las representaciones de Felipe V y la familia real en Nueva España durante la Guerra de Sucesión." *Colonial Latin American Review* 31, no. 3 (2022): 381–410.

Ramos Ávalos, Jorge. "La democracia pendiente." *La Prensa*, July 9, 2010. https://www.prensa.com/impresa/opinion/democracia-pendiente_0_2607489371.html.

Rawlings, Helen. *The Spanish Inquisition*. Malden, MA: Blackwell, 2006.

Recio Mir, Álvaro. "Alamedas, paseos y carruajes: Función y significación social en España y América (siglos XVI–XIX)." *Anuario de Estudios Americanos* 72, no. 2 (2015): 515–43.

Regalado Pinedo, Aristarco. *L'Ouest mexicain à l'époque des découvertes et des conquêtes (XVIe–XVIIe siècle)*. Paris: L'Harmattan, 2013.

Rex Galindo, David. *To Sin No More: Franciscans and Conversion in the Hispanic World, 1683–1830*. Stanford, CA: Stanford University Press; Oceanside, CA: Academy of American Franciscan History, 2017.

Rivero Rodríguez, Manuel. *La edad de oro de los virreyes: El virreinato en la monarquía hispánica durante los siglos XVI y XVII*. Madrid: Ediciones Akal, 2011.

Rodríguez Villa, Antonio. *Don Cenon de Somodevilla, Marqués de la Ensenada: Ensayo biográfico formado con documentos en su mayor parte originales, inéditos y desconocidos*. Madrid: Librería de M. Murillo, 1878.

Romero de Terreros, Manuel. *Una casa del siglo XVIII en Mexico: La del conde de San Bartolome de Xala*. Mexico City: Imprenta Universitaria, 1957.

Rosenmüller, Christoph. *Corruption and Justice in Colonial Mexico, 1650–1755*. Cambridge: Cambridge University Press, 2019.

———. "Friends, Followers, Countrymen: Viceregal Patronage in Mid-Eighteenth Century New Spain." *Estudios de Historia Novohispana*, no. 34 (2006): 47–72.

———. "La 'langosta que arruina': Clero regular y secularización durante el gobierno del primer conde de Revillagigedo." *Historias*, no. 103 (May–August 2019): 29–50.

———. *Patrons, Partisans, and Palace Intrigues: The Court Society of Colonial Mexico, 1702–1710*. Calgary: Calgary University Press, 2008.

Rubial García, Antonio. "Las órdenes mendicantes evangelizadoras en Nueva España y sus cambios estructurales durante los siglos virreinales." In *La iglesia en Nueva España: Problemas y perspectivas de investigación*, edited by María del Pilar Martínez López-Cano, 215–37. Mexico City: Universidad Nacional Autónoma de México, 2010.

———. *Una monarquía criolla (La provincia agustina de México en el siglo XVII)*. Mexico City: Consejo Nacional para la Cultura y las Artes, 1990.

———. "Las virreinas novohispanas: Presencias y ausencias." *Estudios de Historia Novohispana*, no. 50 (January–June 2014): 3–44.

Rubio Mañé, Jorge Ignacio. "Llegada a México del Virrey D. Juan Francisco de Güemes y Horcasitas, 1746." *Boletín del Archivo General de la Nación* 19, no. 1 (January–March 1948): 5–18.

———. *El virreinato*. 4 vols. Mexico City: Fondo de Cultura Económica, 1983.

Ruiz Torres, Pedro. *Reformismo e Ilustración*. Vol. 5, *Historia de España*, edited by Josep Fontana and Ramón Villares. Barcelona: Editorial Crítica; Marcial Pons, 2008.

Sáez-Arance, Antonio. "La Corte de los Habsburgos en Madrid (siglos XVI y XVII): Estado de la cuestión y nuevos planteamientos historiográficos." In *La creatividad femenina en el mundo barroco hispánico: María de Zayas, Isabel Rebeca Correa, Sor Juana Inés de la Cruz*, edited by Monika Bosse, Barbara Potthast, and André Stoll, vol. 1, 1–16. Kassel, Germany: Edition Reichenberger, 1999.

Sala y Vila, Nuria. "Una corona bien vale un virreinato: El marqués de Castelldosrius, primer virrey borbónico del Perú (1707–1710)." In *El "Premio" de ser virrey: Los intereses públicos y privados del gobierno virreinal en el Perú de Felipe V*, edited by Alfredo Moreno Cebrián and Nuria Sala y Vila, 17–150. Madrid: Consejo Superior de Investigaciones Científicas, 2004.

Salazar Andreu, Juan Pablo. "Domingo Pantaleón Álvarez de Abreu, 1743–1763." *Anuario Mexicano de Historia del Derecho*, no. 18 (2006): 253–78.

Salazar Mir, Adolfo de. *Los expedientes de limpieza de sangre de la Catedral de Sevilla: Índice*. Madrid: Ediciones Hidalguía, 1998.

Saldaña, Iván E. "PAN adelanta en el Senado y Diputados rechazo a reforma para 'absorber' a autónomos." *El Heraldo de México*, January 7, 2021. https://heraldodemexico.com.mx/nacional/2021/1/7/pan-adelanta-en-el-senado-diputados-rechazo-reforma-para-absorber-autonomos-242490.html.

Saldaña Solís, Marcela. "El inicio de la secularización de las doctrinas: Arzobispado de México, 1749–1760." Master's thesis, Universidad Nacional Autónoma de México, 2011.

Sánchez Bella, Ismael. *Iglesia y Estado en la América española*. Pamplona, Spain: Ediciones Universidad de Navarra, 1990.

Sánchez Durán, Álvaro. "Interacciones entre hombres de negocios de la nación portuguesa y élites políticas en la Monarquía Hispánica: El doctor Andrés de Fonseca y las rentas reales de Málaga (1645)." In *Estudios sobre la corrupción en España y América (siglos XVI–XVIII)*, edited by Francisco Gil Martínez and Amorina Villarreal Brasca, 81–104. Almería, Spain: Editorial Universidad de Almería, 2017.

Sánchez Santiró, Ernest. *Corte de caja: La Real Hacienda de Nueva España y el primer reformismo fiscal de los Borbones (1720–1755); Alcances y contradicciones*. Mexico City: Instituto Mora, 2013.

———. "La hacienda reformada: La centralización de la renta de alcabalas en Nueva

España (1754–1781)." In *Finanzas y política en el mundo iberoamericano: Del antiguo régimen a las naciones independientes, 1754–1850*, edited by Ernest Sánchez Santiró, Luis Jáuregui, and Antonio Ibarra, 143–78. Cuernavaca, Mexico: Universidad Autónoma del Estado de Morelos; Mexico City: Instituto Mora; Universidad Nacional Autónoma de México, 2001.

———. "El nuevo orden parroquial de la ciudad de México: Población, etnia, y territorio (1768–1777)." *Estudios de Historia Novohispana*, no. 30 (January–June 2004): 63–92.

Sanchiz, Javier, and José Ignacio Conde Díaz Rubín. "La familia Monterde y Antillón en Nueva España: Reconstrucción genealógica (primera parte)." *Estudios de Historia Novohispana*, no. 32 (January–June 2005): 93–164.

———. *Historia genealógica de los títulos y dignidades nobiliarias en Nueva España y México*. Vol. 1, *Casa de Austria*. Mexico City: Universidad Nacional Autónoma de México, 2008.

Sarrablo Aguareles, Eugenio. *El conde de Fuenclara, embajador y virrey de Nueva España, 1687–1752*. 2 vols. Seville: Escuela de Estudios Hispano-Americanos, 1955.

Schreffler, Michael. *The Art of Allegiance: Visual Culture and Imperial Power in Baroque New Spain*. University Park: Pennsylvania State University Press, 2007.

Schroeder, Susan, and Stafford Poole, eds. *Religion in New Spain*. Albuquerque: University of New Mexico Press, 2008.

Schwartz, Stuart B. *Sovereignty and Society in Colonial Brazil: The High Court of Bahia and Its Judges, 1609–1751*. Berkeley: University of California Press, 1973.

Semboloni Capitani, Lara. *La construcción de la autoridad virreinal en Nueva España, 1535–1595*. Mexico City: El Colegio de México, 2014.

Serrano Hernández, Sergio Tonatiuh. "Building an Empire in the New World: Taxes and Fiscal Policy in Hispanic America during the Seventeenth Century." PhD diss., Universidad Carlos III de Madrid, 2020.

Serrano Martín, Eliseo. "La lealtad triunfante: Fiesta, política y sociedad en España en la primera mitad del siglo XVIII." In *España festejante: El siglo XVIII*, edited by Margarita Torrione, 17–36. Málaga, Spain: Centro de Ediciones de Diputación de Málaga, 2000.

Silva Prada, Natalia. "Impacto de la migración urbana en el proceso de 'separación de repúblicas': El caso de dos parroquias indígenas de la parcialidad de San Juan Tenochtitlán, 1688–1692." *Estudios de Historia Novohispana*, no. 24 (January–June 2001): 77–109.

Smith, Robert Sidney. "Sales Taxes in New Spain, 1575–1770." *Hispanic American Historical Review* 28, no. 1 (February 1948): 2–37.

Stangl, Werner. "¿Provincias y partidos o gobiernos y corregimientos? Los principios rectores del desordenamiento territorial de las Indias y la creación de un sistema de información histórico-geográfico." *Jahrbuch für Geschichte Lateinamerikas*, no. 54 (2017): 157–210.

Stein, Stanley J., and Barbara H. Stein. *Apogee of Empire: Spain and New Spain in the Age of Charles III, 1759–1789*. Baltimore: Johns Hopkins University Press, 2003.
———. *Silver, Trade, and War: Spain and America in the Making of Early Modern Europe*. Baltimore: Johns Hopkins University Press, 2000.
Stollberg-Rilinger, Barbara. "Comunicación simbólica en la época premoderna: Concepto, tesis, y perspectivas para la investigación." In *Constitución, poder y representación: Dimensiones simbólicas del cambio político en la época de la independencia mexicana*, edited by Silke Hensel, 33–78. Frankfurt: Iberoamericana Editorial Vervuert, 2011.
———. *Maria Theresia: Die Kaiserin in ihrer Zeit*. Munich: C. H. Beck, 2017.
———. *Rituale*. Frankfurt: Campus Verlag, 2013.
Storrs, Christopher. *The Resilience of the Spanish Monarchy, 1665–1700*. Oxford: Oxford University Press, 2006.
Tanck de Estrada, Dorothy. *Pueblos de indios y educación en el México colonial, 1750–1821*. Mexico City: El Colegio de México, 1999.
———. "El rector desterrado: El surgimiento y la caída de Antonio López Portillo, 1730–1780." In *Permanencia y cambio: Universidades hispánicas, 1551–2001*, edited by Enrique González y González and Leticia Pérez Puente, vol. 1, tome 1, 181–96. Mexico City: Universidad Nacional Autónoma de México, 2006.
Tanck de Estrada, Dorothy, and Carlos Marichal. "¿Reino o colonia? Nueva España, 1750–1804." In *Nueva historia general de México*, edited by Erik Velásquez García et al., 307–53. Mexico City: El Colegio de México, 2010.
Taylor, William B. "'. . . de corazón pequeño y ánimo apocado': Conceptos de los curas párrocos sobre los indios en la Nueva España del siglo xviii." In *Entre el proceso global y el conocimiento local: Ensayos sobre el Estado, la sociedad y la cultura en el México del siglo XVIII*, edited by Brian F. Connaughton, 261–317. Mexico City: Universidad Autónoma Metropolitana, Unidad Iztapalapa, 2003.
———. *Magistrates of the Sacred: Priests and Parishioners in Eighteenth-Century Mexico*. Stanford, CA: Stanford University Press, 1996.
———. "Los pueblos indígenas de Jalisco en una perspectiva comparativa." In *Entre el proceso global y el conocimiento local: Ensayos sobre el Estado, la sociedad y la cultura en el México del siglo XVIII*, edited by Brian F. Connaughton, 107–56. Mexico City: Universidad Autónoma Metropolitana, Unidad Iztapalapa, 2003.
Téllez Alarcia, Diego. *D. Ricardo Wall: Aut Caesar aut nullus*. Madrid: Ministerio de Defensa, 2008.
———. "Guerra y regalismo a comienzos del reinado de Carlos III: El final del ministerio Wall." *Hispania* 61, no. 209 (2001): 1051–90.
———. "Richard Wall: Light and Shade of an Irish Minister in Spain (1694–1777)." *Irish Studies Review* 11, no. 2 (August 2003): 123–36.
TePaske, John J. "General Tendencies and Secular Trends in the Economies of Mexico and Peru, 1750–1810: The View from the *Cajas* of Mexico and Lima." In *The Economies of Mexico and Peru during the Late Colonial Period, 1760–1810*,

edited by Nils Jacobsen and Hans-Jürgen Puhle, 316–39. Berlin: Colloquium Verlag, 1986.

TePaske, John J., and Herbert S. Klein. *Ingresos y egresos de la Real Hacienda de Nueva España*. Vol. 2. Mexico City: Instituto Nacional de Antropología e Historia, 1988.

Torre Curiel, José Refugio de la. *Vicarios en entredicho: Crisis y desestructuración de la provincia franciscana de Santiago de Xalisco, 1749–1860*. Zamora: El Colegio de Michoacán; Guadalajara: Universidad de Guadalajara, 2001.

Tutino, John Mark. "Creole Mexico: Spanish Elites, Haciendas, and Indian Towns, 1750–1810." PhD diss., University of Texas, Austin, 1976.

———. *Making a New World: Founding Capitalism in the Bajío and Spanish North America*. Durham, NC: Duke University Press, 2011.

Urrutia, Javier de. *Descripción histórico-artística de la catedral de Cádiz*. Cádiz: Imprenta, Librería y Litografía de la Revista Médica, 1843.

Valenzuela Márquez, Jaime. "La recepción pública de una autoridad colonial: Modelo peninsular, referente virreinal y reproducción periférica (Santiago de Chile, siglo XVII)." In *México en el mundo hispánico*, edited by Óscar Mazín Gómez, vol. 2, 495–516. Zamora: El Colegio de Michoacán, 2000.

Vallejo García-Hevia, José María. "José Moñino y Redondo." Real Academia de la Historia, *Diccionario biográfico electrónico*. https://dbe.rah.es/.

Valle Menéndez, Antonio del. *Juan Francisco de Güemes y Horcasitas, Primer Conde de Revillagigedo, Virrey de Nueva España: La historia de un soldado (1681–1766)*. In collaboration with Pilar Latasa Vassallo. Santander, Spain: Librería Estudios, 1998.

Valle Pavón, Guillermina del. "Antagonismo entre el consulado de México y el virrey Revillagigedo por la apertura comercial de la Nueva España, 1789–1794." *Estudios de Historia Novohispana*, no. 24 (2001): 111–37.

———. "El consulado de comerciantes, de la ciudad de México y las finanzas novohispanas." PhD diss., El Colegio de México, 1997.

———. *Donativos, préstamos y privilegios: Los mercaderes y mineros de la ciudad de México durante la guerra anglo-española de 1779–1783*. Mexico City: Instituto Mora, 2016.

———. "Los excedentes del ramo Alcabalas: Habilitación de la minería y defensa del monopolio de los mercaderes de México en el siglo XVIII." *Historia Mexicana* 56, no. 3 (January–March 2007): 969–1016.

———. "Ocultación del 'fondo de sobras' del ramo de alcabalas por los priores del Consulado de la ciudad de México." In *Mérito, venalidad y corrupción en España y América: Siglos XVII y XVIII*, edited by Pilar Ponce Leiva and Francisco Andújar Castillo, 323–48. Madrid: Editorial Albatros, 2016.

———. "Relaciones de negocios, familiares y de paisanaje de Manuel Rodríguez de Pedroso, Conde de San Bartolomé de Xala, 1720–1770." In *Redes sociales e instituciones comerciales en el imperio español, siglos XVII a XIX*, edited by

Guillermina del Valle Pavón and Antonio Ibarra, 117–39. Mexico City: Instituto Mora; Universidad Nacional Autónoma de México, 2007.

———. "El respaldo económico del Consulado de México para la Guerra de Sucesión Dinástica." In *La Casa de la Contratación y la navegación entre España y las Indias*, edited by Antonio Acosta Rodríguez, Adolfo González Rodríguez, and Enriqueta Vila Vilar, 941–63. Seville: Universidad de Sevilla; Consejo Superior de Investigaciones Científicas, 2003.

Vázquez Varela, Ainara. "La corte virreinal de Manuel de Guirior en Nueva Granada (1772–1776)." In *Élites, representación y redes atlánticas en la Hispanoamérica moderna*, edited by Francisco A. Eissa-Barroso, Ainara Vázquez Varela, and Silvia Espelt-Bombín, 175–214. Zamora: El Colegio de Michoacán, 2017.

———. *"De la primera sangre de este reino": Composición de las instituciones de justicia y gobierno de Santa Fe de Bogotá (1700–1750)*. Bogotá: Editorial Universidad del Rosario, 2010.

———. "Jorge de Villalonga's Entourage: Political Networking and Administrative Reform in Santa Fe (1717–1723)." In *Early Bourbon Spanish America: Politics and Society in a Forgotten Era (1700–1759)*, edited by Francisco A. Eissa-Barroso and Ainara Vázquez Varela, 111–26. The Hague: Brill, 2013.

———. "Redes de patronazgo del virrey Sebastián de Eslava en Nuevo Reino de Granada." *Príncipe de Viana* 72, no. 254 (2011): 135–47.

Velasco Mendizábal, Gloria Lizania. "Familia, poder y negocios: El conde de San Bartolomé de Xala." In *Genealogía, heráldica y documentación*, edited by Amaya Garritz and Javier Sanchiz, 761–80. Mexico City: Universidad Nacional Autónoma de México, 2014.

———. "Un riojano entre vascos y montañeses: Manuel Rodríguez Sáenz de Pedroso, primer conde de San Bartolomé de Xala." *Estudios de Historia Novohispana*, no. 45 (2011): 123–59.

Velázquez, María del Carmen. *El marqués de Altamira y las provincias internas de Nueva España*. Mexico City: El Colegio de México, 1976.

Vélez-Sainz, Julio. "Anatomía áulica y política de *Fieras afemina amor* de Calderón." *Hispanófila* 161, no. 1 (January 2011): 1–17.

Vilar y Pascual, Luis. *Diccionario histórico, genealógico, y heráldico de las familias ilustres de la monarquía española* . . . Madrid: Imprenta de D. F. Sánchez 1859.

Voekel, Pamela. *Alone before God: The Religious Origins of Modernity in Mexico*. Durham, NC: Duke University Press, 2002.

———. "Peeing on the Palace: Bodily Resistance to Bourbon Reforms in Mexico City." *Journal of Historical Sociology* 5, no. 2 (June 1992): 183–208.

Voltes, Pedro. *La vida y la época de Fernando VI*. Barcelona: Planeta, 1996.

Walker, Charles. "The Upper Classes and Their Upper Stories: Architecture and the Aftermath of the Lima Earthquake of 1746." *Hispanic American Historical Review* 83, no. 1 (2003): 53–82.

Walker, Geoffrey J. *Spanish Politics and Imperial Trade, 1700–1789*. Bloomington: Indiana University Press, 1979.

Walter, Rudolph. "Exkurs: Wirtschaftlicher Liberalismus." In *Geschichtliche Grundbegriffe: Historisches Lexikon zur politisch-sozialen Sprache in Deutschland*, edited by Otto Brunner, Werner Conze, and Reinhart Koselleck, vol. 3, 787–815. Stuttgart: Klett-Cotta Verlag, 1982.

Weber, Max. *Economy and Society: An Outline of Interpretive Sociology*. Edited by Guenther Roth and Claus Wittich. Berkeley: University of California Press, 1978.

Winterling, Aloys. "Der Fürstenhof in der Frühen Neuzeit: Forschungsprobleme und theoretische Konzeption." In *Residenzkultur in Thüringen vom 16. bis zum 19. Jahrhundert*, edited by Roswitha Jacobsen, 29–42. Jena, Germany: Quartus-Verlag, 1999.

Yalí Román, Alberto. "Sobre alcaldías mayores y corregimientos en Indias: Un ensayo de interpretación." *Jahrbuch für Geschichte Lateinamerikas*, no. 9 (1972): 1–39.

Yun Casalilla, Bartolomé. "Introducción: Entre el imperio colonial y la monarquía compuesta; Élites y territorios en la Monarquía Hispánica (ss. XVI y XVII)." In *Las redes del imperio: Élites sociales en la articulación de la Monarquía Hispánica, 1492–1714*, edited by Bartolomé Yun Casalilla, 11–35. Madrid: Marcial Pons; Seville: Universidad Pablo de Olavide, 2009.

Zahino Peñafort, Luisa. "El criollo mexicano Francisco Vives y su correspondencia desde la Francia revolucionaria: De canónigo catedralicio a miembro de una sociedad jacobina." *Estudios de Historia Novohispana*, no. 15 (1995): 113–127.

Zepeda Cortés, María Barbara. "José's Secrets: Minister Gálvez's Master Plan for Spain's Participation in the American Revolution." In *Spain and the American Revolution: New Approaches and Perspectives*, edited by Gabriel Paquette and Gonzalo M. Quintero Saravia, 77–90. London: Routledge, 2020.

———. "Trumped by Politics: Pedro Antonio de Cossío, the Merchant Who Ruled New Spain." *Colonial Latin American Review* 31, no. 4 (2022): 549–72.

Zucker, Mark. "Iconography in Renaissance and Baroque Art." In *A Companion to Renaissance and Baroque Art*, edited by Babette Bohn and James M. Saslow, 359–80. Malden, MA: Wiley-Blackwell, 2013.

Index

Ahumada y Vera, Luisa María del Rosario. *See* Amarillas, Marquise of las
Alameda Square, Mexico City, 4, 51–52, 55, 84
Alburquerque, Duchess of (vicereine): entry to Mexico City, 24, 54; Santa María la Redonda, 76
Alburquerque, Duke of (viceroy), 24, 33, 43; politics, 131–32, 143
alcabala (sales tax): Veracruz, 104–8; conflict with the *consulado* of Mexico City, 89–103; reforms in Spain, 14–15; return to Crown control, 59–60
alcalde mayor / alcaldía mayor (district judge akin to *corregidor*), xii, 12, 16–17, 28, 71, 79, 110, 121; Bolaños, 113–15; Jerez, 112–13; Puebla, 31–32, 131; San Bartolomé Capulhuac, 68–70; viceregal appointments of, 40
alguacil mayor (chief constable) of the Inquisition, 52
Amarillas, Marquis of las, Agustín Ahumada y Villalón (viceroy), 5, 25, 44–45, 65, 102, 121, 127–29, 133, 144–47, 153, 158
Amarillas, Marquise of las, Luisa María del Rosario Ahumada y Vera (vicereine), 25, 44–46, 51, 64, 128, 144–45, 153

Analco (Guadalajara), 110
Andalusia, 2, 126, 134–35, 147, 157–58
Antequera (Andalusia, Spain), 2, 65, 108, 134–35, 158
Antequera de Oaxaca. *See* Oaxaca
appointment of Güemes as viceroy, 89–108
Aragón (Spain), 14, 123, 155, 159
Aranjuez (Spain), 85
Arriaga, Julián (secretary of the Indies), 19–20, 86, 102–3, 105, 107, 127, 130, 134, 146–47, 153
asesor letrado (legal adviser) of Güemes, 104
Atlas (titan), 23, 36–37
Atlihuetzian (Tlaxcala), 28–29
audiencia (high court) of Mexico City, xi–xii, 1–3; rituals, 32–41, 49–50, 57–59; work ethic, 61–63
audiencia of Guadalajara: after Güemes, 120–21; clash with Güemes over jurisdiction, 109–11; conflict over treasury, 116–20; fight over Bolaños, 113–21; work ethic, 60, 63
auditor de guerra (judge advocate) of Güemes, 164-65
Augustinians: Puebla, 82; secularization of *doctrinas*, 72–73, 87; secularization of San Bartolomé Capulhuac, 68–71; secularization of San Mateo Atlatlahucan, 77–78; secularization of Yuririapundaro, 87

Azqueltán (Atzqueltlan), 114

Bajío, El, 137
Banfi y Parrilla, José (chief clerk of the secretary of the Indies), 153
Banfi y Villalobos, Juan, 116, 118–19, 122, 153
Barbara of Bragança. *See* Bragança, Barbara of
Barroeta y Barrenechea, Juan Crisóstomo, 101, 154, 166
Basarte, José (president of the *audiencia* of New Galicia), 109–14, 116, 120–22, 142, 154–55
Basque Country (Spain), 161
Belaunzarán, Juan Bautista, 94, 99, 101–2, 104–8, 142, 154–55
Bobadilla, Count of, 134–36
Bolaños (mining camp), 3, 5, 110, 111–15, 118, 120–21, 123, 141, 143, 147
Bourbon Reforms: assault on Creole autonomy, 147; new interpretations, 5, 20, 141, 147–48; traditional historiographical view, 5, 20; viceregal participation, 148–49
Bragança, Barbara of (queen of Spain), 11; at court, 46–47, 54; birthday, 63; fall of Ensenada, 18–20, 146; portrait in Mexico City, 55
bribes, 89, 118–19, 143
Brihuega (Spain), 9

Cádiz (Spain), 10, 20, 24, 44, 85, 103, 107, 127, 129, 133–34, 146–48, 152
Calatrava (military order), 162–63, 165
Campillo y Cossío, José, 11, 155; *New System*, 12
captain general: of Havana and Güemes, 133; of Old Castile and Güemes, 129
Capuchins, 82, 88
Capulhuac, San Bartolomé, 68–70, 73, 78, 87, 141
Carmelites, Discalced: Madrid, 83; Puebla, 82; Tehuacan de las Granadas, 86–88
Carnival Monday, 60
casaca (embroidered jacket), 40, 56
Casafuerte, Marquis of (viceroy), 24–25, 43, 144
Castillo de Aysa, Marquis of el, Francisco de Aysa Gastón (president of the *audiencia* of Guadalajara), 112, 121, 123, 154–55
Castro Santa-Anna, José Manuel de, 5, 25, 41, 80, 119, 125, 130
Cerralvo, Marquis and Marquise of (viceroy and vicereine), 24–25
Cevallos Villagutierre, Ignacio Felipe, 85, 98–101, 126, 155–56
chancellor of the *audiencia*, 157
Chapultepec, 32
Charles III (king of Spain), 5, 20, 53–54, 108, 129, 139, 141, 147, 156, 179
Charles IV (king of Spain), 42
chief clerk (*oficial mayor*), 153; of *alcabala* administration, 133; of the secretary of the Indies, 85, 98, 116, 120; of the viceregal secretariat, 117
Cholula, 29, 31, 43
civil judge (*oidor*) of the *audiencia*, xii, 33, 41, 48, 57, 62, 103, 109–10, 132, 154, 158–67
classical mythology, 36–38
cofradía (sodality) in Santo Domingo priory, 81
Coliseum Theater, 51
Colonia del Sacramento (Uruguay), 19
confessor, royal, 11, 71, 84, 95, 98, 138, 158, 161
Conquista, Duke of la (viceroy), 62, 161
conquistadors, 23, 28, 32, 34, 43

consulado (merchant guild) of Mexico, 2–3, 20, 29, 32, 106–7; conflict over *alcabala*, 89–104, 147–48; criticism of Ignacio Cevallos, 98–99; rituals, 41, 59–60
consulado of Cádiz, 10, 20, 103, 107
corregidor. See *alcalde mayor*
Cortes (Spanish parliament of estates), 38
Cortés, Hernán, 34
Cosuela, Manuel, 101, 165
Council of Castile, 135, 138
Council of the Indies (appellate court for Spanish America), xi, 11, 13, 39, 48, 53, 65; *alcabala* in Veracruz, 104–6; conflict over Bolaños, 120; opposed to inexperienced officials, 94; opposition to secularization, 71–73, 85–86; praise for Güemes, 133; ruling against Güemes, 133, 138, 146
Council of the Treasury, 11, 15
Council of Trent (1545–1563), 76
Council of War, 126, 136–37, 147, 155
Coyoacán, 80
Creole (Spaniard born in the Americas), 13, 80–81, 87, 147
Croix, Marquis of (viceroy), 58, 136–37, 139, 154–57

doctrinas (Native parishes), vii, 2, 5, 67, 71–75, 77–80, 86–87, 131, 141–42, 158, 196
Dominicans: Mexico City, 48, 80–81; Puebla, 82; secularization, 73, 87

ecclesiastical chapter (*cabildo eclesiástico*): rituals, 31–32, 34, 36–37, 49, 55; tithe, 85
Ensenada, Marquis of la, Zenón de Somodevilla (first minister): exile in Andalusia, 19, 126, 129, 146, 156; fall from power, 3, 6, 18–20, 85–86; tax reforms, 2–3, 14–15, 72, 91–92, 94, 96, 102, 104, 126
Esquilache, the Marquis of (first minister), 88, 136–37, 139, 156

Farinelli (musician), 47
Farnese, Elizabeth (queen of Spain), 11
Ferdinand VI (king of Spain), 11, 45, 60, 64, 83
Franciscans: Mexico City, 34–35; Observant Franciscans in Santa María la Redonda, 75–78; Otumba, 32; Querétaro, 87; Reinosa (Cantabria), 2; Santa María Ozumba, 78; Tlaxcala, 31
Fuenclara, Count of (viceroy), 17–18, 29, 32, 36–37, 52–53, 64, 91, 144, 157, 161, 165

Gálvez, José de, expulsion of Jesuits and partisans, 137–39; judicial investigation, 5, 13, 86, 126, 139, 147–48
Gamboa, Francisco Javier, 166
García Panes y Abellán, Diego, 40
Gelves, Marquis of (viceroy), 48
Godoy, María Antonia de, 26
golilla (black jacket), 56
Gómez de Angulo, Diego Felipe, 156
Gorospe Padilla, Diego José (*alcalde mayor* of Bolaños), 113–15, 120–21, 123
Graneros, Nicolás, 68–70
Guadalajara. See *audiencia* of Guadalajara
Guadalupe, the Virgin of, 84, 128
Guanajuato, 80
Guaraní people, 19
Guatemala, kingdom of, xi, 73, 98–99, 137

272 Index

Güemes y Horcasitas, Juan Francisco de (viceroy): appointment as viceroy of New Spain, 2, 18; arrival in New Spain, 4, 23, 27; departure from New Spain, 5, 20, 126–29, 138; death, 126, 137; governor of Havana, 2, 21, 25, 27; final judicial review, 126, 134–35; knight of the order of Santiago, 18; military career, 2, 9, 20–21; origins and education, 2; salary, 18, 143; title of Count of Revillagigedo, 18, 125; travels to Mexico City as viceroy-designate, 23–24, 28–44; wedding, 2; dean of the Council of War, 5, 126, 129, 138, 147
Güemes, Antonia, 55, 134–36, 138, 236
Güemes, Antonio María, 55
Güemes, Francisca Javiera, 55, 134
Güemes, Josefa Cayetana, 55, 167
Güemes, Juana María, 55, 134
Güemes, Juan Vicente, 55, 59, 100, 136, 163
Güemes, María Francisca, 55, 129
Güemes, Teresa, 55
Gulf of Mexico, 90

Habsburg, House of, 2, 9–10, 15–16, 20, 53, 146, 229n5
Hat and Cloak Revolt, 136, 156
Hesperia, Atlas's lover, 36–37
Hospitallers of San Juan de Dios (order of), 82
House of Trade, 19, 153
Huejotzingo, 29, 31, 43
Huéscar, Duke of, Fernando de Silva Álvarez de Toledo, 126, 157

Immaculate Conception (day of), 48
Inquisition, rituals: 4, 45–46, 49–53, 55, 58, 64, 144–45; secret report about Fuenclara, 17–18
intendants of provinces, 13, 15

Jerez (now de García Salinas), 112–13
Jesuits: expulsion of order, 126, 137–38; general in Rome, 73; missions among Guaraní, 19–20; Profesa Church, 34–35, 60; provincial, 75; royal confessor, 10–11, 95, 138
Jorge, Juan, 13
judicial investigation (*visita general*), of 1716–1727, 61. See also Gálvez, José de
judicial review (*juicio de residencia*): of *alcaldes mayores*, 16–17; of the Marquis of el Castillo de Aysa, 112; of Viceroy Juan Francisco Güemes, 125, 128–33, 146

Keene, Benjamin, 178n41, 178n44

La Joya (Veracruz), 130
La Rioja (Spain), 11, 101, 154
Lagos, 82, 88
Léon (Spain), 101, 156
Linares, Duke of (viceroy), 39, 49, 56, 61

Málaga (Spain), 135, 165
Mariana of Austria (queen of Spain), 148
Martínez de Aguirre, Jacinto, 4, 56, 101, 157, 161
mayordomo (steward) of the viceroy, 18, 53
Meninde, José, 69–70
Metztitlan, 81
Mixtecs, 80
montañés (person from northern Spain), 11, 154, 164
Morlete Ruiz, Juan Patricio, vii, 57–58
Mostenses Square (Madrid), vii, 134–35
municipal council (*cabildo civil*), xii, 106; *alcabala* conflict, 95–97, 102;

construction, 18, 32, 115; of Mexico City, 18, 29, 31–34, 36, 37, 41, 51, 60, 80, 90–91, 113, 142, 145; of Otumba, 32; public safety, 18; of Puebla, 29, 32; of Tlaxcala, 30–31, 41; of Veracruz, 27–28, 105

Narvarete, Juan José, 119
Nayarit Indians, 111
New Galicia, kingdom of, 109–10; see also *audiencia* of Guadalajara
New Granada (viceroyalty), 10, 18, 72
Night of Sorrows (Spanish Conquest), 32
Nuestra Señora del Destierro (Our Lady of the Exile), 82

Oaxaca: *alcabala* of city of Antequera de Oaxaca, 108; bishopric, 81, 134, 161; secularization, 71–74, 131, 143
Observant Franciscans, 75–76, 83
Ocotlan (sanctuary), 31
Octupan, 193
Ortiz, Juan José, 116–17, 154
Otumba (Otompan), 29, 32, 42, 125, 128–30, 133, 138, 145, 157
Our Lady of Guadalupe (basilica), 29, 32, 84, 92, 128–30, 132, 164
Our Lady of Remedies (day of), 60–61
Our Lady of the Assumption (Church in Veracruz), 27
Our Lady of the Exile (Nuestra Señora del Destierro), 82
Our Lady of the O (day of), 63
Our Lady of the Rosary (day of), 63

Padilla Pacheco Aguayo, Antonia Ceferina Paula, Countess of Revillagigedo (vicereine), 158; chilly reception of inquisitors, 45, 50–52; Discalced Carmelites, 83; family in Puebla, 113, 120; fiesta in Otumba, 128; marriage, 2; palace life, 46–55; rituals, 34, 54–55; travel to Mexico, 23, 25–28, 31–32; return to Spain and death, 128–29, 144
palio (portable canopy), 27, 33, 43
Patiño, José, 10, 15, 20–21
Patiño, María Teresa (queen's lady-in-waiting), 17
Pátzcuaro, 137
Perote (Veracruz), 29, 130
Philip V (king of Spain), 2, 9, 14, 53, 91, 131, 134, 156
physiocrats, 12–13, 15
Piedras Negras, 130
portero (audiencia porter), 50
principales (Native nobility), 78, 113
prior (leader of the *consulado*), 101
priory: Augustinian, in San Bartolomé Capulhuac, 68–70; Discalced Carmelite, in Madrid, 83; Dominican, in Mexico City, 48, 80–81; Franciscan, in Mexico City, 34–35; Observant Franciscans, Santa María la Redonda, 75–78; in Otumba, 32; in Puebla, 82–83; in Reinosa (Cantabria), 2; in Santa María Ozumba, 78; in Tehuacan de las Granadas, 86; in Tlaxcala, 31; in Yuririapundaro, 87
provincial (head of a province of a regular order), 74; Augustinian, 69–70; Jesuit, 95, 138
Puebla, *alcabala*, 90, 96, 131; *alcalde mayor*, 131; bishop and secularization, 71–74; governor, 17; priories, 79, 82–83, 86; rituals, 17, 29, 31, 41, 43, 60, 128, 130, 143
pueblo (ethnic polity), 1, 23, 27, 29, 41, 78, 79, 137
Puerta del Sol (Madrid), 38

Puerto de Santa María (Spain), 156

Querétaro, Franciscan priory, 87

Rávago y Noriega, Francisco. *See* confessor, royal
real acuerdo (joint committee of viceroy and civil judges), 49, 62
Reinosa (Cantabria), 2
repartimiento de mercancías (Native trade with district judges), 212n69–213n69
Rubio y Salinas, Manuel José (archbishop), 74, 158, 163

sagrario, newly built parish church, 81; room where the host is kept, 70, 75, 81, 164
Saint Ferdinand's Day, 60, 63
Saint Francis's Day, 60
San Agustín de las Cuevas (Tlalpan), 56, 157, 161
San Ángel, 56, 145, 161
San Antonio of the Viceroys (hacienda), 28–29, 130
San Bartolomé Capulhuac, 68–70, 73, 78, 87, 141
San Bartolomé de los Tepetates, 128–29, 130
San Bartolomé de Xala, Count of, Manuel Rodríguez Sáenz Pedrozo, 100–101, 132, 158, 164, 166
San Cristóbal Ecatepec, 29, 32, 41–42, 128, 130, 142
San Diego Baguedano (hacienda), 130
San Felipe Neri (order), 82
San Felipe Real (Chihuahua), 154
San Francisco Church (Tlaxcala), 30
San Francisco Ixtacuixtla, 41
San Francisco Street (now Madero), 34–35, 52
San Francisco Tepito, 92

San Gaspar de Huilacatitlan, 113–14
San Juan Bautista de Xichu, 80, 199
San Juan de Ulúa (fortress), 17, 42, 69, 119
San Juan Teotihuacan, 130, 142
San Luis Potosí, 76
San Mateo Atlatlahucan, 77–78, 87
San Miguel de Belén, 82
San Miguel el Grande (now Allende), 82
San Miguel Texcalpan, 78
San Sebastián Church (Antequera, Andalusia), 2, 158
Santa Catarina Church (Lagunilla), 34
Santa Cruz, 193
Santa Fe de Bogotá (New Granada), 72
Santa Hermandad (rural police force), 127
Santa María Acuitlapilco, 41
Santa María la Redonda, 75–77
Santa María Ozumba, 78
Santa Rosa de Alburquerque, 111
Santiago (Cuba), 133
Santiago (military order), 18, 55, 162
Santiago de Guatemala, 155–56
Santiago of Calimaya, Count of, 164
Santiago Tianguistenco, 68, 70, 78, 87, 141, 193
Santo Domingo Square, 34, 50–51
semanero (*audiencia* judge on weekly rotation), 62
Sesa (Aragón), 155
Seven Years' War, 103
Sierra Bolaños, 113
Sigüenza y Góngora, Carlos, 38–39
Sinaloa, 17
Smith, Adam, 12
Spanish Conquest, 26, 31, 63, 67
Spanish Empire, xi, 9, 12, 43, 149
Superintendent of mercury distribution, 119, 163
Superintendent of Mexico City's

alcabala (sales tax), 94, 97, 103, 106
Superintendent of the royal mint in Mexico City, 137, 139, 157
Superunda, Count of (viceroy of Peru), 17
súplica (plea), 62, 94

Tacuba, 56
Tehuacan de las Granadas, 86, 88
Tepeyac Hill, 84
Tepeyahualco (Puebla), 29, 130
Thirty Years' War, 90
Three Holy Kings (holiday), 63
tlatoani (Aztec ruler), 1
Tlaxcala, 28–31, 33–34, 41–43, 125, 130, 138, 143, 163–64; governor, 41
Treasurer of ecclesiastical chapter of Mexico City, 3, 98; see also Cevallos Villagutierre, Ignacio Felipe
Treaty of Aix-la-Chapelle (Aachen, 1748), 16
Treaty of Madrid (1750), 19
Tribunal of Accounts, 56, 60, 62, 65, 99, 101, 116–17, 154
Tribunal of the Crusade Indulgence, 50–51

Ulloa, Antonio de, 13
Uruguay River, 19

Uztáriz, Gerónimo de, 156

Valley of Mexico, 32, 43, 128
Veracruz: *alcabala* auctions, 104–09, 142; *común y vecindario* (community), 104–5; jail, 70, 119, 137; merchant fleet, 97–98, 131; viceregal travels, 23–25, 27, 42–43, 127–23, 144; warden of fortress, 17
Villaviciosa (Spain), 9
visita general. See Gálvez, José de; judicial investigation

Wall, Ricardo, 19, 146, 159
War of the Austrian Succession, 91
War of the Spanish Succession, 9–10, 17, 131, 134
Ward, Bernardo, 13, 20

Xalapa, 28–29, 93, 128–30, 145

Yucatán, xi, 73, 87, 137, 156, 159
Yuririapundaro (Augustinian priory), 87

Zacatecas, 111, 119–20, 161
Zapopan, 63
Zapotecs, 80
Zedano, Juana, 109

www.ingramcontent.com/pod-product-compliance
Lightning Source LLC
Chambersburg PA
CBHW021341230426
43666CB00006B/364